EMOTION
IN ADVERTISING

E·M·O·T·I·O·N
IN ADVERTISING

Theoretical and Practical Explorations

Edited by
STUART J. AGRES,
JULIE A. EDELL,
and TONY M. DUBITSKY

QUORUM BOOKS
NEW YORK • WESTPORT, CONNECTICUT • LONDON

Library of Congress Cataloging-in-Publication Data

Emotion in advertising : theoretical and practical explorations /
  edited by Stuart J. Agres, Julie A. Edell and Tony M. Dubitsky.
       p.   cm.
  Includes bibliographical references.
  ISBN 0-89930-537-7 (lib. bdg. : alk. paper)
  1. Advertising—Psychological aspects. 2. Advertising—Research.
  3. Human information processing—Research. I. Agres, Stuart J.
  II. Edell, Julie A. III. Dubitsky, Tony M.
  HF5822.E46   1990
  659.1'01'9—dc20   90-30018   ˑ

British Library Cataloguing in Publication Data is available.

Library of Congress Catalog Card Number: 90–30018
.ISBN: 0–89930–537–7

First published in 1990

Quorum Books, 88 Post Road West, Westport, CT 06881
An imprint of Greenwood Publishing Group, Inc.

Printed in the United States of America

The paper used in this book complies with the
Permanent Paper Standard issued by the National
Information Standards Organization (Z39.48-1984).

10 9 8 7 6 5 4 3 2 1

TP

Contents

Impact of Emotional Advertising on Consumer Responses

Stimulus-Viewer Interactions

Epilogue

Figures and Tables

FIGURES

TABLES

Preface

Emotion and Advertising: A Timely Union

Julie A. Edell

Much of the existing advertising research focuses on how consumers process the brand information conveyed in an advertisement. The consumer has been seen as an active information seeker who views advertising to learn all that can be learned about the brand in order to make the optimal choice. Advertising practitioners have long sensed that the way in which the message is conveyed is at least as important as what the message says. But it has been only in the last few years that researchers have begun to conceptualize about and to attempt to capture emotional reactions to ads. The dominance of learning-based advertising response has shifted to a more balanced approach which includes the evaluation of the ad itself, as well as the emotional reactions to the ad.

Advertising researchers are not alone in shifting some of their attention away from cognitive to affective or emotional reactions. Social psychologists are also embracing the notion that affective reactions have been under-researched. Robert Zajonc (1980) has stimulated much research and thinking with his provocative article that argues that affect and cognition are under the control of independent systems. He concluded that affect and cognition influence each other in numerous ways, and that both effects are important in understanding how people respond to stimuli in the world.

In a more applied setting, R. P. Abelson, D. Kinder, M. D. Peters, and S. T. Fiske (1982) examined the affective and semantic components in people's perceptions of political figures. They concluded that affective reactions are different from cognitive reactions. Affective reactions are more episodic in nature and, as such, are less subject to consistency pressure than are cognitive reactions. Thus, some might easily say that former President Carter has made them feel both angry and proud, but they are quite unlikely to judge him to be both honest and power hungry. Abelson et al. (1982) conclude that not only do affective and cognitive reactions behave differently, but also affective reactions add predictive ability to cognitive reactions.

A growing body of mood research suggests that feelings can change the nature of cognitive processing. Positive affect has been shown to affect risk-taking behavior, decision-making strategies, recall speed, and evaluations of many kinds (Isen, Johnson, Mertz, & Robinson, 1985; Isen & Means, 1983; Johnson & Tversky, 1983). The applicability of this work to advertising is straightforward. The emotional reactions one has in response to an ad may influence what gets activated from memory, increasing the likelihood that valence-congruent thoughts are activated. If the emotional reaction is positive, more positive thoughts may be generated in response to the message of the ad. As a result of this process, more positive beliefs will be formed about the brand's attributes, and the evaluation of the ad itself will be enhanced.

Even in the area of decision making, one finds models that suggest that the basis for most decisions is emotional (Etzioni, 1988). Etzioni suggests that emotions influence decisions in various ways. Emotion may define the objective of the decision maker. Emotional intensity may cause the range of alternatives that would be considered to be narrowed, and emotional factors often intrude upon the decision-making process by curtailing the amount of consideration given to logical factors.

Given the work in other fields and the potential influence of emotions in advertising, it is fitting that more research attention be given to the role of emotions as they relate to advertising. Theories of advertising are incomplete unless they incorporate emotional factors. Any design of advertising research, either theoretical or pragmatic, that does not examine emotional reactions is incomplete at best and risks being invalid. There is clear need for a continued effort to understand how advertising and emotions are linked.

The chapters in this book represent a wide array of approaches to studying the relationship between emotion and advertising. The chapters include both theoretical and empirical approaches and cover a broad spectrum of views about this relationship. Regardless of the particular approach or paradigm used to study the emotion-advertising relationship, the authors are quite uniform in their view that the relationship is an important one and very complex.

The book is organized into six general sections. The first section of Part I consists of chapters that provide an overview or a theoretical perspective on how emotions have their effect in the advertising environment. The second section contains chapters that investigate how emotional responses to advertising can and should be measured. In Part II, the first section comprises empirical chapters each of which examines some structural aspect of the advertisement and how it relates to emotional response. The second section consists of three chapters which examine how the emotional reactions to ads affect other constructs or behavior of interest to the advertiser. The two chapters in the third section explicitly examine how the emotional make-up of the viewer interacts with the emotional fabric of the ad, and the final section is an overview chapter which examines the role of consumer psychology in the social sciences.

The first section includes six chapters. In the first of these, Stuart Agres provides an agency viewpoint about the role of emotion in advertising. In his chapter he presents a dilemma that confronts advertising agencies: emotional advertising does not score well on standard copy-testing systems. Agres goes on to present a research program that concludes that advertising must deliver both rational and psychological benefits to the consumer.

Chris Allen and Terence Shimp discuss how classical conditioning methods can be used to examine a unique set of issues in advertising research. They detail what should and should not be expected of conditioning methods. Allen and Shimp discuss major differences in the general goals and assumptions underlying behaviorist versus cognitivist methods and overview the Pavlovian approach to research. They specify the affective phenomena for which conditioning methods seem especially well suited and describe a general style of television advertising in which conditioning principles may have their greatest applicability.

Thomas Srull develops a general conceptualization of how subjective affective states affect brand evaluations via advertising. He theorizes that information processing models provide the most elegant and comprehensive accounts of affect available today. Srull concludes that a rapprochement between those interested in cognition and those interested in affect is not only possible but also necessary for future advancement. His conclusion is based on empirical as well as theoretical evidence.

David Aaker and Douglas Stayman present a review of their research which focuses on specific feelings, in particular, warmth. They contrast this specific feeling approach to other approaches of studying feelings. Aaker and Stayman discuss the advantages of the specific feeling approach and suggest areas of study in which it would be particularly suitable.

Christopher Puto and Robert Hoyer review the latest thinking about transformational advertising. Since the introduction of the transformation concept in 1980, the concept appears to be engendering an ever-widening variety of usages resulting in a generalized lack of meaning. This chapter traces the development of the transformation construct, delineates its current standing, and presents the results of an exploratory foray into the development of potential measures for it.

Malcolm Smith, Kristina Frankenberger, and Lynn Kahle introduce the literature on emotion attribution. They present the emotion attribution theory as a mechanism for understanding the arousal-inducing effects of fear appeals in advertising. A review of the literature on emotion attribution theory is followed by a review of models that have attempted to explain the effects of fear appeals in communications. Finally, the effects of fear appeals on emotional responses are explained by integrating emotion attribution theory into a model of the effectiveness of fear appeals in advertising.

The problem of measuring emotional response is considered by Trent Punnett and Richard Pollay in chapter 7, which introduces the use of facial expressions to measure emotional response to television advertising. The Facial Action Coding System developed by P. Ekman and W. V. Friesen (1978) is described, and guidelines for pretesting its usefulness are outlined.

J. Edward Russo and Debra Stephens propose that emotional responses to an advertisement be assessed by scales for the specific feelings that the ad was designed to evoke. They compare the ad-specific approach to the general approach that uses the same battery of adjective scales for all ads. The ad-specific feelings predicted attitude toward the ad at least as well as either general adjective list, but it was inferior in predicting attitude toward the brand.

The first chapter in Part II, by Fairfid Caudle, argues that the portrayal of emotion is essential to the success of a persuasive communication. Since magazine advertisements are limited to images and words on a printed page, facial expression is the primary way in which emotion is communicated. Caudle's chapter highlights issues relevant to the potential role of facial expression in the arousal of emotion.

Cheon-Soung Park and Esther Thorson report a study that examines the differences in emotional response related to the different executional style of the ads. They use an advertising taxonomy (Hefzallah & Maloney, 1979) to show that association and satisfaction style commercials produce more emotional responses than do demonstration, testimonial, or comparison style commercials.

Whether storyboards and animatics reliably predict emotional responses to finished television commercials is the focus of chapter 11 by Ronald Goodstein, Julie Edell, and Marian Moore. They present a study that compares the emotional responses to storyboards, animatics, and finished commercials. The findings are that animatics and finished commercials elicit similar emotional reactions, but that storyboards are not good indicators of the feelings generated in response to the finished commercial.

Patricia Stout, Pamela Homer, and Scott Liu report on a study conducted to determine whether differences exist between the emotions individuals see portrayed in a commercial and their own personal feelings. Findings indicate that there are distinct differences between the emotions displayed in the ad and the emotional reactions of the viewers. Additionally, the overall findings partially support the point that personally felt emotions contribute more to making an advertisement effective than do ad-depicted emotions.

Chapter 13, by Julie Edell and Helen Anderson, explores what role the introductory position of the brand name and product category within a commercial have on emotional responses. Models are presented articulating the processing activities possible with each of the three brand name/product category positions tested. Edell and Anderson found that different feelings were generated to the version of the commercials in which the product category and the brand name were introduced at the very end of the ad.

Chapter 14, by Basil Englis, details how emotional reactions to ads may mediate the cognitive outcomes of an ad exposure. Englis reports the results of a study that looked at the effects of emotional reactions on the ability of viewers to recall the message of the ad.

In a related vein, Thomas J. Page, Jr., Esther Thorson, and Maria Papas Heide investigate memory performance. The effects of emotionality of the commercial, of product category involvement, and of brand familiarity are researched in two experiments. In both experiments, emotional commercials were more likely to be recalled earlier in the recall sequence. In neither experiment did product involvement enhance memory performance, but the positive effect of brand familiarity on memory was strong.

T. J. Olney, Rajeev Batra, and Morris Holbrook present a three-component model of attitude toward the ad. A study across advertisements examined the effects of these three subcomponents on a behavioral measure of "looking time." Looking time is operationalized by stimulating both a "zipping" condition and a "zapping" condition. Implications are drawn for the importance of attitude toward the ad as an indicator of which ads will actually be watched and may thus be potentially influential.

Timothy C. Brock, Carol Bridgwater, and Laura A. Brannon demonstrate the role of values by coordinating the content of persuasive messages to previously measured values of recipients. Four experiments were conducted employing messages that either matched or mismatched the recipients' values and temperaments. The matching messages were found to be more effective than nonmatching messages.

Ronald Hill and Debra Stephens present a model of the synergistic relationship between the current mood of the consumer and the mood intrinsic to the advertisement. Their chapter discusses possible mood-management strategies of consumers when they evaluate ads and presents a framework for understanding these phenomena.

The final chapter of the book, by John Maloney, takes a historical view of how consumer psychology has grown, changed, and struggled to understand the communication process. The chapter includes a general "phenomenistic" model. Maloney encourages a renewed emphasis upon nonliteral and nonverbal cognitive processes.

REFERENCES

Abelson, R. P., Kinder, D., Peters, M. D., & Fiske, S. T. (1982). Affective and semantic components in political person perception. *Journal of Personality and Social Psychology, 42* (4), 619–630.

Ekman, P., & Friesen, W. V. (1978). *Facial Action Coding System (FACS): A technique for the measurement of facial action.* Palo Alto, CA: Consulting Psychologists.

Etzioni, A. (1988). Normative-affective factors: Toward a new decision-making model. *Journal of Economic Psychology, 9*, 125–150.

Hefzallah, I. M., & Maloney, W. P. (1979). Are there only six kinds of TV commercials? *Journal of Advertising Research, 19* (4), 57–64.

Isen, A. M., Johnson, M. M., Mertz, E., & Robinson, G. F. (1985). The influence of positive affect on the unusualness of word associations. *Journal of Personality and Social Psychology, 48* (6), 1413–1426.

Isen, A. M., & Means, B. (1983). The influence of positive affect on decision-making strategy. *Social Cognition 2*, 18–31.

Johnson, E. J., & Tversky, A. (1983). Affect, generalization, and the perception of risk. *Journal of Personality and Social Psychology, 45* (1), 20–31.

Zajonc, R. (1980). Feeling and thinking: Preferences need no inferences. *American Psychologist, 35* (2), 151–175.

Acknowledgments

The collection of papers presented in this book is the outcome of a conference on emotions and advertising held at the offices of Lowe Marschalk, Inc., in May 1988. We gratefully acknowledge the sponsorship of Lowe Marschalk, the Consumer Psychology Division (no. 23) of the American Psychological Association, and the Marketing Science Institute.

Many individuals contributed to the success of the conference, notably Philip Herr, senior vice president and director of research at Lowe Marschalk. Philip was the initial coordinator of the conference, helped to select presentations, deftly handled the numerous logistics of setting up the conference, and provided ongoing assistance.

In transforming the conference presentations into an edited volume of chapters, we wish to acknowledge the Fuqua School of Business and the Lowe Marschalk Market Research Department for providing resources for compilation and editing. Thanks also are due to Richard Del Vecchio for helping to prepare illustrations for this work and to Jacqueline Edwards for her insightful copyediting of key sections of the manuscript.

Finally, we wish to acknowledge the continuing enthusiasm of Eric Valentine of Quorum Books.

PART I

Theoretical Approaches

Conceptual Issues

1

Emotion in Advertising: An Agency Point of View

Stuart J. Agres

INTRODUCTION

As the only representative of an advertising agency in this volume, I am taking the opportunity to discuss the issue of emotion in advertising from the practitioner's vantage point. It is, after all, the practitioner who faces the challenges on a daily basis, who applies our findings, and provides the ultimate test of the validity of the theories we generate.

There is a broad range of issues that we as practitioners face and that I know will come up for consideration: First, and perhaps most important, is the question: What do we mean by "emotion in advertising"? It seems like a simple question, but it's not. For example, there is the important subquestion of stimulus versus response. When we speak of "emotion in advertising" are we speaking in terms of what is happening in the film, or in terms of what is happening to the viewer in response to the advertising that was just seen or heard? In other chapters, authors discuss stimulus and response issues, but we should recognize that these issues are confused constantly and we must be very careful to keep clear which issue is under consideration.[1]

Second, whether we consider emotion in advertising to be about the stimulus or the response, we generally are talking about something that I'll label "emotionality" or "mood"—the things that are happening in the stimulus to which we ask viewers to empathize or identify—the emotion that is generated or tapped as a consequence of exposure. But there is something else that is worth dealing with; that something else is the one or more benefits being offered to consumers derived from the use of the product or service which is psychological/emotional in its impact. What psychological need is to be satisfied? What is the consumer attempting to satisfy when using products or services in the category in general, or when using the specific brand in question?

Third, there are measurement issues. There are verbal and verbal-like (rational) measurements of emotional response, an intriguing construct, whether those are rating scales or verbatim responses.[2] Can we rationally process our feelings? What do we get when we ask a typical consumer to do this? How well are we trained in this culture and society to process feelings? Then, there are nonverbal measures including physiological and picture-response methods.[3] Of course, we can choose to forget all of that and go right to the behavioral measurements; go straight to the measurement of the effect. Given that we know that we did something in the stimulus, we could just see what the end effect of that is going to be.[4]

Fourth, there are practical and theoretical implications, which are examined in later chapters in this book.

General discussions often seem to revolve around a nonrational, nontangible kind of communication within a piece of advertising—the kind that is very often done through some semiotic signaling or gesturing. This is not the issue here; rather, let us go past that point and look at the emotional issues that much of that nonverbal communication is intended to trigger.

WHAT IS THE NATURE OF THE PROBLEM?

Advertising has a problem. The advertising problem is that what is deemed to be emotional advertising systematically scores poorly on standard copy-testing systems regardless of the method used. By and large, the copy-testing systems do not seem to reflect what many consider to be the values of emotional advertising. FCB/Leber Katz Partners has talked about this for some time; about "thinking" versus "feeling" advertising. They were one of the first advertising agencies to "go public" with the notion that feeling advertising was facing a negative bias in the testing systems. Yet, agencies are almost unanimously consistent in their belief that emotions are important—positively important—to the persuasion process.

THE ROLE OF ADVERTISING

Most advertising agencies share common beliefs about what advertising is supposed to do: (1) advertising should make a member of the target audience want to use or buy the product or service; (2) advertising should be viewed as an investment rather than merely as a cost of current sales, in that it should help build brand loyalty, and it should also help build resistance to competitive attack in the marketplace.

Although everyone may agree on what advertising is supposed to do, it's not what is actually happening in the marketplace. It is certainly not what we have been seeing over the past decade. Rather, there has been diminishing brand loyalty in virtually every category we have studied. There has been very little apparent resistance to competitive attack. In addition, the increasing use of promotion as an alternative to advertising communications suggests that advertising isn't really viewed as operating as an investment. If it were, those funds would not be shifting from advertising budgets with quite the speed that they are.

How has this come about? If advertising was once viewed as an investment, a way of building brand loyalty and long-term sales—but it isn't anymore— something has happened. To answer this, there are at least two places to look: first, at the consumer. Some years ago, we in the marketing and advertising community used to say, "The consumer is changing," and indeed we now use the term "consumerism." A second possibility is that we, the industry, did the changing—that something we do now is different from what we did before— and perhaps the message itself is different.

At least three kinds of things have occurred. One has been an increase in the use of research as an aid to decision making. In fact, in many cases it is no longer merely an aid—it is the decision maker. Second, there has been a move to shorter commercial lengths; we have moved from sixty seconds to thirty and increasingly now to fifteen. Third, there has been that rise in consumerism. Even though many more events have probably occurred over the years, unscrambling even these eggs is very difficult—to know what led to what, or when, or where.

One way to approach this, and the vantage point that I take, is to look first in our own backyard (at least we know a little bit about it) and see whether it helps explain what has happened. Our collective backyard is research, and I think that without sounding too terribly cynical, it is fair to point out that there are two things that this industry tends to do: (1) answer questions that can be addressed, whether or not those are the questions that were asked, and (2) label the answers in terms of what it is that we wished we could have measured.

Let us take, for example, the issue of "persuasion." The question that is asked by brand management is, "Will the target consumer be persuaded to buy my product?" But the question we try to answer is, "Will consumers, in general, select my product as a door prize?" I would argue that this is not exactly the same issue even if it may be tapping some of the same kinds of notions. There are products that I would buy that I would be unlikely to accept free, and there are products that I would accept free but would not buy without more information.

A second example has to do with "communications testing." I don't think that when communications testing started we had brand managers and others saying, "Gee, I would really like communications testing." In my experience the question that was asked was quite different: "Is my product going to SELL?" In business, there's a tendency to get down to basics.

We, as researchers, on the other hand, ask questions like: "What do you remember being said and shown?" We ask the question, "What in your opinion is the main idea that the sponsor was trying to communicate to you, other than wanting you to buy the product that was advertised?"

Think about those questions. It isn't necessary to go deep into educational theory to know that several things are going to be true about the answers that you get back. First, with regard to what one remembers being said and shown, the more abstract the notion: the harder it is to verbalize, the more idiosyncratic the verbalizations, and the harder it is to code. In fact, verbalizations are exceptionally hard to deal with even if you have been given the right answers.

Second, let's deal with the question of the main idea that the sponsor is trying to communicate. I remember being asked what was essentially that question in high school after reading *Moby Dick* and again after reading *Little Women* and discussing each of them in class for weeks. I thought that I had understood them and then I got that dreaded question on a test: "What is the main idea?" and I couldn't answer it.

Now we show a consumer a typical commercial for thirty seconds and then ask that same question. How much abstraction is a consumer going to be able to do? What kind of playback is he or she going to give you? Probably not a lot.[5]

If those are the questions, what are the effects of copy testing? I would maintain that the effects are not, in general, improved sales or improved persuasiveness. I think that what we get as an effect is an attempt to generate advertising that will survive the test questions. It's not necessary to dig into psychological theory to know that once you set up a structure where there are rewards and punishments, people will go for the rewards—and try to avoid the punishments. So everyone begins to learn some rules about how to get those rewards.

Let me share some of these rules with you. In general, they do work: (A) Try to construct advertising that is verbal, even if it's within a predominantly visual medium, which television is. After all, it can be played back much better by the respondent. (B) Be literal. (C) If you really want to get the main idea played back, tell them your strategy; literally tell them what you want them to tell you.

I believe that if we think about it in this way the other events of the past decade are not terribly surprising. We have been in a mode where a lot of research has been driving a lot of advertising. When one thinks about it, one realizes that many of us following those test results could become very comfortable with a shorter length commercial. As long as we continue to be verbal and literal with consumers, they can play the message back and we can probably tell them our strategy in thirty seconds as well as in sixty seconds and perhaps even in fifteen seconds if we talk fast enough.

The changing consumer behaviors that we have seen are also easy to understand. If we choose to be merely literal and verbal and we tell consumers only the rational reasons why they ought to buy, a consumer would be absolutely crazy not to shift from the detergent that first got clothes clean and white to the one that gets clothes clean, white, bright, fresh smelling, soft, and disinfected. We have created the famous condition of "All else being equal." As a consumer who is being offered only products' rational benefits all the time, I am going to shift.

We at Lowe & Partners think that what happened is that through this process advertisers lost. They lost because, very simply, there was a failure to recognize that consumers are more than the economists' "rational man." They lost because the industry set up that strange condition where all else was left to become equal.

In contrast let me share one main idea that I did take away from two speeches in *Julius Caesar*. At Caesar's funeral, Brutus addresses the crowd saying something like, "Listen to me, reason with me, and I will tell you why it was absolutely necessary to kill Caesar." He reasons with the populace and appears to convince them that he was right. Immediately after, however, Marc Antony comes on the scene and he says something a little different: "I come to bury Caesar, not to praise him, but here are some facts that make it sound as if Caesar was not really all that ambitious." We go on to see that Marc Antony begins with a bit of a logical argument as well. Then he undrapes Caesar's body so that the crowd can view the stab wounds and the blood, and he tells them that they are the beneficiaries of Caesar's will. As you probably recall, the crowd really went for Marc Antony's speech having been convinced by his appeal to both their rational and their more emotional sides.

By the same token, we at Lowe & Partners believe that consumers will buy products, or even go to war, in an effort to satisfy both rational and emotional needs, even if we are talking about what should be the highest involvement, seemingly most rational products like houses or automobiles. Neither one is an exclusively rational purchase. However, we do recognize that for such high-ticket items, it is often necessary to have rational hooks to grab on to. It would be very difficult to tell one's spouse that the reason the new car is in the driveway is because buying it fulfilled your need for self-actualization or even peer group affiliation. Instead, you might say that it has great craftsmanship and great engineering.

All this has led us to a new perspective on the role of advertising itself: it should signal a product's ability to satisfy both emotional and rational needs by delivering both psychological and rational benefits to consumers. As a result, consumers have two ways of associating with the brand or product—on a rational basis and on an emotional basis as well. This double bond of rational and psychological benefits helps insulate the brand or product from competitive activity.

Let us return to the detergent example. Suppose a competitor tries to outdo my detergent's rational benefit with the one-upmanship claim of an even brighter disinfectant? The consumers in my franchise could still retain an emotional linkage to my brand and continue to purchase it, at least long enough for me to make my next "product improvement."

To clarify some potentially confusing terminology, bear in mind that thus far we have not been talking about emotional advertising—the kind that might make one laugh, cry, or become angry. We have been talking about psychological benefits—the kind of benefits derived from the use of a service or product. In contrast, emotionality will be defined as a property of the stimulus execution with which the viewer empathizes or identifies. The distinctioin is one of "benefits" versus "feelings."

Consider the example of a computer that features a bubble memory system. In the event of a power loss, an electrostatic charge remains on the bubble and nothing is lost from that bubble memory. Clearly, the rational benefit is that the user cannot lose his work; the psychological benefit is a sense of safety and security. In our view, the execution of a commercial based on the bubble memory feature could be executed with or without great emotion, so long as the commercial signaled both the rational and psychological benefits that the consumer could expect to derive from the product or service.

LOWE & PARTNER'S RESEARCH PROGRAM ON EMOTIONS AND ADVERTISING

Overview

Up to this point I have discussed this agency's perspective on the advertising research industry and what might amount to some basic tenets of successful advertising. Since we are directly involved in the applications of this, we have recognized the need to go beyond what might be considered armchair philosophizing and to put the theories to the test in a series of "ecologically valid" experiments. We have conducted these studies with typical consumers using typical advertising as well as prototype materials. We have investigated the actual measurement systems that are used by advertising practitioners on a day in and day out basis. The ultimate goal of this program was to explore the benefit to advertisers should they choose to incorporate both rational and psychological benefits in their advertising communications (Agres, 1984, 1988; Agres & Bernstein, 1984, 1985; Bernstein & Agres, 1984).

Since we felt that there were problems inherent in the standard testing systems' abilities to tap into the values that are believed to exist in advertising with a strong emphasis on emotionality, our initial goal was to explore new response methods. We wanted to, as much as possible, bypass consumers' cognitive/rational/logical information processing as it would impact their responding to questions about the advertising stimuli. Subsequent work examined the effects of benefit structures on both emotional and other response measures.

Development of the Marschalk Emotional Expression Deck (MEED)

In the first study, we created our own deck of fifteen different illustrations of facial expressions—each utilizing a male face, and each representing what we hoped would prove to be a distinct emotional state.

The first aspect of the study was conducted to confirm that the pictures created by our illustrator corresponded to consumers' views of emotional states. We knew that we did not want to fall into the trap that I have earlier described, "naming things that we wished we were measuring." We had consumers describe the emotion depicted by each illustrated face; we had them place emotion labels (words) with the illustration that best depicted the emotion; and we also asked for similarity judgments of the faces on a paired basis.

In terms of the verbal descriptions of these emotions, we found something that we had always felt was a problem: consumers have a difficult time generating the emotion labels by themselves. Many consumers responded to the task by giving a running commentary on what they believed must have been going on in the man's life to create the depicted emotion, but failed to ever articulate the emotion itself. We knew from copy-testing experience that responses to the question, "As you saw the commercial, what thoughts and feelings did you have?" rarely had "feelings" played back. We suspected that this might be so because consumers can not articulate feelings very well; we are not, after all, trained in school to be introspective.

One other interpretation that would have been possible from this task alone would have been that the illustrations were not very good. However, when people placed provided word labels with the pictures, we found that the illustrations were understood properly. Some emotional illustrations were easier to label, and some were more difficult. But rather than this being a matter of how good a job the illustrator had done on individual faces, we found that there was a systematic issue at hand. Generally, the milder or more neutral the emotion, the harder it was to label.[6]

Even though the milder expressions were more difficult to label, "mapping" based on similarity judgments yielded a three-dimensional solution: the first dimension was a positive/negative emotional state, and the second was an active/passive or emotional intensity dimension, and the third dimension, a relatively minor one compared to the other two, might best be described as "other-directedness." Certain emotions, such as anger, hostility, and jealousy, require a targeted-other for their expression.

Although these findings were interesting, the most significant understanding came from the overlay of the emotion labels onto our multi-dimensional map. Using a property-fitting procedure, we generated a "Wheel of Emotions" (shown in Figure 1.1) which depicts how emotions are represented in general. The basic dimensions of the wheel appear to range from happy to unhappy (vertical) and from self-confident to fearful (horizontal). There are also some interesting between states worth elaborating. We can describe a combined state of both happy and confident (in the NE quadrant) as "proud/satisfied"; between confident but currently unhappy (in the SE quadrant) as "determined"; between unhappiness and fearful (in the SW quadrant) as "worry/guilt"; and, finally, between fearful and happiness (in the NW quadrant) as "questioning/anxiety/overwhelmed."

Originally we had set out to build a set of illustrations that would allow respondents to communicate to us without having to go through their own ver-

Figure 1.1
The Wheel of Emotions

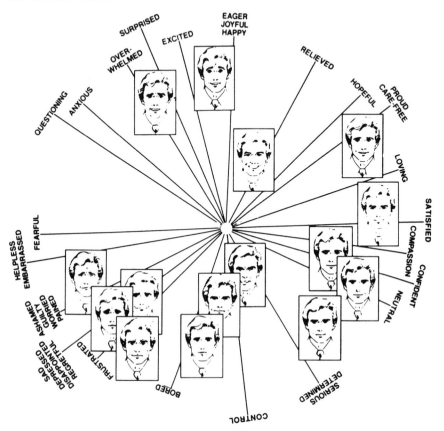

Note: Copyright © 1985 Marschalk Inc. Used With Permission.

balizations, and attendant "rational processing," when dealing with advertising. This Wheel of Emotions told us which MEED illustrations would be appropriate for us to use as positive target illustrations for consumers to select among. For example, if shown a commercial and then asked to respond to a "vicarious product experience" question ("How would you feel if you were to use the product in the commercial?"), one would have to know whether the expression chosen is positive or negative. The results from the first study suggested that we accept as positive those faces in the NE quadrant which span the emotions from "pleasure" to "happiness" and "satisfaction".

Using Facial Expressions to Evaluate Responsiveness to Advertising

The second study used these illustrations to test differences among three types of advertising communications: those with purely rational end benefits; those with purely psychological end benefits; and those with a mixture of rational and psychological end benefits. Using a between-subjects design, we presented male consumers with three versions of rough commercials for three imaginary products: a personal computer, a shampoo for men, and a banking service. We were interested in the percentage of consumers who would select any one of the target faces in response to our "vicarious product experience" question. We also included three conventional cognitive measures of advertising effectiveness: one measure of purchase intent and two measures of cognitive appeal (how much consumers like the product and how much they agree with the statement that the product is for "someone like me").

The key result from this second study was that the mixed-benefit commercials clearly outperformed both the pure rational and pure psychological versions on the "vicarious product experience" measure. A significantly greater proportion of consumers indicated that they would feel like the man in the "happy," "pleased," and "satisfied" pictures when exposed to mixed-benefit advertising.

We also found that purely psychological benefit advertising was least likely to generate selection of the target illustrations: they were outperformed by both mixed and purely rational versions. In fact, they were outperformed on all measures. We suspect this was so because there was no rational hook linking the product to the consumer's needs. Thus it would appear that psychological end benefits are not enough for effective advertising.

Effects of Rational, Psychological, and Mixed Benefits on Brand Loyalty

In the third study, we examined the impact of benefit structure on a key marketing variable: brand loyalty. We retrofitted the shampoo commercial stimuli (used in the second study) to white card concept statements in order to gather evidence for the generalizability of our findings and to allow for greater experimental control over the manipulation of rational, psychological, and mixed benefits.[7] Our surrogate measure of brand loyalty was the extent to which consumers would resist switching to a competitive product that offered additional rational benefits and price discounts.

Using a between-subjects design, consumers were presented with one of four concept statements for Avanti shampoo. Each concept began and ended with identical paragraphs; the experimental manipulation of benefit structure came about through a variation in the fourth paragraph, as shown in Table 1.1.

Specifically, two rational and two psychological benefits were constructed for Avanti shampoo. The purely rational version consisted of both rational benefits; the purely psychological version consisted of both psychological benefits. Each of the two mixed-benefit concepts consisted of one of the two rational benefits and one of the two psychological benefits.

After exposure to a given Avanti concept, consumers responded to the "vicarious product experience" question by selecting three MEED pictures that they felt best represented how they would feel were they to use the product.

Table 1.1

Construction of Pure Rational, Pure Emotional, and Mixed Benefit Concept Statements

==

¶1. When it comes to shampoo, a man's needs are different than a woman's.

¶2. That's why now there's Avanti—the first shampoo designed specially for men.

¶3. Avanti is made with a blend of three essential proteins a man's hair needs most. And it's unique formulation has conditioners that are built right in.

¶4.

Pure Rational Concept

Rational appeal 1: So now with Avanti, you can shampoo your hair as often as you like and know it won't get split, dry out, or get damaged.
Rational appeal 2: And Avanti leaves your hair thick, full of body.

Mixed Concept (a)

Rational appeal 2: So now with Avanti, your hair will be thick, full of body.
Emotional appeal 1: You'll look and feel terrific.

Mixed Concept (b)

Rational appeal 1: So now with Avanti, you can shampoo your hair as often as you like and know it won't get split, dry out, or get damaged.
Emotional appeal 2: Your best will shine through loud and clear, whatever you're doing, whoever you're with.

Pure Emotional Concept

Emotional appeal 1: So now with Avanti, you'll look and feel terrific.

Emotional appeal 2: And your best will shine through loud and clear, whatever you're doing, whoever you're with.

¶5. New Avanti. It's the first shampoo made just for men.

Table 1.2
Competitive Concept Statement

===

Introducing Allegro shampoo for men.

Allegro has everything those other men's shampoos have—like proteins and conditioners built right in—but only Allegro puts the two of them together for a unique, special cleansing power.

That's because Allegro's special formula works to penetrate hair follicles deep down below the scalp. So your hair is not only clean, it's healthier, too.

That's Allegro. For truly healthy hair.

Next, a concept for another men's shampoo (see Table 1.2), was presented. We asked consumers the same "vicarious product experience" question after they read the Allegro concept and again let them select three MEED pictures.

Finally, we measured brand loyalty after exposure to the competitive concept. We operationally defined *brand loyalty* as the number of discount levels prior to brand switching. We felt that brand switching would always occur at some level of discounting. At issue—as a measure—was "how deep the discount" before this switch occurred. Specifically, after our consumer read the Allegro concept, we asked him which of the two shampoos he would purchase at $2.00 for an 11-ounce bottle. His actual choices became the basis for the next question series: "If (brand selected) still costs $2.00, and (other brand) costs $1.90, which one would you now choose?" This question was continued until he chose the other brand or until fifteen discount levels (at 10¢ each) had been offered and rejected.

For the purpose of analysis, we combined responses so that there were two groups to compare: (1) a "pure-benefits" group, made up of both purely rational and purely psychological concepts, and (2) a "mixed-benefit" group, made up of both mixed-benefit concepts. By collapsing, each of the two resulting groups were exposed to identical and the same amount of information. In other words, combining the purely psychological benefits concept with the purely rational benefits concept means that the information elements are identical to those of the two mixed-benefit concept statements when they are combined. As a result any differences obtained between the two groups must be due, not to the information itself, but rather to the order of presentation.

Our results showed that (1) consumers responded to the white card concepts for Avanti in the same way as when the stimuli were filmed, rough commercials. That is, the mixture of rational combined with psychological end benefits had higher proportions of target face illustrations than did the pure end benefits. (2)

Consumers are more resistant to a competitive sales message after having been exposed to a mixed-benefit communication.

If looked at from another perspective, we see real power in the notion of "vicarious product experience." How an individual believes that he will feel should he use a product, relates directly to his degree of "loyalty" to that product when faced with competitive options. This understanding of the power of pre-disposition through a simple communication demonstrates something that advertisers heretofore might only have wished for from their advertising.

Effects of Benefit Structure on Recall and Persuasion

Overview. We have observed something important taking place in advertising. It seems that advertising has changed dramatically over the past few years, from a fairly hard-selling rational benefit approach (in what used to be called Cincinnati or P&G prototype advertising) to something that looks a lot more like the mixed-benefit types we have studied in our research program.

This raised some questions: "What are the typical testing results for this newer kind of advertising?" "Are there enough mixed-benefit commercials available so we can study them?" We realized that if we could investigate a body of copy test data for commercials that had been coded appropriately, we could take a look at the impact of psychological benefits on "recall" and "persuasion" measurements.

Recently, we had the opportunity to analyze a data base of 168 thirty-second finished film commercials for which there were copy test scores from ASI Market Research, a proprietary copy-testing service. This represented the entire set of thirty-second, fully finished commercials for which ASI had collected both their recall and new persuasion measurements. We set up a double-blind procedure so that we could gather objective information on psychological benefits and then linked this information to the recall and persuasion scores. Our coder was blind to the copy test scores for the commercials that were to be content analyzed; we were blind to the actual stimulus commercials, receiving only a data set with copy test scores and the coder's content-analysis codes.

Professor Russell Belk, a scholar in advertising research at the University of Utah, coded ASI's commercials on whether or not each incorporated a rational benefit and/or a psychological benefit, as well as on a third issue of interest: whether the execution was likely to induce an emotional response in the viewer. These latter "emotionality" issues were coded: (1) humor predominating, (2) dynamic emotion (bringing the viewer from one emotional state to another by the end of the commercial), (3) static emotional arousal (i.e., simple mood-generating advertising), or (4) no likely emotional response.

The data set was analyzed on a purely descriptive basis to determine whether there was a sufficient number of pure-benefit and mixed-benefit executions (all of the commercials contained rational benefits). Only 47 of the 168 commercials

(28 percent) were mixed-benefit executions, incorporating a psychological benefit as well as a rational one.

Impact of benefit structure. The first step of analysis mandated the creation of a measure of "advertising success" that could take into account performance on measures of both recall and persuasion. To do this, each ad was judged "successful" only if it scored at or above the mean on both measures.

In confirmation of previous findings, our results showed that commercials incorporating mixed benefits perform better in terms of advertising success than pure-benefit ads (in this case those containing only a rational benefit).

When we further subdivided the mixed-benefit ads into those that directly stated the psychological benefit versus those that merely implied it, we found that ads implying the psychological benefit outperformed the directly stated ads. This finding is not surprising given that we believe that consumers are more likely to engage in defense mechanisms when exposed to overt statements of psychological benefits. What we did find surprising was the level of the improvement achieved. Taking the pure-benefit commercials as the norm (index = 100)—they represent more than 70 percent of the cases—we find that including a psychological benefit increases the advertising success to an index level of 158 (58 percent greater likelihood of advertising success relative to the normative pure-benefit commercials). Further, subdividing these into an implied benefit versus a directly stated benefit yields indices of 171 and 137, respectively.

Impact of emotionality. Although the issue of total effectiveness was of interest to us in reviewing benefit structures, we chose to look at the recall and persuasion scores separately for the commercials in each of the three "emotionality" categories mentioned above (humor, dynamic shift, and static). Both of the emotional response–generating categories (dynamic shift in emotion and simple/sustained mood) tended to generate suppressed recall scores (which require an association of the brand name to the execution), but only the simple mood category was unlikely to generate a high level of persuasion. Apparently there is something about the emotion generation and resolution that creates an environment in which the benefits become more salient or accepted; perhaps the dynamic shift in emotions affects the consumer-respondents in a more involving way.

On the other hand, those commercials in which humor predominated achieved above average recall without simultaneously achieving high persuasion scores. This pattern of scores parallels those of the simple mood-generating commercials, albeit at higher levels.

Coming back, then, to some earlier comments, we find (as had FCB/Leber Katz Partners stated before) that "feeling" advertising does indeed fail to perform well (in terms of total effectiveness) on standard copy-testing systems. However, within this general class of advertising, creating a dynamic shift in viewers' emotions can significantly increase scores. The more important finding, we feel, is that which was stated earlier: consumers respond better to advertising, even within standard copy-testing environments, when that advertising signals a prod-

uct's or a service's ability to deliver both rational and psychological benefits—
an important advance in understanding advertising.

PRACTICAL APPLICATIONS OF THIS RESEARCH

Taken as a whole, this research program provides a better advertising strategy
focus. All of us—research, account, and creative people alike—must be forced
to think more carefully about the psychological and rational needs of our brands'
consumers. Adopting this vantage point mandates uncovering the corresponding
benefits in clients' products and services.

This deeper understanding leads to a heuristic for revealing rational and psychological benefits that I call a "four-box" model. This device forces those who
work on a given brand to consider the psychological and rational benefits for
both the brand and the category.

First, one would attempt to understand the "category generic" benefits why
a person would use this kind of product in terms of psychological and rational
benefits. The next step would be to dig deeper to figure out why the consumer
would use this particular brand. The goal of this exercise is to create a meaningful
differentiation for the brand along the lines of psychological and rational benefits
to consumers. Advertisers usually want to prevent consumers from being convinced merely to buy the category (increasing primary demand) while failing to
understand the benefits associated with buying this brand. This simple exercise
not only maintains our focus but it also drives our advertising.

DIRECTIONS FOR FUTURE RESEARCH

Research programs always seem to have next steps. Areas of inquiry that
earlier might never have been considered seem to spring forth. What follows
are areas that grew out of this work.

Consider the notion of linked versus unlinked benefits, a distinction that captures the difference between psychological benefits coming from the same or
different features of the product or service. We define a linked benefit as a pairing
of psychological and rational benefits deriving from the same feature. An unlinked benefit is a pairing of a psychological benefit from one feature with a
rational benefit from a different feature. While this has not yet been tested
empirically, we would hypothesize that linked benefits will be superior to unlinked benefits.

Is it possible to segment consumers on the basis of psychological needs, going
beyond typologies, such as VALS 2, to the point where we are testing tenets of
Mazlowian theory? It would be fascinating to find out whether these psychologically based segments of consumers are buying different products. Or different
categories of products. Or different forms of products. Are there major new
product opportunities for these segments? How might one direct advertising
against these psychologically based segments?

Is there an interaction between programming environment and a commercial's benefit structure (or emotionality) that leads to advertising effectiveness? Media planners do not select media on the basis of content. They believe it to be inefficient to do so. However, this is true only if one does not get a substantial lift through judicious use of program content—a point that remains to be determined empirically. Further, if there are indeed different psychologically based segments, we might find consumers watching different kinds of programming.

CONCLUSIONS

We believe that this program of research and its underlying theory holds broad implications for the development of advertising, for the understanding of consumers and their behaviors, and for the advertising industry as a whole. The latest study in this program of research, for example, suggests that the advertising industry has yet to come to terms with what at this point should be taken as a "given." That only 28 percent of the commercials incorporated a psychological benefit, while all contained a rational benefit, suggests that the industry has not yet internalized the notion that consumers are human beings. Consumers, because they are human beings, have needs that go beyond the purely rational, and they purchase products in an effort to satisfy these other needs as well. As such, our findings hold at least as much significance for advertising development as they do for the testing of advertising materials.

REFERENCES

Agres, S. J. (1984). *The Marschalk Emotional Expression Deck*. Unpublished manuscript, The Marschalk Company, Inc.

Agres, S. J. (1988). Rational, emotional, and mixed appeals in advertising: Impact on recall and persuasion. In L. F. Alwitt (Ed.), *Proceedings of the Division of Consumer Psychology* (pp. 57–61). Washington, DC: American Psychological Association.

Agres, S. J., & Bernstein, M. (1984, August). *Cognitive and emotional elements in persuasion and advertising*. Paper presented at the 92nd Annual Convention of the American Psychological Association, Toronto, Ontario, Canada.

Agres, S. J., & Bernstein, M. (1985). The use of facial expressions to evaluate emotional responsiveness to advertising. *Proceedings of the Second Annual Advertising Research Foundation Copy Research Workshop*, (pp. 67–74). New York: Advertising Research Foundation.

Bernstein, M., & Agres, S. J. (1984, October). *On assessing emotional responsiveness to advertising*. Paper presented at the Association for Consumer Research, Washington, DC.

Notes

1. See, for example, the distinction raised by Stout, Homer & Liu (Chapter 12) between felt and depicted emotions, as well as the work by Englis (Chapter 14) on the relationship

between emotions judged to be conveyed by commercials and viewers' emotional response to them.

2. With regard to verbal rating scales, Puto and Hoyer (Chapter 5) outline their work in developing a measure of the consumer's brand-experience relationship; while Russo and Stephens (Chapter 8) contrast two types of verbal measures of the emotional impact of advertisements (i.e., ad-specific and general measures).

3. Punnett and Pollay (Chapter 7) advocate the use of and propose guidelines for a rigorous coding system that captures expressive facial movements in order to measure emotional responses to television advertising.

4. For example, Brock, Brannon, and Bridgewater (Chapter 17) "cut straight to the chase" by examining the impact of schema-related and schema-unrelated direct mail solicitations on a behavioral measure—re-enlisting with a weight-loss clinic.

5. The typical consumer may not even remember the main idea of some advertising that is "transformational," the goal of which is to change the experience the consumer has in buying, owning, or consuming a brand. Puto and Hoyer (Chapter 5) further explore this distinction between transformational and informational advertising.

6. There was no difference between males and females in terms of this difficulty in describing the emotional states that were seen.

7. Because the earlier stimuli used a live presenter format throughout, concern was felt that the normal facial and bodily expressions of the presenter could represent a confounding variable and impact on the findings.

2

On Using Classical Conditioning Methods for Researching the Impact of Ad-Evoked Feelings

Chris T. Allen and Terence A. Shimp

In recent years there has been growing interest in affective and emotional topics in advertising research. This "emotion revolution" has provided an important opportunity to explore fundamentally new issues (Holbrook & Hirschman, 1982). For example, ad-evoked feelings have emerged as a mediator of advertising's influence distinct from traditional cognitive considerations (e.g., Batra & Ray, 1986; Edell & Burke, 1987). Interestingly, however, this revolution has had little impact on the knowledge generation strategies utilized by advertising researchers. For the most part, the general methods of cognitive and social psychology continue to be featured in empirical work (cf., Cafferata & Tybout, 1989).

The Seventh Annual Conference on Advertising and Consumer Psychology furnished a forum for discussing a variety of issues under its general theme of Emotions and Advertising. This chapter was developed in response to one of the questions posed by the conference organizers: "How should moods, emotions, and feelings be studied within an advertising context?" The chapter describes an alternative strategy for conducting research on the impact of ad-evoked feelings—a strategy that is best viewed as a potential supplement to more mainstream approaches.

The alternative discussed herein grows out of the set of procedures and assumptions associated with the classical conditioning or Pavlovian research tradition. The fundamental focus of this tradition is the form of learning which occurs when stimuli are encountered in systematic and predictable patterns. Often the pairing of two stimuli—one which is relatively neutral (i.e., the conditioned stimulus) and another which is provocative or at least mildly interesting (i.e., the unconditioned stimulus)—can influence evaluations of the neutral stimulus.

The knowledge products that have emerged from the classical conditioning tradition are generalizations (i.e., learning principles) which prescribe the optimum circumstances for affecting evaluative judgments. When the stimuli are a product or brand on the one hand (serving as the conditioned stimulus) and nonverbal ad elements like pictures or music on the other (i.e., the unconditioned stimulus), the potential applicability of the conditioning framework in advertising applications quickly becomes apparent.

The purpose of this chapter is to explain how classical conditioning methods can be used to examine a unique set of issues in advertising research. This will be accomplished by elucidating what should and should not be expected of conditioning methods. We first discuss major differences in the general goals and assumptions underlying behaviorist versus cognitivist methods and overview the Pavlovian approach to research. Next we specify the affective phenomena for which conditioning methods seem especially well suited. We also describe a general style of television advertisement wherein conditioning principles may find their greatest applicability.

The focus then shifts to more specific concerns about how to properly employ classical conditioning methods in consumer research contexts. This discussion begins with a review of relevant consumer studies. We find that the most recent projects in this area are incorporating the meticulous methodological procedures that characterize the Pavlovian tradition. With this background, opportunities for future research are then considered. The chapter concludes with an attempt to reinforce our theme that conditioning methods can foster examination of a unique set of issues in the advertising domain.

BEHAVIORIST METHODS AND THE PAVLOVIAN TRADITION

While behaviorist and cognitivist research programs are often viewed as incommensurable and even confrontational, we adopt the perspective that competing programs simply represent different ways of seeking knowledge about natural phenomena (cf., Anderson, 1986; Hudson & Ozanne, 1988; Peter & Olson, 1987). Working with a behaviorist approach entails, first and foremost, becoming comfortable with a unique set of research goals and methodological priorities. These result in different knowledge products than those obtained through traditional cognitivist methods. We contend that one of the most appealing aspects of behaviorist methods is the potential they offer for learning something unique about how advertising works.

Contrasting Goals and Assumptions

Cognitivist and behaviorist research programs are motivated by a host of antithetical assumptions and goals (cf., Anderson, 1986; Nord & Peter, 1980; Peter & Olson, 1987; Schwartz, 1978; Zuriff, 1985). We do not attempt to review all points of contention, but instead focus on three major areas: the role of the environment, the role of hypothetical constructs concerning intrapsychic mechanisms, and the nature of the knowledge products produced by the two programs.

Behaviorists work from the presumption that behavior is controlled by stimuli encountered in the environment; thus, they adopt the perspective that satisfactory explanation must link behavior to the external environment. This "externalism" is chosen as the best strategy for advancing the goals of prediction and control (Zuriff, 1985). While behaviorists seek to constrain their use of hypothetical concepts regarding mental states, constructs representing internal, private events are not uncommon in their program (Schwartz, 1978; Zuriff, 1985).

Cognitivist methods originate from a very different metaphysical foundation; they are based on the observation that behavior is often not in one-to-one correspondence with the environment. This prompts the inference that "there must be something else to which behavior corresponds, namely, an internal representation of the world" (Zuriff, 1985, p. 161). It follows, according to this perspective, that an adequate explanation for behavior must appeal to hypothetical constructs regarding internal cognitive processes (Haugeland, 1978; Zuriff, 1985). These abstractions often become reified in the cognitivist program (cf., Hudson & Ozanne, 1988).

Given their diverse metaphysical bases, it should be expected that cognitivists and behaviorists would value and produce different knowledge products. Cognitivists produce theoretical explanations featuring multiple layers or chains of intrapsychic constructs (Nord & Peter, 1980). Behaviorists seek laws of associative learning which include identification of basic elements along with the combinational rules that will foster learning (Schwartz, 1978). The behaviorist's overriding priority is to identify these basic elements in the external environment. The simple fact that the two research programs do yield fundamentally different knowledge products is not a reason to prefer one over the other.

It should be emphasized that behaviorism is a very general label which encompasses the work of many different researchers using diverse empirical paradigms (Schwartz, 1978; Zuriff, 1985). Pavlovian research is just one exemplar of the behaviorist tradition. Pavlovian researchers do emphasize how relations among environmental stimuli affect behavior. An understanding of where Pavlovian methods may prove valuable in the advertising domain must be based on a realistic appraisal of what this tradition does and does not say about learning. In the following section some common misconceptions are addressed.

Misconceptions About the Pavlovian Tradition

In the marketing literature, classical conditioning is often portrayed as a *theoretical explanation* which is particularly germane for low-involvement consumption (e.g., Engel, Blackwell, & Miniard, 1986; Gorn, 1982; Holbrook & O'Shaughnessy, 1984; Kroeber-Riel, 1984). This portrayal contains a hidden assumption about what classical conditioning theory asserts: It is presumed that simple contiguity of a conditioned stimulus (CS) and an unconditioned stimulus (US) will effect a transfer of the unconditioned response directly to the CS (then to be called the conditioned response). Because traditional Pavlovians have chosen not to speculate about intrapsychic mechanisms in explaining conditioned learning, cognitivists often infer that shifting this response from one stimulus (i.e., the US) to another (i.e., the CS) is something which must occur in a noncognitive or mindless process (Allen & Madden, 1985). Thus, if the US (e.g., background music in an ad) produces excitement, the CS (e.g., a new brand) should become exciting (Nord & Peter, 1980). If the US provokes a sense of prestige, the CS will become prestigious (Kroeber-Riel, 1984). It is a prevalent assumption in the consumer behavior literature that almost any hedonic tone will transfer automatically from US to CS (Engel et al., 1986; Gorn, 1982; Holbrook & O'Shaughnessy, 1984; Peter & Olson, 1987). Accordingly, classical conditioning is offered as a primary theoretical justification for the use of emotional ad executions with low-involvement products.

On close inspection, common stereotypes of the Pavlovian tradition contain two misinterpretations. The first is the notion that this tradition implies a theoretical explanation involving a mindless or noncognitive process. Modern Pavlovian researchers contend that conditioning entails learning about relationships among stimuli in one's environment (Rescorla, 1988): a distinguishing characteristic of conditioned learning is the establishment of a *contingency relation* between a CS and a US. In this view, associative learning occurs because the CS provides information about the US and signals that it is forthcoming (Domjan & Burkhard, 1986; Hugdahl, 1987). Rather than being a mindless process, it is to be expected that humans would be fully aware of the contingency relation (Allen & Janiszewski, 1989; Dawson, Schell, Beers, & Kelly, 1982; Stuart, Shimp, & Engle, 1987).

A second common oversimplification is the belief that mere contiguity of a CS and US will shift a response from one stimulus to the other. Whether a particular CS/US pair will yield conditioned learning, and what the actual nature of the conditioned response will be, are strictly empirical questions. As F. K. McSweeney and C. Bierley point out, there are no "rules that would predict which choices of CS's and US's will yield conditioning" (1984, p. 624), and there is no reason to assume that "the response that will be conditioned will necessarily be similar to the response evoked by the US" (p. 621). "Describing Pavlovian conditioning as the endowing of a CS with the ability to evoke the *same* response as the US is a wholly inadequate characterization" (Rescorla, 1988, p. 158).

What Is Conditioned?

If classical conditioning does not involve a simple transfer of response from one stimulus to another, one is left with an important question about what is conditioned. Discussions in the consumer behavior literature are quite vague on this point, and they often refer to the output of successful conditioning as simply a conditioned response. This notion of a response is then interpreted as implicating overt behavior change as the output of conditioned learning. Seeking effects for conditioning treatments simply in terms of overt behavior change is likely to prove too limiting for advertising research and is, in fact, unnecessary.

British researchers A. B. Levey and I. Martin (1975, 1983; Martin & Levey, 1978, 1985, 1987) argue that what is conditioned is an "evaluative response" and not overt behavior per se. These researchers go so far as to claim that the evaluative response, and not overt behavior, is the response that is both necessary and sufficient for conditioned learning. Martin and Levey describe the evaluative response as follows:

> The evaluative response is postulated as a characteristic internal reaction to environmental stimuli in terms of the evaluation of good/bad, liked/disliked, pleasant/unpleasant. It is subjective in the sense that it is unique to the individual and refers to the individual's own internal state; non-specific in that it is not attributable to a particular sensory modality. It is seen as a mechanism which provides the necessary link between immediate and final (unknowable) consequences. (1987, p. 62)

From Levey and Martin's (1975, 1983) perspective, conditioned learning takes the form of alterations in one's general evaluation of some stimulus object. They thus portray the consequences of successful conditioning in very familiar terms for consumer researchers. Indeed, advertising research is likely to be stimulated by adopting the perspective that classical conditioning is best viewed as one basic mechanism for shaping attitudes (*cf.*, Greenwald, 1968; Petty & Cacioppo, 1981); as C. T. Allen and C. A. Janiszewski (1989) have pointed out, research adopting this perspective is appropriately portrayed as being in a seam between the cognitivist and behaviorist research traditions.

The Pavlovian Tradition in Advertising Research

What might one expect of the Pavlovian tradition when attempting to adapt it to the advertising domain? Because behaviorist approaches seek explanations which feature the role of environmental variables, the principal focus will be shifted to the elements and structures of advertising messages. Developing explanations for how advertising works in the form of theories about intrapsychic mechanisms would not be a priority. The Pavlovian approach may ultimately provide insights about how to build and structure ads and ad campaigns to maximize their impact on consumers' attitudes. This can be viewed as a more practitioner-oriented research agenda than those typically pursued through cognitivist methods (Nord & Peter, 1980).

To understand how the patterns and structures of advertisements may serve to influence consumer attitudes, it is necessary to identify the basic, reoccurring elements found in ad stimuli. In the following section we identify these basic elements as those with affect-evoking potential. These affect evokers furnish one building block for implementing a Pavlovian approach to advertising research, and they implicate specific styles of advertisements as appropriate points of reference for conditioning studies.

NONVERBAL AD ELEMENTS AS AFFECT EVOKERS AND UNCONDITIONED STIMULI

In recent years consumer researchers have introduced many forms of emotional concepts into the advertising literature (e.g., Cafferata & Tybout, 1989). Emotional advertisements contain invariably nonverbal elements (NVEs), including colors, sound effects, music, and visual imagery. NVEs serve the role of unconditioned stimuli in the conditioning framework (Edell, 1988) and are of particular interest because of their potential to evoke pleasant feelings that the advertiser hopes will become associated with the brand being advertised.

It follows that certain styles or types of television advertisements exemplify Pavlovian conditioning requirements. Such ads are complex and meticulously constructed and often contain multiple brand (i.e., the CS) presentations interspersed among a series of attractive NVEs (i.e., the USs). These ads commonly feature multiple NVEs like attractive visual images and colors along with robust and appealing background music. Verbal claims about product performance are frequently absent. It certainly seems that advertisers display a kind of "Pavlovian intuition" in this ad style (Peter & Olson, 1987)—at a minimum, the ads illustrate an instinctive reliance on learning via simple association on the part of advertisers (cf., McCracken, 1986).

EXTANT CONSUMER RESEARCH IN THE PAVLOVIAN TRADITION

Advertising and consumer researchers have long been familiar with classical conditioning principles and have acknowledged their potential relevance to advertising contexts. However, classical conditioning's relevance to advertising applications is more a matter of presumption than solid empirical evidence. Indeed, very few studies have direct relevance to advertising settings. This is because most Pavlovian research has studied animal behavior. Moreover, work with humans has emphasized autonomic responses and skeletal behaviors rather than attitudinal conditioning.

The following review is restricted to studies published in marketing and consumer-behavior outlets. Excluded, for example, are the classic attitude studies by the Staatses (e.g., Staats & Staats, 1957, 1958). The review is ordered from studies using nonoptimal conditioning procedures to those using more optimal procedures. Not surprisingly, this ordering is basically chronological since later researchers have benefited from earlier efforts.

Early Conditioning Research in the Consumer Literature

G. J. Gorn (1982) presented subjects with slides of a writing pen (serving as the CS) with *simultaneous playing* of background music (the US). (This format is called "simultaneous conditioning.") His experimental design featured four stimulus combinations: (1) liked music (from the movie *Grease*) served as a positive US and accompanied the presentation of a light blue pen; (2) liked music also accompanied a beige pen; (3) unliked music (classical Indian music) served as the negative US and was displayed alongside a light blue pen, or (4) with a beige pen.

Following exposure to these pen and music combinations, subjects were given an opportunity to select a pen, either light blue or beige, as a gift for participation. Congruent with a conditioning hypothesis, 79 percent of the subjects in the "liked music" conditions picked the pen color associated with that music; only 30 percent in the "disliked music" conditions picked the pen color associated with that music.

Gorn's experiments are noteworthy for several reasons. His is the first major study in consumer research positioned directly as a test of classical conditioning. It is also interesting that Gorn obtained evidence for conditioning using non-optimum procedures. Specifically, (1) the research employed a single pairing of CS and US; (2) the CS and US appeared simultaneously rather than in the superior forward-conditioning order (i.e., CS followed by the US); (3) there is no compelling reason why music and writing pens are relevant stimuli or belong together; (4) the US in the pleasant-affect condition (i.e., the *Grease* music) was familiar to subjects, which diminishes the likelihood that the CS would have established a unique predictive relation with the music; and (5) a behavioral-choice criterion is a demanding measure for the conditioned response.

C. T. Allen and T. J. Madden (1985) systematically replicated Gorn's first experiment and incorporated several new procedures: (1) subjects were processed individually, rather than in groups, because of a concern that Gorn's results may have been contaminated by subjects interacting with one another; (2) humor served as the US instead of music; (3) in addition to using Gorn's pen selection measure to evidence a conditioned response, Allen and Madden employed a "buy-back" measure; and (4) a systematic postexperimental inquiry assessed the potential presence of demand artifacts.

Using a 2 (pen color) by 2 (humor type) design, female subjects viewed one of two pen colors (green or black) while listening to humorous episodes from either of two famous comedians, Bill Cosby or Redd Foxx. Cosby's humor represented a composite, positively valenced US, whereas Foxx's sexist humor was chosen to represent a disliked US. Dependent variables included pen selection and the buy-back measure whereby the experimenter offered to repurchase a subject's pen for 25¢ or, if they refused to sell at that price, for 50¢.

The pen selection results indicated no significant difference between the percentage of subjects selecting either green or black pens as a function of whether pen color was paired with pleasant or unpleasant humor. On the buy-back measure, a greater percentage of the Foxx subjects (27 percent) sold their pens back compared to only 7 percent of the Cosby subjects.

The same deviations from optimal-conditioning procedures characteristic of Gorn's research apply also to Allen and Madden's study. They used a single conditioning trial, familiar USs, a simultaneous-conditioning procedure, behavioral measures of conditioning response, and questionable CS–US belongingness.

Research with Children

M. C. Macklin (1986) researched preschoolers by manipulating the temporal relation between orange and yellow pencils (the CS) and the cartoon character Smurf (the US). The conditioned and unconditioned stimuli were arranged in three orders: simultaneous conditioning, forward conditioning, and a truly random control (discussed more fully below). The CS (pencils) and US (Smurf) were presented to the children as 9-by-12-inch laminated posters. The experiment involved three 5-second exposures to the pictures equally spaced over a 20-minute session.

The key dependent variable was pencil selection. The experimenter presented the orange and yellow pencils side by side and permitted subjects to select one. A second buy-back measure allowed each subject to keep his or her selected pencil or to replace it with a sticker chosen from a variety of popular stickers.

No significant relationship was detected in any of the three treatment groups on pencil-color selection. In terms of the buy-back measure, children in the forward-conditioning group were less likely to trade their selected pencil for a sticker (60.2 percent traded) than were children in the simultaneous group (82.1 percent traded) or control group (89.3 percent traded).

The Macklin study is an important first step toward applying the classical conditioning paradigm in a consumer context with children, but its failure to provide unqualified support for conditioning may again be due to nonoptimal study procedures. Specifically, the procedures were nonoptimal due to both a US-preexposure effect (Smurf is a familiar stimulus) and a CS-preexposure effect (orange and yellow pencils are familiar, nonnovel stimuli).

The Emergence of More Optimal Procedures

A study by C. Bierley, F. K. McSweeney, and R. Vannieuwkerk (1985) used music from *Star Wars* as the US and 12 colored geometric shapes (red, blue, and yellow circles, squares, triangles, and rectangles) as conditioned stimuli. Subjects were assigned randomly to two conditioning groups or one of two control groups. In conditioning group 1 (red predictive), red geometric figures were consistently followed by music in a forward-conditioning fashion (i.e., the red figures predicted the *Star Wars* music in every trial). In conditioning group 2 (yellow predictive), yellow figures were always followed by music. Group 3 (truly random control) received the same numbers of red, blue and yellow figures as presented to groups 1 and 2 and heard music from *Star Wars*, but the figures and music were presented in a random ordering. A fourth group (CS-only control) saw the colored figures but heard no music.

This use of the truly random control group is the first application of this procedure in a consumer research context and deserves special mention. This control procedure, when introduced by R. A. Rescorla (1967), gave researchers an unambiguous mechanism for empirically implementing the concept of *contingency relation*. In a truly random control group, the CS and US are presented to subjects the identical number of times they occur in the experimental, conditioning group, but no contingency whatsoever is established between CS and US. Consequently, any differences in responses between experimental and control subjects is attributable to the contingent relation established, and not to alternative accounts such as mere frequency of CS presentations.

Returning to the Bierley et al. project, the procedure included 28 trials for each of the three colors. Each CS was on the screen for 5 seconds followed by *Star Wars* music for 10 seconds. Magnitude estimation was used to measure color preferences. A mixed model ANOVA tested for a significant group-by-color interaction effect, which was the crucial indicator of whether preferences for colored geometric shapes had been conditioned by their association with the *Star Wars* music. A significant group-by-color interaction effect was obtained; however, this effect was not clear cut but rather represented a combination of a nonsignificant increase of color preference in the conditioning groups compared to the random control group, and a significant *decrease* in preference for red in the yellow-predictive group compared to the random control group. Simple main effect results did indicate, in support of the conditioning prediction, that both red and yellow geometric shapes were more preferred when they preceded the *Star Wars* music.

This study's primary contribution involves the use of experimental procedures that have been shown in prior research to enhance the likelihood of detecting classical conditioning. But even here the procedures are not ideal for maximizing conditioned learning. As with the USs in the previously described studies, *Star Wars* music is a familiar stimulus, which implies that less conditioning probably occurred than would have had an original, novel music arrangement been used. Also, the question remains as to whether music is the most appropriate stimulus to use for conditioning preferences for colored geometric shapes.

Shaping Consumer Attitudes via Pavlovian Methods

E. W. Stuart, T. A. Shimp, and R. W. Engle (1987) undertook four experiments to test different classical conditioning principles in an attitude formation context. In all experiments attractive water scenes (a mountain waterfall, sunset over water, a boat mast against the sky, and a lavendar-hued island) represented a composite US, and "Brand L toothpaste" served as the conditioned stimulus.

A hypothetical brand was chosen to optimize the opportunity for attitudinal conditioning. The experiments were conducted via slide presentations involving pictures of: (1) the CS, Brand L; (2) three other filler products ("Brand M detergent," "Brand J soap," and "Brand R cola"), which served to deflect hypothesis guessing from Brand L; (3) the US scenes; and (4) a variety of filler scenes. The ordering of the various slides was systematically arranged to structure both forward- and backward-conditioning groups (the US precedes the CS in backward conditioning) and truly random and CS-only control groups.

Experiment 1 manipulated the number of trial presentations at four levels: 1,3,10, and 20 pairings of conditioned and unconditioned stimuli. Subjects exposed to the conditioning trials exhibited more positive attitudes toward Brand L toothpaste at all trial levels than the corresponding control group. The amount of conditioning did not increase with progressive increases in the number of CS-US pairings.

Experiment 2 tested the so-called CS-preexposure, or latent inhibition, effect. A latent inhibition group received a number of preexposures to Brand L toothpaste presented by itself *prior to* its being paired with the attractive visuals. This preexposure was expected to inhibit attitudinal conditioning, and in fact this is what the data reflected. However, though conditioning was weaker in the preexposure group than in the non-preexposure group, there was evidence that the preexposure group was conditioned at a 10-trial level.

A third experiment evaluated forward versus backward conditioning, predicting that greater conditioning would occur in the forward group. The data supported this prediction and also demonstrated that the backward-conditioning treatment, though inferior to forward conditioning in affecting attitudes toward Brand L, yielded more favorable attitudes than the random control group (*cf.*, Spetch, Wilkie, & Pinel, 1981).

A potential problem with experiments 1, 2, and 3 was that the CS-US sequencing involved a combination of forward and simultaneous conditioning procedures. Experiment 4 altered the procedure so that the conditioning group received a pure forward-conditioning treatment. Results from this 10-trial experiment demonstrated again the superiority of forward over backward conditioning in influencing attitudes toward Brand L toothpaste, and the superiority of both over a random-control procedure.

Several aspects of these experiments are noteworthy in the context of the brief evolution of classical conditioning studies in consumer behavior. First, having benefited from predecessor studies, Stuart, Shimp, and Engel's use of rigorous conditioning procedures and appropriate control groups permits unambiguous conclusions regarding the conditionability of attitudes. Second, with the possible exception that water scenes (the composite US) may not have been entirely relevant for the conditioned product, toothpaste, the experiments arranged optimal conditions for classical conditioning to occur. Specifically, the CS was a novel, unfamiliar stimulus toward which subjects had no established schemas, no preexisting attitudes, and no previously established associations with other concepts; moreover, the US composite was established via pretesting to represent a relatively novel set of visual scenes. These conditions increased the likelihood that a contingent relation between CS and US would be established, and that the pleasant affect evoked by the USs would serve to condition a favorable evaluation of Brand L toothpaste.

Future Advertising Research in the Pavlovian Tradition

Classical conditioning research is in the introductory stage of a potentially gainful life cycle in consumer behavior. Very little is known at this point about attitudinal conditioning. Future conditioning research in advertising and consumer behavior should consider at least five general classes of factors: (1) person characteristics; (2) stimulus characteristics (i.e., CS, US, and the relationship between them); (3) background, or context factors; (4) mechanical experimental conditions (number of trials, intertrial interval, length of stimulus exposure, and so on); and (5) real world versus laboratory testing.

Person characteristics. People certainly vary in their degree of conditionability as a function of personal characteristics related to the nature of the stimuli involved. For example, in experiments where stimuli are predominantly visual (such as Stuart et al. 1987), it might be expected that subjects who are more visually oriented—for example, as measured by Childers and Houston's (1984) style of processing scale—would be more conditionable than verbally oriented subjects. Likewise, not all subjects would respond favorably to a particular musical arrangement serving as the US, as tastes in music are disparate.

Stimulus characteristics. Decisions concerning the choice of conditioned and unconditioned stimuli are critical to the outcomes of conditioning experiments. Pavlovian psychologists who have studied animal behavior have established that the amount and rapidity of conditioning increase with the intensity of CS, US, or both, and that conditioning is retarded when either the CS or the US is nonnovel or familiar (*cf.*, Domjan & Burkhard, 1986; Mackintosh, 1983; McSweeney & Bierley, 1984).

These requirements create dilemmas for consumer researchers, especially in the choice of USs. On the one hand, we would like to use well-known cultural symbols and artifacts as USs (e.g., popular music, celebrities) because they appear frequently in actual marketing communications; however, such stimuli may be less than ideal for conditioning evaluative responses because of their popularity and celebrity.

The fact that past consumer research has obtained mixed results may be explained by differences in the familiarity of USs. For example, Gorn's (1982) use of classic Indian music was truly an unfamiliar stimulus in comparison to the familiar *Grease* music. Comparatively, Allen and Madden's (1985) use of humorous episodes by Bill Cosby and Redd Foxx was much closer to being equally familiar USs. Thus, whereas Gorn could have expected rapid negative conditioning to the unfamiliar Indian music, but no rapid positive conditioning to the familiar *Grease* music, Allen and Madden could not have expected rapid conditioning for either of the comedians. Macklin (1986) also could not have expected rapid conditioning of her preschoolers to the three-trial contingency between pencils and the familiar Smurf character. Similarly, Bierley et al. (1985) should not have expected rapid conditioning to the well-known *Star Wars* music. This may explain why they felt it necessary to employ 28 repetitions for each color.

In making the preceding comments, we of course are assuming that experimental results with animals translate directly to attitudinal conditioning. This assumption might be unwarranted. The only way that consumer researchers will know whether familiar, nonnovel stimuli are indeed inferior as USs will be through additional research. Researchers need to hold constant the CS, the numbers of trial presentations, and so on, while altering the relative degree of US familiarity. Of course, the same applies on the CS side. Holding all else constant, one can then test whether new, unfamiliar brands do indeed condition more rapidly and more strongly than established brands.

An even more challenging area for research involves the issue of CS-US relevance/belongingness. At present it is not known what makes the CS and US relevant to each other (Domjan & Burkhard, 1986), but intuition would suggest some likely possibilities for consumer research. For example, Stuart et al's. (1987) water scenes were somewhat relevant for toothpaste and perhaps for products like soft drinks and beach equipment, but probably would be much less relevant for, say, electronic appliances. Interestingly, Macklin's (1986) use of the blue-hued cartoon character Smurf may have exhibited greater belongingness had she attempted to condition preference for blue rather than orange and yellow pencils. Clearly more research would be useful in attempting to formalize our understanding of what makes CSs and USs relevant for one another.

Context factors. It was long believed that simple contiguity between CS and US was responsible for conditioning. This notion has largely been discarded. Background conditions and context factors in a conditioning experiment are now known to influence learning. R. S. Sutton and A. G. Barto claim that "Context stimuli can have such large effects on resultant associative strength that they cannot satisfactorily be ignored by a nontrivial theory of classical conditioning" (1981, p. 149). This suggests that contextual factors such as programming (in the case of television advertising) and format (in the case of magazine advertising) may influence the rate of conditioning.

Mechanical experimental conditions. The number of CS-US trials, the length of the intertrial interval, the amount of time given each stimulus presentation, and the overall length of stimulus exposure are all important considerations when designing conditioning research. Unfortunately, there are no guiding principles in providing answers for these issues. "It's an empirical question" is the only possible retort in response to basic concerns such as: "How many trials should I use?", "How long should each slide appear on the screen?", and "How many filler items (cf., Stuart et al., 1987) should be used to deflect hypothesis guessing?''

Real world versus lab testing. Should conditioning research be conducted with real advertisements in natural settings or in laboratories using artificial stimuli? Actually, this is not an either-or proposition, but rather a matter of sequencing. We propose that tightly controlled experiments are essential initially in implementing the meticulous requirements of Pavlovian methods. The problem with testing real commercials is that one cannot be certain whether results are attributable to conditioning effects or to other processes.

Once careful laboratory experiments have provided a sense of how advertising stimuli work within the classical conditioning framework, it will be productive to extend the research to more natural contexts. For example, now that there is some laboratory evidence that forward conditioning is superior to backward conditioning (Stuart et al., 1987), it would be meaningful to test this issue using television commercials. Alternative versions of commercials could be prepared. In one version the CS (i.e., the brand) would appear followed by the US (e.g., attractive visuals or music) in the forward-conditioning arrangement. A second version would reverse this ordering by presenting the brand after the US to produce the backward arrangement. Yet another version might present the brand and other stimuli in a random sequence. Appropriate measures of brand attitudes would then gauge the effects of the various arrangements in an applied test of this basic, Pavlovian principle.

CONCLUSIONS—ASKING A DIFFERENT SET OF QUESTIONS

Structuring advertising research within the classical conditioning framework leads one to focus on a different set of questions than those typically posed by consumer and advertising researchers. These questions are best illustrated by putting them in the context of the prototypical television ad which features brief flashes of attractive or unusual visual images (i.e., the US) interspersed among a sequence of brand (i.e., the CS) presentations. Often such ads also include rhythmic background music or jingles. When using this ad style there are choices to be made about how and how often to show the brand. Is it better to show the brand name, the package, the product in use, or some combination? Should all the images be affect evokers, or just those that follow a brand presentation? How many CS/US presentations are appropriate for a 30-second ad? Can the benefits of repetition be better realized with a flight of ads? Should voice-overs be used to enhance attention when the CS is presented? Might changes in the rhythm, pitch, or loudness of the background music be used to direct viewers' attention to the focal CS/US pairings? Does pleasing background music add to the impact of an affect-evoking visual? Is the novelty of the US, or the affect-evoking potential of the US, more important in shaping attitudes? Will conditioned learning manifest for mature brands as well as new brands? Can brief glimpses of celebrities serve as effective USs? These and many other questions are motivated by the conditioning framework.

The Pavlovian approach to advertising research thus turns one's attention to the basic elements and structures of advertising stimuli, and deemphasizes the more common focus on intrapsychic states and processes. Are there general laws of associative learning that can help consumer and advertising researchers to better understand how advertising works, and assist advertising practitioners in building more effective brand presentations? While the answer at this time can only be a very tentative yes, more empirical work would certainly seem justified in this area.

REFERENCES

Allen, C. T., & Janiszewski, C. A. (1989). Assessing the role of contingency awareness in attitudinal conditioning with implications for advertising research. *Journal of Marketing Research, 26*, 30–43.

Allen, C. T., & Madden, T. J. (1985). A closer look at classical conditioning. *Journal of Consumer Research, 12*, 301–315.

Anderson, P. F. (1986). On method in consumer research: A critical relativist perspective. *Journal of Consumer Research, 13*, 155–173.

Batra, R., & Ray, M. L. (1986). Affective responses mediating acceptance of advertising. *Journal of Consumer Research, 13*, 234–249.

Bierley, C., McSweeney, F. K., & Vannieuwkerk, R. (1985). Classical conditioning of preferences for stimuli. *Journal of Consumer Research, 12*, 316–323.

Cafferata, P., & Tybout, A. M. (1989). *Cognitive and affective responses to advertising.* Lexington, MA: D. C. Heath.

Childers, T. L., & Houston, M. J. (1984). Conditions for a picture-superiority effect on consumer memory. *Journal of Consumer Research, 11*, 643–654.

Dawson, M. E., Schell, A. M., Beers, J. R., & Kelly, A. (1982). Allocation of cognitive processing capacity during human autonomic classical conditioning. *Journal of Experimental Psychology: General, 111*, 273–295.

Domjan, M., & Burkhard, B. (1986). *The principles of learning & behavior.* Monterey, CA: Brooks/Cole Publishing Company.

Edell, J. A. (1988). Nonverbal effects in ads: A review and synthesis. In S. Hecker & D. Stewart (Eds.), *Nonverbal communication in advertising* (pp. 11–27). Lexington, MA: D. C. Heath.

Edell, J. A., & Burke, M. C. (1987). The power of feelings in understanding advertising effects. *Journal of Consumer Research, 14*, 421–433.

Engel, J. F., Blackwell, R. D., & Miniard, P. W. (1986). *Consumer behavior.* New York: Dryden Press.

Gorn, G. J. (1982). The effects of music in advertising on choice behavior: A classical conditioning approach. *Journal of Marketing, 46*, 94–101.

Greenwald, A. G. (1968). On defining attitude and attitude theory. In A. G. Greenwald, T. C. Brock, & T. M. Ostrom (Eds.), *Psychological foundations of attitudes* (pp. 361–388). New York: Academic Press.

Haugeland, J. (1978). The nature and plausibility of cognitivism. *The Behavioral and Brain Sciences, 2*, 215–226.

Holbrook, M. B., & Hirschman, E. C. (1982). The experiential aspects of consumption: Consumer fantasies, feelings, and fun. *Journal of Consumer Research, 9*, 132–140.

Holbrook, M. B., & O'Shaughnessy, J. (1984). The role of emotion in advertising. *Psychology and Marketing, 1*, 45–64.

Hudson, L. A., & Ozanne, J. L. (1988). Alternative ways of seeking knowledge in consumer research. *Journal of Consumer Research, 14*, 508–521.

Hugdahl, K. (1987). Pavlovian conditioning and hemispheric asymmetry: A perspective. In G. Davey (Ed.), *Cognitive processes and Pavlovian conditioning in humans* (pp. 147–182). Chichester, England: John Wiley & Sons Ltd.

Kroeber-Riel, W. (1984). Emotional product differentiation by classical conditioning. In T. C. Kinnear (Ed.), *Advances in consumer research: Vol. XI* (pp. 538–543). Provo, UT: Association for Consumer Research.

Levey, A. B., & Martin, I. (1975). Classical conditioning of human evaluative responses. *Behavioral Research and Therapy, 13*, 221–226.

Levey, A. B., & Martin, I. (1983). Part 1. Cognitions, evaluations and conditioning: Rules of sequence and rules of consequence. *Advances in Behavioral Research and Therapy, 4*, 181–195.

Mackintosh, N. J. (1983). *Conditioning and associative learning*. Oxford, England: Oxford University Press.

Macklin, M. C. (1986). Classical conditioning effects in product/character pairings presented to children. In R. J. Lutz (Ed.), *Advances in consumer research: Vol. XIII* (pp. 198–203). Provo, UT: Association for Consumer Research.

Martin, I., & Levey, A. B. (1978). Evaluative conditioning. *Advances in Behavioral Research and Therapy, 1*, 57–101.

Martin, I., & Levey, A. B. (1985). Conditioning, evaluations and cognitions: An axis of integration. *Behavioural Research and Therapy, 23* (2), 167–175.

Martin, I., & Levey, A. B. (1987). Learning what will happen next: Conditioning, evaluation, and cognitive processes. In G. Davey (Ed.), *Cognitive processes and Pavlovian conditioning in humans* (pp. 57–81). Chichester, England: John Wiley & Sons Ltd.

McCracken, G. (1986). Culture and consumption: A theoretical account of the structure and movement of the cultural meaning of consumer goods. *Journal of Consumer Research, 13*, 71–84.

McSweeney, F. K., & Bierley, C. (1984). Recent developments in classical conditioning. *Journal of Consumer Research, 11*, 619–631.

Nord, W. R., & Peter, J. P. (1980). A behavior modification perspective on marketing. *Journal of Marketing, 44*, 36–47.

Peter, J. P., & Olson, J. C. (1987). *Consumer behavior: Marketing strategy perspectives*. Homewood, Ill.: Richard D. Irwin, Inc.

Petty, R. E., & Cacioppo, J. T. (1981). *Attitudes and persuasion: Classical and contemporary approaches*. Dubuque, IA: Wm. C. Brown Co. Publishers.

Rescorla, R. A. (1967). Pavlovian conditioning and its proper control procedures. *Psychological Bulletin, 74* (1), 71–80.

Rescorla, R. A. (1988). Pavlovian conditioning: It's not what you think it is. *American Psychologist, 43*, 151–160.

Schwartz, B. (1978). *Psychology of learning and behavior*. New York: W. W. Norton and Company, Inc.

Spetch, M. L., Wilkie, D. M., & Pinel, J. P. J. (1981). Backward conditioning: A reevaluation of the empirical evidence. *Psychological Bulletin, 89,* 163–175.

Staats, A. W., & Staats, C. K. (1958). Attitudes established by classical conditioning. *Journal of Abnormal and Social Psychology, 57,* 37–40.

Staats, C. K., & Staats, A. W. (1957). Meaning established by classical conditioning. *Journal of Experimental Psychology, 54,* 74–80.

Stuart, E. W., Shimp, T. A., & Engle, R. W. (1987). Classical conditioning of consumer attitudes: Four experiments in an advertising context. *Journal of Consumer Research, 14,* 334–349.

Sutton, R. S., & Barto, A. G. (1981). Toward a modern theory of adaptive networks: Expectation and prediction. *Psychological Review, 88* (2), 135–170.

Zuriff, G. E. (1985). *Behaviorism: A conceptual reconstruction*. New York: Columbia University Press.

3

Individual Responses to Advertising: Mood and Its Effects from an Information Processing Perspective

Thomas K. Srull

INTRODUCTION

Affect and cognition have each been assumed to play a major, if somewhat ill-defined, role in consumers' reactions to advertising. There are many ways to see this, but one of the most obvious is simply to look at the two historically dominant ways of assessing advertising effectiveness. On the one hand, there are cognitive (especially memory) measures such as day after recall. It is only a slight exaggeration to say that these measures are based on the assumption of the more, the better, although the precise reasons for why this should be the case have never been fully articulated. On the other hand, however, there are also affective measures of advertising effectiveness such as attitude toward the brand, attitude toward the ad, and so on. The theories behind these measures are sometimes more complicated, but it is fair to say that they are also based on an assumption of "the more, the better."

Although scientific interest in them has certainly peaked during the last twenty years, affect and cognition have actually been the objects of scientific study for many decades. And, while the "basic" aspects of affect and cognition have been pursued by psychologists, many of the "applied" aspects have been studied by advertising specialists. In each of these domains, however, there has been an important and common theme. Specifically, those interested in affect and those interested in cognition have operated quite autonomously—one is even

The present chapter benefited substantially from discussions at the Seventh Annual Advertising and Consumer Psychology Conference held at Lowe & Partners. I would also like to thank Sharon Shavitt, my close friend and copacetic colleague, for many helpful discussions.

tempted to say independently. There have, of course, been periodic exceptions to the rule. But, at least until the last twenty years, this was the rule that made any exceptions so noteworthy.

All of this changed dramatically in the 1970s. Up until this time, psychologists usually contrasted *cognition* with *emotion*—very intense states that developed slowly, dissipated slowly, and had very pervasive influences on one's behavior. However, attention eventually began to shift to more mild affective states such as *mood*. There were two reasons for this. One was that mood was found to be affected by relatively minor events such as being given a cookie (Isen & Levin, 1972), hearing pleasant music (Fried & Berkowitz, 1979), or unexpectedly finding a small sum of money (Isen & Levin, 1972). At the same time, however, mood was found to affect a variety of cognitive processes. To give just a few examples, mood affects how we think about ourselves (Schwarz & Clore, 1983), how we think about cars and television sets (Isen, Shalker, Clark, & Karp, 1978), and even how we go about making decisions and solving problems (Isen & Patrick, 1983). Because mood was both a cause and an effect that was associated with so many psychological and situational variables, its role had to be considered in nearly every domain of investigation.

During the same time period similar changes were occurring in advertising and consumer-behavior research. Much of this was a result of the enormous influence of M. Fishbein (Fishbein, 1967; Fishbein & Ajzen, 1975) and other related models of attitudes. After the introduction of such models, there did not seem to be such a strong distinction between affect and cognition. And, to the extent such a distinction was maintained, it was necessary to assume a very strong interdependence between the cognitive and affective systems.

This chapter reviews very briefly why affective states such as mood are important from the perspective of the individual consumer, describes why a consideration of such states has been an important development in our field from a scientific perspective, sketches an integrative model of information processing that simultaneously encapsulates the influence of both affect and cognition, and reports the results of several experiments that were designed to test the major tenets of the model.

MOOD MATTERS

Researchers are now paying considerable attention to the effects of subjective mood states on various aspects of advertising and consumer behavior (*cf.*, Cafferata & Tybout, 1989). The underlying reason for this attention is clear: mood matters. Reliable mood effects, some of which are quite large, have been reported from several different laboratories and by researchers of widely divergent theoretical persuasions. Moreover, a wide array of experimental paradigms and mood manipulations has been employed. In short, people starting at very different places have all come to the same conclusion. Mood is important, and its effects must be taken into account. This is particularly true for anyone interested in developing a complete theory of individual responses to advertising.

Although mood can affect many different facets of consumer behavior (see, for example, Gardner, 1985), most work continues to be conducted in the area of memory and judgment. G. H. Bower and his colleagues have reported an impressive series of studies demonstrating that mood can have strong and consistent effects on memory (Bower, 1981; Bower, Gilligan, & Monteiro, 1981; Bower, Monteiro, & Gilligan, 1978). Other studies have found that these effects extend into the domain of judgment and behavioral decision making (e.g., Isen, 1984; Isen, Clark, & Schwarz, 1976; Isen, Means, Patrick, & Nowicki, 1982).

Researchers concerned with advertising have found many implications of this work. It is possible, for example, that media contexts can create a particular mood state which, in turn, affects a consumer's memory, brand evaluation, and so on. Alternatively, the ad itself may create a mood that has similar effects (cf., Aaker, Stayman, & Hagerty, 1986). In each case, the ultimate effect of ad exposure would be a function of both the information conveyed in the ad and the consumer's affective state. In other words, the affective state of the consumer modulates the effect of the ad. From a historical perspective this is a very important insight.

INFORMATION PROCESSING MODELS: AN UNFULFILLED PROMISE

The effects of mood pose a serious challenge to information processing approaches to advertising and consumer behavior. Philosophers and psychologists have long made a conceptual distinction between cognition and affect, thinking and feeling, and the rational and irrational sides of existence. But how seriously should such dichotomies be taken today? What role, if any, should such distinctions play in our theoretical models? Do they suggest that the "laws" of consumer behavior will be different, depending upon whether the cognitive or affective system dominates?

One might think that mood effects are important because they are outside the boundaries of information processing models. I believe that this is a mistake. If information processing is truly a metatheoretical system, and I believe it is, then mood effects must be accounted for in the same way as any other type of effect, namely by specifying the computational mechanisms that are involved. Mood effects pose an important and difficult challenge because information processing theorists have seldom dealt with the affective system. However, there is nothing in principle that prevents an explanation of such effects in information processing terms. At the very least, it seems to be very premature to conclude otherwise. There simply is no reason why this should not be treated as an open question.

The general issue of whether mood can be accounted for in information processing terms is an extraordinarily difficult one. One might even argue that it is premature to ask such a question at present because so little is known about mood effects and their vicissitudes. Keeping this in mind, and adopting a more modest objective in the remainder of this chapter, I will try to introduce a general approach that can be used to study mood within an information processing framework. I believe that this, in and of itself, is an important contribution.

The Failure of Traditional Memory Models

One of the earliest and most robust mood effects reported in the literature is that one's mood often spills over into evaluations of various objects. For example, when one is in a positive mood state, one is likely to evaluate various products, brands, and ads more positively than when one is in a neutral or negative mood (Ger, 1989). The most common interpretation of this effect continues to be one in terms of a spreading activation model of memory. Specifically, being in a positive mood is said to activate a good mood node in memory. Activation from this node and its associates then spreads through the system. Eventually this will be associated with the particular object one is thinking about (e.g., a particular brand or ad), and the positive aspects of one's experience will rub off onto the object.

One strength of the spreading activation model is that it has a long history of being examined in cognitive psychology (see, for example, Collins & Quillian, 1969); there is a lot of support for it, and we know a considerable amount about the mechanisms involved. Another strength is that it can be used to account for mood effects in free recall (see, for example, Bower, 1981; Bower & Cohen, 1982).

Perhaps because of these reasons there has been no serious challenger to the spreading activation model of memory. Nevertheless, I believe there are a number of serious weaknesses with the model that hitherto have not received serious discussion.

First, there is a serious logical problem. Spreading activation models assume that the activation emanating from any given node spreads down all the paths that are associated with it. This is fine when one is working with semantic concepts, but what happens when one moves into the domain of mood and nodes that might be referred to as "feel good" or "feel bad"? Here, the number of paths to other nodes becomes extraordinarily large. In fact, some have argued that evaluation is a normal part of comprehension and, thus, it occurs when we are exposed to any object at all (e.g., Osgood, 1952; Zajonc, 1980). To the extent that this is true, or that anything even approximating it is true, the "feel good" and "feel bad" nodes will be connected to the representation of roughly half the experiences in our life! What this means is that the amount of activation spreading to any single node will be minuscule. This is a fundamental conceptual problem with using spreading activation models that simply has not been addressed.

There is also a psychological problem with such models that makes them somewhat implausible. Specifically, activation spreads very quickly and dissipates very quickly. This raises two issues. One is that, according to these models, mood will primarily have an effect if the judgment is assessed during that precise time frame in which the activation has spread to a new node. Unfortunately, the most careful and sophisticated examinations of this process have narrowed such a time frame down to a few hundred milliseconds (Kounios, Osman, & Meyer, 1987; Meyer, Yantis, Osman, & Smith, 1985; Yantis & Meyer, 1988). The second issue is that, if one follows the logic, and if one's moods are so easily affected by external events, one's evaluations of objects should be changing almost constantly. Yet there is very little evidence that this is true. In fact, such evaluations are often extremely resistant to change.

Finally, there are a variety of empirical problems as well. For example, the effects of positive and negative moods are not always symmetrical (Isen, 1984), although spreading activation models suggest that they should be. Although there is clear evidence of such asymmetries, however, they have not been used to reject spreading activation models. Rather, the models have been retained while adding on a variety of ad hoc assumptions. For example, people in a negative mood are said to want to eliminate the mood strategically by not thinking negative thoughts or making negative evaluations (the so-called "mood repair" hypothesis). The problem here is that the number of concepts involved can quickly approximate the number of phenomena to be explained.

In short, attempts to account for mood effects in terms of memory processes have more or less been confined to spreading activation models. Yet there are a number of logical, psychological, and empirical problems with the spreading activation approach. None of these problems is fatal in and of itself, but, in combination, they cast doubt on the long-term viability of the approach. In a later section, I describe a very different type of memory model that circumvents many, if not all, of these problems.

The Failure of Classical Judgment Models

An alternative to accounting for mood effects in terms of memory structures and processes (the postulation of nodes, associative pathways that link them, and activation that spreads down the associate paths) is to move to higher order judgment processes. Unfortunately, classical judgment models do not fare any better.

Consider again what is probably the most basic mood effect of all: people in a positive mood give more favorable ratings to objects (e.g., a particular brand or ad) than people in a neutral or negative mood. People in a positive mood are sometimes said to "see the world through rose-colored glasses." However, this phrase also points to the problem that is endemic to classical models of judgment.

According to these models, judgment is a function of the absolute value of any attribute and the context in which a particular stimulus is judged. Consider a subject in a psychophysical experiment who is asked to judge a six-ounce weight either in the context of much lighter weights or much heavier weights.

The weight will be judged as much heavier in the first case than in the second. In other words, the weight is psychologically contrasted away from its context stimuli. This type of "contrast effect" is extremely robust and present in virtually every judgment domain (see, for example, Wyer & Srull, 1989).

Now consider a consumer judging the favorability of a particular brand. The problem is that, if the person is in a positive mood, he or she *will* see the world through rose-colored glasses. In other words, the person will see *all* brands more favorably. It is very likely, however, that when this occurs, the brand being judged will be contrasted away from all of the other (context) brands, and thus receive a more negative rating than it would under other conditions.

In short, classical judgment models have trouble accounting for even the most basic mood effects: the most obvious prediction is a contrast effect when, empirically, we know that assimilation effects are most likely to occur. Once again, this is not necessarily a fatal flaw. But it does suggest that such models will need to be buttressed with some other mechanisms.

A RAPPROCHEMENT

In this section, a very different way of thinking about memory and judgment is developed. First, a relatively formal information processing model is sketched; it is then shown how the model integrates much of the existing literature; and, finally, specific predictions are derived from the model concerning when one's subjective mood should and should not have an affect on brand evaluations.

The model, first developed in a series of papers (Lichtenstein & Srull, 1985, 1987; Srull, 1983, 1989; Srull & Wyer, 1989), begins by distinguishing between on-line and memory-based processing (for related discussions, see Hastie & Park, 1986: Lynch & Srull, 1982). Consider first on-line processing. On-line processing is said to occur whenever a person acquires brand-related information with the (implicit or explicit) objective of making an evaluation of that brand. When this occurs, a global evaluation of the brand will be made at the time of information acquisition and stored in memory separately and independently from the specific information that is acquired (*cf.*, Riskey, 1979). To give just one example, if a person sees or reads an ad with the objective of evaluating the brand, the computational activity involved (e.g., averaging the values associated with each attribute) will occur as the information from the ad is being processed.

Memory-based processing is quite different. In many cases, a person will acquire brand-related information with no specific objective in mind, or only a very general objective such as to comprehend the information being presented in the ad (*cf.*, Srull & Wyer, 1986; Wyer & Srull, 1986). Under these conditions, a global evaluation of the brand will typically not be made at the time of information acquisition. If later asked to make a specific evaluation, the person will be forced to retrieve the previously acquired information from memory, or some subset of it, and use this information as a basis for his or her evaluation of the brand. In other words, a judgment will need to be computed on the spot.

Such a model has been found to be very heuristic. For example, one prediction is that memory-based judgments (because they require both retrieval and computation) should take longer than on-line judgments (because they require only the retrieval of a judgment that has already been made); in fact, this is true (Srull, 1989). Another prediction is that the time required to make memory-based judgments will be affected by the total amount of information presented (e.g., the number of claims in the ad), but on-line judgments will not; this is also true (Lichtenstein, 1987).

Perhaps the most important prediction is that the correspondence between whatever facts are recalled and the global evaluative judgment that is made should be much higher in memory-based than in on-line processing conditions. In an initial test of this hypothesis, M. Lichtenstein and T. K. Srull (1985) found, in 12 out of 12 independent comparisons, that the correlation between recall and judgment was higher in memory-based than on-line conditions. Moreover, the correlations in the memory-based conditions were universally large and statistically different from zero, while those in the on-line condition were not. Specifically, the mean correlation across 12 conditions was .64 in the memory-based condition and .22 in the on-line condition.

More recently, R. Hastie and B. Park (1986) have replicated these effects using a slightly different paradigm. The on-line condition was very similar to that described earlier. However, for a memory-based condition, they had subjects anticipate making one judgment, but later asked them for a different, unrelated judgment. Across four separate experiments, the average correlation between recall and judgment was .51 in the memory-based condition and .16 in the on-line condition.

Conceptual replications of these results using slightly different orienting tasks have been reported by A. Chattopadhyay and J. W. Alba (1988); J. G. Lynch, H. Marmorstein, and M. F. Weigold (1988); Lichtenstein (1987); Lichtenstein and Srull (1987); and Srull (1984, 1989). In short, these findings are very strong and replicate across a variety of laboratories, stimulus sets, content domains, and delay intervals.

Based on this evidence, it is fair to conclude that the model described above has been quite successful in accounting for past research, and it has recently been extended into a number of new domains (see, for example, Srull & Wyer, 1989; Wyer & Srull, 1989). For both of these reasons, it is useful to ask whether the model can also be used to conceptualize the role that subjective affective states such as mood have on brand evaluation. In fact, conceptually extending the model into this domain is a very straightforward endeavor. Specifically, if the processing objectives of the consumer are a determinant of exactly when a brand evaluation occurs, they should also mediate the influence of subjective affective states on any judgments that are made.

In short, the model presented suggests that the affective state of the consumer will have an effect on brand evaluations *if* it is experienced at the time the internal computational procedures are activated. Thus, affective states at the time of encoding will influence the judgments of subjects using on-line processing because the judgment is being formed at the same time the affective state is being experienced. On the other hand, affective states during encoding should not affect the evaluations of subjects using a memory-based processing strategy because the evaluation is not computed until the time of judgment.

Essentially, the opposite is true of mood states that are experienced at the time a judgment is requested. In this case, there should be no effect for consumers who have already formed their brand evaluations on-line. As long as they can easily access their prior evaluation, they can simply report it to the experimenter. However, consumers who are forced to use memory-based processing will be affected by mood states experienced at the time of judgment because that is precisely the time during which the computations are made.

EMPIRICAL EVIDENCE

Four experiments were designed to examine the model; they followed two different research approaches. One was to delineate when mood does and does not have an effect in terms of the cognitive processes that are activated at any given time. This approach was followed in Experiments 1 and 2.

The second approach is to look across groups of subjects when there is reason to believe that the two groups use different processes to perform the same task. I attempted to do this by examining expert-novice differences. In other words, rather than experimentally manipulate processing objectives, they were left free to vary naturally. The general idea is that "experts" already have many prior evaluations and thus will be immune from the effects of temporary mood states. In contrast, "novices" will engage in much more computational activity and thus will be subject to the same processes described above. Experiments 3 and 4, which followed this approach, were designed to provide converging evidence for the model.

Experiment 1

The model presented suggests that affective states at the time of encoding will influence the judgments of subjects using on-line processing because the judgment is being formed at the same time the affective state is being experienced. On the other hand, affective states during encoding should not affect the evaluation of subjects using a memory-based processing strategy because the evaluation is not computed until the time of judgment.

Subjects in the first experiment were undergraduate students who came into the laboratory and were put into a positive, neutral, or negative mood by using the involved recollection procedure previously described by Srull (1983). In brief, subjects enter a quiet, dimly lighted room and are encouraged to relax completely. They are then asked to recall privately everything possible from a previous, strongly affectively toned event in their personal lives (except in the neutral condition). Every few minutes, subjects are given a "probe" that encourages them to concentrate on every detail concerning what they were thinking and how they felt during the actual experience.

The procedure is similar to those that attempt to induce mood states with hypnotic suggestion (see, for example, Bower, 1981), except that subjects are not self-selected and there is no attempt to put them into a true hypnotic trance. Nevertheless, the mood states that result can be quite intense. The procedure has proven to be quite effective, and some of the effects it produces are inconsistent with the demand characteristics of the situation (Srull, 1983). Thus, there is converging evidence that an actual mood state is being experienced phenomenologically.

Following the mood-induction procedure, subjects were shown a single (modified) print ad. It contained 10 separate attribute values for the Mazda RX7. The information was adapted from ads actually used by the company. They were changed simply by revising the sentences and putting them into paragraph form.

Subjects read the information at their own pace under one of two conditions. Subjects in the on-line condition were told to read the ad with the purpose of forming an evaluation of the product so that they would later be able to judge how desirable it would be relative to other competing brands. Subjects in the memory-based condition were told simply to comprehend what was being said.

After subjects had read the ad, they were dismissed and asked to return in 48 hours. At that time, all subjects were put into a neutral mood and, without being reexposed to the original ad, were asked to evaluate the product. Specifically, subjects were asked, "Assuming you wanted to purchase a product similar to the Mazda RX7, how desirable do you think this particular brand would be?" Subjects made their ratings on a scale ranging from 0 (very undesirable) to 20 (very desirable).

The mean ratings are presented in Table 3.1. These results provide considerable support for the model. In the on-line processing condition, the mean evaluative rating was 13.6 in the positive mood condition, 12.4 in the neutral mood condition, and a 10.2 in the negative mood condition. Thus, the mood state of the subject had a strong and consistent impact. Ratings were displaced from their neutral baseline in both the positive and negative mood conditions, indicating that the mood effects were symmetrical.

Ratings in the memory-based condition were quite different; in this case, mood appeared to have no impact at all. In particular, note that memory-based subjects in a positive mood gave somewhat lower ratings than those in the on-line condition, and memory-based subjects in a negative mood gave somewhat higher ratings than those in the on-line condition.

In summary, mood had a much greater influence in the on-line condition than in the memory-based condition. It is important to remember, however, that only mood at the time of encoding was manipulated. Theoretically, subjects in the on-line condition were making their evaluations of the brand at the precise time the mood state was being experienced. According to the model, however, this

Table 3.1
Experiment 1: Mean Brand Evaluations of Subjects in a Positive, Neutral, or Negative Mood at the Time of Encoding as a Function of Initial Processing Objectives

==

Processing Objectives

Mood State	On-Line	Memory-Based
Positive	13.6	12.6
Neutral	12.4	11.9
Negative	10.2	12.2

was not true of those in the memory-based condition. Theoretically, these subjects would be forced to compute their evaluation at the time it was requested, a time at which they were all in a neutral mood.

Experiment 2

The model suggests that the mood state of the subject will have an effect on product evaluation only if the mood is being experienced while the evaluation is taking place. The results of the first experiment are consistent with this in that the mood at the time of encoding had an effect only in the on-line processing condition. Theoretically, those engaged in on-line processing were computing their judgment at the time of input (encoding).

Subjects who engage in memory-based processing are assumed to use a much different process. Because no evaluation is computed on-line, any such judgment must be made at some later time. In order to form a judgment, subjects must search memory for relevant information and integrate the information retrieved using some type of combination rule. In other words, the product evaluation is computed at the time of judgment rather than at the time of input. One implication of this is that affective states at the time of judgment should affect the evaluations of those subjects using memory-based processing. This is so because the computation will be made while the affective state is being experienced. However, when subjects form their evaluations on-line, affective states at the time of judgment should have no effect.

Experiment 2 tested these predictions by using a procedure comparable to that used in the first experiment. All subjects were first placed in a neutral mood. Then they were shown the ad for the Mazda RX7 and told to read the information

Table 3.2
Experiment 2: Mean Brand Evaluations of Subjects in a Positive, Neutral, or Negative Mood at the Time of Judgment as a Function of Initial Processing Objectives

==

Processing Objectives

Mood State	On-Line	Memory-Based
Positive	11.8	12.9
Neutral	11.9	12.2
Negative	12.2	11.1

at their own pace. As before, subjects in the on-line condition were told to read the ad with the purpose of forming an evaluation of the product so that they would later be able to judge how desirable it would be relative to other competing brands. Subjects in the memory-based condition were told simply to comprehend what was being said.

After subjects had read the ad, they were dismissed and asked to return in 48 hours. At that time, they were put into either a positive, neutral, or negative mood and then were asked to evaluate the product without being reexposed to the original ad.

The mean ratings are presented in Table 3.2. Although not quite as strong as in the first experiment, the data are quite consistent with the model here as well. For those subjects who engaged in the on-line processing, the mean brand evaluation was 11.8 in the positive mood condition, 11.9 in the neutral mood condition, and 12.2 in the negative mood condition. Note that the means associated with each of the mood conditions are very close to the neutral baseline. As expected, mood at the time of judgment had no effect when on-line processing had already occurred.

Those subjects who engaged in memory-based processing showed a quite different pattern of results. As predicted, mood had a strong and consistent effect in this case. Theoretically, this is due to the fact that only memory-based subjects were making their evaluations of the brand at the time the mood state was being experienced.

Taken together, the results of Experiments 1 and 2 indicate that one can observe mood effects at either encoding or judgment; however, whether either of these effects occurs depends critically on the way in which the ads are originally processed.

Experiment 3

In the first two experiments, the processing objectives were experimentally manipulated, and comparisons were made across experimental conditions. The philosophy behind the third experiment is somewhat different. Subjects are first classified as either novice or expert, and the comparisons are then made across the groups of subjects. This is relevant to testing the model if one assumes that experts and novices naturally use different processing strategies. In other words, rather than experimentally manipulate processing objectives, they are left free to vary naturally.

It is reasonable to assume that the experts and the novices will process the information obtained from an advertisement differently. Novices, by definition, have little prior information and only limited experience with the product class. As a consequence, they will be forced to find some algorithm to combine specific items of information. In contrast, experts will have a much richer knowledge base to begin with. They will know which attributes are most important; they will have prior beliefs about how attributes are related to one another in a correlational sense; and they will have already formed many brand evaluations. In many cases, brand evaluations will be based on past judgments rather than on new information (see Lynch & Srull, 1982). To the extent each of these propositions is true, mood states at the time of encoding should have little effect.

The procedure of the experiment was similar to that used in the first study. Undergraduate students were first put into a positive, neutral, or negative mood. They were then shown the same ad pertaining to the Mazda RX7 and given the same on-line processing instructions. Subjects were then dismissed and asked to return in 48 hours. At that time, all subjects were first put into a neutral mood and then asked to evaluate the product. At the end of the second session, subjects rated their self-knowledge of automobiles in relation to the rest of the population, and a median split was used to identify novice and expert subjects. This procedure was adapted from that used by E. J. Johnson and J. E. Russo (1981).

It was predicted that mood at the time of encoding would have a strong effect on the judgments of novice subjects but not on those of experts. The data for novices, shown in Table 3.3, offer clear support for the hypothesis. Note in particular that the means in both mood conditions are displaced from their neutral baseline condition. This is theoretically due to the fact that subjects were forming their evaluations at the time they were experiencing the mood state.

The data for expert subjects are a little more ambiguous. Contrary to what was predicted, mood at the time of encoding did have a systematic effect. However, it was extremely small. The mean brand evaluation for experts was 14.24 in the positive mood condition, 14.17 in the neutral mood condition, and 14.03 in the negative mood condition. Relative to the novice condition, mood had the same type of effect, but the magnitude of the differences was much smaller. Thus, qualified support for the more general model was obtained.

Table 3.3
Experiment 3: Mean Brand Evaluations of Subjects in a Positive, Neutral, or
Negative Mood at the Time of Encoding as a Function of Expertise

==

Level of Expertise

Mood State	Novice	Expert
Positive	14.16	14.24
Neutral	12.09	14.17
Negative	10.87	14.03

Experiment 4

The procedure of Experiment 4 was, with two exceptions, identical to that used in Experiment 3. The first alteration was that all subjects were put into a neutral mood at the time of encoding. The second change was that subjects were put into a positive, neutral, or negative mood at the time of judgment. It was assumed that novice subjects would form their evaluations of the brand at the time of input. Thus, when asked to make a specific judgment during the second session, they would simply retrieve the prior evaluation from memory. To the extent this is true, mood at the time of judgment should have no effect.

The prediction for expert subjects is more or less the same. These subjects should also not have to compute their evaluation at the time of judgment. Rather, one would expect that the judgment would have already been formed and stored in memory. If this is true, one would expect that mood at the time of judgment would have no effect on the evaluations of expert subjects.

The data, presented in Table 3.4. offer mixed support for both hypotheses. In both cases, mood at the time of judgment had a systematic effect, but, in each case, the magnitude of the effect was very small. The mean brand evaluation of novice subjects was 14.12 in the positive mood condition, 13.18 in the neutral mood condition, and 12.67 in the negative mood condition. One can see how small these effects are by comparing them to those obtained in Experiment 3.

The data obtained from expert subjects are similar. The mean brand evaluation for expert subjects was 14.63 in the positive mood condition, 14.08 in the neutral mood condition, and 13.76 in the negative mood condition. As in Experiment 3, mood had a systematic effect even though the model predicts otherwise. It is also true, however, that these effects are very small compared to those obtained in the previous experiments.

Table 3.4
Experiment 4: Mean Brand Evaluations of Subjects in a Positive, Neutral, or Negative Mood at the Time of Judgment as a Function of Expertise

===

Level of Expertise

Mood State	Novice	Expert
Positive	14.12	14.63
Neutral	13.18	14.08
Negative	12.67	13.76

CONCLUSIONS

As noted earlier, mood effects are sometimes thought to be outside the boundary conditions of information processing models. Such a conclusion is premature and certainly inconsistent with the data reported in this chapter. In fact, the present results suggest that at least some mood effects can be accounted for quite well in information processing terms. A reasonably simple model was developed and used to illustrate how specific a priori predictions pertaining to mood can be derived. Moreover, the effects reported in this chapter are quite similar to those obtained in many other paradigms. Thus, the generalizability of this approach would appear to be very promising.

Experiments 1 and 2 provided strong support for the model. The data from the last two experiments, both of which pertain to expert-novice differences, were a little more ambiguous. Strong and consistent mood effects were observed in each case the model predicted they would be. However, mood effects were also observed in several cases where the model suggests mood should not have an impact. It is useful to consider why the model broke down under these conditions.

The fact that these mood effects were so small offers some clue. One possibility is that the criterion used to classify subjects as expert was simply too liberal. Upon reflection, is it reasonable to assume that 50 percent of the population is expert in any given domain? If not, some true novices would have been classified as experts, and these misclassified subjects could have produced the small effects that were observed. Consider Experiment 3 for example. If some of the subjects classified as experts were actually computing their evaluation at the time of encoding, the effects observed would not be surprising; indeed, they would be expected.

Another possibility is that the retrieval process attributed to experts is too simple to model their actual performance. As G. D. Logan and W. B. Cowan (1984) have pointed out, there may be a "race" between an algorithm that is used to process new information and an attempt to retrieve a prior evaluation. In most cases, the retrieval process will be faster and will be used to make the judgment. However, retrieval is not perfect, and the algorithm may win the race in a small percentage of cases. This would also produce a mood effect, but one that is much smaller than that observed for novices.

A final possibility is that the judgment and translation assumptions are too simple. The prior evaluation that is retrieved by an expert is unlikely to be in the same form as that requested by the experimenter. Thus, it will need to be translated and mapped onto whatever particular scale is used. It is possible that mood has some effect on this mapping process.

All of these possibilities are viable, and all deserve to be explored in future research. Each provides a mechanism for providing a fuller account of the data. The model will certainly become more complex as a result. However, this is not too surprising since only very simple processing assumptions were made.

It should also be noted that this is a very general information processing model within which more specific theoretical commitments can be made. For example, no assumptions at all were made about the nature of the mental representation of brands and their attributes. More specific models could be built by postulating associative networks, feature lists, bins, schemata, or nearly anything else. Similarly, no assumptions were made about the integration rule; this could be modeled by postulating adding, averaging, weighted averaging, or even a more complicated rule. At this time, and for the purposes of this chapter, such assumptions are unnecessary. As the relevant data base grows, and other types of data need to be accounted for, more specific theoretical commitments will be required (cf. Lichtenstein & Srull, 1987).

The more general point is that information processing approaches to studying mood should not be dismissed prematurely. Accounting for affective processes is a definite challenge, but it is a challenge that must be met. Even if such models are ultimately rejected, we are sure to learn a great deal in the process of exploring their implications.

REFERENCES

Aaker, D. A., Stayman, D. M., & Hagerty, M. R. (1986). Warmth in advertising: Measurement, impact, and sequence effects. *Journal of Consumer Research, 12*, 365–381.

Bower, G. H. (1981). Mood and memory. *American Psychologist, 36*, 129–148.

Bower, G. H., & Cohen, P. R. (1982). Emotional influences in memory and thinking: Data and theory. In M. S. Clark & S. T. Fiske (Eds.), *Affect and cognition* (pp. 291–332). Hillsdale, NJ: Erlbaum.

Bower, G. H., Gilligan, S. G., & Monteiro, K. P. (1981). Selectivity of learning caused by affective states. *Journal of Experimental Psychology: General, 110*, 451–473.

Bower, G. H., Monteiro, K. P., & Gilligan, S. G. (1978). Emotional mood as a context for learning and recall. *Journal of Verbal Learning and Verbal Behavior, 17*, 573–585.

Cafferata, P., & Tybout, A. (Eds.). (1989). *Cognitive and affective responses to advertising*. Lexington, MA: Lexington Books.

Chattopadhyay, A., & Alba, J. W. (1988). The situational importance of recall and inference in consumer decision making. *Journal of Consumer Research, 15*, 1–12.

Collins, A., & Quillian, M. R. (1969). Retrieval time from semantic memory. *Journal of Verbal Learning and Verbal Behavior, 8*, 241–248.

Fishbein, M. (1967). Attitude and the prediction of behavior. In M. Fishbein (Ed.), *Readings in attitude theory and measurement* (pp. 477–492). New York: Wiley.

Fishbein, M., & Ajzen, I. (1975). *Belief, attitude, intention, and behavior*. Reading, MA: Addison-Wesley.

Fried, R., & Berkowitz, L. (1979). Music hath charms . . . and can influence helpfulness. *Journal of Applied Social Psychology, 9*, 199–208.

Gardner, M. P. (1985). Mood states and consumer behavior: A critical review. *Journal of Consumer Research, 12*, 281–300.

Ger, G. (1989). Nature of effects of affect on judgment: Theoretical and methodological issues. In P. Cafferata & A. Tybout (Eds.), *Cognitive and affective responses of advertising* (pp. 263–275). Lexington, MA: Lexington Books.

Hastie, R., & Park, B. (1986). The relationship between memory and judgment depends on whether the judgment task is memory-based or on-line. *Psychological Review, 93*, 258–268.

Isen, A. M. (1984). Affect, cognition, and social behavior. In R. S. Wyer & T. K. Srull (Eds.), *Handbook of social cognition* (vol. 3, pp. 179–236). Hillsdale, NJ: Erlbaum.

Isen, A. M., Clark, M., & Schwarz, M. F. (1976). Duration of the effect of good mood on helping: Footprints on the sands of time. *Journal of Personality and Social Psychology, 34*, 385–393.

Isen, A. M., & Levin, P. F. (1972). The effect of feeling good on helping: Cookies and kindness. *Journal of Personality and Social Psychology, 21*, 384–388.

Isen, A. M., Means, B., Patrick, R., & Nowicki, G. (1982). Some factors influencing decision-making strategy and risk taking. In M. S. Clark & S. T. T. Fiske (Eds.), *Affect and cognition* (pp. 128–146). Hillsdale, NJ: Erlbaum.

Isen, A. M., & Patrick, R. (1983). The effect of positive feelings on risk taking: When the chips are down. *Organizational Behavior and Human Performance, 31*, 194–202.

Isen, A. M., Shalker, T., Clark, M., & Karp, L. (1978). Affect, accessibility of material in memory and behavior: A cognitive loop? *Journal of Personality and Social Psychology, 36*, 1–12.

Johnson, E. J., & Russo, J. E. (1981). Product familiarity and learning new information. In K. B. Monroe (Ed.), *Advances in consumer research* (vol. 8, pp. 151–155). Ann Arbor, MI: Association for Consumer Research.

Kounios, J., Osman, A. M., & Meyer, D. E. (1987). Structure and process in semantic memory: New evidence based on speed-accuracy decomposition. *Journal of Experimental Psychology: General, 116*, 3–25.

Lichtenstein, M. (1987). *Impression formation: The relation between recall and judgment*. Unpublished doctoral dissertation, University of Illinois.

Lichtenstein, M., & Srull, T. K. (1985). Conceptual and methodological issues in examining the relationship between consumer memory and judgment. In L. F. Alwitt & A. A. Mitchell (Eds.), *Psychological processes and advertising effects: Theory, research, and application* (pp. 113–128). Hillsdale, NJ: Erlbaum.

Lichtenstein, M., & Srull, T. K. (1987). Processing objectives as a determinant of the relationship between recall and judgment. *Journal of Experimental Social Psychology, 23*, 93–118.

Logan, G. D., & Cowan, W. B. (1984). On the ability to inhibit thought and action: A theory of an act of control. *Psychological Review, 91*, 295–327.

Lynch, J. G., Marmorstein, H., & Weigold, M. F. (1988). Choices from sets including remembered brands: Use of recalled attributes and prior overall evaluations. *Journal of Consumer Research, 15*, 169–184.

Lynch, J. G., & Srull, T. K. (1982). Memory and attentional factors in consumer choice: Concepts and research methods. *Journal of Consumer Research, 9*, 18–37.

Meyer, D. E., Yantis, S., Osman, A., & Smith, J. E. K. (1985). Temporal properties of human information processing: Tests of discrete versus continuous models. *Cognitive Psychology, 17*, 445–518.

Osgood, C. E. (1952). The nature and measurement of meaning. *Psychological Bulletin, 49*, 197–237.

Riskey, D. R. (1979). Verbal memory processes in impression formation. *Journal of Experimental Psychology: Human Learning and Memory, 5*, 271–281.

Schwarz, N., & Clore, G. L. (1983). Mood, misattribution, and judgments of well-being: Informative and directive functions of affective states. *Journal of Personality and Social Psychology, 45*, 513–523.

Srull, T. K. (1983). Affect and memory: The impact of affective reactions to advertising on the representation of product information in memory. In R. P. Bagozzi & A. Tybout (Eds.), *Advances in consumer research* (vol. 10, pp. 520–525). Ann Arbor, MI: Association for Consumer Research.

Srull, T. K. (1984). The effects of subjective affective states on memory and judgment. In T. C. Kinnear (Ed.), *Advances in consumer research* (vol. 11, pp. 550–553). Ann Arbor, MI: Association for Consumer Research.

Srull, T. K. (1989). Advertising and product evaluation: The relation between consumer memory and judgment. In P. Cafferata & A. Tybout (Eds.), *Cognitive and affective responses to advertising* (pp. 121–134). Lexington, MA: Lexington Books.

Srull, T. K., & Wyer, R. S. (1986). The role of chronic and temporary goals in social information processing. In R. M. Sorrentino & E. T. Higgins (Eds.), *Handbook of motivation and cognition* (pp. 161–197). New York: Guilford Press.

Srull, T. K., & Wyer, R. S. (1989). Person memory and judgment. *Psychological Review, 96*, 58–83.

Wyer, R. S., & Srull, T. K. (1986). Human cognition in its social context. *Psychological Review, 93*, 322–359.

Wyer, R. S., & Srull, T. K. (1989). *Memory and cognition in its social context.* Hillsdale, NJ: Erlbaum.

Yantis, S., & Meyer, D. E. (1988). Dynamics of activation in semantic and episodic memory. *Journal of Experimental Psychology: General, 117*, 130–147.

Zajonc, R. B. (1980). Feeling and thinking: Preferences need no inferences. *American Psychologist, 35*, 151–175.

4

A Micro Approach to Studying Feeling Responses to Advertising: The Case of Warmth

David A. Aaker and Douglas M. Stayman

Advertising that works is advertising that makes somebody feel something.
... All advertising has some emotion. Some advertising is all emotion.

Hal Riney

Most of our (advertising) research tools ... overlook that critical ingredient—human emotion.

Joe Plummer

Advertising practitioners and theorists have long recognized that much effective advertising is based primarily upon feeling or emotional or affective responses as opposed to thinking or rational or cognitive processes. Over the years considerable progress has been made in understanding how the cognitive responses and processes stimulated by the informational aspects of advertising affect persuasion (Bettman, 1979). In addition, much research has suggested what pretesting measures are likely to be valid indicators and predictors of those processes.

In comparison, our knowledge of how the feeling component of advertising works and how it should be tested or evaluated is at best embryonic. In the past half decade, however, substantial interest in the feeling side of advertising has been evidenced among both practitioners and academics (*cf.*, Alwitt & Mitchell, 1985; Cafferata & Tybout, 1989). Progress is being made on a number of fronts including measurement (e.g., Aaker & Stayman, 1989a; Aaker, Stayman, & Hagerty, 1986; Batra & Ray, 1986b; Stayman & Aaker, in press); pretesting (e.g., Alwitt, 1985); model building (e.g., Batra & Ray, 1985; MacKenzie,

Lutz, & Belch, 1986); and moving toward a more comprehensive theory (e.g., Holbrook, 1985).

This chapter reviews our own research focusing on specific feelings in general and one specific feeling in particular, warmth. In addition to summarizing some of our findings to date, we contrast our approach to that of others, pointing out some of its advantages in gaining understanding and suggesting some directions for future research. A review of specific results we have found using our approach is presented. Our research approach is described, positioned, and related to the types of findings we have generated. Finally, several general areas we believe will be productive research directions are identified and discussed.

Before beginning it is important to clarify some terms which will be used and are within the quagmire of the "affective lexicon" (Ortony & Clore, 1981). Terms such as feeling, mood, and affective and emotional response are used broadly to categorize a set of responses different from more "cognitive" mental operations as a set of "hot" phenomena principally linked by some subjective feeling experience. However, these terms can also be distinguished by two dimensions: duration and intensity (for example, Lazarus, Kanner, & Folkman, 1980; Wessman & Ricks, 1966). As used here, emotions are short in duration but relatively intense, whereas feelings are also short term but less intense. In contrast, moods are mild but more long lasting. Affect remains a general term encompassing all responses including a subjective feeling component.

A SUMMARY OF FINDINGS CONCERNING WARMTH

Our research has focused primarily upon three specific feelings: amusement, irritation, and warmth. The emphasis has been upon warmth, partly because it has been understudied and appears to be one of the most common positive feelings used in advertising. It has been identified as one of five or six perceptual dimensions people use to describe advertisements (Aaker & Bruzzone, 1981; Wells, Leavitt, & McConville, 1971). In addition, J. A. Edell and M. C. Burke (1987) identified one of their three feeling response dimensions as warmth.

We define warmth to be "a positive, mild, volatile emotion involving physiological arousal and precipitated by experiencing directly or vicariously a love, family, or friendship relationship" (Aaker et al., 1986, p. 366). Thus, we have defined warmth in terms of its position in the affective lexicon (a mild, volatile emotion), its valence (positive), and certain likely antecedents (love, family, or friendship relationships).

Other specific feelings that have been researched in advertising—amusement, fear, and irritation—are qualitatively different from warmth. Fear appeals (see Sternthal & Craig, 1974) are, of course, negative rather than positive and involve cognitive activity especially as part of the process by which fear is reduced by the communication. Amusement (see Sternthal & Craig, 1973) is complex because of its role as an attention-getting device, because of its fast wear-out, and because much of it involves a play on words and cognitive activity of some kind. Irritation (see Aaker & Bruzzone, 1985) is closely related to the general attitude toward the ad.

A series of studies focusing upon warmth has yielded a set of empirical findings that, taken together, begins to provide an understanding about the nature of warmth as well as how it works to influence and, of course, raises a host of additional questions. Eleven of these findings are discussed below.

About 21 Percent of Prime-Time Commercials Are Warm

A set of 855 prime-time commercials was cluster analyzed on the basis of their score on four perceptual factors: warm, entertaining/humorous, irritating, and informative (Stayman, Aaker, & Bruzzone, 1989). The ads were all tested by Bruzzone Research Corporation (BRC) during their periodic weekly sweeps in which BRC tests all prime-time ads that have been running for several weeks. The test, a mail questionnaire which includes an adjective checklist, is sent to a probability sample of 1,000 households. A total of 21 percent of the commercials fell either into a warm cluster (19 percent) or a very warm cluster (2 percent).

The Warmth Monitor Is a Useful Continuous Measure

The warmth monitor is a continuous measure of viewer-felt warmth first used in D. A. Aaker et al. (1986) who reported a series of tests. The tests suggested that the warmth monitor achieved an acceptable level of test-retest reliability (a correlation of .81) and sensitivity, an ability to discriminate between warmth and amusement and irritation, and an absence of reactivity in at least one context. In another study, the warmth monitor was found to discriminate between warmth and liking (Stayman & Aaker, in press). In the second study, a "humor monitor" did less well on similar tests, and an "irritation monitor" did not perform adequately (Stayman & Aaker, in press).

Felt Warmth Is Accompanied by Physiological Arousal

In a study reported in Aaker et al. (1986), the "warmth monitor" output was compared to galvanic skin response (GSR) as a measure of physiological arousal. Control of sequence effects tended to generate low levels of going-in warmth and thus large changes in warmth during the commercial. The warmth monitor measure had a correlation with subjects' GSR that averaged .67 over four warm commercials, whereas it was zero for irritating and informative ads and .31 for humorous ads (which had a warmth component). In a follow-up study, which did not control the sequence effects (Stayman & Aaker, in press), the average correlation between the warmth monitor and GSR over three ads was .24 for warm ads as opposed to .09 for humorous ads and .04 for irritating ads.

The ability of advertising to generate arousal has also been demonstrated by

G. Meyer-Hentschel (1983) and J. T. Cacioppo and R. E. Petty (1983) using print ads. In the Meyer-Hentschel study, a set of seven self-report scales reflecting surgency and uniqueness dimensions correlated .92 with GSR measures.

The presence of arousal is important conceptually and empirically. A lack of arousal would make it questionable as to whether much of the conceptual work in emotion theory could appropriately be applied in this context. Most emotion researchers (e.g., Lazarus, 1984) state that arousal is a necessary component of emotion, although researchers studying constructs such as general affect do not require arousal for effects (e.g., Isen, 1984). Empirically, the finding suggests that GSR and other arousal measures might play a role in testing communications which are designed to generate a warmth or other feeling response.

Felt Warmth Is Volatile

Felt warmth as measured by the warmth monitor exhibited significant changes within 7 to 15 seconds (Aaker et al., 1986). Such short-term responses are consistent with the findings of Meyer-Hentschel (1983) and Cacioppo and Petty (1983) who observed physiological responses to print media. One implication is that feelings can be generated and changed within a single commercial, even a 30-second commercial and probably within a 15-second commercial. Conceptually, volatility, like arousal, positions warmth within the classic definitions of an emotion.

Felt Warmth Is Affected by Sequence Effects

A warm ad preceded by another warm ad would be less effective than a warm ad preceded by a non-warm ad even if the non-warm ad is equally well liked (Aaker et al., 1986). These results appear to be due to a contrast effect. In part, this finding is probably caused by the volatility of the warmth response. Because the warmth level can change so quickly it may be of limited value to start at a high level, whereas a contrast effect can emerge quickly and last during a substantial portion of the commercial.

An implication is that it is probably of little importance what type of program precedes the commercial unless the portion of the program just preceding the commercial elicits a warm response and the commercial is one of the first ones after the break. It helps to explain the J. Walter Thompson finding that the program type (e.g., situation comedy versus action) had no effect upon commercial effectiveness but that the episode within the program type did have an impact (Yuspeh, 1977).

Warmth Exhibits a Habituation Period over Repetition

Over repetition, the warmth response is initially strong, then exhibits a habituation period with reduced felt warmth before declining with excessive repetition—a very different pattern than that for humorous ads where felt amusement drops off continuously or irritating ads which rise monotonically (Stayman & Aaker, 1987). An implication is that feeling responses differ one from the other in response to repeated exposures. It is likely that identification of a different repetition and effectiveness function will be required for different specific feelings just as past researchers found that affective versus informational appeals may have different response and effectiveness patterns (e.g., Batra & Ray, 1986a).

The Impact of Warm Ads Requires Repetition

One model of how affective advertising works is that affective response is transferred immediately to the brand, and the strength of the association is proportional to the intensity of the affective response. However, in the repetition study (Stayman & Aaker, 1987), a clear finding was that no positive attitude change was observed during the first four exposures even though these exposures were associated with a high level of warmth and liking. A substantial and significantly greater attitude change occurred during the second set of four exposures even though the warmth response had fallen to a moderate though still positive level.

The most reasonable explanation is that affective advertising may require substantial exposure to build up the association between the affective response and the brand. The need for many repetitions is consistent with the work of W. Kroeber-Riel (1979) who found that 30 exposures of print ads were needed to build observed associations. Both associational network (Anderson, 1983) and classical conditioning (Bierley, McSweeney, & Vannieuwkerk, 1985) theories suggest that a number of repeated exposures may be necessary for affective reactions to become associated with brand-related cognitions.

The implications of these findings are rather dramatic for the implementation and testing of affective advertising. Because the study involved forced exposures during a limited three-week period, the repetition function was probably compressed. Therefore, a field test would probably find that many more than eight exposures will be required for even an effective feeling campaign to have an impact. There is the suggestion that fewer than five exposures might be a complete waste of effort. Furthermore, it suggests that ad tests and academic studies which involve only one or two exposures must be interpreted very cautiously when applied to warm advertising. This conclusion can be contrasted to models such as the "three exposures is enough" model advanced by H. E. Krugman (1972).

Warmth Responses Differ from A_{ad}

Most researchers studying affective responses have focused upon attitude toward the ad, A_{ad}. The implicit assumption has been that conceptualizing at the level of the A_{ad} is adequate to model affective responses (Lutz, 1985; Moore & Hutchinson, 1983). Some researchers have conducted studies suggesting that A_{ad}

captures the impact of feeling responses (e.g., Batra & Ray, 1986b; Edell & Burke, 1987; Holbrook & Batra, 1987b).

In the repetition study (Stayman & Aaker, 1988), the positive feelings, warmth and amusement, both had a significant impact upon brand attitudes at both four and eight exposures, an impact that was still significant even with A_{ad} and prior brand attitudes as control variables. In contrast, the A_{ad} variable was either insignificantly related to attitude toward the brand or became insignificant when warmth response was added as a control variable. However, this direct impact of feelings upon attitudes was not observed at 12 exposures where the ability of the commercial to create feelings had diminished and the high repetition level had created a negative A_{ad}. Further, the negative feeling, irritation, was completely mediated by A_{ad} at all exposure levels.

In another study involving nine ads (Stayman & Aaker, in press), subjects used both a warmth monitor and a liking monitor. The test-retest reliability of the warmth monitor was .85, which represents an explained variance of 72 percent. In contrast, the correlation between the warmth monitor and the liking monitor was .61, which represents an explained variance of 37 percent. Thus, in a continuous measure context, warmth and liking are very different.

An implication is that A_{ad} is an inadequate construct on which to base a model of affective advertising and that consideration of specific feeling responses is necessary to develop a more complete model.

Warmth Is Related to Boredom

When respondents were exposed to warm commercials in the repetition study (Stayman & Aaker, 1987), their boredom level increased steadily but exhibited a habituation plateau from exposures four to eight and thus represented a mirror image of the warmth response. In contrast, irritation gradually increased until eight exposures and then exhibited sharper increases. The mean correlation, which measures linear relationships and thus is not well suited to reflect these relationships, was .57 between warmth and boredom over exposures versus .46 between warmth and irritation.

An implication is that boredom is a better indicator of and more closely related to warmth than is irritation. Changes in irritation appear to noticeably lag changes in both boredom and warmth. Such insights may be useful in further studying the nature of warmth. For example, is boredom-related warmth due to a common underlying dimension of both? Or is it due to some other factor such as specific cognitions necessary for warmth but which must be absent for boredom?

Warmth Is Associated with Other Feelings

In an effort to explore the relationship between feelings, a set of 180 adjectives was developed by scaling an original set of 644 adjectives on their relevance to advertising responses (Aaker, Stayman, & Vezina, 1988). Respondents were asked to scale each pair of feelings as to how similar they were. The emotions were then clustered on the basis of these similarity metrics. One of the 31 clusters was a rather tight cluster of 12 feelings which was labeled warm/tender since it contained the feelings warm, warmhearted, and tender. However, it also contained a set of other feelings, such as sympathetic and compassionate, romantic and love, affectionate, and intimate. The study identified other feelings that were relatively close to the warm/tender cluster, such as pride, relaxed, friendly, and delighted.

A study by C. A. Smith and P. C. Ellsworth (1985) suggests that warmth is associated with or similar to happiness and pride, which appeared in the cluster analysis as feeling clusters distinct from warmth. Smith and Ellsworth asked 16 students to recall in detail past experiences associated with each of 15 different emotions. Most of the subjects for the "happy" experience remembered scenes similar to those found in the warm ads in the perception studies. These scenes included times spent with other people, being reunited with close friends or relatives, being at a party with friends, or going out on a pleasant date. When the 15 studied emotions were positioned in a six-dimensional space, Smith and Ellsworth found that pride was very similar to happiness.

The understanding of such relationships should aid efforts to understand how such feelings are created and how diagnostic and evaluative tests can be developed.

Warmth Is Associated with Believability

Some, perhaps most, warm ads portray a scene that is realistic. We have hypothesized that the ability of such warm ads to generate a warmth response will depend upon the ability of the ad to be perceived as believable or true to life (Aaker & Stayman, 1989b). One of the practitioners of emotional advertising, Hal Riney (1981), makes it a point to strive for reality in his ads to the point of using nonactors. He noted that "people cannot relate emotionally to things that are false. You must strive for reality. When you can, use real people. Actors almost never look or act real" (Riney, 1981, p. 6).

Other ads create a warm feeling with a scene that makes no attempt to be realistic. Such an ad might portray a baseball player singing or a Pillsbury "Doughboy" character. For such ads to create warmth, we hypothesize that they must achieve verisimilitude, the willingness of the audience to suspend disbelief. Operationally, they need to avoid creating perception of an ad's being phony, pointless, or contrived; such perceptions could interfere with the emotional response.

Indirect support for this hypothesis comes from data on 80 prime-time commercials obtained by BRC. The ads were all national commercials that had been running for three weeks and appeared on prime time during a 1986 week.

To explore the believability hypothesis, we compared the warmth scores (the percent who checked the warm adjective) for those who checked the adjectives believable and true to life with those who did not. Table 4.1 displays the results. Those checking "believable" showed three times as much incidence (9 percent versus 3 percent) of checking "warm" than those not checking "believable."

Table 4.1
The Influence of Believability and Verisimilitude upon Warmth

Respondent Group	Size (000's)	Percentage Checking Warm
Checked Believable	2.6	9%
Not Checked Believable	21.4	3%
Checked True-to-Life	1.0	13%
Not Checked True-to-Life	23.0	4%
Checked Phony	1.7	1%
Not Checked Phony	22.3	5%
Checked Silly	1.8	2%
Not Checked Silly	22.2	5%

Similarly, those checking "true-to-life" had over three times the incidence of checking warm (13 percent versus 4 percent) than those not checking "true-to-life."

To explore the verisimilitude hypothesis, a similar analysis, also shown in Table 4.1, was conducted with the "phony" and "silly" adjectives since a phony or silly commercial would not have achieved verisimilitude. Again, the data lend support to the hypothesis: those not checking phony were five times as likely to check warm (5 percent versus 1 percent) as those who checked phony. Likewise, those who did not check silly were over twice as likely to check warm (5 percent versus 2 percent) as those who checked silly.

An additional study (Stayman & Aaker, 1989) provided more direct evidence by manipulating believability for warm ads by sensitizing subjects to it in a laboratory setting. All three warm ads in the study exhibited significant differences in literal believability and felt warmth due to the manipulation. In contrast, there were no literal believability differences for the six non-warm ads and no differences in feeling responses for five of the six non-warm ads.

An implication is that believability may play a role in modeling feeling response for ads that generate feelings of warmth and similar feelings. Furthermore, believability, which is a construct that once was an accepted part of ad testing (Maloney, 1963), but fell into disfavor, may be rediscovered as an important construct in the evaluation of the feeling response to advertising.

A MICRO APPROACH TO STUDYING FEELING RESPONSE TO ADVERTISING

The emerging research in studying the feeling response to advertising has involved a variety of research questions, constructs, perspectives, and research approaches. This section describes and positions our approach, relates it to others, and suggests the type of research questions that it is well suited to pursue.

Our research approach has several related characteristics. In particular, it focuses upon (1) specific feelings rather than more macro constructs such as general affect or liking of an ad; (2) audience feelings rather than audience perceptions; (3) a particular feeling, namely warmth, its characteristics and relationships to other feelings; (4) the direct link between specific feelings and attitude/behavior rather than the impact of feelings upon cognitive processing; and (5) the causes and mediators of specific feelings.

The Focus upon Specific Feelings

One way to categorize research on feeling response is to consider the constructs used. There is considerable variation in terms of the level of abstraction and specificity. Some researchers have worked with good versus bad feelings, manipulating people to "feel good" or "not feel good" (cf., Gardner, 1986; Isen, 1984). Physiological arousal has been the central focus of other researchers (e.g., Kroeber-Riel, 1979; Rothschild & Thorson, 1983). Many researchers have used affect toward the ad as the basic construct of interest and thus do not distinguish between whether the affect is caused by humor, entertainment, or some other quality of the ad (e.g., MacKenzie et al., 1986).

In contrast, we have focused upon specific feelings such as warmth, amusement, and irritation. This has permitted us to explore the differences in such factors as repetition functions and impact across feelings, even feelings with the same affect. Assessing effects of independent variables such as repetition through more macro constructs, such as general affect or arousal, may thus mask underlying differences of theoretical and practical importance.

The focus upon specific feelings also permits the study of dimensions of emotions, such as arousal and volatility, with less ambiguity. Physiological measures, such as GSR in particular, are difficult to interpret when general stimuli are applied because it is known that arousal can be stimulated by a variety of sources. However, when the stimuli are focused upon a relatively narrow set (e.g., involving warm commercials only), the interpretation becomes less ambiguous and the test is likely to be more sensitive.

Audience Feelings Rather than Audience Perceptions

Many researchers have assessed evaluations of the advertisement rather than the feeling responses themselves (cf., Edell & Burke, 1987; Madden, Allen, & Twible, 1988). They have measured ad evaluations such as ad liking and to what extent viewers think an ad is humorous or warm (Burke & Edell, 1986) rather than whether viewers were amused or felt warm. Thus, much research has implicitly or explicitly assumed that such evaluations capture the impact of feeling response. R. Batra and M. L. Ray (1986b) and Edell and Burke (1987;

Burke & Edell, 1989) have argued for the importance of studying feeling states rather than perceptions.

In our approach we attempt to measure the audience feelings as they view the ad. Do the audience members feel amused, warm, irritated? The concept is to study their feelings rather than their perceptions or opinions. There is, of course, a dramatic difference in constructs even though they might be related. Feelings imply physiological arousal and the potential of an impact not tied to cognitive processing. Perception is an active cognitive activity and need not involve arousal.

A Particular Feeling—Warmth

There are many lists of emotions and several efforts to provide a theoretical structure (e.g., Plutchik, 1980) that attempt to be comprehensive. In contrast, our effort to explore linkages between emotions has focused upon warmth. We have been interested in how warmth relates to other feelings such as boredom, irritation, pride, and sympathy. The goal is to provide a greater understanding of warmth and how it links to other feelings. For example, our result that warmth appears to be more closely related to boredom than irritation over repeated exposure might help us eventually to develop a greater understanding of at least one small section of the emotion space.

The Direct Link Between Feelings and Attitude/Behavior

There has been substantial interest in the impact of affective response upon cognitive processes and memory (e.g, Bower, 1981; Gardner, 1985; Isen, 1984; Kroeber-Riel, 1979; Thorson & Friestad, 1989). Our focus has been rather upon the direct link between feeling response and attitude and behavior. The question is will a feeling affect attitude and behavior directly by creating associations that may not involve conscious cognitive processing? A related question is whether a feeling will have an impact upon attitude and behavior that is not explained by a more macro construct such as liking of the ad. Our approach has allowed us to identify, as discussed above for example, the differential mediating role of ad liking for warm and humorous versus irritating commercials and at different repetition levels. Hopefully, a further understanding of these direct influence routes may lead to a more integrated, comprehensive model of influence.

Causes and Mediators of Specific Feelings

Much of the research on emotional response in advertising has been concerned with the impact of the feeling response. In contrast, one of our primary interests is to explore the causes and mediators of a specific feeling which has not been examined to date (cf., MacInnis & Jaworski, 1989). The focus on one feeling, in our view, allows much greater insight into the antecedents of feeling responses than is possible when a more macro construct, such as liking the ad, is motivating the analysis or when it is attempted to study all specific feelings in one project. The former incorporates many antecedents which are hard to separate operationally (Lutz, 1985); the latter makes it difficult to incorporate all antecedents for each feeling into one study. This area raises questions such as what independent variables affect warmth responses, and do these effects differ for warmth versus other feelings? For example, how do the programming context and number of exposures affect warmth versus other feelings?

The antecedent role of believability, both literal and verisimilitude (the appearance of truth), and the different response orientations seem to be fruitful areas for research (Aaker & Stayman, 1989b; Stayman & Aaker, 1989). The believability construct appears to influence the warmth response and may help in pretesting contexts. Knowledge of the orientations of response may provide insight into those aspects of the ads that provide connections between the feeling response and the brand.

From the Specific to the General

It is our hope that the focus upon specific feelings in general and warmth in particular will suggest constructs and relationships that will be applicable to other feelings and ultimately to more general models. Hopefully, the merging of micro research such as ours with more macro approaches will lead to more complete models than would otherwise be possible.

FUTURE RESEARCH DIRECTIONS

The research stream reported has identified more questions than it has answered. In particular, five sets of questions should be pursued.

Relationship Among Feelings

We know that some feelings are associated with warmth, but we know little about how they are associated or with what constructs we should be working. One issue is at what level of abstraction emotions should be studied. Should it be broader than warmth? For example, how appropriate is a positive affect which could be generated by warmth but also by other feelings, such as amusement or feeling informed? Or should it be narrower than warmth, such as affection, pride, or love? Is pride a cause of warmth because pride will be accompanied by warmth but warmth will not always or even often involve pride? More generally, what is the causal link between these and other emotions?

Another issue is how feelings interact. Will an affective response be additive or independent with some other individual feelings, or are there interactions? What about the sequencing of emotions? Is a feeling of relief after a fear response different than one after concern or puzzlement? Although we found a contrast effect for dissimilar feelings, are contrast effects always present?

There are a host of theories about basic emotions from which other emotions are based. However, it is not clear that such theories fit our context even if they are valid. First, they tend to be oriented toward negative emotions. Further, their structure is conceptualized at a high level of abstraction. For example, C. E. Izard's (1977) eight core emotions include only joy and happiness on the positive side. In advertising research, it seems likely that we will need micro theories at a more detailed level and a lower level of abstraction. In contrast, the relationship between warmth, pride, happiness, and sympathy may be of interest.

Antecedents

Almost no work has been directed at determining what causes feeling response in advertising (cf., MacInnis & Jaworski, 1989; for an exception, see MacInnis & Westbrook, 1987). Yet, the task of creating feeling advertising and providing diagnostic tests really needs such model building. It now may be appropriate to look backward from feeling response to determine its causal antecedents. We have suggested (Aaker & Stayman, 1989b) that the mediators of warmth responses include audience mediators, situation mediators, stimulus perception mediators, and stimulus orientation mediators. Examples of audience mediators include general audience characteristics, such as emotionality, age, and sex; and ad-specific audience characteristics, such as interest, experience, and similarity. Situation mediators include repetition, setting, product category, and mood. Stimulus perception mediators are cognitive empathy, such as understanding the situation of others; and believability, both literal and verisimilitude. The stimulus orientation mediators are emotional empathy, reliving a prior experience stimulated by the ad, a strong affect toward a character, and a reaction to a behavior or emotion displayed by a character.

Several questions arise. Are these the antecedents of warmth? How do they relate to mediators of other feelings? It seems evident that different feelings will have different antecedents; therefore, a micro approach is probably necessary to study antecedents.

Relationship Between Cognitive Models and Feelings

A host of researchers have explored the role that feelings have upon memory (cf., Gardner, 1985; Isen, 1984). However, they have typically used general affect polarity—do respondents feel good or bad? A real question, especially in the advertising context, is whether specific feelings such as warmth, amusement, and surgency will have different impacts upon memory and cognitive activity. The challenge is to model not only affective response but also its impact upon cognitive processes.

The Process by Which Connections Are Developed

Of perhaps more import is the process by which the associations so important to emotional advertising are created, stored in memory, dissipated or replaced, and retrieved. Are there conditions under which relatively intense feeling responses can inhibit learning by distracting? What is the role of classical conditioning in explaining the process? Is there a way to make use of cues to reduce the repetitions needed to create the associations, to make the associations stronger, or to make the associations more salient at the time of purchase (Keller, 1987; Stayman & Batra, 1989)?

What Feelings Should Be Studied?

What specific emotions should be of interest to advertisers? Is warmth of sufficient interest to be the subject of study? Or would it more productive to study elegance, amusement, worry and worry reduction, or relief? An ad of a safe hair coloring or an insurance program could elicit strong feelings of both worry and worry reduction, for example. Certainly, a number of different feelings that can be elicited by advertising have been developed (e.g., Aaker et al., 1988; Holbrook & Batra, 1987a) as have a number of different types of ads (e.g., Stayman et al., 1989).

Systematic research into response over repetition of different feelings may provide further insight into the relationship between different feelings as well as how feelings in advertising work. For example, feelings which display similar repetition and effectiveness patterns can then be further examined to explore the reasons underlying the similarities. Likewise, if certain feelings display one response-effectiveness pattern (e.g., a need for connections to develop) while other feelings display a different pattern (e.g., an immediate effect of response), then appropriate models can be developed.

CONCLUSIONS

Clearly, we have much to learn about the role of feeling response in advertising. There is a lot of room for researchers to make contributions from a variety of perspectives and methodologies. However, we would encourage some to focus upon a limited range of specific feelings using a more micro approach. Cumulatively, such efforts should lead to the development of models that will some day lead to a more comprehensive understanding of the process, integrate the disparate ways in which different feelings work, and integrate cognitive processes with emotional response.

REFERENCES

Aaker, D. A., & Bruzzone, D. E. (1981). Viewer perceptions of prime-time television advertising. *Journal of Advertising Research, 21* (5), 15–23.

Aaker, D. A., & Bruzzone, D. E. (1985). Causes of irritation in advertising. *Journal of Marketing, 49* (2), 47–57.

Aaker, D. A., & Stayman, D. M. (1989a). *Implementing the concept of transformational advertising.* Working paper, University of California, Berkeley.

Aaker, D. A., & Stayman, D. M. (1989b). What mediates the emotional response to advertising? The case of warmth. In P. Cafferata & A. M. Tybout (Eds.), *Cognitive and affective responses to advertising* (pp. 287–303). Lexington, MA: Lexington Books.

Aaker, D. A., Stayman, D. M., & Hagerty, M. R. (1986). Warmth in advertising: Measurement, impact, and sequence effects. *Journal of Consumer Research, 12* (4), 365–381.

Aaker, D. A., Stayman, D. M., & Vezina, R. (1988). Identifying feelings elicited by advertising. *Psychology and Marketing, 5* (1), 1–16.

Alwitt, L. (1985). *Monitoring the emotional flow of commercials.* Paper presented at the 11th Annual Advertising Research Foundation Midyear Conference, Chicago, IL.

Alwitt, L. F., & Mitchell, A. A. (Eds.). (1985). *Psychological processes and advertising effects.* Hillsdale, N.J.: Lawrence Erlbaum.

Anderson, N. H. (1983). *The architecture of cognition.* Cambridge, MA: Harvard University Press.

Batra, R., & Ray, M. L. (1985). How advertising works at contact. In L. F. Alwitt & A. A. Mitchell (Eds.), *Psychological processes and advertising effects* (pp. 13–44). Hillsdale, N.J.: Lawrence Erlbaum.

Batra, R., & Ray, M. L. (1986a). Situational effects of advertising repetition: The moderating influence of motivation, ability, and opportunity to respond. *Journal of Consumer Research, 12* (4), 432–445.

Batra, R., & Ray, M. L. (1986b). Affective responses mediating acceptance of advertising. *Journal of Consumer Research, 13* (2), 234–249.

Bettman, J. R. (1979). *An information processing theory of consumer choice.* Reading, MA: Addison-Wesley.

Bierley, C., McSweeney, F. K., & Vannieuwkerk, R. (1985). Classical conditioning of preferences for stimuli. *Journal of Consumer Research, 12* (3), 316–323.

Bower, G. H. (1981). Mood and memory. *American Psychologist, 36* (2), 129–148.

Burke, M. C., & Edell, J. A. (1986). Ad reactions over time: Capturing changes in the real world. *Journal of Consumer Research, 13* (1), 114–118.

Burke, M. C., & Edell, J. A. (1989). The impact of feelings on ad-based affect and cognitions. *Journal of Marketing Research, 26* (1), 69–83.

Cacioppo, J. T., & Petty, R. E. (1983). Foundations of social psychophysiology. In J. T. Cacioppo & R. E. Petty (Eds.), *Social psychophysiology: A sourcebook* (pp. 3–36). New York: Guilford.

Cafferata, P., & Tybout, A. M. (Eds.). (1989). *Cognitive and affective responses to advertising.* Lexington, MA: Lexington Books.

Edell, J. A., & Burke, M. C. (1987). The power of feelings in understanding advertising effects. *Journal of Consumer Research, 14* (3), 421–433.

Gardner, M. P. (1985). Mood states and consumer behavior: A critical review. *Journal of Consumer Research, 12* (3), 281–300.

Gardner, M. P. (1986). *Responses to emotional and informational appeals: The moderating role of context-induced mood states.* Working paper, New York University.

Holbrook, M. B. (1985). Emotion in the consumption experience: Toward a new model of the human consumer. In R. A. Peterson, W. D. Hoyer, & W. R. Wilson (Eds.), *The role of affect in consumer behavior: Emerging theories and applications* (pp. 17–52). Lexington, MA: Lexington Books.

Holbrook, M., & Batra, R. (1987a). Toward a standardized emotional profile (SEP) useful in measuring responses to the nonverbal components of advertising. In S. Hecker & D. W. Stewart (Eds.), *Nonverbal communications in advertising* (pp. 95–109). Lexington, MA: Lexington Books.

Holbrook, M., & Batra, R. (1987b). Assessing the role of emotions as mediators of consumer responses to advertising. *Journal of Consumer Research, 14* (3), 404–420.

Isen, A. M. (1984). Toward understanding the role of affect in cognition. In R. S. Wycr, Jr., & T. K. Srull (Eds.), *Handbook of social cognition: Vol. 3* (pp. 179–236). Hillsdale, NJ: Lawrence Erlbaum.

Izard, C. E. (1977). *Human emotions.* New York: Plenum Press.

Keller, K. L. (1987). Memory factors in advertising: The effect of advertising retrieval cues on brand evaluations. *Journal of Consumer Research, 14* (3), 316–333.

Kroeber-Riel, W. (1979). Activation research: Psychobiological approaches in consumer research. *Journal of Consumer Research, 5* (1), 240–250.

Krugman, H. E. (1972). Why three exposures may be enough. *Journal of Advertising Research, 12,* 11–14.

Lazarus, R. S. (1984). On the primacy of cognition. *American Psychologist, 39* (2), 124–129.

Lazarus, R. S., Kanner, A. D., & Folkman, S. (1980). Emotions: A cognitive-phenomenological analysis. In R. Plutchik & H. Kellerman (Eds.), *Theories of emotion* (pp. 189–217). New York: Academic Press.

Lutz, R. J. (1985). Affective and cognitive antecedents of attitude toward the ad: A conceptual framework. In L. F. Alwitt & A. A. Mitchell (Eds.), *Psychological processes and advertising effects* (pp. 12–44). Hillsdale, NJ: Lawrence Erlbaum.

MacInnis, D. J., & Jaworski, B. J. (1989). Information processing from advertisements: Toward an integrative framework. *Journal of Marketing, 53* (4), 1–23.

MacInnis, D. J., & Westbrook, R. W. (1987). The relationship between expectational cues and emotional response to advertising. Paper presented at the 1987 ACR Conference, Boston, MA.

MacKenzie, S. B., Lutz, R. J., & Belch, G. E. (1986). The role of attitude toward the ad as a mediator of advertising effectiveness: A test of competing explanations. *Journal of Marketing Research, 23* (2), 130–143.

Madden, T. J., Allen, C. T., & Twible, J. L. (1988). Attitude toward the ad: An assessment of diverse measurement indices under different processing 'sets'. *Journal of Marketing Research, 25* (3), 242–252.

Maloney, J. C. (1963, June). Curiosity vs. disbelief in advertising. *Journal of Advertising Research, 2,* 2–8.

Meyer-Hentschel, G. (1983). An arousal profile for print ads. Working paper, University of the Saarland, Saarbrüken, West Germany.

Moore, D. L., & Hutchinson, J. W. (1983). The effects of ad affect on advertising effectiveness. In R. P. Bagozzi & A. M. Tybout (Eds.), *Advances in consumer research* (vol. 10, pp. 526–531). Provo, UT: Association for Consumer Research.

Ortony, A., & Clore, G. L. (1981). Disentangling the affective lexicon. In *Proceedings of the Third Annual Conference of the Cognitive Science Society.* Berkeley, CA.

Plummer, J. T. (1972). Evaluating TV commercial tests. *Journal of Advertising Research,* *12* (October), 21–27.

Plutchik, R. (1980). *Emotion: A psychoevolutionary synthesis.* New York: Harper & Row.

Riney, H. (1981). Emotion in advertising. *Viewpoint, 1,* 2–13.

Rothschild, M., & Thorson, E. (1983). Electroencephalographic activity as a response to complex stimuli: A review of relevant psychophysiology and advertising literature. In L. Percy & A. G. Woodside (Eds.), *Advertising and consumer psychology* (pp. 239–251). Lexington, MA: D. C. Heath.

Smith, C. A., & Ellsworth, P. C. (1985). Patterns of cognitive approaches in emotion. *Journal of Personality and Social Psychology, 48,* 813–838.

Stayman, D. M., & Aaker, D. A. (1987). *Repetition and affective response: Differences in specific feeling responses and the mediating role of attitude toward the ad.* Working paper, University of Texas at Austin.

Stayman, D. M., & Aaker, D. A. (1988). Are all of the effects of ad-induced feelings mediated by A_{ad}? *Journal of Consumer Research, 15* (3), 368–374.

Stayman, D. M., & Aaker, D. A. (1989). *The role of believability in the elicitation and effect of feeling responses to advertising.* Working paper, University of Texas at Austin.

Stayman, D. M., & Aaker, D. A. (in press). Continuous measurement of specific emotional response: The emotion monitor. *Psychology and Marketing.*

Stayman, D. M., Aaker, D. A., & Bruzzone, D. F. (1989). The incidence of commercial types broadcast in primetime—1976–1986. *Journal of Advertising Research,* June/July, 26–33.

Stayman, D. M., & Batra, R. (1989). *The encoding and retrieval of ad affect in memory.* Working paper, University of Texas at Austin.

Sternthal, B., & Craig, C. S. (1973). Humor in advertising. *Journal of Marketing, 37* (4), 12–18.

Sternthal, B., & Craig, C. S. (1974). Fear appeals revisited and revised. *Journal of Consumer Research, 1* (3), 22–34.

Thorson, E., & Friestad, M. (1989). The effects of emotion on episodic memory for television commercials. In P. Cafferata & A. M. Tybout (Eds.), *Cognitive and affective responses to advertising* (pp. 305–326). Lexington, MA: D. C. Heath.

Wells, W. D., Leavitt, C., & McConville, M. (1971). A reaction profile for TV commercials. *Journal of Advertising Research, 11,* 11–17.

Wessman, A. E., & Ricks, D. G. (1966). *Mood and personality.* New York: Holt, Reinhart, & Winston.

Yuspeh, S. (1977). *Program environment copy test.* New York: J. Walter Thompson Co.

5

Transformational Advertising: Current State of the Art

Christopher P. Puto and Robert W. Hoyer

Transformational advertising was introduced to the research community by W. D. Wells (1980) as an explanation for one of the ways in which advertising "works," the providing of information being the other. In the interim, there have been a variety of approaches to studying this concept, but transformation has not gained the general acceptance in the academic literature which seemed at one time to be inevitable. Moreover, the concept appears to be engendering an ever-widening variety of usages (*cf.*, Deighton, 1987), which could easily result in a generalized lack of meaning such as has been noted for "involvement" and which could similarly be occurring for "framing." The purpose of this chapter is to trace the development of the transformation construct, to delineate its current standing, and to present the results of an exploratory foray into the development of potential measures for it.

DEVELOPMENT OF THE TRANSFORMATIONAL FRAMEWORK

A transformational advertisement is defined as "one which associates the experience of using (consuming/owning) the advertised brand with a unique set of psychological characteristics, which would not typically be associated with the brand experience to the same degree without exposure to the advertisement" (Puto & Wells, 1984, p. 638). A key aspect of this definition is that it is the advertisement itself that links the brand with the capacity to provide the consumer with an experience that is different from the consumption experience that would normally be expected to occur without exposure to the advertisement. As an example, most football fans can recall the live Schlitz Beer blind taste tests which occurred at half-time intermissions during televised National Football

League games in the early 1980s. The results of the taste tests shown in the commercials indicated that consumers often preferred the taste of Schlitz to that of their own brand, but sales results suggested that this preference disappeared when consumers saw the Schlitz name on the label. Something altered the viewers' perceptions of their own brand in such a way that the experience of drinking it changed once the brand name was removed. That is, with the label intact, the consumer's brand was preferred to Schlitz; with the label removed, Schlitz had a better chance of being preferred. Clearly, one candidate for the cause of this form of preference reversal is the original brand's advertising. It succeeded in transforming the consumers' experiences with their respective brands of beer.

Transformational advertising was first proposed by Wells (1980) as one anchor of an information-transformation continuum along which various forms of advertising could be classified. Thus, advertisements could be classified as either informational or transformational, implying that having more of one characteristic necessitated having less of the other. C. P. Puto and W. D. Wells (1984) later modified the continuum into a two-dimensional space, in which one dimension was transformation (high to low) and the other dimension was information (high to low). They also proposed a scale for measuring the informational and transformational content of television commercials, and they presented the results of a study which purported to differentiate among the four cells of the information/ transformation matrix.

Puto (1986) then posited that the transformation concept, as used in transformational advertising, is a multidimensional concept which contains the following four dimensions: (1) personal relevance, (2) experiential/empathy, (3) informational, and (4) executional. As used here, personal relevance refers to the degree to which the observer (consumer) connects himself or herself with the advertisement. It is important to distinguish personal relevance from the similar appearing experiential dimension. The experiential dimension refers to the advertisement's empathic capabilities, which are defined as the ability to generate "an observer's vicarious emotional identification with the execution of an advertisement" (Puto & Wells, 1984, p. 639). Thus, observers end up sharing the same experiences (albeit vicariously) as do the actors in the advertisement. The distinction, then, is that personal relevance is a necessary, but not sufficient, condition for empathy. Thus, a consumer can connect with an ad (e.g., "They are talking to me") without necessarily generating empathy for the ad (e.g., "That's the kind of experience I'd like to have").

The information dimension applies to the advertisement's ability to provide consumers with factual, relevant brand data in a clear and logical manner in such a way that they have greater confidence in their ability to assess the merits of buying the brand after having seen the advertisement (Puto & Wells, 1984). When this information changes the experience the consumer has in using (buying/ owning/consuming) the brand, it becomes transformational. A good description of this transformational effect with respect to information is given by J. Deighton

(1984a): "any effect on diagnosis . . . is a transformational consequence of advertising provided it would not have occurred in the absence of the advertising."

Thus, a wristwatch, which was originally just a timepiece, can be transformed into a "special statement" by an information-laden advertisement which reveals that the watch is hand crafted in Switzerland from solid gold, certified to function at a depth of 360 feet, and produced in limited quantities. Similarly, advertisements for Mercedes Benz automobiles are typically information oriented, yet the effect of this information is to transform the experience of owning and driving a Mercedes Benz into that of owning and driving a high-performance luxury sedan. Objectively, the car's performance may not be superior to a Chevrolet Eurosport, but its perceived performance may be far superior as a result of the advertisement.

The executional dimension arises from findings reported by W. D. Wells, C. Leavitt, and M. McConville (1971) and from recent work on the attitude toward the ad construct (cf., Edell & Burke, 1986; Mitchell & Olson, 1981). A well-executed ad will, typically, be both likable and memorable, thus increasing the likelihood of the consumer's attending to it and thereby facilitating the transferral of the experience with the ad to the experience with the brand. Examples of elements which may underlie the executional dimension are humor, drama, scenery, and celebrity presenters, essentially anything that contributes to the ad's likability and/or memorability. Puto (1986) did not specify the exact nature of the relationship of each of these four dimensions to the overall transformation concept other than to postulate that increasing levels of each will tend to increase the ad's transformational effect.

In the remainder of this chapter, it is proposed that transformation is a process which can occur as a result of exposure to an advertisement, but it is separate from the characteristics of the ad.

TRANSFORMATION AS A PROCESS

The preceding discussion has relegated transformation to a particular form of advertising when it may indeed be more than that. Transformation of experience may be a fundamental aspect of human behavior, one which can be used to explain, among other things, the basic forces at work when consumers are exposed to advertising messages. Thus, transformation is proposed to be a process whereby past experience with a brand causes a unique set of psychological characteristics to become associated with that brand and influences subsequent experience with it. This experience can be in the form of education (Deighton, 1987), observation, word of mouth, trial, or an advertisement. When this change in experience results from exposure to an advertisement or an advertising campaign, the ad is said to have transformed the consumer's experience with the brand. It is important to note that it is not necessary for the consumer consciously to connect the effect with the advertisement or even to be aware of having been exposed to the advertisement. Certainly, conscious awareness does not preclude the transformation effect—indeed, it may enhance it—but there is ample evidence to suggest that considerable processing occurs below the level of conscious awareness (e.g., Hasher & Zacks, 1979; Kihlstrom, in press; Lewicki, 1986).

A critical aspect of this approach is that transformation is not an executional characteristic of an advertisement such as emotion, information, image, or humor. Rather, it is the process through which advertisements affect consumption behavior. Thus, one does not set out to construct a transformational advertisement since, according to this proposal, ads work by transforming the consumption experience. Hence, one uses knowledge of the transformation process to develop measures of the effectiveness of an advertisement and to diagnose which aspects of the transformation process are functioning in that ad.

A legitimate question, then, concerns how transformation can be distinguished from persuasion (cf., Deighton, 1987). Persuasion is typically viewed as moving an individual to acknowledge a new set of beliefs and behaviors as a result of some form of communication. Thus, the sheer force of argument can cause one to alter one's beliefs regarding an object or behavior. That is one form of persuasion. It may not, however, alter the individual's psychological response to the object or behavior. Transformation is another means of effecting persuasion. Individuals acquiesce to persuasion; they undergo transformation.

THEORETICAL PROPOSITIONS

The foregoing presentation gives rise to several theoretical propositions, each of which is enumerated and discussed briefly below.

> *Proposition 1*: To be effective as an instrument of persuasion, an advertisement must transform the experience of using (consuming) the advertised brand.

This is the basic premise for how advertising works. An ad which does not lead to a change in the consumer's experience with the advertised brand will not be effective as a persuasive medium. There are no restrictions on the executional form of the advertisement. It can evoke strong emotions, mild emotions, or "cold" cognitions.

> *Proposition 2*: The transformational response can be immediate, when based on factual material, or delayed over multiple exposures, when based on emotional executions.

This proposition states that "thinking" ads can produce a rapid transformation effect while "feeling" ads usually will require multiple exposures over time before producing a transformation effect. This differential effect is attributable to the interaction of the advertisements and the environment in which they are processed. Specifically, the environment contains many different stimuli, all of which compete for the consumer's limited attention capacity. Thus, well-executed thinking ads, which are often more direct and easier to process, will produce a more immediate effect than feeling ads, which often involve a higher level of abstraction. This is consistent with the memory differentials for concrete versus abstract stimuli proposed by A. Paivio (1971).

> *Proposition 3*: It is not necessary for the consumer to recall exposure to a specific ad for transformation to occur.

An important aspect of this proposition is that memory for the advertisement (e.g., as measured by day-after recall tests) is not essential for transformation. In other words, although overt or conscious awareness of having been exposed to the ad may enhance or expedite the transformation process, it is not required. This is not an advocation of the "subliminal seduction" process espoused in the popular press. Rather this refers to G. Mandler's (1982) proposed cognitive-interpretive system, which is defined as "an organized system of structures that operates on the input from the external world" (p. 20). The cognitive-interpretive system does not reside wholly within consciousness, and thus it is not subject to introspections. The consumer is capable of expressing cognitions relative to the consumption experience; he or she just may not be capable of reliably tracing the source of those cognitions to the advertisement.

This differs slightly from the approach proposed by Deighton (1984b), in which he hypothesizes that persuasion by advertising occurs in two steps. The first step is the creation of an expectation as a result of exposure to the ad; the second step is an attempt to confirm that expectation based on more objective information, such as evidence or actual brand experience. The difference between Deighton's approach and the one suggested above lies mainly in the thought processes imposed on the consumers. Deighton's approach appears to require at least moderately high awareness levels and a processing effort on the part of consumers (which may indeed be the case when the informational dimension dominates an ad), whereas the more automatic nature of the cognitive-interpretive system appears to be more compatible with the typical advertising exposure environment. The following section describes and gives the results of an exploratory study conducted to learn more about the nature of consumers' responses to advertising campaigns with respect to the multidimensional structure of transformation proposed above.

AN EXPLORATORY STUDY

Empirical work has been stymied by the lack of measures for the transformation construct. Given the complex nature of the process, the measurement difficulty is not surprising. In their original work in this topic, Puto and Wells (1984) proposed two separate scales, one for transformation and one for information, which were used to measure the transformational and informational aspects, respectively, of specific advertisements. Given the current proposed transformation process, applying the scales to individual advertisements may not be the appropriate approach. Since the process is concerned with consumers' changed experiences with the brand as a result of exposure to advertising, a more appropriate measure may be one which is more closely tied to the brand itself. Also, because of the attendant analysis and interpretation problems with open-ended measures (e.g., depth interviews, projective techniques, etc.) and with physiological measures of response to advertising (e.g., galvanic skin response, electroencephalogram, etc.), some form of closed-end measure is desirable.

In keeping with these objectives, the original Puto and Wells (1984) scales have been modified to reflect the brand experience relationship while retaining the desired closed-end form. The 20 items included in the scale are given in Table 5.1. The normal response mode is to indicate the degree of agreement or disagreement with each item on a six-point response scale anchored by "strongly agree" and "strongly disagree." The details of the study are given below.

Method

One hundred fifty male subjects were recruited from the Ann Arbor, Michigan, area under the auspices of participating in a survey on sports viewing habits. The survey took place in two parts: the first one occurred one week prior to the start of the baseball World Series, and the second one occurred approximately one week after the conclusion of the World Series. Subjects were compensated at the conclusion of the second phase of the study.

The pretest instrument consisted of questions regarding product class and brand usage on 10 brands (5 beers, 3 automobiles, and 2 shaving creams), attitudes toward each of the 10 brands, and the transformation scale for each brand. The posttest instrument was identical to the pretest instrument. In each case, the order of the brands in the questionnaire was randomized across subjects to minimize response bias.

Results

Because the transformation process is brand specific, separate factor analyses were conducted for each of the ten brands. Additionally, because the stability of the factors over time is an important issue with regard to the application of the transformation construct, separate factor analyses were conducted for the pretest and the posttest instruments. The goals of the study were to ascertain the robustness of the factor structure across multiple brands and to ascertain its stability over time. The results of these analyses are summarized in Tables 5.2, 5.3, and 5.4. In each analysis, the factor constraints were as follows: minimum eigenvalue exceeds one and factor loading exceeds .70. Table 5.2 provides a frequency tabulation of the number of times an individual scale item met these criteria across the 10 brands for the pretest instrument. Table 5.3 contains the same information for the posttest instrument; Table 5.4 summarizes the results

Table 5.1
Transformation Scale Items

1. People who drink (brand) beer are a lot like me.
2. (Brand) beer fits my life-style very well.
3. My friends see me as the kind of person who drinks (brand) beer.
4. Thinking of (brand) beer brings to mind experiences I've had in my life.
5. Drinking (brand) beer makes me feel good about myself.
6. I probably share a lot of experiences with people who drink (brand) beer.
7. I see myself as the kind of person who drinks (brand) beer.
8. If I could change my life-style, I would make it more like the people who drink (brand) beer.
9. When I see a (brand) advertisement, I often see myself as one of the characters in the ad.
10. There is something special about (brand) that makes it different from other brands of beer.
11. (Brand's) advertisements seem to be talking directly to me.
12. (Brand's) advertisements are meaningful to me.
13. When I think of (brand) beer, I think of their advertising.
14. (Brand's) advertisements are the kind that keep running through my mind after I've seen them.
15. (Brand) can support the claims they make about their advertising.
16. It is difficult to give a specific reason why, but (brand) beer is really not for me.
17. I have confidence in buying (brand) beer.
18. If people thought (brand) was my favorite brand of beer, I'd be a little embarrassed.
19. I think I know a great deal about (brand) beer.
20. I think I know what features to compare when shopping for beer.

---

from both instruments. The Cronbach coefficient alphas given in each table are the averages for the factors over all 10 brands.

Discussion

The results across brands are surprisingly robust. Two findings are particularly noteworthy. One is the inseparability of the personal relevance and experiential dimensions. The other is the emergence of an image/confidence dimension which, even though less stable than the others, nonetheless occurs with a greater than chance frequency.

Although these results do not prove anything regarding the transformation

Table 5.2
Factor Loading Frequencies—Pretest

Item	Personal Relevance	Execution	Image/ Confidence	Information
Like Me	10/10			
Lifestyle	9/10			
Friends	8/10			
My Life	6/10			
Feel Good	10/10			
Share Experiences	8/10			
See Myself	9/10			
Change	7/10			
Characters	6/10			
Special		9/10		
Talking to Me		6/10		
Meaningful		8/10		
Advertisements		7/10		
Keep Running		9/10		
Support Claims			4/10	
For Me			6/10	
Confidence			6/10	
Favorite Brand			8/10	
Know Great Deal				9/10
Know Features				10/10
Alpha	.93	.85	.79	.56

Table 5.3
Factor Loading Frequencies—Posttest

Item	Personal Relevance	Execution	Image/ Confidence	Information
Like Me	10/10			
Lifestyle	9/10			
Friends	8/10			
My Life	7/10			
Feel Good	6/10			
Share Experiences	9/10			
See Myself	8/10			
Change	6/10			
Characters	5/10			
Special		9/10		
Talking to Me		6/10		
Meaningful		9/10		
Advertisements		7/10		
Keep Running		9/10		
Support Claims			9/10	
For Me			9/10	
Confidence			8/10	
Favorite Brand			9/10	
Know Great Deal				10/10
Know Features				10/10
Alpha	.94	.87	.82	.67

Table 5.4
Factor Loading Frequencies—Combined

Item	Personal Relevance	Execution	Image/ Confidence	Information
Like Me	20/20			
Lifestyle	18/20			
Friends	16/20			
My Life	13/20			
Feel Good	16/20			
Share Experiences	17/20			
See Myself	18/20			
Change	13/20			
Characters	12/20			
Special		18/20		
Talking to Me		12/20		
Meaningful		17/20		
Advertisements		14/20		
Keep Running		18/20		
Support Claims			13/20	
For Me			15/20	
Confidence			14/20	
Favorite Brand			17/20	
Know Great Deal				19/20
Know Features				20/20

construct, they do suggest that the individual responses of consumers to brand experience questions produce a relatively stable structure. This is an important first step in exploring the measurement issues concerning the transformation process. However, no information which suggests the nomological validity of the construct has been provided. Thus, although a reliable phenomenon has been measured, it may not be the proposed transformation construct. Considerable work remains before this issue can be satisfactorily addressed. Moreover, there is little evidence to link the construct with the advertising. This linkage requires a series of tightly controlled laboratory experiments which were beyond the scope of this brief, exploratory field study.

These obvious constraints notwithstanding, this work raises several issues of considerable interest to advertising theoreticians and advertising practitioners alike. The first, and most important, is the development of the proposed transformation process which provides a theoretical linkage between advertising exposure and advertising response. By offering a theoretical explanation of the process by which advertisements affect consumers, it is possible to begin developing an understanding of which executional formats may be more effective given knowledge of the current psychological profiles of the target audience. It is also possible to begin the process of developing a measure both to evaluate the relative effectiveness of alternative advertisements and to diagnose the strong/weak elements of a given advertisement or campaign.

REFERENCES

Deighton, J. (1984a). Personal communication with W. D. Wells. Dartmouth College, Hanover, NH.

Deighton, J. (1984b). The interaction of advertising and evidence. *Journal of Consumer Research, 11* (3), 763–770.

Deighton, J. (1987). Two meanings of transformation. In M. Houston (Ed.), *Advances in consumer research*, (Vol. 15, pp. 262–264). Provo, UT: Association for Consumer Research.

Edell, J. A., & Burke, M. (1986). The relative impact of prior brand attitude and attitude toward the ad on brand attitude after ad exposure. In J. Olson and K. Sentis (Eds.), *Advertising and consumer psychology* (vol. 3, pp. 93–107). New York: Praeger.

Hasher, L., & Zacks, R. T. (1979). Automatic and effortful processes in memory. *Journal of Experimental Psychology: General, 108*, 356–388.

Kihlstrom, J. (in press). The psychological unconscious. In L. Pervin (Ed.), *Handbook of personality theory and research*. New York: Guilford.

Lewicki, P. (1986). *Nonconscious social information processing*. New York: Academic Press.

Mandler, G. (1982). *Mind and emotion*. Malabar, FL: Krieger Publishing (first published in 1975).

Mitchell, A. A., & Olson J. C. (1981). Are product attribute beliefs the only mediator of advertising effects on brand attitude? *Journal of Marketing Research, 18* (3), 318–332.

Paivio, A. (1971). *Imagery and verbal processes*. New York: Holt.

Puto, C. P. (1986). Transformational advertising: Just another name for emotional advertising or a new approach? In W. D. Hoyer (Ed.), *Proceedings of the division of consumer psychology* (pp. 4–6). Washington, D.C.: American Psychological Association.

Puto, C. P., Julnes, G., & Wooten, D. (in press). The transformational process in psychology: Implications for advertising. In G. Gorn, R. Pollay, & M. Goldberg

(Eds.), *Advances in consumer research* (vol. 18). Provo, UT: Association for Consumer Research.

Puto, C. P., & Wells, W. D. (1984). Informational and transformation advertising: Differential effects of time. In T. C. Kinnear (Ed.), *Advances in consumer research* (vol. 11, pp. 638–643). Provo, UT: Association for Consumer Research.

Wells, W. D. (1980). How advertising works. Mimeo. Chicago, IL: Needham Harper Worldwide.

Wells, W. D., Leavitt, C., & McConville, M. (1971, December). A reaction profile for TV commercials. *Journal of Advertising Research 11*, 11–17.

6

Fear Appeals in Advertising: An Emotion Attribution Approach

Malcolm C. Smith,
Kristina A. Frankenberger, and
Lynn R. Kahle

Although advertising practitioners have long used emotional appeals in their advertisements, only recently have advertising and marketing researchers paid serious attention to the role that emotions play in advertising. M. B. Holbrook and R. Batra (1987) discuss the emergence of emotions as a topic of interest to consumer-behavior scholars, noting that the role of emotion in advertising has been a central research topic. For example, M. E. Goldberg and G. J. Gorn (1987) recently examined the effects, within the context of happy or sad television programs, of emotional compared to informational ads. J. A. Edell and M. C. Burke (1987) examined how the feelings generated by the ad and thoughts about the ad contribute uniquely to the explanation of the effects of advertising. Other research has investigated the role of emotions in mediating the effects of advertising (Holbrook & Batra, 1987) and the effects of positive affect responses on a consumer's attitude toward the ad, a consumer's attitude toward the brand, and the relative importance of each type of response (Batra & Ray, 1986).

This chapter takes a new approach to the study of emotions and advertising by incorporating emotion attribution theory into a proposed model explaining the effects of fear appeals in advertising. Emotion attribution theory, although no stranger to psychology, is virtually ignored in advertising and marketing literature. Only two known studies in marketing and advertising incorporate emotion attribution theory: G. J. Badovick (1988) uses emotion attribution theory to explain salesperson motivation and performance, and V. S. Folkes (1984) uses attribution theory to explain consumers' reactions to product failure.

This chapter introduces emotion attribution theory as a new approach to understanding the effectiveness of fear appeals in advertising. We present a theoretical framework and briefly discuss the implications for advertising research; review the relevant social psychology literature on emotion attribution theory, then the literature on the effectiveness of fear-arousing communications; and, finally, present an emotion attribution model designed to explain the effects of fear appeals in advertising.

THEORETICAL FRAMEWORK

Although recent research on emotions in advertising has not focused on the specific emotion of fear, advertisers are apparently quite interested in fear appeals. J. R. Stuteville (1970) notes that there is "heavy and continuous reliance on fear appeals in the sale of personal products" (p. 39). H. E. Spence and R. Moinpour (1972) observe that "communications using fear appeals are designed to stimulate anxiety in an audience with the expectation that the audience will attempt to reduce this anxiety by adopting, continuing, discontinuing, or avoiding a specified course of thought or action" (p. 40). That is, the use of fear appeals in advertising is a deliberate attempt to arouse anxiety. Emotion attribution theory, which is an attempt to explain emotional reactions to arousal, is therefore well suited to explain consumers' reactions to fear appeals in advertising.

Emotion attribution theory postulates that arousal resulting from ads is generic, or nonspecific, and the attributions the consumer has about the arousal determine the quality and quantity of the resulting emotions. In our model, the threatening ad message induces varying levels of arousal in the ad recipient, depending on the perceived level of fear in the ad. Arousal triggers the attribution process, which influences emotional responses to the ad. The higher the level of ad-induced arousal, the stronger the need for attribution and the more (or less) intense the emotional response.

M. B. Holbrook and J. O'Shaughnessy (1984) have recognized that cognition is part of the emotional process, but they have not explicitly used emotion attribution as a means of examining the effects of emotion in advertising. Emotional responses are recognized as explicit mediators of advertising effectiveness in a model by Holbrook and Batra (1987) that is intended to "portray the role that emotions play in determining advertising effectiveness" (p. 406) (see Figure 6.1). Although empirical support was found for the model, they omitted two important steps: (1) the initial arousal induced by the ad and (2) the attributions made to explain induced arousal. These phenomena occur before attitudes are formed toward the ad or the brand.

EMOTION ATTRIBUTION THEORY

Theory Overview

Emotion attribution theory is an extension of attribution theory, which attempts to understand our perceptions of causality (Harvey & Weary, 1984). F. Heider

Figure 6.1
Communication Model of Advertising Effectiveness

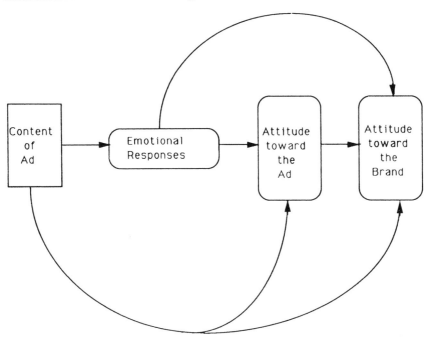

(1958) inspired attribution theory. He believed that the causal conditions of an action depend upon the person (internal factors) and the environment (external factors). Whereas attribution theory asks why and how people make attributions about themselves and others based on observations of overt behavior, emotion attribution theory asks how emotional (physiological) arousal affects attributions about affective reactions. According to R. A. Dienstbier (1979), emotion attribution theory "depends upon the premise that some physiological arousal is a part of all experience appropriately characterized as emotional" (p. 237). Given evidence that emotional reactions are biochemically similar, with nearly indistinguishable physiological characteristics (Freedman, Sears, & Carlsmith, 1981), emotion attribution theory is an attempt to explain how we make sense of our emotional reactions to arousal.

Much of the research on attributions and emotions in the 1960s and 1970s followed what we can call the traditional approach. Researchers were primarily interested in physiological manipulations of initial emotional arousal, such as drug injections, physical exercise, and placebo-induced and startle-induced emotional states. Many studies of this nature appeared in attribution literature until the early 1980s, when a marked change in theory and procedure occurred. Recent research is less concerned with peripheral arousal; it focuses instead on "feelings of emotional tension'' (Dienstbier, 1984, p. 507) or other self-reported, externally induced arousal symptoms.

The following section briefly reviews the literature on emotion attribution theory from its beginnings in the traditional school, to the recent, modified approach to emotion attribution theory and practice.

Traditional Emotion Attribution Theory

Traditional emotion attribution theory began in the work of S. Schacter and his colleagues in the 1960s. Schacter and J. E. Singer (1962) linked cognitive, situational, and physiological characteristics to explain emotional reactions to arousal. In their classic study, emotional arousal was induced through epinephrine (adrenaline) injections. Subjects aroused by the epinephrine without knowledge of its effects were more likely to respond to angry or euphoric confederates than subjects who attributed emotional responses to the effects of the drug. These findings supported the hypothesized emotional sequence: subjects encountering physiological (internal) arousal attempt to identify the source of arousal based on situational cues. This cognitive labeling process, along with the arousal state, is an important determinant of resulting affective reactions (Weiner, 1985). Subjects experiencing a state of physiological arousal "will behave most emotionally if they identify an emotional stimulus as the source of their arousal" (Valins & Ray, 1967, p. 345).

Until the late 1960s and early 1970s, Schacter and S. Valins conducted much of the major research on emotions and arousal. Schacter's studies essentially confirmed the emotion theory first proposed in Schacter and Singer (1962) (Latané & Schacter, 1962; Nisbett & Schacter, 1966; Schacter & Wheeler, 1962). R. E. Nisbett and Schacter (1966) also demonstrated that perceived intensity of the emotional stimulus mediates cognition about emotional reactions. In their study, fear-induced subjects correctly attributing pain to a shock rather than to a placebo pill experienced more pain than subjects in the placebo condition.

Valins strengthened the foundation laid by Schacter by studying the cognitive effects of internal events on emotional responses. Valins (1966) manipulated the extent to which male subjects believed their hearts were reacting to photographs of seminude females and measured the effects of "liking" for each of the slides. The hypothesis suggested that those who attributed changes in heart rate to the women in the photographs would find those women more appealing than the remaining women whose photographs were not paired with bogus heart rates. The experiment revealed that, relative to slides for which no change in heart rate was perceived, increased or decreased bogus heart rates induced subjects to rate slides as significantly more attractive during the experiment. The same women were rated more attractive in an interview four to five weeks later. Valins and Ray (1967) reported related findings in a study on avoidance behavior. Fear aroused subjects "who thought that snake stimuli did not affect them internally were more likely to hold a live snake" (p. 349) than subjects given no prior information about their internal reactions. Here attributions about fear to emotional (internal) or nonemotional (external) sources affected the degree of avoidance behavior exhibited by the subjects.

As demonstrated by Valins and A. A. Ray (1967), and later by M. D. Storms and Nisbett (1970), undesirable emotional responses may be reduced by inducing subjects to misattribute the source of arousal to external rather than internal sources (Harvey & Weary, 1984). Storms and Nisbett (1970) induced insomniac subjects to attribute their inability to sleep to external factors by telling them that placebo pills would either cause arousal or reduce arousal. Subjects in the arousal conditions who attributed their internal physiological arousal to the placebo got to sleep more quickly than they had on nights without the pills, "presumably because they attributed their arousal to the pills rather than to their emotions" (p. 319). In the reduced arousal condition, subjects had more trouble sleeping, presumably because they experienced intense emotional states even after they took a (placebo) sedative. Although these findings suggest possible therapeutic implications, J. H. Harvey and G. Weary (1984) note that the reported misattributions have been difficult to replicate. At least one study found results contrary to the reverse placebo effect reported by Storms and Nisbett (Kellogg & Baron, 1975).

Much of the research conducted in the 1970s on sexual arousal is linked with traditional emotion attribution theory. For example, consistent with D. Zillman's (1983) excitation-transfer theory,[1] J. R. Cantor, Zillman, and J. Bryant (1975) found enhanced sexual arousal reported by subjects who misattributed arousal from physical exercise to an erotic film. Male subjects were exposed to an erotic film in one of three phases: (1) immediately following physical exercise; (2) long enough after exercise that subjects believed they had recovered, but recent enough so that residual excitation remained; and (3) long enough after exercise so that complete recovery from physical arousal was maintained. Subjects in the second phase rated the film more exciting than the other groups, demonstrating a propensity to misattribute enhanced emotional response to an unrelated source of arousal.

Other studies on sexual arousal attempt to link it to aggression. There are generally three schools of thought in this area: (1) that exposure to erotic stimuli leads to aggressive behavior (Jaffe, Malamuth, Feingold, & Feshbach, 1974; Meyer, 1972; Zillman, 1971; Zillman, Hoyt, & Day, 1974); (2) that sexual arousal actually inhibits aggression (Baron & Bell, 1977); and (3) that the likelihood of aggressive behavior depends on the degree of erotica, where mild erotica inhibits aggression but strong erotica facilitates aggression (Donnerstein, Donnerstein, & Evans, 1975). In these studies, male subjects are provoked or annoyed in some fashion prior to viewing erotica (typically nude females or heterosexual couples engaged in sexual activity) or nonerotica. Subjects then experience either increased or reduced levels of aggression, depending on the experiment. Regardless of conflicting results, it is clear that subjects have a propensity to misattribute feelings of aggression (either enhanced or reduced) to something other than the actual source of arousal, consistent with emotion attribution theory. Some of the inability to obtain consistent results in sex-aggression studies has been attributed to the excitatory potential of the stimuli, the level of involvement (degree of absorption in the material), and the hedonic valence of the material (Zillman & Sapolsky, 1977). Zillman and B. S. Sapolsky report no differences in involvement potential, minimal differences in excitatory potential, and significantly less annoyance in erotic versus nonerotic conditions. Although results imply support for the view that erotica reduces aggression, the authors hesitate to reach that conclusion because retaliatory behavior was the same in both the erotic and nonerotic conditions.

Much of the important work on emotion attribution theory was contributed by Dienstbier through his work on temptation (Dienstbier, 1972; Dienstbier, Hillman, Lehnhoff, Hillman, & Valkenaar, 1975; Dienstbier, Kahle, Willis, & Tunnell, 1980; for a detailed review of emotion attribution theory through 1978, see Dienstbier, 1979). Dienstbier (1972) demonstrated that cheating on an exam was more likely when the arousal induced by the temptation to cheat could be attributed to external factors (a placebo pill) rather than internal factors. In addition, subjects in a control group who were given no placebo, but requested to act as if they had been given an arousal drug, cheated less than subjects who attributed arousal to the placebo.

A subsequent study hypothesized that children would react differently to internal versus external attributions of negative emotions to forbidden behavior (Dienstbier et al., 1975). Same-sex twins were asked to aid the experimenter in a boring task (watching a slotcar so that it did not crash). The car crashed when the children diverted their attention for a criterion period of time, and then the experimenters induced internal (the children were made to feel bad for what they had done) or external (made to feel bad because they were caught) attributions. As predicted, children who attributed the crash to external factors differed significantly from their twin counterparts who made internal attributions. When asked to repeat the task, the internal condition twins transgressed less.

An experiment on moral schema activation (Dienstbier et al., 1980) demonstrated similar results. This study manipulated initial arousal in college students by having them read passages relevant to morality (experimental conditions) or passages irrelevant to morality (control conditions). Internal-attribution conditions were evoked by having students read passages about emotional consequences of acting contrary to moral values. External-attribution conditions were evoked through passages relating immoral behavior to punishment in children. As reported by the authors, "even when moral schemas are elicited under conditions favoring moral behavior, those schemas will lead to reduced cheating most effectively under conditions in which subjects attribute their arousal to their own behavior rather than to external causes" (p. 193).

In an imaginative series of experiments on misattribution, it was hypothesized that startle-induced arousal would increase attraction for an opposite-sexed experimenter but decrease attraction for a same-sexed experimenter (reported in

Dienstbier, 1979). Study 1 placed blindfolded male subjects in a barber chair and spun it nine times before the chair suddenly tilted backward to the simultaneous sound of a loud noise. Compared to subjects in the control condition (no tilt or noise), subjects rated the female experimenter more attractive. Study 2 found that male subjects in the same experimental condition liked a male experimenter less. While there was not a significant difference between experimental and control conditions for female subjects in Study 3, it was noted that "male and female subjects made dramatically different attributions of their arousal in the presence of the same attractive male in the two studies" (p. 291).

As attribution research moved into the 1980s, researchers changed their focus, primarily by studying emotions and attributions in the context of achievement motivation studies. With this shift came a modified procedural and theoretical approach to the study of emotions and attributions. The modified approach, discussed primarily in the context of B. Weiner's cognitive-emotion theory, is reviewed next.

Modified Emotion Attribution Approach

In the last decade, traditional Schacterian emotion attribution theory has largely been advanced to a modified approach. As discussed previously, Schacter's emotional sequence begins with internal, peripheral physiological arousal. Respondents looking for a source for their arousal attribute it to situational cues; hence, cognitive labeling, in conjunction with situational cues, leads to an emotional state based upon a person's attributions (or misattributions) about the source of arousal.

Reexamination of his own research led Dienstbier (1984) to observe that arousal similar to the dimensional, peripheral arousal of Schacter's experiments could be induced by discussing symptoms with child subjects (as in Dienstbier et al., 1975) or by presenting internal and external manipulations to college students in textual format (as in Dienstbier et al., 1980). This observation led to the conclusion that placebo-induced arousal symptoms were "nonessential" in studies that "appeared to support the peripheral-dimensional view" (Dienstbier, 1984, p. 507). Subsequently, Dienstbier sought a "modification of emotion attribution theory away from the 'classic' notion that one's understanding of the causes of one's peripheral arousal symptoms determines the quality of emotional experienced," suggesting instead that "one's ideas about the source and meaning of one's emotional experience . . . determines the quality of that experience and the impact of that experience on behavior" (Dienstbier et al., 1984, p. 508)

The primary difference between the traditional and modified views of emotion attribution theory, that peripheral arousal (via drug injections, placebos, physical exercise, or startle) is unneeded, is embraced in the approach of Weiner. Weiner's (1986) cognition-emotion sequence stems from extensive research on achievement motivation and is more clearly defined than previous emotion attribution theory. Weiner identified two achievement-related affects: outcome-dependent affect and attribution-dependent affect. Outcome dependent–attribution independent emotions are based on desired goals of the outcome. For example, after winning an athletic event, a person will be happy regardless of the cause attributed to his or her success. Attribution-dependent emotions are influenced by the causal attributions ascribed to the event by the individual. For example, if a salesperson attributes lack of ability to an outcome of failure, he or she may feel guilt, shame, or fear about future sales attempts.

Weiner also identifies three causal dimensions that influence attribution dependent affects: a locus dimension, which determines whether causes are internal or external to the person; a stability dimension, which indicates whether causes are thought to be stable (persistent) or unstable (changing); and a controllability dimension, which indicates the extent to which an individual believes he or she has control over the causes of success or failure.

A simplified account of Weiner's (1986) extended model suggests that causal attributions and causal dimensions operate to influence affective reactions to an outcome. An example of a finding that is fairly robust in empirical research supporting the model is that people tend to attribute success to internal factors and failure to external factors (Baumgardner, Heppner, & Arkin, 1986; Harvey & Weary, 1984; McFarland & Ross, 1982). Although statistical methods have verified the structure of various components of Weiner's model (Reisenzein, 1986; Russell & McAuley, 1986; see also Weiner, 1986), no studies to date have attempted to verify the complete theory (as presented in Weiner, 1986).

Weiner's theory predominates the literature on emotions and attributions in the 1980s, particularly in the contexts of achievement motivation (Weiner, Russell, & Lerman, 1978, 1979; Weiner, 1985, 1986; Wong & Weiner, 1981) and helping behavior (Weiner, 1980a, 1980b). These studies are consistent with the modified view in their approach. For example, Weiner, D. Russell, and D. Lerman (1978, 1979) asked subjects to indicate on rating scales "the intensity of affect that they thought would be experienced" or to recall "the emotions that they did experience" in situations of success and failure (Weiner, 1986). While at least two studies have examined actual outcomes in relation to causal attributions (McFarland & Ross, 1982; Russell & McAuley, 1986, Study 2), most researchers have been content to use self-reported measures.

Summary

Emotion attribution theory is a significant and supported attempt to explain how we make sense of our perceptions of emotional reality. Although it has undergone change in the last decade, Weiner's cognition-emotion sequence is fairly consistent with the traditional emotion attribution view. What traditionalists labeled "arousal," Weiner calls "outcome-dependent" affect. Both traditional and modified theories posit a cognitive, attributional process that influences affective reactions to events.

THE EFFECTIVENESS OF FEAR APPEALS

M. Burgoon and E. P. Bettinghaus (1980) note a sizable body of research concerning fear appeals in persuasive messages. In addition, they point out that the effects of fear-arousing material in a persuasive message have been debated frequently. The most controversial point is the relationship between the level of fear and the amount of persuasion (Gelb, Hong, & Zinkhan, 1985).

Direct Links

Drive Explanation Model. The Drive Explanation Model is based on the premise that the perceived fear, which is aroused by the persuasive message, creates a state of drive that is unpleasant to the receiver (Boster & Mongeau, 1984). The receiver must perform some action in order to reduce the drive. This theory claims that the receiver will change his or her attitudes and behaviors as a means of drive reduction.

The Drive Explanation Model predicts that the higher the fear content, the higher the perceived fear of the audience. This fear is predicted to be positively related to the audience's attitude toward the topic. In fact, I. L. Janis and S. Feshbach (1953) have pointed out that implicit in the use of fear appeals is the assumption that, when emotional tension is aroused, the audience will become highly motivated to accept the reassuring beliefs or recommendations advocated by the communicator in order to reduce the tension. In other words, as perceived fear increases, the attitudes of the audience will more closely approach the recommended attitude of the message.

This model is in agreement with the findings of K. H. Beck and A. K. Lund (1981), C. Colburn (1967, as cited in Boster & Mongeau, 1984), and H. Leventhal (1970). F. Sternthal and C. Craig (1974) claim that many recent studies show this positive correlation between fear and persuasiveness.

Leventhal, M. A. Safer, and D. M. Panagis (1983) claim two types of factors may reduce the effectiveness of a fear-arousing message. First, the fear may be associated with different components of the message and therefore may direct behavior in unexpected ways. Second, the fear may arouse feelings of hopelessness or feelings that one cannot cope with the threat. Leventhal et al. (1983) go on to say that fear is a powerful motive and it may stimulate various coping mechanisms and defensive strategies which would not be observed under nonfearful circumstances. In fact, F. J. Boster and P. Mongeau (1984) point out that there are probably many potential drive-reducing actions possible; therefore, Leventhal et al. (1983) claim that this serial model, in which one stage leads to the next, is inadequate to explain the relationship between the level of fear in a message and the corresponding level of persuasion.

Resistance Explanation Model. Janis and Feshbach (1953) note that the receiver of a fear-arousing message may have defense mechanisms that occur and could give rise to highly undesirable effects from the standpoint of the communicator. These mechanisms include resistance to the message (evasiveness, mishearings, etc.), hostility (defiance, contempt, etc.), and avoidance. G. R. Miller (1963) states that "a strong fear appeal is not effective in producing audience response, but this conclusion is tempered by personality differences among audience members, the relevance and interest value of the communication for the audience and other relevant factors that affect the relationship'' (p. 122). Thus, the process of defense avoidance produces resistance (i.e., the receiver is motivated to ignore, minimize, or deny the importance of the threat). According to this Resistance Explanation Model, as outlined by Miller (1963), the receiver will pay attention to persuasive messages with low fear content, which are, therefore, likely to be more effective than messages with high fear content. This model predicts a negative relationship between the amount of fear-arousing material in a persuasive message and the receiver's conformity to the recommended action.

Janis and Feshbach (1953), in one of the first studies investigating this relationship, found that a minimal appeal was most effective in gaining conformity with the recommended message. They claim that their findings consistently indicated that the inclusion of more fear-arousing material not only failed to increase the effectiveness of the communication but also actually interfered with its overall success. Similar findings are found in R. E. Williams (1983, as reported in Gelb et al., 1985) and are reported in Burgoon and Bettinghaus (1980).

Curvilinear Model. Janis and Leventhal (1968) were apparently the first to propose a curvilinear hypothesis to explain the relationship between fear and persuasion. This explanation posits that as the fear-arousing content of a persuasive message increases, the amount of perceived fear also increases, but as perceived fear increases, the amount of attitude change increases and then begins to decrease. That is, the relation function is that of an inverted "U". Thus, when a receiver is extremely fearful or has very little fear, according to this hypothesis, little attitude or behavioral conformity or change toward the recommendation in the message will occur; however, the optimal amount of conformity is produced when the listener is moderately fearful.

At least three different variations of this hypothesis seek to explain why this relationship might take place. The first, put forth by Janis and Leventhal (1968), predicts that, at low levels of fear, the audience is unaffected because they dismiss all information as being inconsequential by means of blanket reassurances (we need not change because we are not convinced, for example). At high levels of fear, the audience exhibits defense mechanisms (denial, detachment, and minimizing rationalization, for example), and these interfere with the acceptance of the message. At moderate levels of fear, "the average person's vigilance and reassurance tendencies are stimulated which is the optimal condition for developing compromise attitudes of the type required for acceptance [of the recommended action]'' (p. 1056).

W. J. McGuire (1969) also has an explanation for such a curvilinear rela-

tionship. He claims that fear acts as both a drive and a cue. As a drive, the
perceived fear increases the probability of an individual's yielding to the message.
As a cue, it increases the probability of that individual's resisting the message.
Together, McGuire proposes that these produce "an overall nonmonotonic relationship between anxiety and influenceability . . . with maximum susceptibility
at intermediate levels of anxiety" (p. 173).

A third variation has been put forth by K. L. Higbee (1970), who claims that
the severity of the threat and the probability that the threat will occur again if
no action is taken are two factors that bring about the curvilinear relationship.
Higbee hypothesizes that these two factors are negatively correlated, and the
inverted "U" comes from the assumption that as the level of perceived fear
increases, the perceived severity increases exponentially while the probability
of occurrence decreases exponentially. F. A. Powell (1965) and Leventhal and
J. C. Watts (1966) report findings that agree with this curvilinear hypothesis.

Indirect Links

The preceding three hypotheses of how fear and persuasibility are related
assume a direct link between fear and attitudinal or behavioral changes that
occurs in order to reduce the state of tension brought about by the fear-arousing
message. Most of the newer theories agree that the link is not this simple and
that other variables combine with fear to influence persuasibility.

Protection Motivation Model. P. W. Rogers (1975) claims that fear-arousing
persuasive messages are composed of three factors: (1) levels of noxiousness of
an event, (2) the probability that the event will occur without behavioral change,
and (3) the availability and effectiveness of a coping response that can reduce
or eliminate the noxious event. The more these factors are present in a persuasive
message, the greater the extent that they will be perceived by the receiver who
will develop a drive to avoid the potential threat. Therefore, the Protection
Motivation Hypothesis claims that the greater the above three factors, the greater
the aroused protection motivation. However, if any of these factors are missing,
the fear appeal will have no effect at all. Therefore, the attitude toward the
message is predicted to be a function of the amount of protection motivation
produced in the listener by the fear-arousing message. M. Menasco and P. Baron
(1983) have reported some support for this theory in a commercial context. Their
results confirmed the possibility that fear of a physical or social threat may
operate only indirectly on persuasion via such mediational responses.

Boster and Mongeau (1984) point out that this model involves many causal
links between fear arousal and behavior; therefore, any correlations between the
two may be quite low. Leventhal et al. (1983) claim that this model does a poor
job in accounting for the consequences of emotional arousal and therefore leaves
the receiver "lost in thought" since it does not predict what actions will take
place (i.e., what is the actual relationship predicted to be?).

Parallel Response Model. Leventhal et al. (1983) claim that the Parallel Response, or Dual Process Model, is a first step toward the integration of the previously mentioned directive models (e.g., Fear-Drive Model) and intensive models (e.g., Protection Motivation Model), and it also takes into account that fear interacts with other variables to affect attitudes and behavior.

Leventhal (1970) states that this explanation asserts that fear-arousing persuasive messages activate two primary processes: (1) fear control, which is subjective, and (2) danger control, which is objective. Both assist in coping with the fear. The receiver's attitude and behavior are influenced by the amount of fear control and danger control aroused by the message.

The danger control produces processes that are instrumental in averting the threat. Leventhal et al. (1983) say that this averting is done based on current experience and past history. They claim that this objective-cognitive process generates a representation of the threat, and it also generates action plans to cope with the threat based on its representation.

The fear control is an emotion-coping process in which the receiver strives to reduce the fear. Emotions are aroused by the message independent from thought, and behaviors are needed to cope with and control these emotions, which are different than those behaviors needed to cope with the threats (Leventhal et al., 1983). These two processes interact to affect the extent to which the receiver conforms to the recommendation in the message (Leventhal, 1970).

It is hypothesized that, if fear arousal only generates a danger control process, the relation between the amount of fear-arousing material in the message and the receiver's attitude toward the message will be positive; however, if only a fear control process is generated, then an inverse relation is predicted (Leventhal, 1970).

Leventhal (1970) claims that this model explains the findings which show a positive relationship between fear and persuasion because, in most cases, the two processes interact in ways that are either mutually interfering or mutually facilitating. However, Sternthal and Craig (1974) argue that this model is predictive of a curvilinear function between the level of fear-arousing material and the attitude toward the topic in question. They claim that, at moderate levels of fear, the danger control mechanism overrides the fear control process, and listeners concentrate on reducing the threat by accepting the recommendations; however, at low levels of fear, the threat does not appear to be serious, and the listener has no reason to accept the message's recommendation because both processes are weak. On the other hand, at high levels of fear, both processes are strong, the tendency to control fear interferes with the process of danger control, and little attitudinal or behavioral change occurs.

Many authors claim that this hypothesis is not testable because the model is ambiguous in its linking statements and concepts, and precise predictions regarding the relationship between fear and persuasion cannot be made (Beck & Frankel, 1981; Boster & Mongeau, 1984; Rogers, 1975). That is, this explanation does not specify under what conditions the different outcomes will occur.

Threat Control Model. Beck and Frankel (1981) postulate that the response to fear appeals depends entirely on cognitive rather than emotional factors. The Threat Control Explanation claims that fear-arousing messages bring about two processes in the receiver. The first is response efficacy, which is the perceived relation between doing the recommended action and the reduction of the noxious event. For this to be high, the receiver must perceive that doing the action will indeed reduce or eliminate the probability of the threat's occurrence.

The second process is a personal efficacy, or the receiver's perceived ability to perform the recommended action successfully. The recommendation must be perceived as "doable" by the receiver for this process to be high.

Beck and Frankel (1981) claim that these two processes combine to create the perceived threat control (i.e., the receiver's perception of success in controlling the threat). The perceived threat control, not the level of fear, has a relation with persuasion. They hypothesize that the relation is most likely positive and linear, but they also point out that it could be negative if the fear appeal has an inverse impact on either the response efficacy or personal efficacy.

Other Factors. Other researchers also propose that certain factors moderate the way in which fear-arousing messages affect our behavior. W. J. McGuire (1969) claims that the effect of the fear appeal is directly related to the simplicity of the message. M. J. Goldstein (1959) has hypothesized that the effect of the level of fear may be related to the personality of the receiver. Colburn (1967) found that high levels of fear appeal become more effective as the topic becomes increasingly important to the receiver. Sternthal and Craig (1974) and Miller and M. A. Hewgill (1966) cite evidence that the credibility of the source of the message has an impact on persuasibility. Boster and Mongeau (1984) argue that age, anxiety level before exposure to the message, and whether the listener volunteered for the study (i.e., methodological issues) could play a role.

FEAR APPEALS IN ADVERTISING

Marketing and advertising practitioners are constantly looking for more effective ways to persuade consumers to buy their products (Sternthal & Craig, 1974). After M. L. Ray and W. L. Wilkie (1970) reviewed the literature on the potential use of fear appeals in marketing, marketing academics renewed their interest in fear as a relevant variable for motivating purchase and consumption behavior (Sternthal & Craig, 1974).

However, this spark of interest seems to have been short lived. Little research has investigated the effects of fear-arousing content and resulting attitude and behavior in a commercial mass-persuasion context. This chapter now reviews the studies that have investigated various aspects of the use of fear appeals in marketing communications.

Research on fear appeals in advertising has investigated both physical and social threats to the receiver. Physical fear would include harm to the body; social fear is fear of disapproval by peers or other associates of some action or characteristic possessed by the receiver of the message (e.g., bad breath or ring around the collar). As in the psychological literature, there are conflicting results.

According to Menasco and Baron (1983), most fear appeal research in marketing has focused on physical threat; however, L. S. Unger and J. M. Stearns (1983) have stated that "in the field," the most common use of fear is social disapproval. Moderate levels of fear are most often used. Products such as insurance, toothpaste, deodorants, mouthwash, and detergents commonly use fear appeals in their advertising. Public service announcements also sometimes use fear appeals in their messages to try to reduce the viewer's risk of getting cancer, to discourage driving while drinking alcohol, or to increase the use of seatbelts. Recently, fear appeals have been used in advertisements that promote the use of condoms to prevent the spread of AIDS.

R. Evans, R. Rozelle, T. Lasater, T. Dembroski, and B. Allen (1970) found that fear was more effective in persuading potential consumers when it dealt with social rather than physical threats. Menasco and Baron (1983) measured subjects' level of social and physical anxiety and exposed them to advertisements that either contained negative consequences for not using the product advertised (a threat) or a positive consequence for using it (a reward). Both physical threats/rewards and social threats/rewards were used. They found that people who measured high in physical anxiety were most persuaded by high-level physical threats and low-level social threats. People who were rated as low in social anxiety were most persuaded by threats in general rather than rewards. People who are low in social anxiety and high in physical anxiety are most easily persuaded by fear-arousing messages. In fact, these people might be most influenced by advertisements that are strongly physically threatening or mildly socially threatening. Ray and Wilkie (1970) state that fear appeals are most likely to be persuasive when the receiver is self-confident and less subject to anxieties. Stuteville (1970), on the other hand, claims that fear appeals are more likely to be effective when the level of anxiety is moderate, rather than high or low, and when the consumer can take some action based on the appeal.

THE PROPOSED EMOTION ATTRIBUTION MODEL

As discussed previously, an emotion attribution process is an antecedent to the formation of an attitude toward the ad. Therefore, we are proposing a new model that utilizes emotion attribution to explain the extent to which threatening or fear-inducing ads influence our emotions (see Figure 6.2).

The process begins with exposure to the fear-arousing ad. Given that the recipient pays attention to it, he or she perceives a level of threat in the ad. Recipient characteristics play a role in influencing this perceived level of threat (i.e., what is perceived to be a mild threat by one person may be considered moderate or even strong by another due to individual differences). The perceived level of threat will determine the intensity of arousal that consequently occurs (minimum to intense). Arousal leads to conscious or subconscious attributions,

Figure 6.2
Proposed Model of Fear Appeals: Emotion Attribution Approach

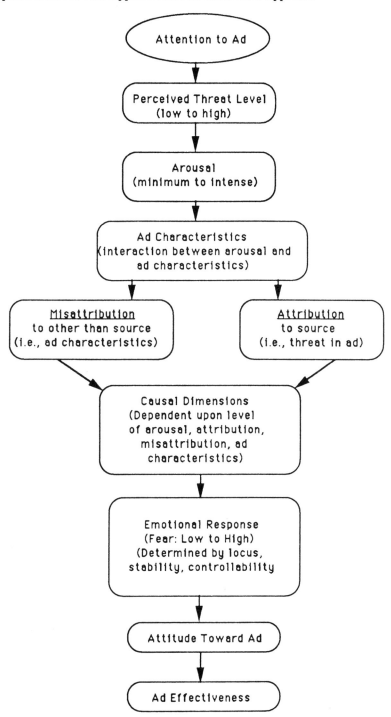

by the recipient, about the cause of arousal. Attributions or misattributions about the source of arousal may be influenced by the intermediary characteristics of the ad itself (e.g., music, spokesperson). Attribution of arousal to the message of the ad, or misattribution of the arousal to something other than the message (e.g., characteristics of the ad), along with the level of arousal, determines the recipient's categorization of the causal dimensions as outlined by Weiner (1985, 1986) (i.e., locus of causality, stability, and controllability). These categorizations in turn determine the emotional response and its intensity. Finally, in accordance with Holbrook and Batra's (1987) model, emotional responses influence attitudes toward the ad, attitudes toward the brand, and, ultimately, the effectiveness of the ad.

The underlying principle of the proposed model is that the effectiveness of the ad depends on whether the recipient attributes the resulting arousal to the fear-laden message (i.e., the message intended by the advertiser) or misattributes the arousal to something else. The following examples illustrate the curvilinear relationship between the level of fear in the ad and the effectiveness of that ad, using the model.

If attributions to low to medium arousal are made to the message, the recipient finds the situation easy to resolve cognitively. For example, for an ad dealing with body odor or a dull laundry, the locus of causality is internal ("it is my fault"), the stability dimension is changing, and the situation is controllable. The recipient probably experiences increasing emotional levels of fear as the arousal goes from mild to moderate, because the situation may become increasingly uncontrollable. However, this is moderated by the degree to which the recipient of the ad is interested in the given message (e.g., "I am worried that the color of my family's laundry is not bright enough" versus "My kitchen floor never needs waxing, so why should I worry about it?").

When the recipient attributes moderate to high arousal to the message (as is the advertiser's intention), causal dimensions begin to be influenced by the situation or the elements in the ad. The controllability dimension probably plays a major role here. Whether the locus of control is deemed to be internal or external and whether the situation is deemed to be persistent or changing play a minor role. If the ad delivers information that can help the recipient alleviate the arousal, the situation is controllable (e.g., "you can help prevent AIDS by using condoms"). However, if the ad offers no methods or inadequate methods of reducing the arousal, there is a risk that misattribution away from the dangerous portrayal will take place because the situation is perceived as uncontrollable. (This situation is more fully addressed below.) The higher the level of arousal, the more likely the recipient will view the situation as uncontrollable, and the less effective the ad will be.

Ineffectiveness of fear-laden ads results from likely misattribution of arousal away from the intended message of the ad. If the arousal is from low to moderate, the recipient may be aware of the threat but does not attribute arousal to the threat. In this case, the recipient may attribute arousal to the portrayal of the event or the characteristics of the ad. If arousal is low and misattribution takes place (e.g., "I do not like that spokesperson," or "Body odor is a stupid topic for advertising," or "The music used in the ad irritates me"), the recipient finds the situation annoying to some extent. In this case, it will not matter whether the locus of causality is internal or external, or whether the situation is persistent or changing. The resulting emotional response may be frustration, annoyance, or perhaps low levels of anxiety, and the ad will therefore be ineffective.

As the arousal moves from moderate to high, misattribution depends upon the amount of information given to deal with the threat. The less information is given, the stronger is the tendency to misattribute the cause of arousal away from the message. If no techniques are offered to deal with the situation (e.g., "You may be the victim of a drunk driver at any time"), danger control, as outlined by Leventhal et al. (1983), is not possible and fear control is evoked. In this situation, the recipient is prone to attribute arousal to whatever reasonable source allows him or her to best cope with it (e.g., "The ad is very graphic and therefore not believable") rather than attribute it to the danger in the message (Dienstbier, 1988, personal communication). That is, the recipient will try to turn the situation into one that can be controlled, even though the danger may really be external, persistent, and uncontrollable. In doing so, arousal is attributed to something over which the recipient has more control. Therefore, as arousal approaches a high level, the effectiveness of the ad decreases.

This model gives rise to the following propositions, which may direct future research in this area:

> *Proposition 1*: The greater the arousal to a fear-laden ad, the more intense the response to the ad.

> *Proposition 2*: The effectiveness of the ad will depend on whether arousal is attributed to the threatening message or misattributed away from that message, where attribution leads to an effective ad and misattribution leads to an ineffective ad.

> *Proposition 3*: The level of arousal will interact with the characteristics of the ad to influence the causal attributions that are made about the arousal.

DISCUSSION

Application of emotion attribution theory to advertising research problems regarding the study of emotions carries with it a broad range of theoretical implications. For example, D. C. Eisert and L. R. Kahle (1986) and Kahle, Eisert, and K. E. Piner (1986) have proposed that the developmental stage influences the attributions that are made about the sources of arousal. In consumer life stage research, applications of the model may vary as a function of developmental level. Preoperational children may respond differently to certain types of fear appeals than concrete or formal operational level children. At a formal operational level, persuasive intent is more likely to be a discounting cue in processing fear stimuli. The use of emotion attribution theory in the study of advertising may also lead to a better understanding of such topics as information processing, motivation, and the issue of high versus low involvement.

The model described here presents a new method of examining fear appeals in advertising by using the novel approach of integrating emotion attribution, as outlined by Dienstbier (1979) and Weiner (1986), with the communication model proposed by Holbrook and Batra (1987). The general model has the advantage of being flexible, and it can be used to explain the effects of a variety of emotions in advertising. It is not meant to explain the effects of all advertising on attitude formation. However, this model does help to shed light on the apparent complexity of the roles emotions play as mediators on the effects of advertising.

NOTE

1. Excitation-transfer theory, as described by Zillman (1983), "projects the intensification of subsequent emotional behaviors and emotional experiences as a function of residual sympathetic excitation from preceding emotional reactions" (p. 215).

REFERENCES

Badovick, G. J. (1988). *The impact of emotional reactions on salesperson motivation following inadequate sales performance*. Unpublished doctoral dissertation, University of Oregon.

Baron, R. A., & Bell, P. A. (1977). Sexual arousal and aggression by males: Effects of type of erotic stimuli and prior provocation. *Journal of Personality and Social Psychology, 35*, 79–87.

Batra, R., & Ray, M. L. (1986). Affective responses mediating acceptance of advertising. *Journal of Consumer Research, 13* (2), 234–246.

Baumgardner, A. H., Heppner, P., & Arkin, R. M. (1986, March). Role of causal attribution in personal problem solving. *Journal of Personality and Social Psychology, 50*, 636–643.

Beck, K. H., & Frankel, A. (1981). A conceptualization of threat communication and protective health behavior. *Social Psychology Quarterly, 3*, 204–217.

Beck, K. H., & Lund, A. K. (1981). The effects of health threat seriousness and personal efficacy upon intentions and behavior. *Journal of Applied Social Psychology, 1*, 401–415.

Boster, F. J., & Mongeau, P. (1984). Fear arousing persuasive messages. *Communications Yearbook, 8*, 330–375.

Burgoon, M., & Bettinghaus, E. P. (1980). Persuasive message strategies. In M. E. Roloff & G. R. Miller, (Eds.), *Persuasion: New directions in theory and research* (pp. 141–169). Beverly Hills, CA: Sage.

Cantor, J. R., Zillman, D., & Bryant, J. (1975). Enhancement of experienced sexual arousal in response to erotic stimuli through misattribution of unrelated residual excitation. *Journal of Personality and Social Psychology, 32*, 69–75.

Colburn, C. (1967). *An experimental study of the relationship between fear appeal and topic importance in persuasion*. Unpublished doctoral dissertation, University of Indiana.

Dienstbier, R. A. (1972). The role of anxiety and arousal in cheating. *Journal of Experimental Social Psychology, 8,* 168–179.

Dienstbier, R. A. (1979). Emotion-attribution theory: Establishing roots and exploring future perspectives. In H. E. Howe, Jr., & R. A. Dienstbier (Eds.), *1978 Nebraska Symposium on Motivation* (pp. 237–306). Lincoln: University of Nebraska Press.

Dienstbier, R. A. (1984). The role of emotion in moral socialization. In C. E. Izard, J. Kagan, & R. B. Zajonc (Eds.), *Emotions, cognition, and behavior* (pp. 484–514). Cambridge, England: Cambridge University Press.

Dienstbier, R. A., Hillman, D., Lehnhoff, J., Hillman, J., & Valkenaar, M. C. (1975). An emotion-attribution approach to moral behavior: Interfacing cognitive and avoidance theories of moral development. *Psychological Review, 82,* 299–315.

Dienstbier, R. A., Kahle, L. R., Willis, K. A., & Tunnel, G. B. (1980). The impact of moral theories on cheating: Studies of emotional attribution and schema activation. *Motivation and Emotion, 4* (3), 193–216.

Donnerstein, E., Donnerstein, M., & Evans, R. (1975). Erotic stimuli and aggression: Facilitation or inhibition? *Journal of Personality and Social Psychology, 32,* 237–244.

Edell, J. A., & Burke, M. C. (1987). The power of feelings in understanding advertising effects. *Journal of Consumer Research, 14* (3), 421–433.

Eisert, D. C., & Kahle, L. R. (1986). The development of social attributions: An integration of probability and logic. *Human Development, 29,* 61–81.

Evans, R., Rozelle, R., Lasater, T., Dembroski, T., & Allen, B. (1970). Fear arousal, persuasion and actual vs. implied behavioral change. *Journal of Personality and Social Psychology, 16,* 220–227.

Folkes, V. S. (1984). Consumer reactions to product failure: An attributional approach. *Journal of Consumer Research, 10* (4), 398–409.

Freedman, J. L., Sears, D. O., & Carlsmith, J. M. (1981). *Social Psychology* (4th ed.). Englewood Cliffs, NJ: Prentice Hall.

Gelb, B. D., Hong, J. W., & Zinkhan, G. (1985). Communications effects of specific advertising elements: An update. In J. H. Leigh & C. R. Martin, Jr. (Eds.), *Current issues in research in advertising* (vol. 2, pp. 75–98). University of Michigan, The Division of Research, Graduate School of Business.

Goldberg, M. E., & Gorn, G. J. (1987). Happy and sad TV programs: How they affect reactions to commercials. *Journal of Consumer Research, 14* (3), 387–403.

Goldstein, M. J. (1959). The relationship between coping and avoiding behavior and response to fear-arousing propaganda. *Journal of Abnormal and Social Psychology, 58,* 247–252.

Harvey, J. H., & Weary, G. (1984). Current issues in attribution theory and research. In M. R. Rosenzweig & L. W. Porter (Eds.), *Annual review of psychology* (pp. 427–460). Palo Alto, CA: Annual Reviews.

Heider, F. (1958). *The psychology of interpersonal relations.* New York: Wiley.

Higbee, K. L. (1970). Fifteen years of fear arousal: Research on threat appeals: 1953–1968. *Psychological Bulletin, 72,* 426–444.

Holbrook, M. B., & Batra, R. (1987). Assessing the role of emotions as mediators of consumer responses to advertising. *Journal of Consumer Research, 14* (3), 404–420.

Holbrook, M. B., & O'Shaughnessy, J. (1984). The role of emotion in advertising. *Psychology and Marketing, 1* (2), 45–64.

Jaffe, Y., Malamuth, N., Feingold, J., & Feshbach, S. (1974). Sexual arousal and behavioral aggression. *Journal of Personality and Social Psychology, 30,* 759–764.

Janis, I. L., & Feshbach, S. (1953). Effects of fear-arousing communications. *Journal of Abnormal and Social Psychology, 48,* 78–92.

Janis, I. L., & Leventhal, H. (1968). Human reaction to stress. In E. Borgatta & W. Lambert (Eds.), *Handbook of personality theory and research* (pp. 1041–1085). Chicago: Rand McNally.

Kahle, L. R., Eisert, D. C., & Piner, K. E. (1986). The growth of social attributions. *Journal of Social Psychology, 126* (2), 151–159.

Kellogg, R., & Baron, R. S. (1975). Attribution theory, insomnia, and the reverse placebo effect: A reversal of Storms and Nisbett's findings. *Journal of Personality and Social Psychology, 32* (2), 231–236.

Latané, B., & Schacter, S. (1962). Adrenaline and avoidance learning. *Journal of Comparative and Physiological Psychology, 65,* 369–372.

Leventhal, H. (1970). Findings and theory in the study of fear communications. In L. Berkowitz (Ed.), *Advances in experimental social psychology*, Vol. 15. New York: Academic.

Leventhal, H., Safer, M. A., & Panagis, D. M. (1983). The impact of communication on the self-regulation of health beliefs, decisions and behavior. *Health Education Quarterly, 10,* 3–29.

Leventhal, H., & Watts, J. C. (1966). Source of resistance to fear-arousing communications on smoking and lung cancer. *Journal of Personality, 34,* 155–175.

McFarland, C., & Ross, M. (1982, November). Impact of causal attributions on affective reactions to success and failure. *Journal of Personality and Social Psychology, 43,* 937–946.

McGuire, W. J. (1969). The nature of attitudes and attitude change. In G. Lindzey & E. Aronson (Eds.), *The handbook of social psychology* (2nd ed., vol. 3). Reading, MA: Addison-Wesley.

Menasco, M., & Baron, P. (1983). Threats and promises in advertising appeals. *Advances in Consumer Research, 9,* 221–227.

Meyer, T. P. (1972). The effects of sexually arousing and violent films on aggressive behavior. *Journal of Sex Research, 8,* 324–333.

Miller, G. R. (1963). Studies on the use of fear appeals: A summary and analysis. *Central States Speech Journal, 14,* 117–125.

Miller, G. R., & Hewgill, M. A. (1966). Some recent research on fear-arousing message appeals. *Speech Monographs, 33,* 377–391.

Nisbett, R. E., & Schacter, S. (1966). Cognitive manipulation of pain. *Journal of Personality and Social Psychology, 2,* 227–236.

Powell, F. A. (1965). The effects of anxiety-arousing messages when related to personal, familial and interpersonal referents. *Speech Monographs, 32,* 102–106.

Ray, M. L., & Wilkie, W. L. (1970). Fear: The potential of an appeal neglected by marketing. *Journal of Marketing, 34,* 54–62.

Reisenzein, R. (1986, June). A structural equation analysis of Weiner's attribution-affect model of helping behavior. *Journal of Personality and Social Psychology, 50,* 1123–1133.

Rogers, R. W. (1975). A protection motivation theory of fear appeals and attitude change. *Journal of Psychology, 91*, 93–114.

Russell, D., & McAuley, E. (1986, June). Causal attributions, causal dimensions, and affective reactions to success and failure. *Journal of Personality and Social Psychology, 50*, 1174–1185.

Schacter, S., & Singer, J. E. (1962). Cognitive, social, and physiological determinants of emotional state. *Psychological Review, 69*, 379–399.

Schacter, S., & Wheeler, L. (1962). Epinephrine, chlorpromazine, and amusement. *Journal of Abnormal and Social Psychology, 65*, 121–128.

Spence, H. E., & Moinpour, R. (1972). Fear appeals in marketing—A social perspective. *Journal of Marketing, 36*, 39–43.

Sternthal, F., & Craig, C. (1974). Fear appeals: Revisited and revised. *Journal of Consumer Research, 7*, 22–34.

Storms, M. D., & Nisbett, R. E. (1970). Insomnia and the attribution process. *Journal of Personality and Social Psychology, 16* (2), 319–328.

Stuteville, J. R. (1970). Psychic defenses against high fear appeals: A key marketing variable. *Journal of Marketing, 34*, 39–45.

Unger, L. S., & Stearns, J. M. (1983). The use of fear and guilt messages in television advertising: Issues and evidence. In P. E. Murphy et al. (Eds.), *Proceedings of the American Marketing Association Educators Conference* (Series no. 49, pp. 16–20).

Valins, S. (1966). Cognitive effects of false heart-rate feedback. *Journal of Personality and Social Psychology, 4*, 400–408.

Valins, S., & Ray, A. A. (1967). Effects of cognitive desensitization on avoidance behavior. *Journal of Personality and Social Psychology, 7*, 345–350.

Weiner, B. (1980a). A cognitive (attribution)-emotion-action model of motivated behavior: An analysis of judgments of help giving. *Journal of Personality and Social Psychology, 39*, 186–200.

Weiner, B. (1980b). May I borrow your class notes? An attributional analysis of judgments of help giving in an achievement related context. *Journal of Educational Psychology, 72*, 676–681.

Weiner, B. (1985). An attributional theory of achievement motivation and emotion. *Psychological Review, 92*, 548–573.

Weiner, B. (1986). *An attributional theory of motivation and emotion.* New York: Springer-Verlag.

Weiner, B., Russell, D., & Lerman, D. (1978). Affective consequences of causal ascriptions. In W. J. Ickes & R. F. Kidd (Eds.), *New directions in attribution research* (vol. 2, pp. 59–90). Hillsdale NJ: Erlbaum.

Weiner, B., Russell, D., & Lerman, D. (1979). The cognition-emotion process in achievement-related contexts. *Journal of Personality and Social Psychology, 37*, 1211–1220.

Williams, R. E. (1983). *Elements of persuasion: An analysis of the effects of communication credibility, fear appeal of the message and channel of communication upon cognitive and behavioral change.* Unpublished doctoral dissertation, Washington State University.

Wong, P.T.P., & Weiner, B. (1981, April). When people ask "why" questions, and the heuristics of attributional search. *Journal of Personality and Social Psychology, 40*, 650–663.

Zillman, D. (1971). Excitation transfer in communication-mediated aggressive behavior. *Journal of Experimental Social Psychology, 7,* 419–434.

Zillman, D. (1983). Transfer of excitation in emotional behavior. In J. T. Cacioppo & R. E. Petty (Eds.), *Social Psychophysiology* (pp. 215–240). New York: Guilford.

Zillman, D., Hoyt, J. L., & Day, K. D. (1974). Strength and duration of effect of aggressive, violent and erotic communications on subsequent aggressive behavior. *Communication Research, 1,* 286–306. (as cited in Zillman & Sapolsky, below).

Zillman, D., & Sapolsky, B. S. (1977). What mediates the effect of mild erotica on annoyance and hostile behavior in males? *Journal of Personality and Experimental Social Psychology, 35,* 587–596.

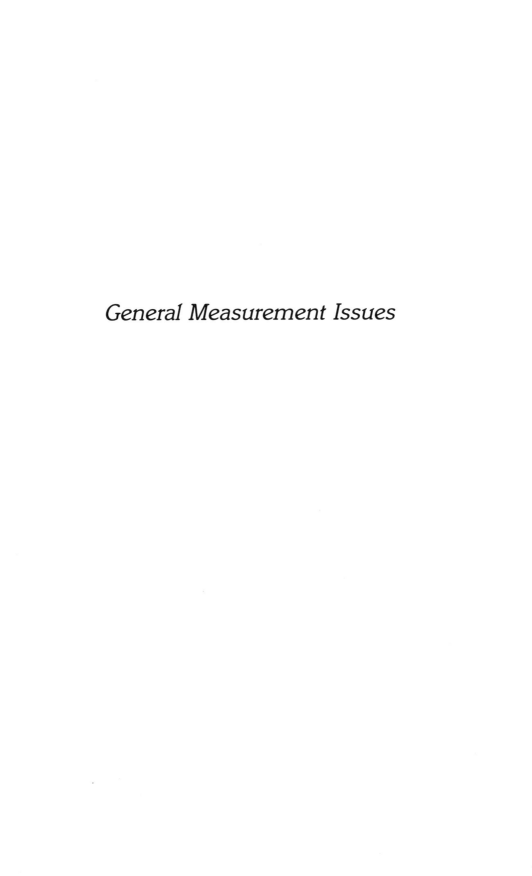

General Measurement Issues

7

Facing up to the Challenge of Measuring Emotional Response to Advertising

Trent H. Punnett and Richard W. Pollay

INTRODUCTION

As a measure of emotional response to television advertising, the measurement and interpretation of facial expressions holds great hope. The use of facial expressions to measure emotion is grounded in the expressiveness of the human face. These expressions can be very complex given the sending capacity of the face and the information it can convey. The human face can have hundreds of expressions, and it can display different expressions extremely rapidly. In literate cultures researchers have found distinctive and consistent facial expressions for anger, disgust, happiness, sadness (or distress), fear, and surprise (Ekman, 1972, 1973; Izard, 1971; Saha, 1973).

Facial expressions, being a behavioral measure, offer several advantages over other measures of emotional response that are based on cognitions, affect, or physiological response. Used in a controlled situation, facial expressions are an unobtrusive measure which can provide continuous information about emotion as it occurs in response to television advertising, at an automatic level.

The use of facial expressions to measure emotional response is an established research topic in psychology, and several coding methods have been developed to determine emotion from displayed facial expressions. Most notable among these methods, in terms of its ability to capture the full range of facial expressions and the types of emotional response that can be interpreted, is the Facial Action Coding System (FACS) developed by Ekman and Friesen (1978).

As facial expressions have not previously been used to measure emotional response to television advertising, this chapter introduces the FACS method by describing the method, discussing its advantages over traditional measures, and outlining guidelines for using the measure in a research situation. The chapter concludes with specific recommendations for future research in measuring emotional response to television advertising.

THE FACIAL ACTION CODING SYSTEM

The primary goal of FACS is to distinguish all visible facial movements. In developing FACS, P. Ekman and W. V. Friesen (1978) based the system on muscular action because each muscle in the face has the potential to change visible appearance. To decompose complex facial muscular actions into component elements, the face was described in terms of what Ekman and Friesen (1978) call action units (AUs).

AUs describe the muscle movements that change the expression of the face. This approach allows a wide variety of possible actions to be captured and separates inference from the description of facial expression. Almost all other descriptive systems of facial expressions use descriptions confounded with inference, an example of which is the "aggressive frown" (Grant, 1969).

Single AUs were the first step in developing FACS. Developing their method by drawing upon anatomy texts, cameras, mirrors, and a learned ability to fire their facial muscles voluntarily, Ekman and Friesen identified 33 AUs, most of which involve a single muscle. FACS names for AUs, like any short title, aid recall but are not fully descriptive.

The procedure of moving the muscles and then photographing the results was repeated for combinations of two, three, and four single AUs. In total, between 4,000 and 5,000 facial combinations were performed and examined. After identifying the most common and meaningful combinations, another 44 AU combinations were included in the FACS system. Table 7.1 provides one example of a FACS AU description, a lip movement expressing a negative reaction. To gain an idea of the difficulty involved in learning to fire facial muscles separately, readers might attempt to mimic this action unit.

Using the FACS system, any complex facial expression can be analyzed into its component AUs. Since FACS emphasizes the scoring of movement, it is particularly well suited for scoring facial actions seen on film or video records. The FACS scoring system allows for measuring facial symmetries, where different AUs appear on each side of the face. The scoring of facial expression using FACS, besides providing a description of muscular action, provides data on intensity (for selected AUs), frequency, and duration of AU movement when motion records are used.

Validation

FACS can be used to measure emotional response by linking the movement of AUs to emotion through a set of hypotheses about what movements represent

Table 7.1
Sample Action Unit

==

Action Unit 15 - Lip Corner Depressor

The muscle underlying AU 15 emerges from the side of the chin and runs upward attaching to a point near the corner of the lip. The action manifestations are:

(1) Pulls the corners of the lips down.

(2) Changes the shape of the lips so that they are angled down at the corner and usually stretched horizontally.

(3) Produces some pouching, bagging, or wrinkling or skin below the lip corners. This may not be apparent unless the action is strong.

(4) May flatten or cause bulges to appear on the chin boss. May also produce depression medially under the lower lip.

(5) If the nasolabial furrow (a wrinkle from beyond the nostril wings) is permanently etched, it will deepen and may appear lengthened or pulled down.

How to do Action Unit 15

Pull your lip corners downward. Be careful not to raise your lower lip at the same time. If you are unable to do this, place your fingers above the lip corners and push downward, noting the changes in appearance. Now, try to hold this appearance when you take your fingers away.

Note: This is based upon Ekman and Friesen (1978).

specific emotions. The problem in validating these hypotheses has been the difficulty in finding valid, independent measures of emotion states, intensities, and durations. In studies using spontaneous emotional behavior, Ekman, Friesen, and S. Ancoli (1980) found that FACS hypotheses of emotional experience predicted the reported experience recorded on multidimensional scales imme- diately after viewing pleasant and unpleasant films. FACS was able to discrim- inate the intensity of negative feelings, the intensity of happy feelings, and which two happy experiences made up the happiest, as well as the occurrence of disgust as compared with fear, anger, or sadness.

Procedures

When motion records of facial expressions are used, the amount of time spent on coding FACS depends on the density of the facial behaviors in the time sample to be scored. A 15-second film segment that is densely packed with behavior may take 10 hours to score if all AUs and combinations are identified, but if only one or two actions occur, scoring could take as little as one minute using scorers familiar with the system.

If selective scoring is done, the time required can be much lower. If only certain emotions are to be scored from facial expressions, then actions that are typical for that emotion are selected. K. R. Scherer and Ekman (1982) estimate that a 2:1 ratio (i.e., 30 seconds of scoring for each 15 seconds of live action) is a reasonable estimate to identify a single emotion. Using this guideline, the scoring for eight emotions for a 30-second advertisement would take approximately eight minutes.

Scherer and Ekman (1982) report that the Emotion Facial Action Coding System (EMFACS) has recently been developed to take advantage of selective coding. In this method, only occurrences of actions considered to be the most common signs of anger, fear, distress, sadness, disgust, contempt, surprise, and happiness are noted.

Scoring for this short list of emotional states with EMFACS is based upon grouping of related AUs. If any action in the grouping is seen, a check is made for that grouping. All other actions are ignored. In addition, the intensity of action is not scored, although intensity is included in the requirements for a particular action within a grouping; and the timing of actions is not measured, only a frequency count is taken. These procedures streamline the scoring task considerably.

The benefits associated in using FACS as a measure of emotional response are that it captures emotions as they happen, without requiring the subject to be cognitively engaged in the measurement task, and that it can be unobtrusive. The system can also identify specific emotions and give indications of intensity. No other measurement instrument, whether it involves a paper and pencil, thought verbalizations, or physiological response, offers all of these benefits. The use of FACS in consumer-behavior research is to date limited, and as a result the validity and reliability in measuring emotional response are unknown. Scherer and Ekman (1982) report, however, that FACS has shown reliability in measuring spontaneous behavior and identified the emotions of interest, anger, disgust, fear, happiness, sadness, and surprise. Since FACS has not been used yet to measure emotional response to television advertising, the value of this method should be established through a pretest designed to assess the validity and reliability of the measure.

GUIDELINES FOR PRETESTING FACS

In a pretest for FACS, individual subjects could be set up to watch a television program with advertisements. The subjects' facial expressions could be videotaped unobtrusively through a one-way mirror while they watch the program. The success in capturing specific emotional responses attributable to the advertisement will depend in large part on the setting used, the selection of advertisements, and the program these advertisements are embedded within. The laboratory setting should approximate a normal viewing environment to encourage natural viewing behavior in subjects. Subjects should sit directly in front of the television, with the one-way mirror located directly above the set to facilitate the videotaping of their facial expressions. The pretest should maximize the variability in potential emotional response to an advertisement to gauge the initial sensitivity of FACS. Since FACS has identified the emotions of interest, anger, disgust, fear, happiness, sadness, and surprise, advertisements that represent primarily one of the seven emotional categories and elicit a strong reaction in the emotional category represented should be selected. The nature of the selected advertisements implies that there should be maximum variability in the predominant emotional reaction between advertisements. As a result, pretest findings may lack external validity, since not all television commercials will be as powerful and vivid as those used in the pretest. The sensitivity of FACS under situations of less variability between advertisements should be investigated in later studies. To avoid other confounding effects, selected advertisements should also meet the following criteria: (1) they are of the same length; (2) they do not represent products or services that are sex specific in their purchase, application, or use; and (3) the advertisements be new or novel to the experimental subjects.

This last criterion, that the advertisements be new or novel to the experimental subjects, is important if frequency biases are to be avoided. An advertisement that has been viewed before has the potential to evoke boredom and inattention in the viewer, or a learned response. The effects of advertisement frequency and wear-out can be investigated in subsequent studies and should be avoided in the pretest.

As emotional responses may be influenced by prior emotions, moods, or feelings (Holbrook & O'Shaughnessy, 1984), contextual effects should be controlled for in the pretest. Context effects may be generated by the program the advertisements are embedded in, or by other advertisements embedded in the same program. Context effects can be reduced in the pretest by selecting a program that is neutral in terms of the emotional response it evokes and by spacing the advertisements apart in the program.

The accuracy and reliability of FACS scorers is important in any study that uses this measurement instrument. The scorers must be properly trained in the FACS method, and they should have experience in using the system prior to scoring pretest videotapes. The accuracy and reliability of scoring can be improved by using two scorers and comparing their scoring results.

One possible influence on experimental results, the Amount of Involved Mental Effort (AIME) (Saloman, 1981), deserves comment by nature of its potential impact on measuring emotional response to television advertising. The concept of AIME recognizes the differences required in cognitive processing levels associated with different tasks. AIME increases when information does not fit easily into existing schemata, or when the information requires internal elaboration before it is assimilated. With television, the nature of the medium requires little internal elaboration, and information typically fits with prelearned schemata. As a result, most television viewing requires low levels of involved mental processing. In terms of sensitivity, FACS may be biased toward advertisements that provoke strong emotions and high levels of AIME. Mediocre or worn-out advertisements may involve low levels of AIME, which may result in no facial expressions being displayed during viewing. As a result, facial expressions indicating emotions may occur only when the advertisement requires a higher than normal level of AIME on the part of the viewer. Although this may be a bias in the method, it may also be useful in identifying effective advertisements.

Initial directions for research should focus on establishing the sensitivity, validity, and reliability of FACS to television advertisements.

To structure and delineate areas for new research, emotional response to television advertising can be approached from the viewpoint of what could impact or influence the response. This leads to the definition of the following areas of influence: the advertisement, the group of advertisements the advertisement is placed in, the program, the viewing environment, and the viewer.

Emotional response to the advertisement can be influenced by the formal features of the ad (motion, sound, number of cuts, color, length, brightness) and its content or theme. At this level, research may focus on evaluating the effects of the individual, specific, formal, and content features on emotional response. This may lead to an investigation of whether emotional response is influenced by specific advertising features or by the advertisement as a whole.

For the group of advertisements an advertisement is placed in, research may investigate order effects on emotional response, whether emotional response carries over from one advertisement to the next, and whether emotion is additive across advertisements. This type of research would, in part, investigate the contextual effects of the advertisements within a group on each other. The program in which advertisements are embedded may also influence emotional response to advertisements through context. Research in this area might focus on whether emotions in response to the program carry over and influence emotional response to advertisements.

Research on the effect of the viewing environment might investigate the effects of viewing group size and content on emotional response and whether factors such as time of day, room brightness, and privacy influence the response. Research may also focus on the viewer in terms of how viewer characteristics may influence a viewer's capacity and type of response and whether different viewer characteristics imply that different types of advertisements are required to provoke an emotional response.

Clearly, much work remains to be done before emotion and its role in advertising are defined and understood. The use of facial expressions in measuring emotional response provides a direct, unobtrusive, behavioral measure of emotion

(Punnett, 1988). As a new measurement method with much potential, facial expressions deserve further investigation.

REFERENCES

Ekman, P. (1972). Universals and cultural differences in facial expressions of emotion. In J. Cole (Ed.), *Nebraska Symposium on Motivation* (vol. 19). Lincoln: University of Nebraska Press.

Ekman, P. (1973). Cross-cultural studies of facial expression. In P. Ekman (Ed.), *Darwin and facial expression: A century of research in review.* New York: Academic Press.

Ekman P., & Friesen, W. V. (1978). *Facial Action Coding System (FACS): A technique for the measurement of facial action.* Palo Alto, CA: Consulting Psychologists Press.

Ekman, P., Friesen, W. V., & Ancoli, S. (1980). Facial signs of emotional experience. *Journal of Personality and Social Psychology, 39* (6), 1125–1134.

Grant, N. G. (1969). Human facial expression. *Man, 4,* 525–536.

Holbrook, M. B., & O'Shaughnessy, J. (1984). The role of emotion in advertising. *Psychology and Marketing, 1* (2), 45–64.

Izard, C. E. (1971). *The face of emotion.* New York: Appleton-Century-Crofts.

Punnett, T. H. (1988). *Measuring emotional response to television advertising.* Unpublished master's thesis, University of British Columbia, Vancouver British Columbia.

Saha, G. B. (1973). Judgment of facial expression of emotion—A cross-cultural study. *Journal of Psychological Research, 17* (2), 59.

Saloman, G. (1981). Introducing AIME: The assessment of children's mental involvement with television. In H. Gardner & H. Kelly (Eds.), *Children and the worlds of television.* San Francisco: Jossey-Bass.

Scherer, K. R., & Ekman, P. (1982). *Handbook of methods in nonverbal behavior research.* Cambridge, England: Cambridge University Press.

8

Ad-Specific Emotional Responses to Advertising

J. Edward Russo and Debra L. Stephens

In the last few years, viewers' emotional responses to advertisements have joined "cognitive responses" as important predictors of post-exposure attitudes. This naturally leads to the consideration of how best to assess emotional responses. The current approach is to record subjects' ratings of a relatively long list of emotional adjective scales. Because such a list is alleged to be comprehensive, it is applied to all ads without modification. We propose the use of a briefer list of feelings that have been selected to apply to an individual ad.

AD-SPECIFIC FEELINGS

The rationale for a tailored set of emotional responses or feelings[1] is straightforward. We assume that advertisements produce a positive attitude toward the brand by evoking an intended sequence of emotion (and cognitive) responses in viewers. Ad-specific feelings are designed to measure the particular emotional responses intended by the advertiser. As such, these responses should be good predictors of the resulting overall attitudes.

Consider the television commercial summarized in Table 8.1. It is a simple depiction of a young woman who has supposedly benefited from plastic surgery.

This work was supported by a grant from the Marketing Science Institute, Cambridge, Massachusetts. Additional funding was provided by the Johnson Graduate School of Management of Cornell University and by the Computer Science Center of the University of Maryland. The authors thank E. Scott Lathrop for his assistance in data analysis.

Table 8.1
Synopsis of a Representative Advertisement: Total Information Plastic Surgery

===

An attractive woman in her mid-twenties strolls through a country setting - a grassy field with a pond in the background. Her skirt is long, white and slit up the side. Her top is short, revealing her midriff.

A voice-over assures listeners that plastic surgery can and does benefit a wide range of people.

A close-up of the woman includes her waist and a leg revealed as the skirt's slit opens briefly.

The announcer urges viewers to telephone for full information as a close-up of the woman's smiling face appears.

From many viewers, this commercial elicits positive feelings that were intended by the advertiser, for example,

• Hope, optimism
• A sensual feeling
• Trust, credibility
• Being impressed.

If an ad is well-executed, most intended responses should be obtained. If the execution is flawed, however, unwanted emotional responses may be elicited from a substantial segment of viewers. For the plastic surgery commercial, we have observed the following responses,

• Not enough information before the number to call
• Too ridiculous to give it attention
• A little revealing
• Similarity of the symbol to a Federal Express logo.

The first three of these responses are general in that they or their equivalent were given by several pretest subjects and seem predictably related to the commercial itself. The last response, though equally unintended, is idiosyncratic. It was generated by only one viewer and seems to reflect personal factors. The former three qualify as ad-specific responses and play a role in our scheme for predicting post-exposure attitudes; the fourth does not.

This approach stands in contrast to other ways of measuring emotional responses to advertisements. Some advertising researchers have assessed emotion as a general affective response (such as the warmth measure of Aaker, Stayman, & Hagerty, 1986). More common are typologies of emotional responses to ads (e.g., Batra & Holbrook, 1988; Batra & Ray, 1986; Burke & Edell, 1989; Edell & Burke, 1987; Holbrook & Batra, 1987). These typologies are applied to all ads in that every item is assessed for every ad viewed. They claim to be a complete assessment of the emotional response to any ad.

The study reported here represents a preliminary effort to determine which approach to measuring emotional responses to ads, ad specific or general, yields more accurate predictions of post-exposure attitudes. We selected two general typologies against which to test our ad-specific approach: those of R. Batra and M. B. Holbrook (1988) and those of J. A. Edell and M. C. Burke (1987). Below is a brief description of each.

Holbrook and Batra (1987) perused the literature on emotion, mood, affect, and drive in order to construct a list of affective responses meant to cover the full range of consumers' emotional responses to ads. This search produced a list of 29 a priori categories of affect, and 3 or 4 words or phrases representing each category (yielding a total of 94 items). The authors then had 12 respondents rate how strongly they experienced each of the 94 feelings for every one of 72 ads. Tests of reliability and validity revealed that, of the initial 29 categories, 12 were highly reliable and also demonstrated convergent, discriminant, concurrent, and predictive validity (Batra & Holbrook, 1988). Furthermore, the 34 items of these 12 categories fell into 12 distinct clusters. These 34 items were used in the experiment that follows.

Unlike Batra and Holbrook, Edell and Burke (1987) constructed their initial list of 169 feelings from published sources, their own intuition, and pretest data. They focused on the possible emotional responses to advertisements only and not to other stimuli. From the first two sources, they constructed an initial list of 169 feelings. Sixty subjects noted each of the listed feelings they had ever experienced while watching a television commercial. Edell and Burke then selected the 60 items checked by at least 50 percent of men or women. The same 60 subjects also saw 16 commercials and reported their feelings to each ad immediately after seeing it. From these responses, Edell and Burke selected 9 additional items. A new group of 29 subjects then rated how strongly they experienced each of the 69 items as they viewed 10 commercials. Thirteen of these items were eliminated as being redundant. A factor analysis of the remaining 56 items revealed three underlying factors, two positive and one negative. In the experiment reported below, the second general typology we tested comprised these 56 items.

AN EMPIRICAL STUDY OF TWO GENERAL TYPOLOGIES

Method

Design. The basic strategy is to compare the emotion lists of Batra and Holbrook (1988) and of Edell and Burke (1987) with our ad-specific approach. As described below we generated for each ad several intended feelings as well as one or more common unwanted feelings. The rated emotional responses of each of the three schemes are used to predict attitudes toward the ad and brand.

The three schemes were compared in a between-subjects design. This is a conservative approach, chosen to eliminate any carryover effects from responding to more than one set of scales. It also reduced the time spent rating the items after having seen an ad, thereby reducing memory loss. The costs of a between-subject design are the additional variance (from differences among the three subject groups) and the exclusion of complementary analyses. The latter means that it is not possible to ask how well the different approaches complement each other and how superior, if at all, a combination of approaches might be.

This preliminary study employed only four television commercials. However, to ensure a minimum range of variation, two were chosen to be of medium quality and two of high quality, as described below.

Stimuli. An initial set of 51 ads was assembled, about half of which had won an Addy, Ad Age, or Clio award. All were expected to be unfamiliar to most subjects, since all were for regionally distributed brands, far distant from the subjects' current residential area. We chose unfamiliar brands in order to observe each commercial's impact on attitudes undiluted by prior brand knowledge (e.g., Machleit & Wilson, 1988).

Each ad was judged by between 28 and 31 pretest subjects on three measures of professional quality: overall impact, professionalism, and "moving people toward purchase." The average rating over the three 1-to-7 scales measured ad quality. We created a double criterion for ad quality by requiring that all award-winning ads receive quality scores above 4.5 and all non-award-winners score below 4.5. This reduced the initial set of 51 candidate ads to 33. A second group of 26 pretest subjects judged the remaining ads on the three quality scales. Four ads were selected whose quality ratings were consistent across both pretest groups. They consisted of two high-quality ads (with scores of 5.1 and 5.3) and two medium-quality ads (scores of 2.9 and 3.1).

To determine the feelings expected to be aroused in viewers by each ad, the first pretest subjects were also asked to describe in writing "each of the emotions you felt during the ad." This generated unwanted as well as intended feelings in response to all ads. The main reason for the second group of 26 pretest subjects was to perform a recognition task for the feelings associated with each of the 33 commercials. All emotions obtained in the free elicitation task were listed for each ad, and the new subjects were instructed to "mark the three feelings that most strongly occurred as a part of your personal, internal response to the ad.'' Furthermore, subjects were told to rank these three feelings in strength.

Based on these rankings, the six to eight most frequently occurring feelings for each of the four test ads were selected for use in the experiment proper. For a given ad, four to six of these were judged to be intended, and one to four as unwanted. In addition, for each ad we provided two distractor feelings that seemed unrelated to the ad and had not been listed by any subject. The distractors served as a control. Subjects genuinely responding to the ads should not experience the distractor feelings.

Subjects. The experimental subjects were 68 undergraduate students who were attending a large Eastern university. Each of three groups of subjects participated in a 45-minute session administered in a classroom setting. The number of subjects ranged from 19 using the Edell and Burke typology to 25 using Batra and Holbrook's.

Procedure. Subjects were instructed to watch the commercials as they naturally would at home, that is, in a relaxed, nonanalytic manner. The four test commercials were preceded by one practice ad which was not used in any data analysis. The two medium-quality ads were shown before the two high-quality ads to reduce any carry over effects. We expected that subjects would notice the quality variable more if a high-quality ad was followed by one of lower quality than if the reverse order were used.

Immediately after each ad was shown, subjects provided intensity ratings for their respective lists of feelings on a 1 (not at all) to 7 (very strongly) unipolar scale. After the intensity ratings, subjects reported all their internal responses to the ad they had just viewed. (These verbal reports were collected as part of another study and are not discussed further here.) Finally, after all four test ads had been shown, brand and then ad attitudes were measured. To measure attitude toward the brand, we used three 1-to-7 semantic differential scales: negative-positive, good-bad, and dislike-like. The measure of brand attitude used in all analyses was the mean rating on these three scales. To measure attitude toward the ad, the scales used were not interesting-interesting, good-bad, and dislike-like. Ad attitude was the mean of these three responses.

Results

General versus Ad-Specific Approaches. Models to predict ad and brand attitude were constructed as follows. We followed Batra and Holbrook's procedure for constructing 12 predictors by summing the ratings of the items in each of their 12 clusters. We also collapsed the 56 scales of Edell and Burke as they did, by summing the ratings classified under each of their three factors. To represent our ad-specific typology, we simply used the ratings of the six to eight nondistractor feelings for each ad.

The direct comparison of the predictive power of the three models is distorted by one inequity. Because ad-specific feelings are nested within an ad, they can account for effects of the different ads (on attitude) derived from other causes such as nonemotional responses. We attempt to redress this imbalance in two ways. First, dummy variables for ads are added to the models with feelings only. Second, the beta coefficients of the general predictors are indexed by ad. In the case of Edell and Burke's three scales, this yields 12 predictors. For Batra and Holbrook, the number of predictors would leap from 12 to 48, which seems unreasonably large and, in any case, is not estimable given only half that number of subjects. So the second tactic for introducing ad-specific prediction into the models based on general emotions is applied only to the Edell and Burke scheme. Finally, we also test models with subject dummy variables to remove any group differences derived from our between-subjects design.

The adjusted R^2s of the Ordinary Least-Squares (OLS) regressions of all models on both ad and brand attitude are reported in Table 8.2. In addition, the results of a partial F-test show whether adding ad and subject variables significantly increased R^2. (For brevity we will henceforth drop the qualifier "adjusted"; all reported R^2s are adjusted for the number of parameters in the model.)

The overall pattern of values in Table 8.2 shows that the ad-specific approach predicts ad attitude as well as either general typology, but it seems to be inferior as a predictor of brand attitude. For all three models, the ad-specific R^2 exceeds those of both batteries of general emotions when ad attitude is predicted. For brand attitude, the Batra and Holbrook scheme is superior; the comparison between Edell and Burke and Russo and Stephens is mixed. However, this generalization must be qualified by its lack of uniformity across the individual ads. For instance, the feelings-only model for brand attitude contains three pairwise comparisons among the R^2s (e.g., the Batra and Holbrook scheme versus the Russo and Stephens scheme). Of these three, not one was unanimously confirmed by all four ads (all were violated by one of the four ads, but not the same ad in all three comparisons). This variation emphasizes how ad dependent the predictive power of each scheme may be and the consequent need for a broader base of ads before comparative performance is concluded.[2]

Intensity of Feelings. Given that ad-specific feelings are able to predict attitudes (at least near the level of two batteries of general feelings), we now turn to an examination of these feelings. First, are intended feelings more intensely activated than unwanted ones? Second, is any differential intensity mediated by ad quality? Specifically for medium-quality ads, are intended feelings less intense or are unwanted feelings more intense? The relevant data are displayed in Figure 8.1. Feeling intensity is very much affected by the quality of ad execution. Figure 8.1 can be described mainly as a crossover interaction between ad quality and intended versus unwanted feelings. These data were subjected to a two-way analysis of variance (with unequal cell sizes). The main effects of both intentionality and quality, as well as their interaction, were significant (all three p's $<.001$). In addition, this crossover interaction was found in all four ads when examined individually. Finally, the intensity ratings of the distractor feel-

Table 8.2
Adjusted R²'s of Models Predicting Attitudes

ATTITUDE TOWARD THE AD

Model	Batra & Holbrook	Edell & Burke Dummy variables for ads	Betas indexed by ads	Russo & Stephens
Feelings +ads +subjects	.74	.56	.52	.79
Feelings +ads	.72*	.54	.55	.74
Feelings	.68	.54		.75

ATTITUDE TOWARD THE BRAND

Model	Batra & Holbrook	Edell & Burke Dummy variables for ads	Betas indexed by ads	Russo & Stephens
Feelings +ads +subjects	.68	.42	.44	.56
Feelings +ads	.66*	.46	.51*	.44
Feelings	.60	.39		.44

*p < .05, partial F test of the additional variance accounted
for relative to the model listed directly beneath

ings are appropriately low. For high-quality ads, however, the distractors' ratings are not as low as the mean level of unwanted feelings, which testifies to how well these two ads avoided unwanted emotional responses. These results suggest that ads of lower quality are inferior in two ways: they fail to activate the feelings intended by the advertiser, and they evoke more unwanted feelings.

DISCUSSION

With only four ads, our experiment was limited in scope, and conclusions must be drawn cautiously. It does appear that our proposed ad-specific approach

Figure 8.1
The Intensity of Feelings by Type of Feeling and Advertisement Quality

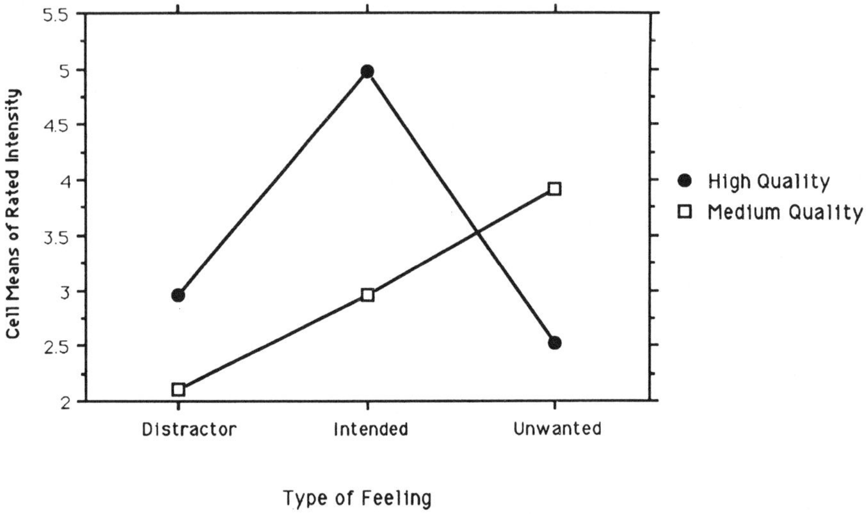

Type of Feeling

has demonstrated enough merit to justify further exploration. With an eye toward future work, we discuss three aspects of the present findings.

The Diagnostic Role of Ad-Specific Feelings

We have limited our comparison of the ad-specific and general approaches to their ability to predict attitudes; however, researchers may be more concerned with how much each reveals about the process whereby ads influence attitudes, and advertising practitioners may care more about each approach's ability to diagnose an ad's executional flaws than their relative R^2s. In both respects, the assessment of ad-specific feelings may offer a diagnostic advantage over general typologies.

Because intended feelings capture a major component of the responses intended by the creator of the ad, their intensity should reveal details of the process of influence. This may be especially important for intended sequences of feelings. A common ad strategy is to begin with a problem description, which often activates unpleasant feelings in viewers. The product is then presented as a solution to the problem, and an emotionally satisfying resolution is portrayed. In such an ad, achieving positive attitudes may depend on the complete sequence of emotional responses.

Similarly, the weak evocation of intended feelings and, even more so, the strong activation of unwanted ones may serve as useful diagnostic aids to practitioners seeking to identify and eliminate flaws in ad execution. For instance, in the plastic surgery ad (described in Table 8.1), a feeling of embarrassment runs counter to the advertiser's goal of persuading viewers that plastic surgery can be for all women, not just the rich or famous. One of our subjects responded, "TIPS, kind of sounds like tits [sic] - suggestive." If this response had been received from a substantial proportion of viewers (which it was not), a redesign of the ad might be in order, e.g., not pronouncing the acronym TIPS or embedding it in a phrase like "information TIPS."

In sum, because they are directly tied to the responses intended by the advertiser, ad-specific feelings may offer a useful view of the advertising influence process. This includes both how it works and when it fails. We note also that this advantage may be enhanced in conjunction with other data like a prompted retrospective protocol that reveals cognitive responses (Stephens & Russo, 1989). To the extent that additional data are ad specific, as are verbal protocols, ad-specific feelings may be more easily coordinated with them to generate further insights.

Ad versus Brand Attitude

All three of the schemes we tested predicted ad attitude better than brand attitude. This is a familiar finding that accords well with a hierarchy of effects explanation. However, the decrement from ad to brand attitude is noticeably greater for the ad-specific approach. Using the "feelings plus ads" model as the basis of comparison, the ad to brand decrease in R^2 is .31 for Russo and Stephens versus .06 for Batra and Holbrook and .08 and .04 for the two Edell and Burke models. As before, these results must be qualified by their limited data base. However, should this phenomenon be found in future work, it may help illuminate the difference between the ad-specific and general approaches. For instance, does the designed robustness of general emotional scales across ads lead somehow to a robustness across the hierarchy of effects? Alternatively, does the general approach predict better because of a greater capacity to capture nonemotional components of brand attitude? Or is the link between ad and brand attitudes less close for emotional responses than for cognitive ones? These questions may be at least partly answered by further investigation of the differential ability of the ad-specific and general approaches to predict brand attitudes.

Joint Approaches

Our between-subjects design did not permit joining the ad-specific and general approaches in a single predictive model. Might the two approaches capture different (though overlapping) components of the emotional response to an ad? For instance, might ad-specific feelings form a kind of emotional foreground while general feelings compose the background, with each providing an essential part of the whole picture? Certainly, future work should collect both kinds of responses from the same subjects to enable a test of joint models. Furthermore, the presence of predictive ability unique to each approach may not only increase their combined R^2, but may also help reveal the mechanism whereby emotional responses influence attitudes.

Finally, we note that joint approaches might include not only both kinds of emotion scales, but also nonemotional responses. We have recently addressed the problem of maximizing the predictive power of a retrospective verbal report (Stephens & Russo, 1989). The present work focuses on the related problem of how best to assess emotional responses. The ultimate goal is to combine both data sources into a unified model of maximum predictive power.

NOTES

1. We shall use the terms emotional responses and feelings interchangeably. However, following Ortony, Clore, and Foss (1987), we distinguish feelings from emotions. The latter are narrower in that being [an emotion] always implies feeling [the same emotion], but not vice versa. Thus, being homesick or irritated automatically means feeling so. In contrast, being attractive or lucky may or may not correspond to feeling attractive or feeling lucky. Thus, the word feeling can endow many phrases with an emotional status. For this reason, feeling is the broader term. We recognize that our distinction between emotions and feelings is not universally accepted, but we believe that it is useful.

2. In this regard it is also worth noting that Edell and Burke's own work (1987, Experiment 2) yielded higher R^2s than those reported here, namely .67 for ad attitude and .50 for brand attitude (without ad or subject variables in the model). The lower R^2s for the Edell and Burke models in Table 8.1 may also be partly attributable to fewer subjects in the Edell and Burke group and to smaller variances in those subjects' attitudes (which would tend to make the prediction task more difficult). The variances in ad attitude for the three groups were 3.1 for Edell and Burke versus 3.6 for both Batra and Holbrook and Russo and Stephens. The corresponding variances of brand attitude were 2.3 versus 3.0 and 2.9.

REFERENCES

Aaker, D. A., Stayman, D. M., & Hagerty, M. R. (1986). Warmth in advertising: Measurement, impact, and sequence effects. *Journal of Consumer Research, 12* (4), 365–381.

Batra, R., & Holbrook, M. B. (1988). *Developing a typology of affective responses to advertising: A test of validity and reliability.* Working paper, Columbia University.

Batra, R., & Ray, M. L. (1986). Affective responses mediating acceptance of advertising. *Journal of Consumer Research, 13,* 234–250.

Burke, M. C., & Edell, J. A. (1989). The impact of feelings on ad-based affect and cognition. *Journal of Marketing Research, 26* (1), 69–83.

Edell, J. A., & Burke, M. C. (1987). The power of feelings in understanding advertising effects. *Journal of Consumer Research, 14* (3), 421–433.

Holbrook, M. B., & Batra, R. (1987). Assessing the role of emotions as mediators of consumer responses to advertising. *Journal of Consumer Research, 14* (3), 404–420.

Machleit, K. A., & Wilson, D. R. (1988). Emotional feelings and attitude toward the advertisement: The roles of brand familiarity and repetition. *Journal of Advertising, 17*, 27–35.

Ortony, A., Clore, G. L., & Foss, M. A. (1987). The referential structure of the affective lexicon. *Cognitive Science, 11*, 341–364.

Stephens, D. L., & Russo, J. E. (1989). *Predicting post-advertisement attitudes*. Working paper, University of Maryland, College of Business.

PART II

CURRENT RESEARCH ON AD STIMULI AND VIEWER CHARACTERISTICS

Ads as Emotional Stimuli

9

Communication and Arousal of Emotion: Some Implications of Facial Expression Research for Magazine Advertisements

Fairfid M. Caudle

INTRODUCTION

The convincing portrayal of emotion is essential to the success of virtually every form of persuasive communication. The arguments of the politician, the lawyer, the preacher, the debater, the actor, and the wooer may be enhanced or diminished by the degree to which they appear sincere to the recipient, who responds to the message within its emotional setting.

Advertising, as another form of persuasive communication, also relies on the portrayal and arousal of emotion. However, whereas television commercials can utilize both visual and auditory messages over a period of time, magazine advertisements are limited to images and words on a printed page and to a static rather than dynamic portrayal. In some instances facial expression is the primary way through which emotion and feelings are communicated.

Expression of emotion in the face has intrigued theorists and researchers for the better part of two centuries, and it is currently the focus of a flourishing theoretical and experimental literature. The intent of this chapter is to draw upon this literature in order to highlight issues relevant to the potential role of facial expression in the communication and arousal of emotion in magazine advertisements.

REPRODUCTION AND RECOGNITION OF EMOTIONAL EXPRESSIONS

Historical Perspectives

The study of facial expression has been characterized by recurring phases of interest in similar problems. Both the accurate reproduction of emotional facial expressions and the recognition of such reproductions have been of interest as scientific problems at least since the early nineteenth century, and as an artistic concern for considerably longer than that. In 1806, the anatomist Sir Charles Bell published his *Anatomy and Philosophy of Expression*, with drawings of the facial muscles and their role in emotional expressions, noting the value of this knowledge for the painter (Woodworth, 1938).

Charles Darwin himself was familiar with the work of Sir Charles Bell and reproduced several of his anatomical drawings in *The Expression of the Emotions in Man and Animals* (1872/1898). The continuing interest in knowledge of underlying musculature as a basis for the accurate portrayal of emotion is evidenced by such contemporary works as W. E. Rinn's review of neurological and psychological mechanisms for producing facial expressions (1984) and S. R. Peck's *Atlas of Facial Expression* (1987).

The creation of representative emotional facial stimuli for use in the experimental study of emotion also has a long history. (For reviews of this earlier literature, see Ekman, Friesen & Ellsworth, 1972; and the classic texts of Woodworth, 1938; and Woodworth & Schlosberg, 1954.) Among the early workers of interest to the present discussion was T. Piderit, a German anatomist who wrote on facial expression in 1859, with a number of later editions. Of particular interest is the fact that Piderit proposed a number of elementary emotional expressions, illustrating them with simple line drawings (Woodworth, 1938), which were adapted by later experimenters for use in a number of studies. For example, E. G. Boring and E. B. Titchener (1923, cited by Woodworth, 1938), prepared a number of "Piderit features" that could then be inserted into a profile drawing of a human face (see Figure 9.1). In this way, they could create some 360 combinations to depict various expressions of emotion. These stimuli were used in a number of studies, both by Boring and Titchener and by other experimenters, to investigate such variables as which faces were accepted as genuine, which were labeled correctly most often, and how suggestion affected the labeling of the faces. A number of additional series of facial expressions were created in the early twentieth century. These included both line drawings of the emotional expressions and posed photographs, such as those assembled by J. Frois-Wittmann (1930).

H. Schlosberg (1941, 1952) examined relationships among emotions in a way that anticipated current consumer research. Using subjects' ratings of the Frois-Wittmann pictures and a classification method developed by Woodworth (1938), Schlosberg arranged the pictures on a circular scale having axes corresponding

Figure 9.1
Individual Facial Features and Composite Facial Profiles Created from Them

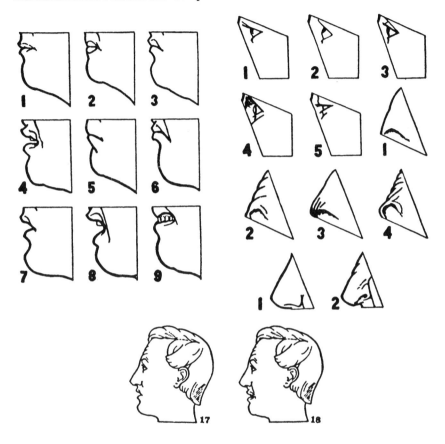

These drawings were prepared by Boring and Titchener (1923) based on illustrations by the anatomist Piderit. Each numbered facial feature was designed to express one element in an emotional facial expression as follows: *Mouth*: 1. normal, 2. sweet, 3. bitter, 4. very unpleasant, 5. stubborn, 6. stubborn and unpleasant, 7. attentive, 8. unpleasant and attentive, 9. snarl or sneer; *Eyes*: 1. normal, 2. exalted, 3. attentive, 4. very attentive, 5. inattentive, withdrawn; *Brows*: 1. normal, 2. attentive, 3. unpleasant or thoughtful state, 4. unpleasant attention; *Noses*: 1. normal, 2. unpleasant attention. The two facial profiles provide examples of the way that Boring and Titchener combined individual features into complete facial expressions. Those shown depict bewildered (17) and amazed (18) expressions. (Reproduced form Woodworth [1938].)

Figure 9.2
One Approach to the Classification of Emotional Facial Expressions

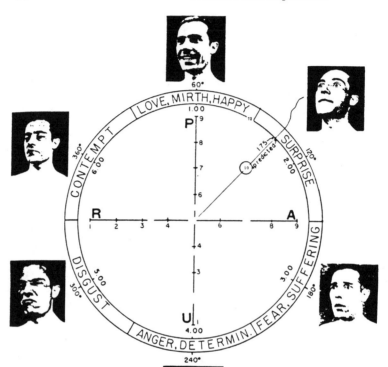

This scale was initially developed by Woodworth (1938) and modified by Schlosberg (1941, 1952) to enable quantitative classifications and comparisons of emotional facial expressions according to ratings along the dimensions of pleasantness-unpleasantness and acceptance-rejection. This figure, which illustrates various locations along the circular scale with photographs from the Frois-Wittmann series, was adapted by Izard (1977) from Woodworth and Schlosberg (1954). (Reproduced with the permission of Dr. Carroll Izard and Plenum Press.) Compare this figure with the Wheel of Emotions (Figure1.1).

to pleasantness-unpleasantness and acceptance-rejection and having the following general sections: (1) love, mirth, happy; (2) surprise; (3) fear, suffering; (4) anger, determination; (5) disgust; and (6) contempt. Within each section, pictures had similar qualitative expressions but varied in intensity. See Figure 9.2 (from Izard, 1977) for an adaptation of Schlosberg's scale indicating relationships among a few of the Frois-Wittmann pictures.

The recurring nature of research on facial expression is illustrated by the contemporary work of S. Agres (1988), who has presented a Wheel of Emotions, which depicts relationships among both the patterns of facial expressions and their intensity within a consumer psychology framework. In addition, detailed guides have been developed for the use of the Facial Action Coding System, a method of assessing emotional facial expressions in which muscular actions in each section of the face are scored separately in order to indicate patterns of muscular response corresponding to emotional facial expressions (Ekman & Friesen, 1978a; 1978b). Rinn (1984) has described several additional methods of facial assessment.

Several reviews have summarized recent research on facial expression and emotion, including P. K. Adelmann and R. B. Zajonc (1989), H. L. Leventhal and A. J. Tomarken (1986), and P. Ekman and H. Oster (1979; 1982). Ekman and Oster (1979) have succinctly stated several conclusions of interest to the present discussion: "Observers label certain facial expressions of emotion in the same way regardless of culture" (p. 529); "members of different cultures show the same facial expressions when experiencing the same emotion unless culture-specific display rules interfere" (p. 530); and "individuals differ in facial 'expressiveness' (encoding ability) and in their ability to judge facial expressions (decoding ability)" (p. 542). These points will be discussed more fully in the following discussion.

Easily Recognized Emotional Expressions in Art and Advertising

It would appear that, since the most basic patterns of emotional facial expression, such as happiness and sadness, can readily be identified, their recognition and identification are not at issue. For example, Figures 9.3, 9.4, and 9.5 each present a representation of sorrow. Pablo Picasso's *Weeping Woman* (1937, Figure 9.3) was painted in the angular Cubist style. It does not in any way appear to be a real face and yet the emotion of sorrow is easily recognized by means of the angles of the eyebrows, the vertical lines on the forehead, the open, downturned mouth, and the tears. Because of these facial cues, we recognize this emotion despite such distortions as the misalignments of eyes and eye sockets, the many geometric lines in the face, and (in the actual work) the painting's nonrealistic color.

In an advertisement for *Sunlight* liquid dishwashing detergent (Figure 9.4), a cartoon medium is utilized to show a woman sobbing because the spots on her glasses are driving away her boyfriend. Notice the many similarities, not in artistic style but in facial features, in comparing this representation with that of Picasso: frown lines, eyebrows, and downturned mouth. Although these images are qualitatively different, they depict similar emotions.

Of these three figures, the most abbreviated representation of sadness is found in Figure 9.5, one of a series of advertisements for Bertolli olive oil. Each advertisement in this series featured a face constructed from foods that the product

Figure 9.3
Weeping Woman **(1937) by Pablo Picasso**

The emotion of sorrow is easily recognized despite the angular distortions that result from the artist's cubist style (Copyright 1990 ARS N.Y./SPADEM)

could be used to prepare. The face in Figure 9.5 was created from salad components of lettuce hair and tomato eyes, with the green stems serving as pupils and drops of moisture for tears. A curved stalk of green onion forms a downturned mouth. In another example in this series, the face was formed from a veal cutlet beret, lemon slice eyes (one shedding a tear), an onion slice mouth, and a beard of chopped garlic. Other ads featured a smiling or frowning Little Orphan Annie–type face formed from different kinds of pasta, and each ad in the series featured copy explaining the face (e.g., ''Sad is the salad never seasoned with Bertolli'').

It is of interest, and possibly of importance, to note that emotional expressions

Figure 9.4
Cartoon Representation of a Sorrowful Facial Expression

Compare the expression of the woman in this ad for *Sunlight*-liquid dishwashing detergent with emotional expression with that shown in figure 9.3 and note the similarities in the configurations of facial features. In addition to the obvious feature of tears, both expressions have been depicted with upturned eyebrows, forehead wrinkles, and open, down-turned mouths. (Reproduction courtesy of Lever Brothers Company, owner of the trademark *SUNLIGHT*.)

Figure 9.5
Representation of Sadness Created Through Combining Vegetable Elements into a Facial Configuration

Notice how readily the illustration is accepted as a sad face despite the minimal and non-realistic information it provides. (Reproduced with the permission of Bertolli USA, Inc.)

in the preceding examples have been employed in a *symbolic* way and were deliberately created for the purpose of representing an emotion. In addition, such emotional expressions are readily recognized, however minimal the information used to create them and whatever the medium in which they appear: painting, cartoon, or vegetable construction.

While the preceding figures may readily be categorized as symbolic portrayals of emotion, the occurrence of such symbols in social interaction is less apparent. However, one could argue that such basic expressions as smiling and frowning appear in so many contexts and so often that they have become symbols of emotion. Indeed, R. Buck (1984) has noted that a ritualized smile of greeting acts as a symbol when it is done intentionally rather than spontaneously. However, as we will see, since basic emotions can readily be recognized and interpreted, the ability to identify an emotion correctly may, in some instances, be less important in advertisements than whether the portrayed emotion was genuinely experienced rather than artificially posed or constructed for the occasion.

GENUINE VERSUS NON-GENUINE EMOTIONAL FACIAL EXPRESSIONS

Historical Perspectives

Just as the reproduction and recognition of facial expressions have a long history as scientific problems, so also does the differentiation of genuine and posed expressions. In *The Expression of the Emotions in Man and Animals* (1872/1898), Darwin reported his explorations of this problem, in the course of which he presented photographs of emotional expressions to observers for their reactions. Since the photographs were provided by others, Darwin had to rely on their judgments that the expressions were or were not genuine. A series of photographs from this book is reproduced in Figure 9.6. On the left are three figures which show different degrees of moderate laughter and smiling. The top and bottom pictures were taken by one person; "the figure of the little girl, with the hat" was taken by someone else. Nevertheless, Darwin assures us, "the expression was a genuine one" (1872/1898, p. 200).

Of greater interest are the three photographs on the right, which show "an old man . . . in his usual passive condition" (top right), "and another of the same man" (middle right), and "naturally smiling" (1872/1898, p. 201), about which Darwin noted, "The latter was instantly recognized by everyone to whom it was shown as true to nature" (p. 201). The bottom right photograph is also "of the same old man, with the corners of his mouth strongly retracted by the galvanization of the great zygomatic muscles" (p. 201). Although many observers recognized it as being "of the nature of a smile" (p. 202), the falseness of the expression was clearly noted. Thus, with these crude stimuli, Darwin investigated a problem that continues to interest contemporary researchers and that may be

Figure 9.6
Genuine and Non-Genuine Expressions of Emotion

Examples of photographs that Darwin employed to investigate the extent to which genuine and non-genuine expressions of emotion could be distinguished. The three photographs on the left show different degrees of moderate laughter and smiling in a little girl, while those of the man on the right show passive (top) and naturally smiling (middle) expressions. The remaining photograph presents a smiling expression artificially induced through electrically stimulating the facial muscles. (Reproduced from *The Expression of the Emotions in Man and Animals* [Darwin, 1872/1898].)

of potential importance to the effectiveness of advertisements: the extent to which genuine versus nongenuine expressions of emotion can be distinguished.

Distinguishing Between Genuine and Non-Genuine Emotional Expressions

Among contemporary researchers, the genuineness of emotional facial expressions is an issue that has been addressed at length by Ekman and W. V. Friesen (1975) and by Ekman (1985). These investigators have amassed considerable evidence to the effect that individuals acquire a variety of management techniques that enable the intensification or masking of their spontaneous displays of emotion and that, within a given culture, display rules influence the way in which basic emotions are expressed.

With regard to distinguishing between genuine versus non-genuine facial expressions, one category of emotional expression that has received considerable attention is the smile. Several studies have, in fact, differentiated among types of smiles. Ekman and Friesen (1982) distinguished between genuine smiles reflecting positive feelings (termed a "felt" smile) and two categories of false smiles:

> In a phony smile nothing much is felt but an attempt is made to appear as if positive feelings are felt. In a masking smile strong negative emotion is felt and an attempt is made to conceal those feelings by appearing to feel positive. (p. 244)

In a follow-up study, Ekman, Friesen and M. O'Sullivan (1988) measured facial characteristics when experimental subjects followed instructions to lie deliberately by concealing negative emotions resulting from watching a stressful film. They found that masking smiles occurred more often than felt happy smiles when subjects attempted to conceal their feelings. These authors noted that their findings confirmed that "the face may display subtle clues that can provide accurate information about felt emotions despite concealment efforts" (p. 418).

With regard to the portrayal of such masking smiles in advertising, an advertisement for Head & Shoulders (Figure 9.7) illustrates a social situation in which such a masking smile might occur: the woman on the left is worried about whether her dandruff is apparent to the woman on the right but tries to smile to conceal her concern.

Although the preceding example illustrates the deliberate use of a less-than-genuine smile, an issue that remains is whether, when genuine smiles are wanted for an advertisement, they are in fact produced. Earlier it was noted that such facial expressions as smiling and frowning can serve a ritualized symbolic function in communication and that such emotional expressions are easily identified in whatever medium or context in which they occur. However, even if such expressions can be readily identified, the question remains whether symbolic smiles (or other expressions) elicit the same response as spontaneous facial

Figure 9.7
Example of an Advertisement Depicting a Social Situation in Which a Masking Smile Might Occur

The woman on the left is worried about whether her dandruff is apparent to the woman on the right but tries to smile to conceal her concern. Notice the unconvincing nature of the smile. (Reproduced with the permission of the Procter & Gamble Company, Inc.)

expressions of emotion. Before addressing this question, however, it may be useful to reexamine the very basic role of emotional expressions in day-to-day communication.

THE ADAPTIVE VALUE OF EMOTIONAL COMMUNICATION FOR SOCIAL BEHAVIOR

In essence, the natural expression of emotion through facial expression and gesture enables others to know our internal state at that moment and to respond appropriately. This view was central to the theory of Darwin, one of the most influential antecedents of contemporary research on facial expression. Although his views are widely known, it is useful for this discussion to reiterate them for the sake of emphasis.

In *The Expression of the Emotions in Man and Animals* (1872/1898), Darwin argued that the communication of emotion has adaptive value since it aids in the coordination of social behavior. In the concluding chapter he noted:

> The movements of expression in the face and body, whatever their origin may have been, are in themselves of much importance for our welfare. They serve as the first means of communication between the mother and her infant; she smiles approval, and thus encourages her child on the right path, or frowns disapproval. We readily perceive sympathy in others by their expression; our sufferings are thus mitigated and our pleasures increased; and mutual good feeling is thus strengthened. (p. 364)

> Expression in itself, or the language of the emotions, as it has sometimes been called, is certainly of importance for the welfare of mankind. (p. 366)

Evolutionary Perspectives in Contemporary Research on Emotion

Among contemporary researchers investigating emotion, there has been a resurgence of interest in the study of emotion from an adaptive, functional, or evolutionary perspective. For example, A. Ohman (1986) has analyzed the emotion of fear, placing both the stimuli that evoke it and the role of angry facial expressions as social stimuli within an evolutionary perspective. In a study of relationships between the appraisal of situations and physiological response, C. A. Smith (1989) noted that:

> In developing additional hypotheses, exploitation of the functional perspective is likely to prove valuable. In addition to drawing on Darwin's ... original observations ..., a careful analysis of the functions served by specific facial actions, or their progenitors, in our evolutionary past may suggest appraisal-related meanings currently communicated by those components. (p. 351)

Finally, J. T. Cacioppo, J. S. Martzke, R. E. Petty, and L. G. Tassinary (1988) have noted "the value of adopting psychophysiological and ethological analyses to enrich rather than to compete with traditional theoretical and situational analyses of social behavior" (p. 602). Additional reviews indicating the importance of Darwin's contributions and the value of an adaptive perspective for the study of emotion can be found in Ekman (1973) and R. Plutchik (1984), among others.

Implications for consumer psychology. As Darwin noted, emotional expressions evolved because they had adaptive value. Editorializing for a moment, one could argue that the effectiveness of some advertisements depends in part on the adaptive value to the consumer of the conveyed message. Although advertising has often been criticized for providing less-than-useful information, it is also the case that a great deal of valuable information is communicated. Advertisements for products with a potentially high adaptive value for society might gain added impact from the portrayal of appropriate, genuine emotions. Such products might include, for example, those that facilitate a parent's caring for a child, maintaining family or social relationships, avoiding threatening situations, and improved health and quality of life.

However, just as advertising can utilize emotion in adaptive and relevant ways, it is not uncommon to find portrayals of emotion in advertising that are false, inappropriate, or exaggerated to such an extent that they do not convey useful information. Attention to adaptive value in product design and to genuine and appropriate expressions of emotion in advertising research may generate tangible benefits through increased consumer response.

SPONTANEOUS (UNPOSED) VERSUS SYMBOLIC (INTENTIONAL) FACIAL EXPRESSIONS

The Spontaneous Communication of Emotion

Returning to the issue of spontaneous versus symbolic communication of emotion, Buck (1984) has proposed that a fundamental distinction exists between them. Defining communication as "occurring whenever the behavior of one individual (the sender) influences the behavior of another (the receiver)" (p. 4), and drawing upon Darwin's analysis of the adaptive value of emotion, Buck has argued that the spontaneous communication of emotion evolved as a biologically shared signal system in which nonintentional external gestures or facial expressions correspond to internal states, which are in this way communicated to others. Buck has proposed that the facial expressions, gestures, and vocalizations that occur in the genuine and nonintentional spontaneous communication of emotion are read and understood directly by a receiver without intervening cognitive judgments (see also Zajonc, 1980).

The Concept of Social Affordance

In developing this line of reasoning, Buck (1984) utilized J. J. Gibson's ecological theory of perception (1977, 1979) in which a major thesis proposed that perceptual systems evolved to extract survival-relevant information directly from the environment, without the need for additional transformations or interpretations. Gibson advanced the concept of "affordance," which might be thought of as a characteristic of the environment having potential value or utility for the perceiver. An affordance is thus something that the environment "affords" or enables, a potential for action that does not require further cognitive restructuring to be perceived. For example, in perceiving a surface such as a wooden floor, the affordance (or attribute) of firmness can be perceived immediately; one can step on the floor confidently without the need for prior experience or cognitive judgment at that moment.

Of interest to the current discussion, Gibson noted that, in addition to the physical environment, such affordances might consist of characteristics of persons and their behavior. Buck cited Gibson's theory as follows:

> Gibson proposed that sexual behavior, nurturant behavior, cooperative behavior, and so forth, can be treated as affordances in which the sender provides possibilities for interaction that can be directly perceived by the receiver. It could be argued that the process of spontaneous communication may be viewed in terms of such "social affordances." (Buck, 1984, p. 42)

Implications for consumer psychology. The concept of affordance is still somewhat controversial; however, the existence of social affordances would have a number of implications for consumer psychology. If such affordances could be identified and represented in a sufficiently spontaneous manner, their incorporation into advertisements might provide a more direct route for communicating emotional content to the consumer and a powerful means of eliciting an emotional response. For example, examine the advertisement for *Curad Bandages* in Figure 9.8. In this example, *Curad Bandages* has contrasted the faces of three tearful, pouting children (who, it is implied, experienced pain when a bandage was removed) with the smiling face of a little boy who instead had been given a *Curad* "Ouchless" bandage. Earlier, the possible relationship between advertising effectiveness and its socially adaptive value was noted. One might extend this idea and speculate that the sight of a genuinely tearful child suggests the possibility of a "social affordance" that might elicit nurturing behavior (in this instance, avoiding a child's pain through the use of this product).

Figure 9.8
Advertisement Contrasting Tearful and Smiling Facial Expressions to Illustrate Potential Product Benefits

Such an advertisement might communicate a social affordance in that the tearful children's need for nurturing may readily be perceived. Thus, this advertisement for *Curad Ouchless Bandages* might elicit nurturing behavior in parents who wish to use this product in order to avoid the pain that could result when removing other brands of bandages. (Reproduced with the permission of Kendall-Futuro, Inc., © 1988 The Kendall Co.)

The Symbolic Communication of Emotion

In contrast with spontaneous communication, Buck (1984) argued that *symbolic* communication involves a voluntary, socially shared system of symbols having arbitrary relationships with their referents. Although language is the most obvious example of symbolic communication, there are nonverbal components as well. As noted earlier, a ritualized smile of greeting is considered to be a symbol when it is done intentionally rather than spontaneously. Symbolic communication does not necessarily provide an external display corresponding to an internal state and, since it is intentional, may be true or false.

Cultural Display Rules in Symbolic Communication

In developing a distinction between spontaneous and symbolic communication, Buck (1984) has drawn upon Ekman and Friesen's (1975) concept of display rules, noted earlier, which essentially consist of cultural rules that govern proper and improper ways to express emotion. In effect, these may alter or inhibit the direct expression of emotion in order to conform to the expectations of a social situation. Even though such emotional communications (altered by display rules) may involve facial expressions or gestures, Buck has included them within the category of symbolic communications, since such alterations are intentional.

Potential Impact of Spontaneous versus Symbolic Communication

Buck argues that differences between spontaneous and symbolic communication result in part from differences in their neural basis. These two forms of communication did not evolve simultaneously. Although the neural relationships between them are very complex, the neural basis of spontaneous communication evolved earlier and thus is associated with older subcortical and paleocortical brain structures and with the right hemisphere. In contrast, as the neural basis of symbolic communication evolved, while it was more or less superimposed upon existing mechanisms of spontaneous communication, it developed associations with the neocortex and with the left hemisphere.

Of particular interest to this discussion is one of Buck's proposals: Since spontaneous and symbolic communication are each more closely associated with different brain centers, the information they convey is thus processed differently. Drawing upon a number of studies concerning hemispheric lateralization and emotional response, Buck has proposed that the meanings conveyed by the spontaneous communication of emotion are immediately accepted and understood, whereas the symbolic, intentional communication of emotion is evaluated through further cognitive interpretation and judgment. As a possible illustration of Buck's argument, recall that President Jimmy Carter was often commented upon because, in public appearances, his smile sometimes appeared to include his mouth but not his eyes. Thus, it would seem that reactions by the public to his facial expression when smiling were frequently dominated by judgments rather than emotional responses. Together with studies of smiling cited earlier, this anecdotal example suggests that the face does provide clues to genuine and non-genuine smiles which may achieve differing impacts upon observers.

It is of interest that this discrepancy between displayed and felt emotions has been recognized and creatively utilized within advertisements. For example, Fleischmann's margarine transformed this discrepancy into a visual metaphor in order to underscore the importance of taking control of cholesterol. One advertisement portrayed the somber face of a male heart attack victim to illustrate the point that "High cholesterol is no laughing matter." This point was dramatized by contrasting one half of the face containing a clown's painted-on smile (symbolizing the displayed emotional expression) with the other half of the face portraying a sober, unsmiling expression (representing the emotion that is actually experienced). In a second advertisement in this series, the traditional symbol of comedy, a smiling mask, was held away from the sober face of a heart attack victim to illustrate that "There's no hiding from cholesterol." Both advertisements illustrate the point that, although one can intentionally display one emotion, a contrasting emotion can still be experienced.

Implications for consumer psychology. The distinction proposed by Buck between the spontaneous and symbolic communication of emotion has several implications for the use of emotional facial expressions in magazine advertisements. Genuine facial expressions corresponding to internal states may be directly understood and thus may elicit qualitatively different responses than the intentional, symbolic expression of emotion.

It need hardly be said that advertisements, whether for magazines or television, feature professional actors, models, and others who have been employed to generate emotional behavior in artificial situations, on demand, and with products with which they may be less than familiar. The objective, of course, is to create an image or segment of behavior that appears genuine and spontaneous. Despite the fact that professionals may be trained to produce designated emotional expressions on demand and to mask their own feelings, it is nevertheless the case that spontaneous feelings may "leak out." As Buck (1984) has noted, "Symbolic communication is always accompanied by tendencies toward spontaneous expression, however hidden and apparently inconsequential" (p. 10).

It would appear that little is known concerning whether Buck's distinction between spontaneous and symbolic emotional communication is paralleled by corresponding differences in advertising effectiveness when one or the other is incorporated into an advertisement. Little is known, as well, about the consumer's ability to recognize emotional "leakage" when models impersonating emotional expressions are photographed for advertisements.

Improving the Spontaneity of Facial Expressions in Magazine Advertisements

It must be acknowledged that achieving the goal of spontaneous emotional expressions in magazine advertisements poses numerous difficulties. In discussing posed versus spontaneous expressions from the perspective of neuropsychology, Rinn (1984) has pointed out, "To ensure that an expression is purely spontaneous-emotional it is necessary that the subject be unaware that he or she is being observed" (p .74). Clearly, this criterion cannot be met by most situations in which photographic materials for advertisements are created. However, given the limitations imposed by the realities of the photographic studio, several suggestions come to mind for improving the genuineness of emotional facial expressions.

Increased familiarity with product. One wonders whether a period of time to develop "product bonding" and familiarity would be useful to those asked to produce expressions indicating reactions to a product. This might facilitate the development of genuine positive feelings concerning the product and reduce the need to impersonate emotional expressions.

External affective stimuli. A number of studies have elicited spontaneous expressions in the laboratory by presenting subjects with various types of emotionally loaded visual stimuli. These have included slides (e.g., Buck, Savin, Miller, & Caul, 1972), videotaped scenes (e.g., Zuckerman, Hall, DeFrank, & Rosenthal, 1976), and audio tapes (e.g., Sullivan & Brender, 1986), among others. Rather than simply instructing a photographic subject to pose in a certain way; the subject could be photographed while watching or listening to an appropriate affective stimulus, thus achieving more natural expressions.

Internal mental stimuli. Other studies have generated quasi-spontaneous facial expressions by providing a self-induced context for the evocation of emotions. In this respect, Ekman, J. C. Hager, and Friesen (1981) have noted that:

> When asked to pose an emotion, a person can either deliberately move particular facial muscles, or, like a Stanislavski actor, attempt to relive or imagine a situation to create the emotional experience from which the expression will flow. (p. 102)

For example, D. W. Harmon and W. J. Ray (1977) asked subjects to recall "actual events in their life, in which they had sincerely felt sad, happy, fearful or angry" (p. 458); Cacioppo, Martzke, Petty, and Tassinary (1988) used a self-disclosure interview in which subjects were asked a range of questions designed to elicit reflections about themselves and past experiences. Other devices designed to elicit spontaneous facial expressions of emotion have included administration of an imagery inventory instructing subjects to imagine being in a situation and to experience feelings associated with that situation (Fridlund, Schwartz, & Fowler, 1984).

It would seem possible to adapt such approaches for use during photographic sessions. In the examples described earlier for Fleischmann's margarine, it is of interest to note that the person pictured in the advertisements was an actual heart attack victim. It is possible that these advertisements may have had greater impact because the model's facial expression reflected his own feelings and memories.

Independent measurement of facial expression. In view of the sophisticated measurement tools available, such as the Facial Action Coding System (Ekman & Friesen, 1978a, 1978b), some consideration might be given to its use as a check on the genuineness of facial expressions of models prior to their final selection for use in an advertisement.

Sensitivity to emotion in facial expressions. Earlier it was noted that individuals differ in their ability to express (encode) or judge (decode) facial expressions. In addition, a number of studies have found gender differences in these characteristics (e.g., Buck et al., 1972; Zuckerman et al., 1976). Although the preceding suggestions focused on improving the spontaneity of emotional expressions in those photographed for advertisements, it is important to keep in mind that the creation of such materials constitutes only one step in the completion of a finished advertisement. At each stage of the production process, judgments are made concerning the appropriateness of photographed expressions. Prudence suggests that some attention be given to the varying sensitivities of those who make such judgments so that the final choice will be the most effective example for a particular situation.

One could argue that, to the extent that an advertising model or spokesperson is genuinely emotionally involved or moved, the consumer's emotional response to the advertisement may be enhanced. After all, it is through just such communication of genuine emotions that advertisements may succeed in making significant statements having high social value. As an example, consider an advertisement for Kinder-Care Learning Centers (Figure 9.9). It would seem that the portrayal of genuine and appealing emotional expressions of children participating in activities such as those provided by such a center might be especially valuable in assisting parents to choose an appropriate caretaker to whom they can safely entrust their children.

RESPONSES TO FACIAL STIMULI

The preceding discussion of emotional responses to advertisements suggests a second issue that consumer psychology might well find of value to address: the extent to which facial stimuli arouse emotional responses. As Ohman and U. Dimberg (1978) have noted concerning research on facial expressions:

> Most of the work with humans in this area has been directed towards the dimensions and the identification of facial expressions, and the problem of emotional reactions to these stimuli has been given but little attention. (p. 1251)

Figure 9.9
Examples of Emotional Facial Expressions that May Enhance the Socially Adaptive Value of an Advertising Message

The appealing facial expressions of these children support the claim that *Kinder-Care Learning Centers* will provide child care that can be trusted. This advertisement illustrates one way in which emotional facial expressions can enhance an advertising message that contains information having potentially adaptive value to society. (Used by permission of Kinder-Care Learning Centers, Inc. Agency: Hutcheson Shutze, Atlanta.)

Although this state of affairs is not quite as stark today, nevertheless it is still true that far less attention has been given to responses to facial stimuli. However, several emerging areas of study suggest issues that might be followed up within an advertising context.

Historical Perspectives

Earlier in this chapter it was noted that social affordances occur when facial expressions provide readily perceived information concerning possibilities for social interaction. A predecessor of this concept of social affordance, and an appropriate starting point in discussing emotional responses to facial stimuli, is the ethological concept of innate releaser stimuli, especially those associated with the face and head. The ethologist Konrad Lorenz proposed that juvenile features, including large heads and eyes and protruding foreheads, trigger innate releasing mechanisms for nurturing behavior and affection (Lorenz, 1971; see Figure 9.10).

Contemporary Examples of Ethological Releaser Stimuli

With regard to the incorporation of such facial characteristics into printed communications and mass media, S. J. Gould (1979) has noted that, whether intentionally or not, Mickey Mouse has "evolved" since his 1928 debut and has become progressively more juvenile, with steadily increasing head and eye size. The use of such juvenile characteristics by greeting card companies and magazines has also been noted (Gould, 1979; Eibl-Eibesfeldt, 1975). Such features have very likely contributed to the great popularity and emotional appeal of such characters as ET (the extraterrestrial) and the Snuggle Bear (Figure 9.11), with its large head, forehead, and smile.

Such juvenile characteristics may occasionally be seen in adults. One wonders whether the perceived sincerity and capacity to attract a large, loyal following evidenced by Tammy and Reverend Jim Bakker were in part due to their physical features; both are characterized by large eyes, large foreheads, and other childlike facial features.

The influence of juvenile facial characteristics on the social perception of adults has been investigated by D. S. Berry and L. Z. McArthur (1985). These authors examined the relationship between the perceived babyishness of a face and the psychological traits associated with it. Babyfacedness in photographs of male subjects was measured, both with subjective ratings and through objective physiognomic measurements; it was found to be positively correlated with perceptions of honesty, warmth, kindness, and naiveté. In contrast, these authors found that faces rated as highly angular were also rated as being more mature, less warm, and less honest. Berry and McArthur (1986) have cited several additional studies in which angularity in facial features influenced ratings of age and personality traits, and in which faces with angular jaws were perceived as

Figure 9.10
Contrasting Head Proportions in Juveniles and Adults

The juvenile forms on the left are characterized by heads that are large in proportion to the rest of the body, and by large, protruding foreheads, large eyes, and rounded shapes among other characteristics. Lorenz (1971) proposed that juvenile head proportions release, or activate, emotional responses and behavior patterns of caring for the young, whereas adult proportions do not do so. See also Eibl-Eibesfeldt (1975) and Gould (1979) for additional discussions of this figure. (Reprinted by permission of the publishers from *Studies in Animal & Human Behaviour,* Vol. II, by Konrad Lorenz, translated by Robert Marti, Cambridge, Mass.: Harvard University Press, Copyright © 1971 by Konrad Lorenz.)

Figure 9.11
Example of an Advertisement Containing Ethological Releaser Stimuli

The *Snuggle* Bear has a large head, relative to its body, as well as a large forehead and rounded body shape. These might be viewed as releaser stimuli that contribute to the *Snuggle* Bear's emotional appeal. (Reproduction courtesy of Lever Brothers Company, owner of the registered trademarks *Snuggle* and *Snuggle* Bear Design.)

older and more dominant than faces with curved jaws. These authors have also cited intriguing unpublished findings in which angular geometric shapes were perceived as older and more dominant than curved ones.

Angularity was also found to affect responses to facial patterns in a study by J. Aronoff, A. M. Barclay, and L. A. Stevenson (1988), who examined the configurations that constitute a threatening facial display. These authors developed a ''Threat Characteristics Scale'' to distinguish threatening and nonthreatening masks from a number of widely differing cultures. Further investigation indicated that geometric patterns of diagonality and angularity embedded within a threatening display were instrumental in creating a sense of threat in the observer, in contrast with curvilinear patterns. The authors speculated that such configurations might affect responses to items as diverse as the design of eyeglasses and architecture.

Implications for consumer psychology. These research findings related to babyfacedness and to the distinction between angularity and curvilinearity in facial features suggest several implications for consumer psychology. The demonstrated relationships between facial features and perceived personality traits suggest that such characteristics might well influence viewers' emotional responses to photographic representations of models or spokespersons in advertisements.

With regard to nonfacial linear or geometric configurations that arouse emotional responses or that are perceived as having particular traits, one might speculate still further that the use of such configurations might influence responses to a number of types of designs of interest to consumer psychology, including packaging, toy design, automobile shapes, and patterns of clothing fabric, to suggest a few. Although developing these ideas further is beyond the scope of this chapter, such speculations do illustrate the potential value, alluded to earlier, of applying an ethological/evolutionary perspective to the study of emotion and the stimuli that arouse it.

Responses to Emotional and Nonemotional Faces

Several studies utilizing emotional and nonemotional faces as stimuli have obtained results that may be relevant to the choice of faces for magazine advertisements. Among these, a number of studies have found that responses to negative facial expressions are more pronounced than responses to other expressions.

In a classical conditioning study, Ohman and Dimberg (1978) employed happy, angry, and neutral faces as conditioned stimuli and shock as the unconditioned stimulus. They found that angry facial expressions were more effective as conditioned stimuli than neutral or happy expressions and, furthermore, that the effect was more pronounced when the face was male than when the face was female. A later study, using only angry faces, found that ''the orientation of angry facial expressions was a critical dimension when faces served as CSs [conditioned stimuli] in aversive classical conditioning'' (Dimberg & Ohman,

1983, p. 165). However, these effects were obtained only when the faces were directed toward the subject. When the faces were directed away from the subject, differential effects of the types of faces were greatly reduced or eliminated.

C. H. Hansen and R. D. Hansen (1988) explored hypotheses derived from the perspective of the adaptive significance of facial stimuli in a study of the ability to pick out discrepant happy and threatening faces from a crowd of nine faces. They found that, when subjects surveyed photographs of crowds, threatening faces embedded in them seemed to pop out, although this was not the case for other discrepant expressions. These results were interpreted as supporting the view that face processing is highly efficient for features of facial threat.

Implications for consumer psychology. Earlier in this chapter, two additional studies were cited in which threatening facial features were explored, and it is of interest to refer to them within the present context. Aronoff, Barclay, and Stevenson (1988) derived configurations widely found in threatening displays; Ohman (1986) provided an evolutionary analysis of fear stimuli that discussed responses to facial expressions within the broader context of the social submissiveness system which, through gesture, facial expression, and other expressive displays, functions to establish social order.

These studies, together with those just noted, suggest that a potentially fruitful direction for consumer research would be the exploration of the effects of threatening and nonthreatening facial stimuli on consumer response to advertising. To give but one example: a tough, threatening facial expression was the dominant feature in an advertisement for Hanes underwear which contrasted this tough expression with a gentle, smiling one to illustrate how one can be a tough man on the outside but prefer softer things underneath. In view of studies indicating that threatening displays are picked out more efficiently, one wonders whether such effects might influence consumer response to advertisements, or whether they might be utilized in other ways.

Hemispheric Lateralization and Asymmetries in Responses to Facial Stimuli

Additional evidence for distinctions in responses to positive and negative facial expressions has been obtained through studies exploring this problem from the perspective of hemispheric lateralization. R. J. Davidson (1984) has noted a number of studies of responses to a variety of affective stimuli, including facial expression stimuli, indicating that the left and right hemispheres may be differentially specialized for the regulation of positive and negative affect, respectively. For example, M. Suberi and W. F. McKeever (1977) presented emotional and nonemotional faces to subjects who memorized them and subsequently discriminated them from nontarget faces. The faces were presented to each visual field, and reaction time was then measured in a recognition memory test. When faces were presented to the left visual field, emotional faces were recognized with faster reaction times than nonemotional faces; sad faces got faster reaction times than happy or angry faces.

R. Reuter-Lorenz and R. J. Davidson (1981) simultaneously presented emotional and neutral facial expressions of the same individual, one to each visual field. Happy faces presented to the left hemisphere were perceived more quickly than sad faces; the opposite was found true for faces presented to the right hemisphere.

Finally, it is also of interest to note that asymmetries occur not only in responses to facial stimuli but also in the production of facial expressions. R. Campbell (1986) has cited a number of studies which indicate that both posed and spontaneous facial expressions tend to show ''left-facedness'' or greater motility in the left half of the face.

Implications for consumer psychology. Although the study of hemispheric differences is by now a well-established technique in consumer research (see F. Hansen, 1981), it may provide a useful tool for the further exploration and assessment of reactions to emotional facial stimuli. It should be noted, however, that the existence of such differential lateralization remains controversial. R. G. Ley and E. Strauss (1986) have cited a number of studies of this problem which have obtained contradictory results.

In view of a general tendency toward left-facedness in facial expressions, and in view of the findings cited earlier in which classical conditioning effects were not found when faces were directed away from subjects (Dimberg & Ohman, 1983), it would be of interest to determine whether responses differ to full or partial left or right views of the face when incorporated into advertisements.

Finally, it would also be of interest to determine whether the location of a face within an advertisement (and thus within the visual field in which the viewer is more likely to view it initially) affects the viewer's response. It has already been found that location of a pictorial advertisement on a simulated newspaper page is related to its evaluation (Janiszewski, 1988). When the advertisement was located within the left visual field (a location designed to maximize right hemisphere processing), it was evaluated more favorably than when it was located within the right visual field (a location maximizing left hemisphere processing). If similar effects were found for facial stimuli in general, an additional question would concern whether such responses differed according to whether positive or negative facial expressions were depicted.

The Facial EMG in the Study of Emotional Facial Expressions

The facial electromyogram (EMG), which indicates those facial muscles that respond when stimuli are perceived or experienced, has become widely used for the study of facial expressions (see Tassinary, Cacioppo, & Geen, 1989, for guidelines in the use of this technique; and see also Cacioppo, Tassinary, & Fridlund, 1990, for a general overview).

Within a large body of studies utilizing the facial EMG, one focus may have special relevance to consumer psychology: studies of relationships between patterns of response in facial muscles and experienced emotions; a number of these studies have been cited earlier (e.g., Cacioppo, Martzke, Petty, & Tassinary, 1988; Fridlund, Schwartz, & Fowler, 1984). Of particular interest to this discussion of facial responses to facial stimuli is a study by Dimberg (1982) who assessed facial muscle reactions in observers of emotional facial expressions. One notable finding was that subjects made covert facial expressions that tended to mimic the happy or angry faces shown in photographs. It was suggested that facial EMG recordings provide a means to distinguish between patterns of response to positive and negative emotional visual stimuli. Since mimicry (assessed through coding by observers) has been found in neonates (Field, Woodson, Greenberg & Cohen, 1982), it would appear to be an elemental response to emotional facial expressions; it might be considered for use as an assessment tool.

Implications for consumer psychology. One might speculate that the assessment of facial mimicry in those observing emotional facial expressions, using either the facial EMG or ratings of observers' facial expressions, might provide a means of exploring several questions suggested earlier. For example, might the extent of such mimicry enable distinctions to be made between responses to spontaneous and posed emotional facial expressions? At some risk, one might go even further afield and ask whether such mimicry, since it does produce muscular responses, might contribute in some way to the subjective experience of emotion as a result of efference from facial muscles, and thus enhance an observer's response to an emotional facial expression (see Adelmann & Zajonc, 1989). At present, these remain only tantalizing questions; however, they do suggest avenues for further investigation.

DISCUSSION

This chapter has been concerned primarily with indicating the relevance to consumer psychology of research on those aspects of facial stimuli that serve to communicate emotional states or to elicit emotional responses, and, throughout this discussion, a number of questions and consumer research issues have been noted. Now let us consider a theoretical framework through which these diverse aspects of emotion and facial expression can be related.

The Ecological Theory of Social Perception

In a paper having potentially great relevance to consumer psychology, L. Z. McArthur and R. M. Baron (1983) have drawn upon the ecological theory of perception proposed by Gibson (1977, 1979), cited earlier in this chapter, and they have applied this ecological approach to the perception of the *social* environment.

In their advocacy of an ecological theory of social perception, these authors have not only stressed the adaptive function of perception, but also have emphasized that perception involves "discovering and adjusting to . . . the useful, structured information in the environment" (p. 216) rather than how such information is processed or structured "in the head" (p. 216). Noting that "we have learned much about the processing of information and little about what that information is" (p. 215), McArthur and Baron (1983) have thus distinguished between an ecological approach and one that stresses information processing:

> Whereas current research in social perception has concentrated on the cognitive processing of social information—how schemata, memory, and various cognitive heuristics influence the meaning we extract from the social environment—research within the ecological approach will reveal what it is in a person's movements, gestures, voice, and facial appearance that communicates to us that person's momentary intentions, emotional state, or more stable qualities. (pp. 216–217)

It is not possible within this brief chapter to do justice to the depth and richness of McArthur and Baron's (1983) theory of social perception. Nevertheless, some indications of the value of this framework can be noted, both with regard to consumer psychology in general and to the particular focus of this chapter, the communication and arousal of emotion.

Three proposals made by McArthur and Baron's theory are of immediate interest. One is that, as we perceive events, we are able to perceive those aspects that remain the same; these might be things (*structural invariants*) or styles or patterns of change (*transformational invariants*).

The second concept of importance to McArthur and Baron is one discussed earlier in this chapter, that of environmental *affordance*, which might be thought of as "the action possibilities provided by an object in the environment as well as the consequences of interacting with that object" (p. 217). In the social environment, such affordances might include a person's movements, facial expressions, gestures, or other characteristics that communicate to us those possibilities or consequences of action that we might take toward that person, or that might be taken toward us.

The third concept of immediate interest is that of *attunement*. As McArthur and Baron have proposed, perception of environmental and social affordances is in turn viewed as being dependent upon the perceiver's attunements, or "the particular stimulus invariants to which the perceiver attends" (p. 216).

Let us return to some of the characteristics of emotional facial expressions discussed earlier. We have noted the ease with which basic emotional facial expressions are identified. We have also noted that non-genuine emotional expressions can be detected, and thus the impact of genuine emotional expressions may differ from non-genuine ones. In addition, evidence has been cited indicating that certain facial configurations such as babyfacedness or angularity elicit differing responses and that some facial expressions (e.g., threatening ones) may be processed more readily than others.

If we now reconsider these observations in the light of McArthur and Baron's theory (1983), a number of relationships among them become apparent. Both the particular configurations of emotional facial expressions and the juvenile facial features noted earlier would then constitute examples of perceptual invariants for which it is highly adaptive for perceivers to be attuned to detect. As McArthur and Baron (1983) have noted, "According to the ecological position, we are sensitive to adaptively relevant information, as opposed to all possible information . . . what we perceive in the social environment is likely to be first and foremost that which is most essential to adaptive action" (p. 219).

One limitation of McArthur and Baron's theory should be noted. This chapter has been concerned with magazine advertisements, and it was noted that these constitute static rather than dynamic stimuli. McArthur and Baron have noted specifically that their theory is most applicable to ongoing events rather than to static stimuli. They have noted that such events provide much richer information than is contained in such stimuli as words or pictures.

Implications for consumer psychology. Earlier in this chapter was noted the potential value of social affordances for communicating emotional content and eliciting emotional responses. Consumer research is needed to determine the invariant stimulus properties, not only of facial expression but also of the person within a social environment, that are readily detected by consumers as affording potential actions or consequences. In other words, advertisements should utilize information that is most likely to be detected and acted upon by consumers.

The ecological concept of attunement is of particular interest to consumer psychology. In a sense, one could argue that consumer psychologists have been utilizing this concept for some time under the guise of demographics which are used to tailor advertisements to the sensitivities and interests of particular target populations. What is needed is research that enables greater correspondences to be established between such attunements and adaptive value, both of the advertising messages themselves and of the products they present to the public.

Furthermore, in view of the limitations imposed by the types of static stimuli that can be incorporated into magazine advertisements, research is needed to determine those types of emotional stimuli and facial expressions that are most readily detected by consumers. In addition, the application of McArthur and Baron's theory of social perception to research concerning the impact of stimulus information provided in television commercials should prove to be a fruitful direction for the future.

FINAL THOUGHTS

The goal of this chapter has been to utilize studies of facial expression from a number of perspectives to suggest issues for consumer psychology. From the studies cited (and the many others that could not be included), one theme might be identified as having potentially great significance for consumer psychology: the importance of approaching the study of emotion in consumer behavior in ways that acknowledge its evolutionary and biological origins. The communication and arousal of emotion can be powerful advertising tools. It is likely that their value will be enhanced when they are utilized in ways that reflect their functions in adaptive social behavior.

REFERENCES

Adelmann, P. K., & Zajonc, R. B. (1989). Facial efference and the experience of emotion. *Annual Review of Psychology, 40*, 249–280.

Agres, S. (1988, May). *Emotion vs emotionality*. Paper presented at the Seventh Annual Conference on Advertising and Consumer Psychology, New York, NY.

Aronoff, J., Barclay, A. M., & Stevenson, L. A. (1988). The recognition of threatening facial stimuli. *Journal of Personality and Social Psychology, 54*, 647–655.

Berry, D. S., & McArthur, L. Z. (1985). Some components and consequences of a babyface. *Journal of Personality and Social Psychology, 48*, 312–323.

Berry, D. S., & McArthur, L. Z. (1986). Perceiving character in faces: The impact of age-related craniofacial changes on social perception. *Psychological Bulletin, 100*, 3–18.

Boring, E. G., & Titchener, E. B. (1923). A model for the demonstration of facial expression. *American Journal of Psychology, 34*, 471–486.

Buck, R. (1984). *The communication of emotion*. New York: Guilford Press.

Buck, R. W., Savin, V. J., Miller, R. E., & Caul, W. F. (1972). Communication of affect through facial expressions in humans. *Journal of Personality and Social Psychology, 23*, 362–371.

Cacioppo, J. T., Martzke, J. S., Petty, R. E., & Tassinary, L. G. (1988). Specific forms of facial EMG response index emotions during an interview: From Darwin to the continuous flow of affect-laden information processing. *Journal of Personality and Social Psychology, 54*, 592–604.

Cacioppo, J. T., Tassinary, L. G., & Fridlund, A. J. (1990). The skeletomotor system, In J. T. Cacioppo & L. G. Tassinary (Eds.), *Principles of psychophysiology: Physical, social, and inferential elements*. New York: Cambridge University Press.

Campbell, R. (1986). Asymmetries of facial action: Some facts and fancies of normal face movement. In R. Bruyer (Ed.), *The neuropsychology of face perception and facial expression*. Hillsdale, NJ: Erlbaum.

Darwin, C. (1898). *The expression of the emotions in man and animals*. New York: Appleton. (Originally published 1872).

Davidson, R. J. (1984). Affect, cognition, and hemispheric specialization. In C. E. Izard, J. Kagan, & R. B. Zajonc (Eds.), *Emotions, cognition & behavior*. New York: Cambridge University Press.

Dimberg, U. (1982). Facial reactions to facial expressions. *Psychophysiology, 19*, 643–647.

Dimberg, U., & Ohman, A. (1983). The effects of directional facial cues on electrodermal conditioning to facial stimuli. *Psychophysiology, 20*, 160–167.

Eibl-Eibesfeldt, I. (1975). *Ethology, the biology of behavior* (2nd ed.). New York: Holt, Rinehart and Winston.

Ekman, P. (Ed.). (1973). *Darwin and facial expression: A century of research in review*. New York: Academic Press.

Ekman, P. (1985). *Telling lies: Clues to deceit in the marketplace, politics, and marriage.* New York: W. W. Norton.

Ekman, P., & Friesen, W. V. (1975). *Unmasking the face: A guide to recognizing emotions from facial clues.* Englewood Cliffs, NJ: Prentice-Hall.

Ekman, P., & Friesen, W. V. (1978a). *Investigator's guide to the Facial Action Coding System.* Palo Alto, CA: Consulting Psychologists Press.

Ekman, P., & Friesen, W. V. (1978b). *Manual for the Facial Action Coding System.* Palo Alto, CA: Consulting Psychologists Press.

Ekman, P., & Friesen, W. V. (1982). Felt, false and miserable smiles. *Journal of Nonverbal Behavior, 6,* 238–252.

Ekman, P., Friesen, W. V., & Ellsworth, P. (1972). *Emotion in the human face.* Elmsford, NY: Pergamon.

Ekman, P., Friesen, W. V., & O'Sullivan, M. (1988). Smiles when lying. *Journal of Personality and Social Psychology, 54,* 414–420.

Ekman, P., Hager, J. C., & Friesen, W. V. (1981). The symmetry of emotional and deliberate facial actions. *Psychophysiology, 18,* 101–106.

Ekman, P., & Oster, H. (1979). Facial expressions of emotion. *Annual Review of Psychology, 30,* 527–554.

Ekman, P., & Oster, H. (1982). Review of research, 1970–1980. In P. Ekman (Ed.), *Emotion in the human face* (2nd ed.). New York: Cambridge University Press.

Field, T. M., Woodson, R., Greenberg, R., & Cohen, D. (1982). Discrimination and imitation of facial expressions by neonates. *Science, 218,* 179–181.

Fridlund, A. J., Schwartz, G. E., & Fowler, S. C. (1984). Pattern recognition of self-reported emotional state from multiple-site facial EMG activity during affective imagery. *Psychophysiology, 21,* 622–637.

Frois-Wittmann, J. (1930). The judgment of facial expressions. *Journal of Experimental Psychology, 13,* 113–151.

Gibson, J. J. (1977). The theory of affordances. In R. E. Shaw & J. Bransford (Eds.), *Perceiving, acting and knowing: Toward an ecological psychology.* Hillsdale, NJ: Erlbaum.

Gibson, J. J. (1979). *The ecological approach to visual perception.* Boston: Houghton-Mifflin.

Gould, S. J. (1979). Mickey Mouse meets Konrad Lorenz. *Natural History, 88(5),* 30, 32, 34, 36.

Hansen, C. H., & Hansen, R. D. (1988). Finding the face in the crowd: An anger superiority effect. *Journal of Personality and Social Psychology, 54,* 917–924.

Hansen, F. (1981). Hemispheral lateralization: Implications for understanding consumer behavior. *Journal of Consumer Research, 8,* 23–36.

Harmon, D. W., & Ray, W. J. (1977). Hemispheric activity during affective verbal stimuli: An EEG study. *Neuropsychologia, 15,* 457–460.

Izard, C. E. (1977). *Human emotions.* New York: Plenum.

Janiszewski, C. (1988). Preconscious processing effects: The independence of attitude formation and conscious thought. *Journal of Consumer Research, 15,* 199–209.

Leventhal, H. L., & Tomarken, A. J. (1986). Emotion: Today's problems. *Annual Review of Psychology, 37,* 565–610.

Ley, R. G., & Strauss, E. (1986). Hemispheric asymmetries in the perception of facial expressions by normals. In R. Bruyer (Ed.), *The neuropsychology of face perception and facial expression.* Hillsdale, NJ: Erlbaum.

Lorenz, K. (1971). *Studies in animal and human behaviour* (vol. 2), (R. Martin, Trans.). Cambridge, MA: Harvard University Press.

McArthur, L. Z., & Baron, R. M. (1983). Toward an ecological theory of social perception. *Psychological Review, 90*, 215–238.

Ohman, A. (1986). Face the beast and fear the face: Animal and social fears as prototypes for evolutionary analyses of emotion. *Psychophysiology, 23*, 123–145.

Ohman, A., & Dimberg, U. (1978). Facial expressions as conditioned stimuli for electrodermal responses: A case of "Preparedness"? *Journal of Experimental and Social Psychology, 36*, 1251–1258.

Peck, S. R. (1987). *Atlas of facial expression: An account of facial expression for artists, actors, and writers.* New York: Oxford University Press.

Plutchik, R. (1984). Emotions: A general psychoevolutionary theory. In K. R. Scherer & P. Ekman (Eds.), *Approaches to emotion.* Hillsdale, NJ: Erlbaum.

Reuter-Lorenz, R., & Davidson, R. J. (1981). Differential contributions of the two cerebral hemispheres to the perception of happy and sad faces. *Neuropsychologia, 19*, 609–613.

Rinn, W. E. (1984). The neuropsychology of facial expression: A review of the neurological and psychological mechanisms for producing facial expressions. *Psychological Bulletin, 95* (1), 52–77.

Schlosberg, H. (1941). A scale for the judgment of facial expressions. *Journal of Experimental Psychology, 29*, 497–510.

Schlosberg, H. (1952). The description of facial expressions in terms of two dimensions. *Journal of Experimental Psychology, 44*, 229–237.

Smith, C. A. (1989). Dimensions of appraisal and physiological response in emotion. *Journal of Personality and Social Psychology, 56*, 339–353.

Suberi, M., & McKeever, W. F. (1977). Differential right hemispheric memory storage of emotional and non-emotional faces. *Neuropsychologia, 15*, 757–768.

Sullivan, M. J. L., & Brender, W. (1986). Facial electromyography: A measure of affective processes during sexual arousal. *Psychophysiology, 23*, 182–188.

Tassinary, L. G., Cacioppo, J. T., & Geen, T. R. (1989). A psychometric study of surface electrode placements for facial electromyographic recording: I. The brow and cheek muscle regions. *Psychophysiology, 26*, 1–16.

Woodworth, R. S. (1938). *Experimental psychology.* New York: Holt.

Woodworth, R. S., & Schlosberg, H. (1954). *Experimental psychology* (rev. ed.). New York: Holt, Rinehart and Winston.

Zajonc, R. B. (1980). Feeling and thinking: Preferences need no inferences. *American Psychologist, 35*, 151–175.

Zuckerman, M., Hall, J. A., DeFrank, R. S., & Rosenthal, R. (1976). Encoding and decoding of spontaneous and posed facial expressions. *Journal of Personality and Social Psychology, 34*, 966–977.

10

Influences on Emotional Response to Commercials of Different Executional Styles

Cheon-Soung Park and Esther Thorson

Extensive research in the last few years has demonstrated that the impact of television commercials is probably mediated through emotional and involvement responses made to commercials, through brand familiarity, and through attitude toward the ad (A_{ad}). Although there has been exploration of how processing varies as a function of whether commercials are informational or transformational (Edell & Burke, 1987), or whether their products are highly involving or not (Thorson & Page, 1988), for the most part, there has been little study of how the processing of commercials varies as a function of detailed characterizations of their executional styles. To help fill this gap, the study presented in this chapter sampled numerous exemplars of five differing executional styles (Hefzallah & Maloney, 1979) and then examined the relationships among how involving their products were, how familiar their brands were, the attitude toward the ad, and the emotional impact that the commercials created in viewers.

The research reported in this chapter is based on a simple characterization of an advertising strategy problem as it exists for professionals. An account executive has a brand to sell. The product category to which that brand belongs has a particular level of product involvement for the consumer (Kapferer & Laurent, 1986; Laurent & Kapferer, 1985; Zaichowsky, 1985, 1987). The brand itself has a particular degree of familiarity to the consumer. The account executive knows, if he or she reads the advertising literature, that he or she is more likely to have a successful commercial if it is liked (e.g., see A_{ad} studies such as Shimp, 1981; MacKenzie, Lutz, & Belch, 1986) and if it creates an emotional response in viewers (e.g., Aaker, Stayman, & Hagerty, 1986; Batra & Ray, 1986; Edell & Burke, 1987; Holbrook & Batra, 1987; Holbrook and Westwood, in press;

Stephens & Russo, 1987; Thorson & Friestad, 1989). Given that this is the case, the job for the executive is to decide upon and have executed some kind of commercial that succeeds in making people like the commercial and experience a positive emotion in response to it.

Is there any reason to believe that the natural limitations of product category and brand familiarity will interact with the style of a commercial to influence the likelihood that it will succeed in creating an emotional response and a positive A_{ad}? Although several studies focusing on emotion have compared different kinds of commercials—for example, R. Batra and M. L. Ray (1986) compared rational and informational commercials and J. A. Edell and M. C. Burke (1987) compared transformational and informational commercials—the comparisons mainly have been concerned with whether interrelationships among the processing responses to commercials change as a function of what type of commercial is being tested. There has been no study of whether executional style mediates the impact of product involvement and brand familiarity on any dependent processes.

To examine executional style as a mediator of commercial processing, a decision must be made about which classification scheme to use for characterizing commercials. There are many ways to classify the executional style of a commercial (see Thorson, 1989, for a review of these taxonomies). One of the most popular taxonomies, among both practitioners and those academics who teach advertising copy and layout, is the classification scheme of I. M. Hefzallah and W. P. Maloney (1979). These researchers reviewed the main content-based taxonomies of television commercials and then attempted to merge all the variations in these taxonomies into six categories of executional style. Five of their commercial categories were used in this research.

Associational commercials were defined as those that link the brand with emotional attributes (such as margarine linked with "country sunshine") that are usually extrinsic to the product. Demonstration commercials show what the brand can do or how it performs. Satisfaction commercials show people who use the brand to achieve goals and thereby experience personal gratification. Testimonial commercials feature an individual who claims to use the product and vouches for its quality. Comparison commercials directly compare the product to its competitors. Hefzallah and Maloney defined a sixth category, informational commercials, but, because the category is so broad and because it seems to overlap with demonstrations, testimonials, and comparisons, it was omitted from the present application of the taxonomy.

Several hypotheses and experimental questions were tested in the study. A first and very basic question concerned whether people would agree on categorizing commercials into the classifications proposed by Hefzallah and Maloney. Given Hefzallah and Maloney's claims that their categories are mutually exclusive, Hypothesis 1 suggested that there would be clear interobserver reliability in classifying commercials into the five executional style categories.

The second hypothesis suggested that, because of the intrinsic emotional nature of the satisfaction and association styles of commercials, these styles would produce more emotional responding by viewers. Consistent with the findings that emotional commercials are better liked, Hypothesis 3 suggested that satisfaction and association commercials would show more positive A_{ad} scores.

Hypothesis 4 was very general and did not predict specific directions of effects. Essentially, it suggested that the effects of product involvement and brand familiarity on emotional response and A_{ad} would be mediated by executional style. That is, it was expected that the relationships of the two antecedent variables, product involvement and brand familiarity, to the two dependent variables, emotional response and A_{ad}, would vary as a function of different executional styles of the commercials.

These four hypotheses were tested in a study of 74 commercials that represented multiple instances of each of the five executional styles. Student subjects each watched approximately half of the commercials and evaluated their involvement with the advertised products, their familiarity with the advertised brands, their A_{ad}, and their emotional responses to the commercials. Finally, these same subjects were asked to learn the Hefzallah and Maloney taxonomy and to categorize each commercial into one of the five executional styles.

METHOD

Subjects

Thirty-six students from an introductory communication class of a large midwestern university participated in the study. They received points toward their grade in the course as compensation.

Commercials

Seventy-four commercials for a wide variety of products and with many different executional styles were randomly divided into one grouping of 36 and one grouping of 38 commercials. The sample of commercials was divided in half because a pretest indicated that subjects became fatigued and bored when they had to watch all 74 of the commercials. Two orders of each of the groups of commercials were dubbed onto ¾-inch video tape.

Procedure

Small groups of students watched one of the commercial tapes in a comfortable viewing room. At the beginning of each testing session, the five categories of executional styles were explained, and the students were given a reminder sheet with a short definition of each commercial type. Each commercial was then shown once. Immediately afterward, the students responded to the product involvement, brand familiarity, commercial involvement, and emotional response items. Finally, they decided which of the five executional categories best characterized the commercial. The students were given two minutes to respond to each commercial. No one had difficulty filling out the items in that time. After viewing all of the 36 or 38 commercials, the subjects were thanked and excused.

Dependent Measures

All scales were 7-point scales. Product involvement was measured with six of the semantic differential items from Zaichowsky's (1985) product involvement scale (irrelevant-relevant, means nothing to me—means a lot to me, doesn't matter to me—matters to me, insignificant-significant, superfluous-vital, and nonessential-essential). Brand familiarity was measured with a single semantic differential item (very unfamiliar—very familiar). Attitude toward the ad was measured with seven semantic differential items: boring-interesting, unexciting-exciting, unappealing-appealing, mundane-fascinating, bad-good, dislike very much—like very much, and unpleasant-pleasant. Emotion was measured with three semantic differential items: neutral-emotional, impersonal-personal, and cold-warm. Each commercial was categorized as one of the five executional types: association, satisfaction, demonstration, comparison, and testimonial.

RESULTS

Concept Scales

A factor analysis was conducted on all the semantic differential items. As expected, the three factors described above emerged: product involvement, emotion, and A_{ad}. The coefficient alphas were all satisfactorily high, indicating that the internal consistency and reliability of each of the four scales were acceptable as can be seen in Table 10.1. A_{ad} accounted for 44.4 percent of variance among the scales; product involvement and emotion explained 18.3 percent and 8.1 percent of variance each.

Hypothesis 1 posited interobserver agreement on the categorization of the 74 commercials into the five executional style categories. Given the significant level of disagreement about the categorization of the commercials by executional style, however, it must be concluded that here was little support for the hypothesis. Only one of the 74 commercials showed perfect interobserver agreement (an association commercial). Thirty-three of the commercials showed 70 percent or greater agreement on the categorization of the commercial into one of the executional styles. Commercials that were classified with this degree of agreement were fairly evenly distributed across the five executional style categories. Twenty-six of the commercials were nearly evenly divided into categorization of two categories. Twelve commercials were nearly evenly divided into cate-

Table 10.1
Regressions Predicting Emotional Responding as a Function of Product Involvement, Brand Familiarity, A_{ad}, and Executional Style

Predictors	Beta	Adj R^2	F	Significance
All commercials				
Aad	.52	.34	679.93	.0000
Satisfaction	.28	.35	356.54	.000
Familiarity	.06	.36	246.334	.000
Prod Inv	.02	.36	187.71	.000
Demonstration	-.017	.36	152.03	.000
Association commercials				
Aad	.54	.35	143.25	.000
Familiarity	.10	.37	77.66	.000
Comparison commercials				
Aad	.57	.36	81.50	.000
Demonstration commercials				
Aad	.52	.33	207.05	.000
Prod Inv	.08	.34	107.63	.000
Satisfaction commercials				
Aad	.51	.37	147.09	.000
Prod Inv	.11	.39	79.60	.000
Familiarity	.08	.40	55.77	.000
Testimonial commercials				
Aad	.45	.25	78.48	.000

Table 10.2
Means of Emotional Response and A_{ad} by Executional Style

Commercial Style	Emotion Score	Aad Score
Association	4.41	4.72
Satisfaction	4.48	4.35
Comparison	3.94	4.00
Demonstration	3.95	4.25
Testimonial	4.05	4.11

gorization into three categories. Two commercials showed an even distribution of categorization into four styles.

Overall, 20 percent of the commercials were coded as associational, 11 percent as comparison, 32 percent as demonstration, 19 percent as satisfaction, and 18 percent as testimonial.

Given that so few commercials could be clearly categorized as a single style, it was decided that executional style would be treated as an individual variable. In other words, all of the subsequent analyses would use the individual choice of executional style that each subject chose for a particular commercial.

Effects of the Executional Styles on Emotion and A_{ad}

Hypotheses 2 and 3 suggested that association and satisfaction commercials would be more likely to produce emotional responses and positive attitudes toward the commercials. Table 10.2 shows the mean emotional response and A_{ad} values for commercials coded into each of the five styles. (Recall that each commercial was cast into a style by individual response.) Two analyses of variance, one for each of the dependent measures, showed significant main effects of executional style. As predicted, for emotion ($F = 9.7$, $p < .000$) the association and satisfaction commercials scored higher than the other three categories.

Hypothesis 3 received only partial support. For A_{ad} ($F = 9.016$, $p < .000$) association was the highest (as predicted); satisfaction and demonstration were intermediate; and comparison and testimonial commercials showed the lowest A_{ad} values.

Predicting the Variance in Emotional Responding

Although not specifically hypothesized, a reasonable next question concerned the degree to which emotional response to the commercials could be predicted

Table 10.3
Factor Analysis of Closed-Ended Items (Principle Components Analysis with Varimax Rotation)

	Aad	Product Involvement	Emotion
Boring-Interesting	.88		
Unexciting-Exciting	.87		
Mundane-Fascinating	.85		
Like very much-Dislike very much	.83		
Appealing-Unappealing	.82		
Good-Bad	.79		
Unpleasant-Pleasant	.62		
Insignificant-Significant		.89	
Irrelevant-Relevant		.86	
Matters to me-Doesn't matter to me		.85	
Means a lot to me-Means nothing to me		.84	
Nonessential-Essential		.81	
Vital-Superfluous		.81	
Cold-Warm			.82
Personal-Impersonal			.80
Emotional-Neutral			.51
Eigenvalue	7.55	3.11	1.38
% of variance accounted for	44.4	18.3	8.1

n=1340

from executional style, brand familiarity, product involvement, and A_{ad}. It was also asked how well A_{ad} brand familiarity, and product involvement could predict emotional response within each category of executional style. The results of stepwise regressions for all commercials combined and for each of the five executional styles individually are shown in Table 10.3. In the overall analysis, A_{ad} accounted for most of the variance in emotional response to the commercials. Brand familiarity and product involvement also contributed significantly to the variance accounted for, but their contribution to R^2 was smaller than that of A_{ad}. Knowing that the commercial was perceived as a satisfaction execution added significantly to R^2, and its effect was positive. In contrast, categorization of a commercial as a demonstration, while significant, was associated with a negative

Figure 10.1
Path Model for All Commercials Merged

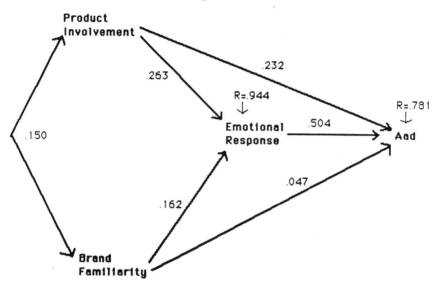

beta. Overall, slightly more than a third of the variance in emotional response could be predicted by the other variables.

Looking next at the commercials as categorized into executional types, prediction of emotional response from A_{ad}, brand familiarity, and product involvement varied from accounting for 25 percent of the variance (testimonial commercials) to 40 percent (satisfaction commercials). As would be expected from the overall results, A_{ad} accounted for most of the variance; product involvement and brand familiarity put in small appearances for the association, demonstration, and satisfaction commercials.

The Impact of Brand Familiarity and Product Involvement as Mediated by Executional Style

Hypothesis 4 suggested that executional style would change the relationships among brand familiarity, product involvement, and A_{ad}. A path analysis was conducted for the data for each of the executional styles and then for all of the commercials merged. In each path analysis, two separate linear regression analyses were run. In each analysis, the dependent variable was emotional response or A_{ad}. The results are shown in Figures 10.1 through 10.6.

As can be seen for the overall model (Figure 10.1), product involvement had direct effects on emotional response (beta = .263, $p < .0000$) and A_{ad} (beta = .232, $p < .0000$). Brand familiarity also had direct effects on emotional response (beta = .162, $p < .0000$) and A_{ad} (beta = .047, $p < .05$). The effects

Figure 10.2
Path Model for Association Commercials

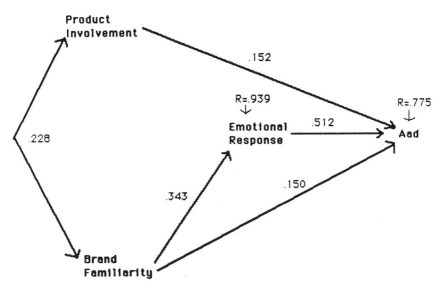

of product involvement were clearly stronger than those of brand familiarity. In addition, the direct effects of product involvement and brand familiarity were greater on emotional response than on A_{ad}. There was a significant, though weak, correlation between product involvement and brand familiarity ($r = .150$, $p < .001$). These results indicate that for a large and diverse sample of commercial executions, product involvement and brand familiarity both influence the likelihood of an ads eliciting positive emotional responding and a positive A_{ad} from viewers. The strong predictability of emotional response from A_{ad} was exhibited in this analysis and in all the other analyses by executional style.

We turn next to the path analyses conducted individually for each of the five executional types. As can be seen by comparing Figures 10.2 through 10.6, the interrelationships of the four variables of interest were clearly influenced by how people categorized the executional style of the commercial.

For commercials categorized as associational (Figure 10.2), brand familiarity had direct effects on both emotional response (beta $= .343$, $p < .0000$) and A_{ad} (beta $= .150$, $p < .00$). Product involvement, however, did not have independent effects on emotional response, even though it had a direct effect on A_{ad} (beta $= .152$, $p < .00$). This result indicates that, when commercials are perceived as associational, product involvement becomes irrelevant to the production of emotional response directly. However, we cannot exclude the possibility of an indirect effect of product involvement on emotion and A_{ad} through the significant correlation with brand familiarity ($r = .228$, $p < .001$).

There was a different pattern for comparison commercials (Figure 10.3).

Figure 10.3
Path Model for Comparison Commercials

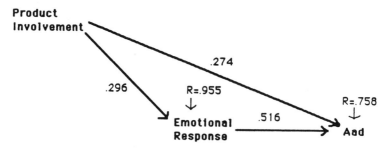

Product involvement had direct effects on emotion (beta = .296, p <.000) and A_{ad} (beta = .274, p <.000). However, brand familiarity had no direct or indirect effects on emotion and A_{ad}. There was no significant correlation between product involvement and brand familiarity. This result indicates that for comparison commercials, brand familiarity does not explain any variation in emotional response and A_{ad}. Only considerations of product involvement level are relevant.

In demonstration commercials (Figure 10.4), the pattern of effects showed that product involvement directly affected emotion (beta = .308, p <.0000) and A_{ad} (beta = .249, p <.0000), and brand familiarity affected only emotion (beta = .117, p <.05). There was no significant correlation between product involvement and brand familiarity.

Two executional styles showed the same pattern of effects. For both satisfaction (Figure 10.5) and testimonial (Figure 10.6) commercials, product involvement had direct effects on emotion (beta = .364, p <.0000 for satisfaction; beta = .182, p <.01 for testimonial commercials) and A_{ad} (beta = .259, p <.0000 for satisfaction; beta = .266, p <.0000 for testimonial commercials). Brand familiarity, however, had a direct effect only on emotion (beta = .163, p <.01 for satisfaction; beta = .145, p <.05 for testimonial commercials) even though, again, there is the possibility of indirect effects of brand familiarity on A_{ad} through the significant correlation between brand familiarity and product involvement (r = .270, p <.001 for satisfaction; r = .152, p <.01 for testimonial commercials).

Figure 10.4
Path Model for Demonstration Commercials

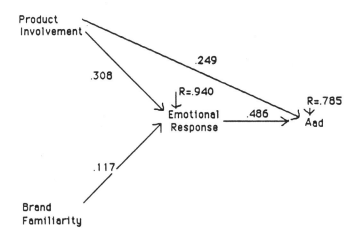

Figure 10.5
Path Model for Satisfaction Commercials

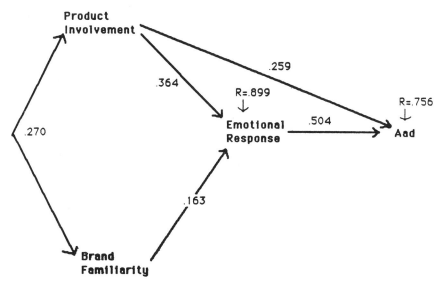

Figure 10.6
Path Model for Testimonial Commercials

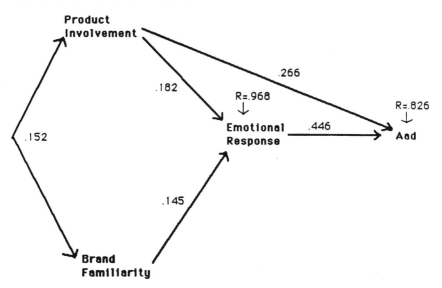

DISCUSSION

The results of this study are of interest to both the practitioner and the theorist. Just as those who have studied the varying taxonomies of commercial executional styles predicted (e.g., Thorson, in press), simple categorization schemes for commercials often fail to find agreement in their application. Half of the commercials in the sample were not consistently cast into a single classification cell; instead, subjects classified them differently. The pattern of classifications suggested that the majority of these commercials were blends of the categories. Presumably, subjects simply selected the aspects of the commercials that were most salient to themselves in order to decide into which category each commercial should be assigned.

A second point of interest was the fact that classification into two of the executional styles was associated with more emotional responding than classification into the other styles. Classification as satisfaction and associational commercials was consistently more likely to be perceived as having created an emotional response. The associational commercials also produced more positive A_{ad} responses; satisfaction and demonstration commercials ran a close second.

Perhaps most important, perception of a commercial as belonging to a particular executional style clearly mediated the impact of product involvement and brand familiarity on emotional responding and A_{ad}. Given this mediating role of executional style, it is interesting to note that, when the sample was analyzed as a whole, it showed product involvement and brand familiarity acting directly and independently on both emotional responding and A_{ad}. It was only when the sample was divided into executional styles that the fact emerged that product involvement and brand familiarity did not always influence the two dependent variables. For example, in the association commercials, product involvement was irrelevant to emotional responding, but in the comparison commercials, product involvement had effects on emotion and A_{ad}; however, brand familiarity had no effects on either of the two responses. In the demonstration, satisfaction, and testimonial commercials, product involvement affected both emotional response and A_{ad}, but brand familiarity affected only the production of emotional response.

These results are especially informative for the practitioner who is interested in creating commercials that elicit emotional responses and positive attitudes toward the commercials. If the familiarity of a brand is low, as, for example, with a new product introduction, then association commercials will be less likely to yield positive A_{ad} and emotional responding because significant amounts of the variance in these commercials are directly related to brand familiarity. On the other hand, brand familiarity is unrelated to emotional responding for comparison commercials, and it does not affect A_{ad} in demonstration, satisfaction, and testimonial commercials. Comparison, demonstration, satisfaction, and testimonial commercials would then seem to be good candidates for the initial round of commercials in a new product campaign.

The mediating role of executional style is also informative for the advertising theoretician interested in the links between exogenous variables, such as brand familiarity and product involvement, and endogenous variables, such as A_{ad} and emotional response. In much of modern research on television commercials, the assumption is that commercials should be sampled so that the results of the information processing studies can be generalized to "commercials." But the present results suggest that this approach may be mistaken. Commercials of different executional styles may not be processed equivalently. Hints of this result can be found in research such as that conducted by Edell and Burke (1987), who showed that, for highly transformational commercials, feelings are better predictors of A_{ad} than are judgments, whereas the opposite is true for highly informational commercials. Together with the present results, the implications seem strong. While it is perhaps true that a rose is a rose is a rose, when it comes to understanding how people process commercials, it may not be true that a commercial is a commercial is a commercial. It may be, then, that we need to develop a science of advertising based on the assumption that the first question to ask of a commercial is to what executional type it belongs. Only then can its emotional and A_{ad} impact be accurately predicted.

REFERENCES

Aaker, D. A., Stayman, D. M. & Hagerty, M. R. (1986). Warmth in advertising: Measurement, impact and sequence effects. *Journal of Consumer Research, 12* (4), 365–381.

Batra, R., & Ray, M. L. (1986). Affective responses mediating acceptance of advertising. *Journal of Consumer Research, 13* (2), 234–249.

Edell, J. A., & Burke, M. C. (1987). The power of feelings in understanding advertising effects. *Journal of Consumer Research, 14* (3), 421–433.

Hefzallah, I. M., & Maloney, W. P. (1979). Are there only six kinds of TV commercials? *Journal of Advertising Research, 19* (4), 57–64.

Holbrook, M. B., & Batra, R. (1987). Assessing the role of emotions as mediators of consumer responses to advertising. *Journal of Consumer Research, 14* (3), 404–420.

Holbrook, M. B. & Westwood, R. A. (in press). The role of emotion in advertising revisited: Testing a typology of emotional responses. In P. Cafferata & A. Tybout (Eds.), *Cognitive and affective responses to advertising.* Lexington, MA: Lexington.

Kapferer, J., & Laurent, G. (1986). Consumer involvement profiles: A new practical approach to consumer involvement. *Journal of Advertising Research, 25* (6), 48–56.

Laurent, G., & Kapferer, J. (1985). Measuring consumer involvement profiles. *Journal of Marketing Research, 21* (1), 41–53.

MacKenzie, S. B., Lutz, R. J., & Belch, G. E. (1986). The role of attitude toward the ad as a mediator of advertising effectiveness: A test of competing explanations. *Journal of Marketing Research, 23* (2), 130–143.

Shimp, T. A. (1981). Attitude toward the ad as a mediator of consumer brand choice. *Journal of Advertising, 10* (2), 9–15.

Stephens, D. L., & Russo, J. E. (1987). Predicting post-advertising attitudes. Working paper, University of Maryland, College of Business.

Thorson, E. (in press). Television commercials as mass media messages. In J. J. Bradac (Ed.), *Messages in communication science: Contemporary approaches to the study of effects.* Beverly Hills, CA: Sage.

Thorson, E., & Friestad, M. (1989). The effects of emotion on episodic memory for television commercials. In P. Cafferata and A. M. Tybout (Eds.), *Cognitive and affective responses to advertising* (pp. 305–325). Lexington, MA: Lexington.

Thorson, E., & Page, T. J., Jr. (1988). Effects of product involvement and emotional commercials on consumers' recall and attitudes. In Sidney Hecker and David W. Stewart (Eds.), *Nonverbal communication in advertising* (pp. 111–126). Lexington, MA: Lexington.

Zaichowsky, J. L. (1985). Measuring the involvement construct. *Journal of Consumer Research, 12* (3), 341–352.

Zaichowsky, J. L. (1987). The emotional aspect of product involvement. In Melanie Wallendorf and Paul F. Anderson (Eds.), *Advances in consumer research* (vol. 14, pp.32–35). Provo, UT: Association for Consumer Research.

11

When Are Feelings Generated? Assessing the Presence and Reliability of Feelings Based on Storyboards and Animatics

Ronald C. Goodstein, Julie A. Edell,
and Marian Chapman Moore

Exploring the role of feelings and emotions in advertising effectiveness has been one of the hot topics of the 1980s (Aaker, Stayman, & Vezina, 1988; Burke & Edell, 1989; Holbrook & Batra, 1986; Stephens & Russo, 1987). The net result is an expanded view of how people react to ads that incorporate both affective and cognitive reactions. Accordingly, the issues of whether and how an ad "works" are now investigated using more than the traditional learning-based measures such as recall. This chapter addresses a question that is especially important today, given that emotions have been established as important advertising outcomes: Can pretest versions of ads generate emotional responses that reliably predict the level of emotional responses that will be generated by the finished version of the ad?

We draw on the literature in message modality—both in psychology and in advertising—to address that question. Our interest differs slightly from that of most modality researchers, however. We do not contrast different final versions of a communication stimulus, say, a television ad versus a print ad, or a television ad versus a radio ad. We are not addressing the question of which media to use. Rather, our interest is in contrasting the responses to different stages of the development of a television commercial. We focus on whether the emotional responses to two unfinished versions of a television ad—storyboards and animatics—can be used reliably to assess the probable emotional reactions to the finished, commercialized version of the ad.

BACKGROUND AND HYPOTHESES

Feelings and Preproduction Versions of Ads

The print versus audio versus audio-visual distinctions among stimuli that are usually made when contrasting differential effects of message modality do not map directly onto the stimulus differences here. Although storyboards may be considered "print" versions of a television ad, they contain visual cues in addition to a written script. Animatics add the element of audio, but not without visual cues. Finished versions of television ads contain both audio and video (i.e., moving pictures). The applicability of the findings of past research to the problem at hand is, therefore, somewhat limited. There are two more subtle distinctions that are intriguing, however. These have to do with (1) the increased richness of the stimulus as one moves from storyboards to animatics to television and (2) the fact that storyboards can be digested at a pace established by the respondent, whereas the pace of animatics and television commercials is controlled by the ad. We expect that both of these factors, which are not independent, influence the extensiveness of the feelings responses that consumers will generate in response to the stimulus.

Storyboards can be read at the subject's own pace, but animatics and television commercials are presented at a predetermined pace. This self-pacing feature has been used to explain the greater comprehension of facts when stimuli are presented in written form rather than in audio or audiovisual form (Chaiken & Eagly, 1976). S. Chaiken and A. H. Eagly found that this was true for inherently difficult-to-understand material. J. Jacoby, W. D. Hoyer, and M. R. Zimmer (1983) found the same effect—increased comprehension of facts when the stimulus material was in print format—for relatively simple material, notably an ad. This was true both when the subjects were given an unlimited amount of time to read the ad and when they were given only 30 seconds to read the ad. Therefore, at least with respect to recall of facts, the evidence leads to the conclusion that storyboards will outperform animatics and television commercials.

But what about feelings? We expect that any stimulus has the potential to generate feelings in the perceiver. C. E. Izard (1972) stated it well when he said, "It seems highly unlikely that a person can complete an appraisal without some interaction between emotion and cognition" (p. 67). Further, we expect that the feelings generated by various preproduction versions of a television ad will affect the attitude toward the ad (A_{Ad}) (where the ad is the preproduction version) and the attitude toward the brand (A_b) in a manner that is similar to the influence of the feelings generated by the finished version of the ad on A_{ad} and A_b. Our formal hypothesis is as follows:

Hypothesis 1: The impact of feelings generated by a storyboard, an animatic, and a finished version of a television ad on attitude toward the ad and attitude toward the brand will be consistent across the three formats.

The Level of Feelings in Preproduction Versions of Ads

Although we believe that storyboards, animatics, and finished versions of commercials will generate feelings, there is some evidence to suggest that the overall level of feelings experienced by the viewer will vary with the form of the commercial.

In 1980 M. J. Schlinger and L. Green raised the question of whether storyboards could predict reactions to finished commercials. Due to stimulus constraints, the "finished commericals" in their study were storyboards that were put on film strips and accompanied by an amateur soundtrack. Although they were not, therefore, able to answer the exact question they posed, they did find a reasonable amount of correlation between the storyboards and the commericals on the Viewer Response Profile. They also identified interesting differences: the commercials (which were much like crude animatics) were more stimulating, more attractive, less irritating, and less confusing, and they created more empathy than the storyboards. They also conclude that "commercials are better able to create 'soothing, dreamy moods than storyboards' " (p. 22). Their subjects, responding as ad critics, reported judgments of the ads' characteristics rather than how the ads made them feel. Nevertheless, most of the differences can be characterized as judgments about the affective dimensions of the ad. This suggests that assessing the viability of responses to preproduction forms of television commercials is especially important when it comes to predicting affective reactions.

Why would an animatic or a finished television commercial generate more feelings than a storyboard? Perhaps the viewers actually do less deliberate processing of the information presented in the ad because they receive the stimulus passively. B. Reeves, E. Thorson, M. L. Rothschild, D. McDonald, R. Goldstein, and J. Hirsch (1985) note that television adds information in the form of ready-made images; television ads "do our thinking for us." Jacoby, Hoyer, and Zimmer (1983) suggest that the audio and video elements of communication stimuli may distract the viewer from the message content. This, again, could result in more affective processing of the stimulus. P. R. Warshaw (1978) found that either audio-only or video-only messages outperformed audiovisual messages on short-term recall. Thus, there does seem to be some distraction from message content when a message involves both audio and video, as is the case for animatics and finished television commercials. In fact, Chaiken and Eagly (1983) found that audio and video communications are better at *persuasion* than print communications.

These "distractions"—audio and video—enhance the vividness of the stimulus. Chaiken and Eagly (1983) contend that vivid information extends a disproportionate impact on people's judgments. We feel that this is true for feelings as well as judgments, especially for a relatively simple, low-involvement stimulus such as a television ad. J. R. Rossiter (1982), in fact, suggests that television is superior to other modalities in accurately communicating emotions. S. S. Liu and P. A. Stout (1987) contrasted audio and audiovisual messages which were either emotional or rational and found that an audiovisual emotional message was best at eliciting positive emotions. Because finished commercials are "richer" than animatics and, therefore, more likely to distract and to elicit emotions, we expect the finished versions of ads to generate a higher level of overall feelings than their animatic versions.

Our formal hypotheses regarding the level of the feelings that will be generated by the various forms of a television commercial are as follows:

> *Hypothesis 2*: The animatic version of a television commercial will generate more feelings responses than the storyboard version of the commercial.

> *Hypothesis 3*: The final version of a television commercial will generate more feelings responses than the animatic version of the commercial.

Purpose of the Study

The primary purpose of this study is to contrast the overall level of feelings generated by three versions of the same television ad—a storyboard, an animatic, and the finished version—and to assess the influence of those feelings on attitude toward the ad and attitude toward the brand. Since feelings are the focus of this study, we do not formally address an obvious related issue, that is, whether cognitive reactions will vary across the three formats of the ad. We thought it was important, however, to determine whether the ads used in this study conformed to the pattern of cognitive-based findings identified in earlier research that contrasted reactions to self-paced stimuli with those of researcher-paced stimuli. Based on the research discussed above, more information processing should occur when the stimulus is the storyboard version of the ad than when the stimulus is the animatic or the finished version. This issue was addressed by examining the differences in brand claim recall across the three versions of the television ads.

METHOD

Overview

Subjects in the experiment were assigned to one of three ad-format groups. Each group was exposed to six ads in the storyboard, the animatic, or the finished form. The design, a 3-by-6 repeated measures, follows B. J. Winer's plan

7 (1971, pp. 519–524) with one between-subjects factor (format) and one within-subject factor (ad). Our primary dependent variables are attitude toward the brand, attitude toward the ad, feelings, and claims recalled.

Format

Three formats were used in this experiment: storyboard, animatic, and finished versions. The content of the ads was identical across format. There was a storyboard and a finished version for all six ads. An animatic was available for only three of the ads used in this study. Subjects in the animatic condition viewed the three animatic ads followed by the finished ads for the other three products. Data for the finished ads from subjects in the animatic condition were not included in the analyses.

Ads

Ads for five products and one public service campaign (antismoking) were used in the study. The products were a tuna dinner mix, a hamburger dinner mix, an allergy medicine, a temperature indicator, and a household cleanser. Although the brands were available locally, none of the ads had aired in the viewing area. The order of ad exposure was the same across the groups.

Subjects

Subjects were recruited by distributing announcements on a university campus. Seventy-eight subjects participated in the 45-minute study and were paid 10 dollars. Subjects were randomly assigned to the format conditions.

Measures

Attitude Toward the Brand. Attitude toward each of the brands was measured before seeing the ad (Prior Ab) and after seeing the (A_b). On both occasions, attitude toward the brand was measured as the average of three 7-point scales (very favorable–very unfavorable, like very much–dislike very much, very good–very bad).

Attitude Toward the Ad. Attitude toward each of the ads (A_d) was measured as the average of three 7-point scales (very favorable–very unfavorable, like very much–dislike very much, very good–very bad).

Feelings. The feelings inventory included 63 items: the 55 items used by Burke and Edell (1989) plus 8 new items; that is, afraid, anxious, edgy, tense, troubled, uncomfortable, uneasy, and worried. These new items were added because fear, a negative feeling, could have an effect on attitude (Dabbs & Leventhal, 1966; Ray & Wilkie, 1970). The following instructions were given for completing the feelings inventory:

We would like you to tell us how the commercial for (Brand Name) made you *feel*. Here we are interested in *your reactions* to the ad *not* how you would describe it. Please tell us how well you think each of the words listed below describes your feelings in response to the ad you just saw. If the word describes the way you feel extremely well . . . put a 5; very well . . . put a 4; fairly well . . . put a 3; not very well . . . put a 2; not well at all . . . put a 1.

Recall of Brand Claims. Subjects were asked to write down all of the claims and the statements made about the products that they could remember from the ads. The number of correct claims listed was used as the recall score.

Procedure

The experiment was conducted in a theater setting with groups of from three to ten subjects viewing the ads at the same time. Prior to viewing the ads, subjects indicated their attitudes about the brands and activities for which they would see ads. Then the first ad was shown. After each ad had been shown, subjects responded to the A_{ad} items and the feelings inventory. After all six ads had been shown, subjects wrote down all of the claims they could recall from each of the six ads. This was followed by the completion of the attitude measures for the six brands or activities. Then subjects were debriefed, paid, and dismissed.

RESULTS

The Structure of Feelings

A factor analysis was conducted on the 63 feeling items using the responses of the subjects who viewed the finished version of the ads. These factor loadings were used to define the feelings scales used in the rest of the analysis. The finished versions of the ads were used to establish the baseline feelings structure and scales for the comparison of feelings across formats.

Four feeling factors were derived: upbeat, warm, disinterested, and uneasy (see Table 11.1). Items loading greater than .5 on a factor were used to define a scale. The upbeat, warm, and disinterested scales closely resemble those found in prior research (Burke & Edell, 1989; Edell & Burke, 1987). The eight new items included in the feelings inventory, along with some items from the negative scale used in earlier research, loaded together and formed the uneasy feelings scale. Scores on each scale for each stimulus were determined by summing the subjects' ratings on the feelings items that make up each scale. Coefficient alpha for the scales ranged from a low of .86 for the disinterested feelings scale to a high of .96 for the upbeat feelings scale (see Table 11.1).

Table 11.1
Feelings Scales

Upbeat Feelings	Warm Feelings	Disinterested Feelings	Uneasy Feelings
Active	Affectionate	Bored	Afraid
Alive	Calm	Critical	Anxious
Amused	Emotional	Defiant	Concerned
Attentive	Hopeful	Disinterested	Contemplative
Attractive	Kind	Dubious	Depressed
Carefree	Moved	Dull	Edgy
Cheerful	Peaceful	Skeptical	Lonely
Creative	Sentimental	Suspicious	Pensive
Delighted	Warmhearted		Regretful
Elated			Sad
Energetic			Tense
Happy			Troubled
Humorous			Uncomfortable
Independent			Uneasy
Industrious			Worried
Inspired			
Interested			
Joyous			
Lighthearted			
Playful			
Pleased			
Proud			
Satisfied			
Stimulated			
Strong			

Note: Coefficient alphas are .96 for the Upbeat Feelings Scales, .87 for the Warm Feelings Scales, .86 for the Disinterested Feelings Scales, and .93 for the Uneasy Feelings Scales. Confident, convinced, lazy, offended, silly, and surprised were items measured that did not load greater than .5 on any factor.

The Influence of Feelings Across Formats

Hypothesis 1 predicted that the influence of feelings on A_{ad} and A_b would be the same across formats. To test whether each of the feelings scales has a similar effect regardless of the format of the ad, pooling tests were conducted for A_{ad} and A_b (Neter & Wasserman, 1974). The constrained models included a dummy variable for each ad, a dummy variable for each ad format, prior A_b, and the four feelings scales. The R-square of the constrained model for A_{ad}, was .59, and the R-square for A_b was .55. The unconstrained models, which allowed the impact of the feelings scales on A_{ad} and A_b to vary by the format of the ad, did not result in significantly more variance being explained than the constrained models (for A_{ad}: $R^2 = .60$, $F_{add} = 1.347$; for A_b: $R^2 = .56$, $F_{add} = .943$). This indicates that feelings have the same impact on A_{ad} and A_b regardless of whether the format of the television ad is a storyboard, an animatic, or the finished form. Hypothesis 1 is supported.

Level of Feelings Across Formats

Analysis of covariance (ANCOVA) was used to test Hypotheses 2 and 3. Tests of the main effect of format (storyboard, animatic, or finished) on the level of overall feelings experienced used the between-subjects error sum of squares. Tests of differences among ads and tests of the format by ad interaction used the within-subject error sum of squares. The covariate was prior attitude toward the brand.

Hypothesis 2 predicts that the animatic versions of television commercials will elicit more feelings than the storyboards will. Hypothesis 3 predicts that the finished version of an ad will elicit more feelings than its animatic version. To assess the extent to which subjects generated feelings (rather than the nature of these feelings) the scores from all 63 items on the feelings inventory were summed into an overall feelings measure. The ANCOVA of this overall feelings measure indicates that ad format is insignificant ($F = 1.56, p > .10$). The interaction of format by ad, however, is significant ($F = 3.96, p < .001$), indicating that, for some ads, the influence of format on the aggregate level of feelings generated is significant.

Further inspection of these results, which essentially disconfirm the main effect of format predicted in Hypotheses 2 and 3, proved enlightening. We reasoned that, since some ads elicit low aggregate levels of feelings, even in the finished form, it is unlikely that significantly fewer feelings would be generated in response to the preproduction forms of those ads. However, the preproduction versions of the finished ads that generate high overall feelings levels should generate significantly lower overall feelings than their finished form. In other words, unless the final version of an ad elicits feelings, no other version of the ad is expected to elicit feelings. If the final version elicits high levels of feelings, the preproduction versions of the ad will underestimate the level of feelings of the final form.

To test this more explicit form of Hypotheses 2 and 3, which contrast the two preproduction versions of the ad with the final version, we first analyzed whether the finished form of the ads used in this study varied significantly in the extent of feelings that were generated by the subjects. Three of the ads elicited significantly higher levels of overall feelings in their finished form ($\bar{x} = 124.63$) than did the other three ads ($\bar{x} = 100.70$). The storyboard version of the three "high feelings" ads generated a significantly lower level of overall feelings than the finished form ($F = 4.35, p < .05$). Comparing animatics and the finished form, the difference in the extent of feelings generated was not significant ($F = .46$). A similar analysis was conducted for the "low feelings" ads. No differences due to format were found. The overall feelings scores are displayed in Table 11.2.

Table 11.2
Total Feelings Means

Ad Format	High Feeling Ads (n=3)	Low Feeling Ads (n=3)
Storyboards	116.00^a	107.64^a
Animatics	133.19^b	115.77^a
Finished	124.63^b	100.70^a

Note: Total Feelings score is the sum of the response to all of the feelings items. The range of possible values are 63 to 315.

Values in a column with the same superscript are not significantly different from one another ($p < .05$), while those with different superscripts are significantly different.

Thus, we find support for our revised, more explicit form of Hypothesis 2 but not for the revised version of Hypothesis 3. Storyboards underestimate the overall level of feelings that are actually generated by finished ads when the finished form of the ad is one that generates a relatively high level of feelings. Animatics, however, accurately predict the high level of overall feelings for these ads. When the ads were ones that generated low levels of overall feelings in their final form, both storyboards and animatics yielded accurate estimates of the level of feelings.

Supplementary Analysis—Specific Feelings Types

We investigated the ad by format interaction further. We ran the ANCOVA model described above twice for each feelings scale—once for those finished ads that generated a high level of the particular feeling and a second time for those finished ads that generated a low level of that feeling. These results are presented below for each of the feelings scales.

An additional interesting issue is whether the pretest feelings scores can be used to predict whether the final form of an ad will generate a high or a low level of each type of feelings. In order to examine the discriminating power of feelings responses to storyboards and animatics, discriminant analysis was used. Of the subjects who saw the storyboards or the animatics, half were used to derive the discriminant functions. Data from the other half of these subjects were used for the classification analysis. The goal was to classify ads rather than respondents. Thus, each ad was classified as one that would generate either a high level or a low level of each type of feeling based on the average response to the finished form of the ad. Two discriminant analyses are presented for each feelings scale: one for the responses to the storyboard and one using the feelings generated by the animatics.

Upbeat feelings. The finished form of two ads generated significantly greater upbeat feelings scores than the other four ads. The ANCOVA for the two high upbeat feelings ads showed a significant difference owing to format ($F = 3.47$;

Figure 11.1
Upbeat Feelings

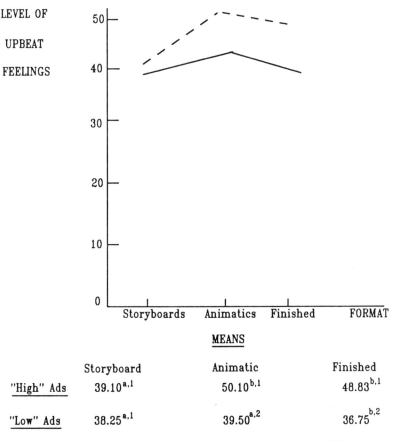

MEANS

	Storyboard	Animatic	Finished
"High" Ads	$39.10^{a,1}$	$50.10^{b,1}$	$48.83^{b,1}$
"Low" Ads	$38.25^{a,1}$	$39.50^{a,2}$	$36.75^{b,2}$

Notes: Means with the same letter superscript in a *row* are not significantly different from one another, while those with different letter superscripts in a row are significantly different ($p<.05$). Means with the same number superscript in a *column* are not significantly different from one another, but those with a different number in a column are significantly different. Comparisons are not to be made on the diagonal.

$p < .05$). For these ads, storyboards resulted in significantly lower upbeat feelings scores ($\bar{x} = 39.10$) than the finished ads ($\bar{x} = 48.83$), whereas animatics ($\bar{x} = 50.10$) were equivalent to the finished form in generating upbeat feelings. For the four low upbeat feelings ads, the effect of format was not significant ($F = .32$). These results are presented graphically in Figure 11.1.

Discriminant analysis was used to examine whether the upbeat feelings scores of the subjects who saw storyboards or animatics could distinguish between high upbeat feelings ads and low upbeat feelings ads. The two finished ads that generated high upbeat feelings were categorized as the high upbeat feelings ads, and the remaining four ads were classified as the low upbeat feelings ads.

The results of the discriminant analysis for storyboards indicates that upbeat feelings scores cannot distinguish ads that generate many upbeat feelings in their final form from ads that will generate few upbeat feelings (chi-square = .22, p = .64). Only three of the six ads could be correctly classified. In the case of animatics, however, the upbeat feelings score is significant in discriminating between high and low upbeat feelings ads (chi-square = 3.97, p <.05). All of the ads were correctly classified using the upbeat feelings scores generated by the animatic version of the ads.

Storyboards underestimate the extent of the upbeat feelings generated by a finished ad and are not able to predict whether a finished ad will generate a high or low level of upbeat feelings. Animatics perform much better. Not only can they predict whether the finished ad will generate a high or low level of upbeat feelings, animatics can also accurately estimate how high or how low the upbeat feelings generated will be.

Warm feelings. The finished form of two ads elicited significantly greater warm feelings scores than the other four ads. The ANCOVA for the two high warm feelings ads showed a significant difference by format (F = 7.54, p <.001): storyboards resulted in significantly lower warm feelings scores ($\bar{x}$ = 27.81) than the finished ads ($\bar{x}$ = 37.85), whereas the warm feelings scores elicited by animatics ($\bar{x}$ = 37.48) were equal to those generated by the finished ads. For the four ads generating low warm feelings scores, the effect of format was not significant (F = .58). Figure 11.2 displays these results.

The discriminant analysis for storyboards indicates that warm feelings scores can distinguish ads that generate high levels of warm feelings in their final form from ads that will generate low levels of warm feelings (chi-square = 15.90, p <.0001). Five of the six ads were correctly classified using the warm feelings scores elicited from the storyboards. The warm feelings scores from the subjects seeing the animatics could also discriminate between high warm feelings ads and low warm feelings ads (chi-square = 21.12, p <.0001. All of the ads were correctly classified using the warm feelings scores generated by the animatic version of the ads.

Although the storyboards underestimate the level of warm feelings that are generated by a finished ad, the storyboard reactions do predict when a finished ad will generate a high level of warm feelings. Animatics predict not only whether warm feelings generated by the finished form will be high or low, but also can accurately estimate how high or how low the warm feelings generated will be.

Uneasy feelings. One finished ad generated significantly higher uneasy feelings scores than the other five ads. There was no animatic version of this ad, so comparisons are made only between the storyboard and the finished version of the ad. The ANCOVA for the high uneasy feelings ad showed no difference owing to format (F = .80). Figure 11.3 shows that subjects generated as many uneasy feelings to the storyboard version of the ad ($\bar{x}$ = 32.77) as to the finished

Figure 11.2
Warm Feelings

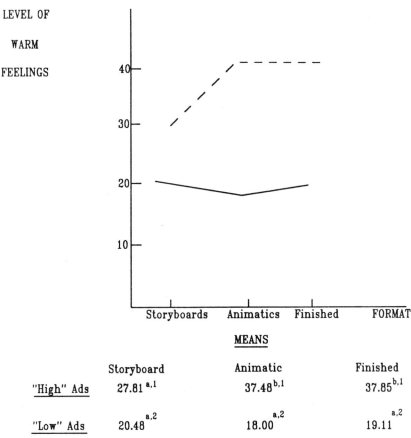

LEVEL OF

WARM

FEELINGS

MEANS

	Storyboard	Animatic	Finished
"High" Ads	27.81 [a,1]	37.48 [b,1]	37.85 [b,1]
"Low" Ads	20.48 [a,2]	18.00 [a,2]	19.11 [a,2]

Note: Means with the same letter superscript in a *row* are not significantly different from one another, while those with different letter superscripts in a row are significantly different (p<.05). Means with the same number superscript in a *column* are not significantly different from one another, but those with a different number in a column are significantly different. Comparisons are not to be made on the diagonal.

ad ($\bar{x} = 36.11$). The effect of format was also insignificant for the five low uneasy feelings ads ($F = 1.82$).

The discriminant analysis for storyboards indicates that uneasy feelings scores are significant in distinguishing the high uneasy feelings ad from the low uneasy feelings ads (chi-square = 15.28, $p < .0001$). All six of the ads could be correctly classified as high uneasy feelings ads or as low uneasy feelings ads using the discriminant function derived from the storyboard data.

Storyboards are good predictors of the amount of uneasy feelings that the finished ads will elicit. The uneasy feelings scores from subjects seeing the

Figure 11.3
Uneasy Feelings

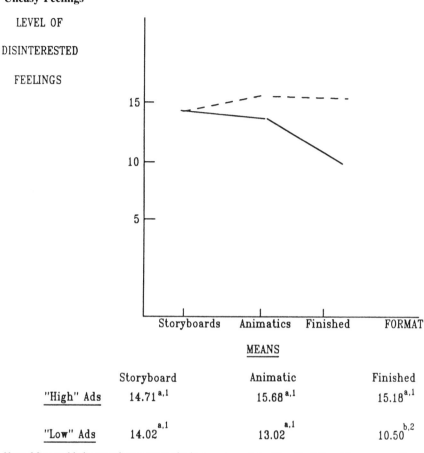

LEVEL OF

DISINTERESTED

FEELINGS

MEANS

	Storyboard	Animatic	Finished
"High" Ads	14.71[a,1]	15.68[a,1]	15.18[a,1]
"Low" Ads	14.02[a,1]	13.02[a,1]	10.50[b,2]

Note: Means with the same letter superscript in a *row* are not significantly different from one another, while those with different letter superscripts in a row are significantly different (p<.05). Means with the same number superscript in a *column* are not significantly different from one another, but those with a different number in a column are significantly different. Comparisons are not to be made on the diagonal.

storyboards indicated whether the finished ads would generate a high or a low level of uneasy feelings. The uneasy feelings scores from the storyboards were also accurate in estimating how high or how low the uneasy feelings scores would be.

Disinterested feelings. The finished form of two ads generated significantly greater disinterested feelings scores than the other four ads. Using an ANCOVA to analyze the two high disinterested feelings ads, differences in the disinterested feelings scores owing to format were not significant ($F = .15$): storyboards ($\bar{x} = 14.71$) and animatics ($\bar{x} = 15.68$) were equivalent to the finished form

Figure 11.4
Disinterested Feelings

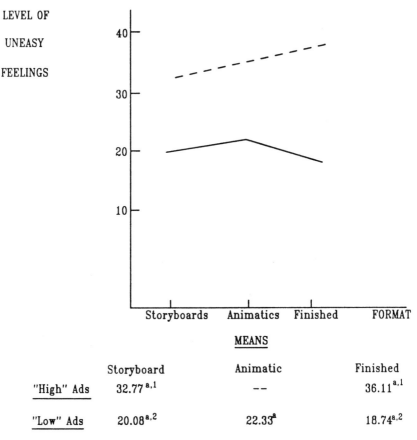

MEANS

	Storyboard	Animatic	Finished
"High" Ads	32.77 [a,1]	--	36.11 [a,1]
"Low" Ads	20.08 [a,2]	22.33 [a]	18.74 [a,2]

Note: Means with the same letter superscript in a *row* are not significantly different from one another, while those with different letter superscripts in a row are significantly different (p<.05). Means with the same number superscripts in a *column* are not significantly different from one another, but those with a different number in a column are significantly different. Comparisons are not to be made on the diagonal.

($\bar{x}$ = 15.18). For the low disinterested feelings ads, the effect of format was significant (F = 5.16, p <.01): both storyboards ($\bar{x}$ = 14.02) and animatics ($\bar{x}$ = 13.02) predicted higher levels of disinterested feelings than subjects experienced while viewing the finished ads ($\bar{x}$ = 10.50). Figure 11.4 presents these results graphically.

The discriminant analysis of the storyboard data indicates that the disinterested feelings generated by storyboards cannot discriminate between finished ads that result in high levels of disinterested feelings and those that result in low levels of disinterested feelings (chi-square = .04, p = .83). The discriminant function derived using the animatic data is more encouraging. The discriminant function is significant (chi-square $= 4.10$, $p < .05$); however, one-third of the ads were misclassified for both the storyboards and the animatics.

Storyboards are not able to predict whether a finished ad will generate a high or a low level of disinterested feelings. Animatics are only slightly better in making this prediction. With both the storyboards and the animatics, disinterested feelings are overestimated for finished ads that generate few disinterested feelings.

Brand Claim Recall

Analysis of covariance, as described above, was used to test the informal hypothesis regarding variability in brand claims recall across ad formats. The number of brand claims correctly recalled varied significantly by format ($F = 3.39$, $p < .05$). Subjects recalled more correct claims when the stimulus was a storyboard ($\bar{x} = 2.0$) than when the stimulus was an animatic ($\bar{x} = 1.7$) or the finished version of the ad ($\bar{x} = 1.5$); the difference in number of correct claims recalled between animatics and the finished versions is not significant.

The analysis of the specific feelings types described above led to a related question regarding brand claims recall: Do subjects recall claims better if the ads do not generate high levels of feelings? In other words, do feelings get in the way of recall? To investigate this issue, we again used ANCOVA and contrasted the high feelings ads to the low feelings ads (as described above). The findings were consistent with the overall findings: Significantly more correct claims were recalled for storyboards than for either animatics or the finished versions of the ad for both high feelings ads ($F = 2.62$, $p < .08$) and low feelings ads ($F = 2.76$, $p < .07$). We also explored this issue for ads that generated high and low levels of each feelings type. Importantly, there were no significant differences in the recall of correct brand claims that could be explained by the interaction of format and level of specific feeling type. Thus, the level of feelings—overall feelings or specific feelings type—that are generated by an ad does not influence the number of correct claims that are recalled for any of the three formats investigated here. There is a main effect of format, however, which suggests that the ads used in this study do not differ from the stimuli used in past research in some fundamentally important way which could have biased our results.

DISCUSSION

The Structure of Feelings

Adding several items to the feelings inventory to capture feelings associated with fear resulted in a four-factor structure for feelings rather than the three-factor structure that had been found in earlier research (Burke & Edell, 1989;

Edell & Burke, 1987). The three factors identified earlier were upbeat feelings, warm feelings, and negative feelings. The four-factor structure includes upbeat and warm feelings but distinguishes between two types of negative feelings: feelings of disinterest (e.g., bored, critical, dull) and feelings of uneasiness (e.g., tense, edgy, concerned). We expect that this distinction will be an important one because, although both types of feelings are negative, uneasy feelings might very well have a positive impact on attitudes—both the attitude toward the ad and the attitude toward the brand or position advocated in the ad (as was the case for our antismoking ad). Advertisers may intend for ads to generate uneasy feelings, but it is hard to imagine their designing ads to generate disinterested feelings. It is important, therefore, that tests of advertising effectiveness distinguish between the two types of negative feelings as well as between the two types of positive feelings and between positive and negative feelings.

The Influence of Feelings Across Formats

The fact that the influence of feelings on A_{ad} and A_b did not differ by format is also encouraging. Our results indicate that preproduction versions of television ads can be used to assess the nature of the influence of feelings on preproduction A_{ad} and A_b. Preproduction versions of a television ad, however, will not always generate the same overall level of feelings that the final ad will.

Feelings Levels Across Formats

High feelings ads. The upbeat, warm, and disinterested feelings responses to animatic versions of ads predicted the level of those feelings responses to the finished version of the ads. (There was no animatic version of the ad that generated high levels of uneasy feelings.) Storyboard responses were able to predict high levels of disinterested and uneasy feelings.

These results have important implications for testing advertising. For instance, if the ad in question was designed to elicit high levels of the positive feelings (i.e., upbeat and warm feelings), storyboard responses would be a misleading indicator of how well the final version of the ad would perform. One could get a good idea of the likely positive emotional reactions to the finished version by testing an animatic, however. On the other hand, one can determine whether the finished version of an ad will generate high levels of disinterested feelings or uneasy feelings at the storyboard stage. Apparently, even the addition of audio and video cannot overcome a fundamental level of disinterest or obscure uneasy feelings for the ads that scored high on the negative feelings. This may be due to the particular ad, the brand, or perhaps the product category. It would be useful to examine this issue more completely in the future and to account for factors such as category knowledge or interest, brand usage, and so forth.

Low feelings ads. When the final version of an ad scores low on upbeat, warm, or uneasy feelings, both the storyboard and the animatic version of the ad score low as well. Thus, low levels of these feelings can be reliably predicted with the least rich (and least expensive) form of the ad. The story is different for ads that score low on disinterested feelings; for these ads, storyboards and animatics overestimate the level of disinterested feelings that will be generated by the final version of the ad. For ads of this type, the additional richness provided by audio and video does ameliorate disinterest. Advertisers must take care, therefore, in evaluating disinterested feelings that are generated in response to storyboards and animatics because the finished version of the ad may actually generate a lower level of disinterested feelings.

Discriminatory power of format. In addition to differing in how well they could predict the overall levels of particular types of feelings that would be generated by the finished version of a television ad, the two preproduction formats also differed in how well they could discriminate between ads that would elicit high and low levels of particular types of feelings. Storyboards can distinguish ads that will generate high rather than low levels of warm and uneasy feelings but not high or low levels of upbeat or disinterested feelings. Responses to animatic versions of television commercials are able to discriminate between ads that will generate high and low levels of upbeat, warm, and disinterested feelings in their final form, although the data are less equivocal for disinterested feelings. (Again, remember that there was no animatic version of the ad that scored high on uneasy feelings.)

CONCLUSIONS

These results provide two important contributions. First, a fourth feelings factor—uneasy feelings—was identified. This is an interesting factor because it is a negative feeling that could easily have a positive effect on attitude. Second, the results provide insight into the applicability of using preproduction versions of television ads to assess the probable feelings responses to the finished version of the ads. We recommend that storyboards be used with caution but are encouraged about the potential of animatics for evaluating emotional responses. The findings, of course, are tentative and subject to certain limitations. Subjects saw the ads only once, and ad exposure and testing were conducted in a laboratory environment.

The findings do, however, suggest interesting hypotheses for the future that go beyond replication. For instance, it seems that the richness that comes from the addition of audio and video enhances the ability of the stimulus to generate high levels of feelings. Understanding what that richness actually adds would provide useful information regarding the design of advertisements in general. D. A. Aaker and J. G. Myers (1987) state that ads must elicit empathy and have verisimilitude in order to generate feelings. Does audio and video richness provide these features? An especially intriguing issue is whether there are individual difference variables that might explain feelings responses to the preproduction versions of television ads or explain assessments of empathy or verisimilitude of the preproduction versions. For instance, people who are visualizers rather than verbalizers (Childers, Houston, & Heckler, 1985) may generate as many feelings in response to a storyboard as they do to the finished version of an ad.

REFERENCES

Aaker, D. A., & Myers, J. G. (1987). *Advertising management* (3rd ed.). Englewood Cliffs, NJ: Prentice-Hall.

Aaker, D. A., Stayman, D. M., & Vezina, R. (1988). Identifying feelings elicited by advertising. *Psychology and Marketing, 5* (1), 1–16.

Burke, M. C., & Edell, J. A. (1989). The impact of feelings on ad-based affect and cognition. *Journal of Marketing Research, 26* (1), 69–83.

Chaiken, S., & Eagly, A. H. (1976). Communication modality as a determinant of message persuasiveness and message comprehension. *Journal of Personality and Social Psychology, 34*, 605–614.

Chaiken, S., & Eagly, A. H. (1983). Communication modality as a determinant of persuasion: The role of communicator salience. *Journal of Personality and Social Psychology, 45* (2), 241–256.

Childers, T. L., Houston, M. J., & Heckler, S. E. (1985). Measurement of individual differences in visual versus verbal information processing. *Journal of Consumer Research, 12* (2), 125–134.

Dabbs, J., & Leventhal, H. (1966). Effects of varying the recommendations in a fear-arousing communication. *Journal of Personality and Social Psychology, 4*, 525–531.

Edell, J. A., & Burke, M. C. (1987). The power of feelings in understanding advertising effects. *Journal of Consumer Research, 14* (3), 421–433.

Holbrook, M. B., & Batra, R. (1986). *Assessing the role of emotions as mediators of consumer responses to advertising.* (Research Working Paper No. 86–AV–10), Columbia University.

Izard, C. E. (1972). *Patterns of emotions.* New York: Academic Press.

Jacoby, J., Hoyer, W. D., & Zimmer, M. R. (1983). To read, view, or listen? A cross-media comparison of comprehension. In J. H. Leigh & C. R. Martin, Jr. (Eds.), *Current issues and research in advertising* (pp. 201–217). Ann Arbor, MI: University of Michigan.

Liu, S. S., & Stout, P. A. (1987). Effects of message modality and appeal on advertising acceptance. *Psychology and Marketing, 4* (3), 167–187.

Neter, J., & Wasserman, W. (1974). *Applied linear statistical models: Regression, analysis of variance, and experimental designs.* Homewood, IL: Irwin.

Ray, M. L., & Wilkie, W. L. (1970). Fear: The potential of an appeal neglected by marketing. *Journal of Marketing, 34*, 54–62.

Reeves, B., Thorson, E., Rothschild, M. L., McDonald, D., Goldstein, R., & Hirsch, J. (1985). Attention to television: Intrastimulus effects of movements and scene changes on alpha variation over time. *International Journal of Neuroscience, 25*, 241–256.

Rossiter, J. R. (1982). Visual imagery: Applications to advertising. In A. A. Mitchell (Ed.), *Advances in consumer research* (vol. 9, pp. 101–106). Ann Arbor, MI: Association for Consumer Research.

Schlinger, M. J., & Green, L. (1980). Art-work storyboards versus finished commercials. *Journal of Advertising Research, 20* (6), 19–23.

Stephens, D. L., & Russo, J. E. (1987). *Predicting post-advertising attitudes.* Working paper, University of Maryland.

Warshaw, P. R. (1978). Application of selective attention theory to television advertising displays. *Journal of Applied Psychology, 63* (3), 366–372.

Winer, B. J. (1971). *Statistical principles in experimental design* (2nd ed.). New York: McGraw-Hill.

12

Does What We See Influence How We Feel? Felt Emotions Versus Depicted Emotions in Television Commercials

Patricia A. Stout, Pamela M. Homer, and Scott S. Liu

Research on the role of feelings and emotion in consumer response to advertising has examined emotion using such global measures as attitude toward the ad (e.g., Gardner, 1985), different categories of affective responses evoked by ads (Batra & Ray, 1986), specifically defined advertising effects such as warmth (Aaker, Stayman, & Hagerty, 1986), and various classifications of basic emotional categories (Havlena & Holbrook, 1986; Holbrook & Batra, 1987). Recent research has investigated differences in advertising effectiveness as a result of the kinds of emotions elicited and ad evaluations (Edell & Burke, 1987). Much of this work has focused on such topics as the relative impact of differences in advertising appeals and the attempts to categorize ads as informational/transformational, warm/irritating, factual/emotional, and so forth.

However, previous work has not explored how ads categorized as representing a specific appeal might elicit certain types of emotions or feelings. Although a possible solution may lie in specific executional factors, our intent here is not to examine such variables. Rather, we are interested in the relationship between the emotions depicted in television commercials and the emotions elicited as personally felt by viewers.

From a practical standpoint, ads (especially emotional appeals such as ''warm'' ads) are created with the intent of eliciting specific emotional responses. The present study sought to enhance understanding of the role of emotional response in advertising by focusing on the following research questions. Is there a difference between emotions individuals see portrayed in the commercial and their own personal feelings? Does this pair of feelings possess distinct dimensions? Does a difference exist for all emotions or just for specific types (e.g., joy but not sadness or guilt)? Are some emotions portrayed in ads "reflected" by the viewer with less distortion than others? And, how do these emotions impact viewers' attitudes and behavioral responses?

BACKGROUND

The psychological literature reporting on the relationship of facial expressions and expressed emotions provides a framework for conceptualizing the relationship between the emotions depicted in a commercial and those felt personally by the viewer. Two decades of research on individual nonverbal cues such as gaze, body movement, and facial expression have established that these cues are often closely tied to emotions and that they can dramatically affect the nature of social interaction (Riggio & Friedman, 1986). G. W. Allport (1961) considered expressive behavior to be the most important element in person perception. Because expressive behavior is likely to have a marked impact on the social reality that emerges between people, the topic has figured prominently in research on face-to-face interaction (see Goffman, 1959, 1971; Rosenthal, 1979).

Television commercials are actually a special case of face-to-face interaction since the combination of sight, sound, and movement can place the viewer in the midst of the action of the commercial. Television commercials may possess a unique ability to capitalize on the potential powers of various nonverbal communication cues, but essentially all media can derive benefits from the effective utilization of nonverbal cues. Nonverbal cues are often suggested as a method of attracting a particular audience, for communicating feelings, for designating the source of the information, and for showing information about the brand's attributes and benefits (Edell, 1988).

This chapter focuses on facial expression nonverbal cues; however, it is acknowledged that the scope of behavioral expression is much broader than facial expressions alone.

Facial Expression and Emotion

That emotional states could be differentiated by postural and facial expression is a long accepted belief. Actors at the Dionysian Theatre some 2,500 years ago wore facial masks from which the audience inferred the actors' emotional states or dispositions (Cacioppo & Petty, 1979). Charles Darwin's (1872) collected observations of emotional expressions provided evidence for universal facial patterns in emotion and suggested a functional importance to the various patterns. Although Darwin's assumptions about the sequence of facial expression and prior unanalyzable feelings is outdated as a theory of emotion (see Candland, Fell, Keen, Leshner, Plutchik, & Tarpy, 1977), most of his conclusions still apply if one views his book as a history of primitive communicative acts.

S. S. Tomkins (1962, 1963) provided a theoretical rationale for studying the face as a means of understanding personality and emotion. His work greatly influenced both P. Ekman and C. E. Izard. In particular, Ekman's (1977) writings illustrate the secular trend toward viewing facial expressions as communicative acts that categorize broad categories of situations. The interpretation is that these facial movements are correlated with certain situations that often lead to particular "emotional" experiences. As communicative acts, they frequently provide information about the actor's evaluation of the situation.

It is also thought that these expressions probably belong to a large class of behaviors that determine the content and quality of emotions. Thus, research in psychology has attempted to identify the link between facial expression and emotional experience by examining how facial feedback effects are mediated. J. D. Laird (1974) postulates that the quality of emotional expression is mediated by expressive behavior, that is, movements of the face affect mood by means of a self-attribution process. From this perspective, facial feedback effects may be regarded as a special case of S. Schachter's (1964) theory of emotion, which views emotional arousal as undifferentiated; our experience of a particular emotion, it is argued, comes from interpretation of situational cues. Alternatively, Schachter's views can be recast in the language of self-perception theory (Bem, 1972).

Others (e.g., Laird, 1984) have shown that the act of physically expressing an emotion (like happiness through smiling) can mediate the experience of the emotion. The facial feedback theorists (e.g., Ekman, Friesen, & Ancoli, 1980; Izard, 1971, 1977; Tomkins, 1962, 1963) contend that proprioceptive and cutaneous feedback from the face is capable of fostering categorical affective experiences. This theory postulates that we experience discrete, differentiated emotions via feedback from innately patterned facial expressions. Recent research utilizes electromyographic (EMG) responses to provide a powerful supplement to the verbal and more overt behavioral responses used in studies of affective reactions (Cacioppo, Petty, Losch, & Kim, 1986; Schwartz, Fair, Salt, Mardel, & Klerman, 1976).

Thus, theory suggests that the response to emotions depicted in a commercial may mediate viewers' felt emotions toward the commercial. This mechanism may work in one of two ways. By inclusion of, for example, babies or puppies in the commercial, the physical act of a smiling response by the viewer may mediate her or his feelings of happiness, leading to a felt happy emotional response. In another way, by seeing happy, smiling characters portrayed in a commercial, the viewer may respond to this communicative act by feeling happy herself or himself and, perhaps, by also smiling (as an additional mediator of the felt emotional response). Therefore, the use of human models may provide a more meaningful social context for the product in commercials by arousing more emotional and attitudinal reflections from viewers who pay greater attention to the commercial (Kanungo & Pang, 1973). Affect transfer (Gresham & Shimp, 1985; Holbrook & Batra, 1987) suggests that these pleasant feelings would be attached or transferred to the ad and the brand.

RESEARCH HYPOTHESES AND RATIONALE

There is a widespread assumption that facial expression can be used by individuals to infer the emotional experiences of others with a reasonable degree of accuracy. One growing stream of research in psychology focuses on the accuracy of identification of facial expression for establishing which emotion is being experienced at the moment of facial expression. Generalization of findings from studies is limited by several design problems (Wagner, MacDonald, & Manstead, 1986), yet ample research has acknowledged and investigated the link between (1) the emotional quality of the stimulus (or the emotion portrayed) and (2) the accurate identification of this depicted emotion. Our review of the literature failed to locate evidence that examines the relationship between identifying the emotion portrayed and the emotion personally felt by the receiver. In this chapter, the aim is to explore the relationship between the emotion shown (emotional quality of the stimulus) and its identification by the receiver, and the emotion personally felt by the receiver.

The current study further examines the notion of three different ways an individual can interact with advertising (Stout, 1985; Stout & Leckenby, 1984, 1985, 1986). Previous research analyzing open-end verbatims indicates three different modes of emotional response to television commercials (i.e., experiential, empathic, and descriptive). Here we first look at *personally felt* emotions expressed by respondents (i.e., experiential emotional response) versus emotions recognized as *depicted in the commercial* (i.e., descriptive emotional response). With an aim of validation, we use adjective checklists to explore whether these are two different constructs. If they are different, we are concerned about whether the differences are systematic for all emotions.

The following exploratory hypothesis was developed after a review of the facial expression literature:

> *Hypothesis 1*: Emotions depicted in commercials and personally felt emotions represent distinct constructs.

Consensus regarding conclusions resulting from previous studies on the use of facial expressions to communicate emotional experiences is limited by several design issues (see Wagner, MacDonald, & Manstead, 1986). However, there is some agreement among findings indicating greater accuracy of identification for basic or primary emotions, such as happiness, surprise, fear, sadness, anger, and disgust (see Ekman & Friesen, 1975; Ekman, Friesen, & Ellsworth, 1972; Izard, 1971). There also tends to be a greater match between sender and receiver when emotional dimensions (such as pleasant/unpleasant or positive/negative affect) are examined in contrast to discrete categories of emotion (like disgust versus sadness) (Winton, 1986).

A second research question looks at the relative impact of these two emotional response modes on dependent measures including attitude toward the ad, brand attitudes, and purchase intentions. Several studies have looked specifically at emotional response to television advertising. Using verbal measures, R. Batra and M. L. Ray (1986) delineated three categories of affective response (SEVA, Deactivation, and social affection), which were thought to mediate response to advertising. They appear to be antecedents of attitude toward the ad (A_{ad}) and to have a weak but significant impact on brand attitudes. Using both verbal and physiological measures, D. Aaker, D. M. Stayman, and M. R. Hagerty (1986) investigated "warmth" (defined as a positive, mild emotion). They reported that enhanced warmth had a positive impact on attitude toward the ad and purchase likelihood; however, warmth did not have a similar positive influence on recall.

Specific dimensions of emotion, such as pleasure, arousal, and domination, have also been found to mediate the effects of ad content on A_{ad} (Holbrook & Batra, 1987). Additionally, these three dimensions along with A_{ad} partially mediate the effects of ad content on attitude toward the brand (A_b). Examination of positive and negative feelings (Edell & Burke, 1987) indicates that these feelings co-occur and that such feelings influence beliefs about the brand as well as A_{ad} and A_b. The emotional quality of the stimulus, in this case the extent to which the ads were informational or transformational, also had an effect on the feelings generated (Edell & Burke, 1987).

Previous research does suggest that emotional responses personally felt by the viewer have an impact on response to an advertising message. Attention has tended to focus on various general "dimensions" of emotion, however. Furthermore, there is evidence that the emotional quality of the stimulus influences the advertising response (e.g., Edell & Burke, 1987). Based on this review of the literature, we propose that:

> *Hypothesis* 2: Emotions will contribute to explaining variance in advertising effects (i.e., A_{ad}, brand attitudes, and purchase intent).

Previous research provides little guidance for postulating the relative importance of depicted emotions versus personally felt emotions. Personally felt or "experiential" emotions are thought to be more self-relevant depending upon the individual's interpretation of the event as it relates to the meaning he or she assigns to it (Stout & Leckenby, 1986). Thus, we would expect these feelings to be "deeper" than simple recognition of depicted emotions and to contribute more to explaining the variance in advertising effects.

> Hypothesis 3: Personally felt emotions will be more important in explaining advertising effectiveness (i.e., A_{ad}, brand attitudes, and purchase intent).

Advertising executions are created to elicit different responses from viewers. Intuition and classical conditioning learning theory would suggest that commercials with a more emotional appeal (as compared to an informational or factual appeal) are designed to elicit emotions from viewers that reflect those depicted on the screen.

Hypothesis 4: Emotions will be more important in explaining the effects of emotional versus factual executions.

METHOD

Overview of Variables

Two levels of the single independent variable, type of appeal, were created by selecting one emotional commercial and one factual commercial for the same brand of instant coffee. The dependent measures included emotional responses, attitudes toward the ad, brand attitudes, and behavioral intent.

Pretest

Six pairs of professional television commercials (aired prior to the experiment) were selected as potential stimulus materials based on the criteria that each pair contained alternative executions for the same brand. Initially, six graduate advertising students were invited to rate each of the twelve commercials on a seven-point "primarily factual" to "primarily emotional" scale. The two pairs that were perceived to be most different were then evaluated by 20 undergraduate students from the same population as the experimental sample. These students rated the information content of the four commercials on four seven-point bipolar scales (tangible/intangible, logical/emotional, objective/subjective, factual/nonfactual). They also evaluated each ad in terms of overall tone and degree of liking. Examination of these judgments indicated that the two commercials for a brand of instant coffee best represented the emotional/factual dimension distinction. Specifically, the emotional appeal was rated as being more emotional/intangible/nonfactual/subjective (alpha = .94, t (36) = 5.96, p <.001). The two executions also varied in terms of overall tone (t (36) = 5.8, p <.001) but did not elicit differing levels of affect (t (36) = 1.7, ns).

Subjects

A total of 213 male and female undergraduate students volunteered to participate in the main experiment. Subjects were randomly assigned to one level of the experimental manipulation (i.e., type of commercial appeal).

Procedure

The experiment was administered in groups of approximately 25 subjects per session. First, each participant was told to read an instruction sheet that asked him or her to view the commercial in "a natural, relaxed way as if he/she were in his/her own home." Then each group was exposed to one of the two professionally produced television commercials for the same brand of instant coffee. The ads were essentially equivalent in terms of production quality, length (both were 30-second spots), and musical tone (i.e., the music served a background role).

After viewing the commercial, respondents completed a questionnaire containing the dependent variables of interest. Participants were debriefed and thanked for their cooperation at the conclusion of the experiment.

The administrator was blind to the hypotheses, and the groups were exposed to one of the two appeals randomly.

Stimulus materials. The two commercials were professional, 30-second television spots. The scenario in the emotional appeal involved a couple returning home late at night from a costume party. It is apparent that they have had an enjoyable evening and that they care deeply for each other. After "toying" with his costume hat, they make a pot of coffee to share by the fire.

The factual appeal presents a bust shot of a male talking to the camera about coffee. There are shots of a fire and a coffee pot to symbolize the key copy point, deep roasted coffee beans.

Dependent variables. The two identical emotional response scales each consisted of 23 items. Emotion items were selected primarily from the Differential Emotions Scale (DES) (Izard, 1971, 1977). The DES is a self-report instrument designed to assess an individual's experience of fundamental emotions, including interest, joy, distress, shyness, surprise, fear, guilt, and anger. Only items reflecting the first five emotions (plus their synonyms) were included in the checklist. The three extremely negative emotions (i.e., fear, guilt, and anger) were excluded because it was deemed unlikely that subjects would experience these emotions in response to the types of commercials tested.

The DES and other similar checklists use affective word prompts as an aided-recall measure. These cues have enhanced the accessibility of past emotional experiences in studies of autobiographical memory retrieval (Robinson, 1976, 1980). Self-report instruments based on versions of the DES scale descriptors have also been shown to coincide with external observations of emotional facial expressions (Ekman et al., 1980).

The checklist also incorporated emotion or feeling items used or suggested in previous research (e.g., Batra & Ray, 1986; Stout & Leckenby, 1984, 1985; Wells, Leavitt, & McConville, 1971). These included "vigor" or "surgency" related items (i.e., playful and amused) and "sensuousness" and "deactivation" related items (i.e., tender, relaxed, and quiet and their opposites, uneasy and tense).

Respondents completed the scale first in response to (1) how they personally felt while watching the commercial and (2) how they felt the words corresponded to the emotions depicted in the commercial (i.e., the items were identical, but the focus changed). Attitudes toward the ad were assessed with three semantic-differential measures (good/bad, foolish/wise, and convincing/not convincing) as were brand attitudes (good/bad, dislike/like, and favorable/unfavorable). Purchase intent was also evaluated in terms of likely/unlikely along with measures of product and brand usage and familiarity. The emotional response items and other dependent measures were assessed via six-point and seven-point continuums, respectively.

RESULTS

Consistent with the pretest evaluations, a Multivariate Analysis of Variance (MANOVA) involving the number of emotions checked as being personally felt and the number checked as being depicted in the ad identified differences between the two commercial executions (Wilks' lambda (2,214 = .960, p = .012). Those exposed to the emotional execution checked more emotions as being personally felt (mean = 13.32) and more ad-depicted emotions (mean = 14.54) than those shown the factual execution (means = 11.68 and 12.18, respectively). A second MANOVA indicated that the two executions also differed in their ability to evoke enhanced ratings on the emotion items as measured by the sum of the 23 individual ratings (Wilks' lambda (2,212) = .932, p = .001). Specifically, viewers of the emotional commercial gave a higher rating sum to both the personally felt (mean = 37.05) and ad-depicted (mean = 44.78) emotion scales than the viewers of the factual commercial (means = 29.70 and 34.98, respectively). Thus, it appears that the two commercials do indeed vary in their level of emotional appeal.

A MANOVA incorporating the average rating on the 23 items in each emotion scale also demonstrated that the two commercials varied in their level of emotional appeal (Wilks' lambda (2,212) = .953, p = .006). The average ratings of the emotional execution for the 23 ad-depicted emotions (mean = 2.21) was greater than the average ad-depicted emotion rating for the factual execution (mean = 1.76).

The final set of analyses verifying that the ads differed in terms of their emotional level involved a MANOVA with the 23 ad-depicted emotions as independent variables. Similar to the previous analysis, the vector of means for the 23 items varied between the two commercials (Wilks' lambda (23,182) = .449, p < .001). The emotional appeal was rated on depicting higher emotion levels for tender, playful, amusing, joyful, surprise, elated, merry, exciting, and shy and lower emotion levels for concentration.

Structure of Emotions

The next task was to determine whether experimental emotions (i.e., those personally felt) and descriptive emotions (i.e., emotions depicted in the commercials) are different constructs. A series of analyses was performed to examine this rationale, as proposed in Hypothesis 1. Initially, paired t-tests compared the means for each corresponding pair of emotions (i.e., 23 total pairs) in the two scales. Fourteen of these 23 pairs (61 percent) were significantly different ($p < .01$) and one pair was marginally so ($p < .06$), implying that these are two distinct sets of measures.

As a second test to examine whether the two emotion constructs were distinct, a factor analysis was performed on all 46 variables (23 personally felt emotions and 23 ad-depicted emotions). Seven underlying factors were identified that explained 65.5 percent of the variance (see Table 12.1 for a summary of the analyses). Of these seven factors, two consisted of only personally felt emotions, two consisted of only ad-depicted emotions, and three were a mixture of items from both emotion scales. In the majority of cases on these mixed factors, the corresponding items from the two lists loaded on the same factor (e.g., "surprised" from both the personally felt and ad-depicted scale loaded on factor 5). The factor structure is overall consistent with the proposition that the two sets of measures represent differing constructs; they do not merely provide duplicate information.

Based on the individual factor components and previous research, the seven factors were labeled as "arousal," "alienation," "attention," "warmth," "amusement," "upbeat," and "uneasy." The individual components associated with each factor were summed, thereby yielding seven scales (coefficient alphas = .92, .86, .88, .81, .83, and .75, respectively), which served as input in subsequent analyses.

Impact of Emotions on Advertising Effectiveness

The seven emotion scales created from the factor analysis results were incorporated as the independent variables in a series of regression analyses. Three dependent variables—attitudes toward the ad (alpha = .89), brand attitudes (alpha = .92), and purchase intent—completed the regression input.

The three resulting models reached statistical significance for the total sample, but only the attention emotion scale contributed significantly to explaining the variance across the three models (see Table 12.2). The R^2 was most impressive for the attitude toward the ad (A_{ad}) effectiveness measure and, for this model, the arousal and amusement scales also made important contributions. These results do support Hypothesis 2, but not overwhelmingly.

The overall findings demonstrate only partial support for Hypothesis 3: personally felt emotions will be more important contributors to advertising effectiveness (as measured by A_{ad}, brand attitudes, and purchase intentions) than ad-depicted emotions. The most important scale, attention, is composed of both types of emotions. The second most influential contribution was made by the first identified factor (i.e., arousal), which consisted of seven personally felt emotions. The remaining significant effects were derived from the mixed factor scales.

Table 12.1
Factor Analysis Results

Emotion	Arousal (AR)	Aliena-tion (AL)	Atten-tion (AT)	Warmth (WM)	Amuse-ment (AM)	Up-beat (UP)	Un-easy (UN)
			Factor Loading				
Merry (F)	.806						
Elated (F)	.751						
Joy (F)	.738						
Exciting (F)	.725						
Delighted (F)	.690						
Energized (F)	.662						
Playful (F)	.580						
Insulting (D)		.797					
Confused (D)		.773					
Disappointed (D)		.742					
Tense (D)		.709					
Downhearted (D)		.701					
Uneasy (D)		.636					
Shy (D)		.552					
Attention (F)			.747				
Interest (D)			.727				
Concentrated (F)			.714				
Interest (F)			.688				
Attention (F)			.678				
Concentrated (D)			.615				
Relevant (D)				.833			
Soothing (D)				.797			
Quiet (D)				.774			
Tender (D)				.698			
Quiet (F)				.633			
Relevant (F)				.631			
Playful (D)					.714		
Amusing (D)					.706		
Amusing (F)					.644		
Surprising (F)					.599		
Surprising (D)					.556		
Energizing (D)						.762	
Elated (D)						.681	
Excited (D)						.673	
Merry (D)						.551	
Uneasy (F)							.747
Tense (F)							.691
% Variance Explained	28.6	13.2	7.4	5.7	4.3	3.7	2.7

(F) = personally felt emotion
(D) = depicted emotion

Table 12.2
Summary of Regression Analyses

Dependent Variable	Standardized Coefficients							
	AR	AL	AT	WM	AM	UP	UN	R^2
Total Sample								
A_{ad}	$.34^a$	-.05	$.52^a$	.04	$-.41^a$	-.01	-.06	.44
A_{brand}	$.18^b$	-.07	$.32^a$	-.07	-.09	.15	-.08	.19
BI	$.17^b$	.09	$.33^a$	.01	$-.17^b$	.06	-.12	.19
Emotional Ad								
A_{ad}	$.42^a$	.02	$.52^a$	.09	$-.22^a$	-.08	$-.22^a$	.60
A_{brand}	.16	-.06	$.47^a$	$-.30^a$	-.18	.18	-.04	.25
BI	$.26^b$	-.03	$.35^a$	$-.21^b$	-.19	.03	-.18	.19
Factual Ad								
A_{ad}	$.26^b$	-.18	$.39^a$	.09	-.02	-.02	.01	.27
A_{brand}	$.26^b$	-.16	$.26^a$	.07	-.03	.09	-.11	.20
BI	.03	.20	$.28^a$	$.18^b$	-.03	.10	-.09	.28

a: $p < .05$
b: $p < .10$

Differences Between Executional Appeals

When the regression analyses were replicated for the separate executional subsamples, additional differences did emerge for the contributions made by the emotion scales. The attention emotion factor consistently contributed to the three pairs of analyses. For the emotional commercial, the warmth emotion also proved valuable for explaining brand attitudes. Most impressive were the multiple contributors in the A_{ad} model (i.e., arousal, attention, amusement, and uneasy were significant additions).

The only emotion scale other than attention that helped explain the variance in the A_{ad} and brand attitude effectiveness measures for the factual execution was arousal. Purchase intent was affected significantly only by attention. Overall, these between-execution analyses support that emotional responses play a more important role in accounting for the effects of emotional versus factual appeals, as proposed in Hypothesis 4.

This was further substantiated by a MANOVA incorporating the seven emotion scales. As expected, the emotional appeal elicited more favorable responses for six of the seven scales (Wilks' lambda $(7,194) = .583, p < .001$). Contrary to expectations, the factual ad stimulated enhanced attention levels (F $(1,200) = 4.43, p = .04$). This may have been due to an inaccurate match between the audience and the scenario depicted in the emotional commercial, thus hindering the interest levels among the viewers. Significantly more favorable reactions were identified for the emotional execution in terms of arousal ($p = .003$), amusement ($p < .001$), and upbeat ($p = .017$).

DISCUSSION

It appears that, for certain emotions, there are distinct differences between emotions experienced as personally felt and emotions identified as depicted in the commercial. For example, words like ''depicted merry,'' ''depicted excited,'' and ''depicted energetic'' loaded consistently together on one factor and ''felt merry,'' ''felt excited,'' and ''felt energetic'' loaded together on a second factor. This suggests that, for these basic categories of emotions, what individuals see depicted in the ads does not directly reflect what they feel. For other emotions, however, like ''depicted quiet,'' ''depicted relaxed,'' and ''felt quiet,'' ''felt relaxed,'' a mixed set of emotions loaded together on one factor. This seems to indicate that, for these emotions, the reflection from portrayal to feeling is less distorted. That is, if an ad portrays warm feelings, individuals will feel warm feelings. This interpretation is suggested both intuitively and through empirical research on warmth in advertisements (e.g., Aaker, et al., 1986).

Results of this study further suggest that depicted and personally felt emotions are two distinct constructs, which supports the first hypothesis. Furthermore, the distinction between the two is clearer for some emotions (like the depiction of upbeat feelings and personally felt arousal) than for others. A plausible explanation for these findings may be related to the relationship between the extinction of emotional response in the presence of expression of certain emotions (see Orr & Lanzetta, 1984). For example, fear facial expressions have been found to intensify the emotional reaction, but it is not clear whether happy facial expressions inhibit or intensify emotional reaction.

Results of analyses examining the two different commercial executions indicated that the more emotional commercial did elicit a greater range of personally felt emotions from the audience compared to viewers of the most factual commercial. Overwhelmingly, these responses also tended to be of higher magnitude for the emotional commercial's audience.

The factor analysis also supported past research findings (e.g., Holbrook & Batra, 1987) that there are some basic, identifiable categories of emotional responses. In turn, these displayed varying influences on the measures of advertising effectiveness, that is, A_{ad}, brand attitudes, and behavioral intent (i.e., indicating partial support for Hypothesis 2). The most influential factor was the attention dimension because of its pervasive effects across these measures. This was coupled with arousal, which achieved secondary importance among the seven identified factors. Conclusive evidence that personally felt emotions account for more of the explained variance in measures of advertising effectiveness than ad-depicted emotions did not emerge (Hypothesis 3). But, as one might expect, a broader range of emotions did impact ad attitudes relative to brand attitudes or behavioral intent. Not only does this suggest a more peripheral influence, but it also supports both the notion of a cognitive and affective distinction and the A_{ad} > brand attitude > behavioral intent processing sequence.

The executional comparison coincided with the proposition that emotional responses explain more variance in advertising effectiveness for emotional versus factual appeals (also evidenced by Edell & Burke, 1987), but the differences were not as great as intuition (and Hypothesis 4) would suggest. The key distinction between the two appeals was related to the warmth factor. As expected, that emotion contributed significantly toward the explained variance in brand attitudes and behavioral intent for the emotional execution. For the factual execution, no additional value was derived from including warmth in the brand attitude model. Furthermore, amusement and upbeat contributed to A_{ad}, and arousal contributed to behavioral intent in the emotional appeal models, but these influences were not apparent in the factual models.

Some of the less than impressive results may have been due to an inaccurate match between the audience and the scenario depicted in the commercials. The emotional appeal might have been more effective at eliciting certain emotions (e.g., attention) if the ad-depicted emotions had better represented those typically understood by the audience. The relative youth of the respondents may have influenced their abilities to empathize with a couple so deeply committed to each other (i.e., attraction that goes beyond infatuation). In addition, the factual commercial depicted a male "relaxing" in front of a fire talking to the camera about coffee. This "relaxed" atmosphere may have given the commercial an aura that reduced the perceived informational value for the audience (the executions were rated as different along a factual/emotional continuum, but this was a relative difference). Evidence for this rationale was demonstrated by the MANOVA for the ad-depicted items—the two executions were not evaluated as different for the relaxed emotional item.

The aim of future research should be to examine a broader range of commercials to determine whether the constructs are different for different executions and product categories. Further refinement of the emotion scale should be explored to determine whether there is a consistency in the categories of basic emotions that are associated exclusively with one of the constructs versus those emotions that tend to mix.

REFERENCES

Aaker, D., Stayman, D. M., & Hagerty, M. R. (1986). Warmth in advertising: Measurement, impact, and sequence effects. *Journal of Consumer Research, 12* (4), 365–381.

Allport, G. W. (1961). *Patterns and growth in personality.* New York: Holt, Rinehart & Winston.

Batra, R., & Ray, M. L. (1986). Affective responses mediating acceptance of advertising. *Journal of Consumer Research, 13* (2), 234–249.

Bem, D. J. (1972). Self-perception theory. In L. Berkowitz (Ed.), *Advances in experimental social psychology,* (vol. 6, pp. 1–62). New York: Academic Press.

Cacioppo, J. T., & Petty, R. D. (1979). Neuromuscular circuits in affect-laden information processing. *Pavlovian Journal of Biological Science,* (July–September), 177–185.

Cacioppo, J. T., Petty, R. E., Losch, M. E., & Kim, H. S. (1986). Electromyographic activity over facial muscle regions can differentiate the valence and intensity of affective reactions. *Journal of Personality and Social Psychology, 50* (2), 260–268.

Candland, D. K., Fell, J. P., Keen, E., Leshner, A. I., Plutchik, R., & Tarpy, R. M. (1977). *Emotion.* Monterey, CA: Brooks/Cole.

Darwin, C. (1872). *The expression of the emotions in man and animals.* London: John Murray, 1904 (first edition, 1872).

Edell, J. A. (1988). Nonverbal effects in ads: A review and synthesis. In S. Hecker & D. W. Stewart (Ed.), *Nonverbal communication in advertising* (pp. 11–27). Lexington, MA: Lexington.

Edell, J. A., & Burke, M. C. (1987). The power of feelings in understanding advertising effects. *Journal of Consumer Research, 14* (3), 421–433.

Ekman, P. (1977). Biological and cultural contributions to body and facial movement. In J. Blacking (Ed.), *Anthropology of the body.* London: Academic Press.

Ekman, P., & Friesen, W. V. (1975). *Unmasking the face.* Englewood Cliffs, NJ: Prentice-Hall.

Ekman, P., Friesen, W. V., & Ancoli, S. (1980, December). Facial signs of emotional experience. *Journal of Personality and Social Psychology, 39,* 1125–1134.

Ekman, P., Friesen, W. V., & Ellsworth, P. (1972). *Emotion in the human face.* Elmsford, NY: Pergamon.

Gardner, M. P. (1985). Does attitude toward the ad affect brand attitude under a brand evaluation set? *Journal of Marketing Research, 22* (2), 192–198.

Goffman, E. (1959). *The presentation of the self in everyday life.* Garden City, NJ: Doubleday Anchor.

Goffman, E. (1971). *Relations in public.* New York: Basic Books.

Gresham, L. G., & Shimp, T. A. (1985). Attitude toward the advertisement and brand attitudes: A classical conditioning perspective. *Journal of Advertising, 14* (1), 10–17, 19.

Havlena, W. J., & Holbrook, M. B. (1986). The varieties of consumption experience: Comparing two typologies of emotion in consumer behavior. *Journal of Consumer Research, 13* (3), 394–404.

Holbrook, M. B., & Batra, R. (1987). Assessing the role of emotions as mediators of consumer responses to advertising. *Journal of Consumer Research, 14* (3), 404–420.

Izard, C. E. (1971). *The face of emotion.* New York: Appleton-Century-Crofts.

Izard, C. E. (1977). *Human emotions.* New York: Plenum Press.

Kanungo, R. N., & Pang, S. (1973). Effects of human models on perceived product quality. *Journal of Applied Psychology, 57,* 172.

Laird, J. D. (1974). Self-attribution of emotion: The effects of expressive behavior on the quality of emotional experience. *Journal of Personality and Social Psychology, 29,* 475–486.

Laird, J. D. (1984). The real role of facial response in the experience of emotion: A reply to Tourangeau and Ellsworth, and others. *Journal of Personality and Social Psychology, 47,* 909–917.

Orr, S. P., & Lanzetta, J. T. (1984). Extinction of an emotional response in the presence of facial expressions of emotion. *Motivation and Emotion, 8,* 55–66.

Puto, C. P., & Wells, W. D. (1984). Informational and transformational advertising: The differential effects of time. In T. C. Kinnear (Ed.), *Advances in consumer research* (vol. 11, pp. 572–576). Provo, UT: Association for Consumer Research.

Riggio, R. E., & Friedman, H. S. (1986). Impression formation: The role of expressive behavior. *Journal of Personality and Social Psychology, 50,* 421–427.

Robinson, J. A. (1976, October). Sampling autobiographical memory. *Cognitive Psychology, 8,* 578–595.

Robinson, J. A. (1980, June). Affect and retrieval of personal memories, *Motivation and Emotion, 4,* 149–174.

Rosenthal, R. (1979). *Skill in nonverbal communication.* Cambridge, MA: Oelgeschlager, Gunn, and Hain.

Schachter, S. (1964). The interaction of cognitive and physiological determinants of emotion. In P. H. Leiderman & D. Shapiro (Eds.), *Psychobiological approaches to social behavior.* Stanford, CA: Stanford University Press.

Schwartz, G. E., Fair, P. L., Salt, P., Mardel, M. R., & Klerman, G. L. (1976, April). Facial muscle patterning to affective imagery in depressed and nondepressed subjects. *Science, 192,* 489–491.

Stout, P. A. (1985). *Emotional response to advertising.* Unpublished doctoral dissertation, University of Illinois.

Stout, P. A., & Leckenby, J. D. (1984). The rediscovery of emotional response in copy research. In D. Glover (Ed.), *Proceedings of the 1984 Convention of the American Academy of Advertising* (pp. 40–45). Lincoln: University of Nebraska, School of Journalism.

Stout, P. A., & Leckenby, J. D. (1985). The pendulum swings—A return to emotion in copy research. In N. Stephens (Ed.), *Proceedings of the 1985 Convention of the American Academy of Advertising* (pp. 39–43). Tempe: Arizona State University, College of Business.

Stout, P. A., & Leckenby, J. (1986). Measuring emotional response to advertising. *Journal of Advertising, 15,* (4), 35–42.

Tomkins, S. S. (1962). The positive affects. *Affect, imagery, consciousness: Vol. 1.* New York: Springer.

Tomkins, S. S. (1963). The positive affects. *Affect, imagery, consciousness: Vol. 2.* New York: Springer.

Wagner, H. L., MacDonald, C. J., & Manstead, A.S.R. (1986). Communication of individual emotions by spontaneous facial expressions. *Journal of Personality and Social Psychology, 50* (4), 737–743.

Wells, W. D., Leavitt, C., & McConville, M. (1971). A reaction profile for commercials. *Journal of Advertising Research, 11* (December), 11–17.

Winton, W. M. (1986). The role of facial response in self-reports of emotion: A critique of Laird. *Journal of Personality and Social Psychology, 50* (4), 808–812.

13

Affect and Attitudes in Advertising: The Impact of Brand Name and Product Category Introductory Position

Julie A. Edell and Helen H. Anderson

The linkage of the brand name to the ad in memory underlies any measure of advertising effectiveness. Ad responses cannot have an impact without being associated with the brand in some way. Research on memory processes indicates that the way in which information is presented influences the way in which it is processed and stored. K. L. Keller (1987) suggested that, in processing an ad, the links between the brand name and the ad elements will depend upon the positioning, number, and prominence of the brand references within the ad. This chapter examines how the introductory position of the brand name and the product category affect the processing of television commercials. Introductory position is the first mention of the brand name or product category in either the video or audio portions of the commercial.

A commercial is an opportunity for the consumer to reinforce, alter, or update his or her attitude about the advertised brand. How might this attitude change take place? We present three models of attitude change and describe how the introductory position of the product category and brand name within a commercial would influence the likelihood of the viewers using that attitude change strategy.

The traditional information processing perspective predicts brand attitude would be modified by critically evaluating the attributes of the brand given in the commercial. In order to critically evaluate the information being provided about the brand, the viewer needs to know to what product category this brand belongs. For example, being thin and light may be positively evaluated attributes of a potato chip, but negatively evaluated attributes of a cookie. Thus, without knowing the product category, the viewer is limited in the extent to which he or she can do on-line brand evaluative processing.

Is there any opportunity for attitude change when neither the product category nor the brand name is identified early in the commercial? R. E. Petty and J. T. Cacioppo (1981) describe a more peripheral route to attitude change which does not require the viewer to critically evaluate the attributes of the brand. Rather, by using peripheral processing, the brand attitude may be altered based on cues within the ad or on an evaluation of the ad itself.

In both of the situations described above, the viewer is processing the ad. In the first situation, the focus of that processing is on the brand; in the second situation, the focus of the processing is on the ad. Alternatively, the viewer may never really process the ad. Rather, if a familiar brand name is introduced early in the commercial, the viewer may immediately activate the evaluation or attitude associated with that brand. In this situation, the only change in brand attitude is a reinforcement of the linkage in memory between the brand name and the brand evaluation.

BACKGROUND

Three attitude change processes have been suggested to explain how consumers process advertisements and form evaluations of the products advertised. These are the central route, the peripheral route, and the schema-triggered affect. Each of these is discussed in more detail below.

Central Route and Peripheral Route

Petty and Cacioppo (1981) presented a model of attitude change which stated that there are two distinct routes to persuasion. Petty, Cacioppo, and D. Schumann (1983) defined the central route to be the result of "diligent consideration of information that is central to what the person feels are the true merits of a particular attitudinal position" (p. 135). This approach to attitude change is consistent with the information processing perspective of J. R. Bettman (1979) and P. L. Wright (1980).

Petty, Cacioppo, and R. Goldman (1981) described the peripheral route to be one in which attitudes change because the "attitude object has been associated with either a positive or negative cue" (p. 847). Thus, if one changes her attitude about a brand because it is advertised by her favorite actor, we would say that the attitude change in the *brand* occurred via a peripheral route; however, the formation of her attitude about the actor could have occurred through diligent evaluation of the actor's skills and abilities. The attitude toward the actor would have been formed via the central route.

When we apply this basic model to an ad situation, the "attitudinal position" the viewer is focusing on may or may not be the brand (Mitchell, 1983). When the consumer is trying to evaluate the product by diligently considering the brand claims within the ad, then *brand central* processing is said to occur (Burke & Edell, 1986). However, when the viewer is diligently considering the executional elements of the ad and forms an attitude toward the ad (A_{ad}), then we consider the processing to be *ad central*. The impact of A_{ad} on attitude toward the brand (A_b), however, would be via the peripheral route. It is also the case that A_{ad} may be formed via the peripheral route. Rather than critically evaluating the attributes of the ad, one's attitude toward the ad may be based on the feelings one experienced while viewing the ad (Edell & Burke, 1987). We call this type of processing *ad peripheral* processing (Burke & Edell, 1986).

Schema-Triggered Affect

S. T. Fiske and M. A. Pavelchak (1986) present a model called schema-triggered affect. Their model assumes that memory is structured in categorical form, that is, memory comprises category labels on one level and specific attributes affiliated with that category at a lower level. A unique feature of this concept is that affective "tags" are associated with both levels of the memory structure. In other words, separate affective associations are stored for both the category label and each of the attributes of that category.

Applying this notion to an advertising context, we assert that individuals may have category labels for various product categories and brands. Associated with each product category would be a category evaluation as well as attributes of the category and their evaluations or affective tags. A person might have a negative evaluation of light beer but evaluate the attribute "less filling" as a positive one. Within this product category structure, one might also have typical brands as attributes of the category. Again, each of these brands could have its own affective tag as well as attributes and their affective tags.

Processing in the schema-triggered affect model involves two stages: schema activation and affect transfer. What schema is activated will be, in part, a function of the ad structure. If the brand name is introduced early in the ad, then the brand schema will be activated. If the brand has been evaluated previously, the affective reaction associated with the brand may be activated and processing may end.

RESEARCH PROPOSITIONS

The goal of our research is to examine the influence that introductory positioning of the product category and brand name within a commercial has on the processing activities and outcomes of the ad. Because the research is exploratory, we cannot develop unequivocal hypotheses about how all of an ad's properties and a person's characteristics interact to affect the processing and outcomes. In this section, we outline the research propositions that follow from the various attitude change models.

A brief overview of the introductory position conditions used in the study is presented to facilitate the understanding of the propositions presented below. Three introductory position conditions are compared.

PC-BN-Body: The product category (PC) introduction is in the first 5 seconds, the brand name (BN) introduction is in the next 5 seconds, and the body of the ad is the last 20 seconds.

PC-Body-BN: The product category introduction is in the first 5 seconds, the body of the ad is the next 20 seconds, and the brand name is introduced in the last 5 seconds.

Body-PC-BN: The body of the ad is the first 20 seconds, the product category is introduced in the next 5 seconds, and the brand name is introduced in the last 5 seconds.

It is also important to note that all of the product categories and brands used in our study were familiar to all of the subjects.

How might a television commercial be processed when the introductory position of the brand name and product category occurs early in the ad? The presentation of the brand name early in the commercial is likely to activate the brand schema in memory. This schema may include usage experiences, brand attributes and their evaluations, other ad executions, and an overall brand evaluation. If the viewer saw the task in processing the commercial as forming an evaluation of the brand, then, as soon as the familiar brand name was encountered he or she could stop processing the ad and activate from memory the brand attitude. If the viewer continued to view the ad, one would not expect departures from the stored brand attitude as long as the information in the ad is consistent with the schema for that brand. Thus, the first proposition is that:

> *Proposition 1*: The PC-BN-Body structure will result in little brand or ad evaluative processing, low recall of ad information, few feelings reactions, and post-exposure brand and ad attitudes that are based on pre-exposure brand attitudes, as is consistent with the schema-triggered affect model.

A television commercial structured with the introductory position of the product category early in the ad and the introductory position of the brand name late in the ad may be processed quite differently. The presentation of the product category early in the commercial is likely to activate the product category schema in memory. This schema may include a list and evaluation of attributes of the product category, the brand names that are members of the category, a description of typical ad executions, and an overall product category evaluation. If the viewer saw her task in processing the commercial as forming an evaluation of the brand, then she could activate the attributes and begin to process the ad to evaluate how well the advertised brand does on these attributes. If the viewer was less focused on evaluating the brand and instead watched the ad to find out the brand name, she may have evaluated the ad and be able to recall more of the ad information and execution than the subjects seeing the PC-BN-body condition. Thus,

Proposition 2: The PC-Body-BN structure will result in brand and ad evaluative processing, good recall of ad information, few feelings reactions, ad attitudes that are based on ad evaluative processing, and post-exposure brand attitudes that are influenced by evaluations of the product information in the ad as well as pre-exposure brand attitudes.

What processing can the viewer be expected to do when both the product category and the brand name are introduced late in the commercial? The viewer cannot activate his or her previously stored brand attitude and cannot evaluate the brand information. In the case in which the television commercial has the Body-PC-BN structure, more peripheral processing is expected. This structure may allow the consumer to focus more on the ad itself or on his or her reactions to it. In this case, the viewer may view more of the ad than the viewer seeing the other conditions. Thus:

Proposition 3: The Body-PC-BN structure will result in few brand or ad evaluative thoughts, more feelings reactions, attitudes toward the ads that are based on the feelings reactions, and post-exposure brand attitudes that are influenced by A_{ad}, as well as pre-exposure brand attitudes.

METHOD

Experimental Design

The experimental design used in the study is a 3-by-3-by-2 design with the following factors: *introductory position* of the product category and the brand name (product category/brand name/body, product category/body/brand name, and body/product category/brand name); *valence* of the attitude toward the brand being advertised (good brand and bad brand); and *product category* being advertised (light beer, frozen dinner entrees, and presweetened cereal). Introductory position and product category are within-subject variables; the valence is a between-subjects variable. Subjects were assigned to one of six groups. Table 13.1 details the combination of the factors seen by each group.

Introductory position. Three formats varying the position where the product category and brand name were first mentioned (in both the audio and video portions of the ad) were used in this study. In each format the introduction of the product category preceded the introduction of the brand name. In the PC/BN/Body format the product category was introduced as the ad begins. It was immediately followed by the introduction of the brand name, and then the body of the ad was presented. In this format the viewer knows immediately what product category is being advertised and what brand the ad is for prior to receiving any "information" about the brand. The second format, PC/Body/BN, begins the same as the first format. However, the brand name is not introduced until the last few seconds of the ad. Here the viewer knows what product category is being advertised but not the brand within that category. In the third format,

Table 13.1
Experimental Design

Group	Set	Valence of Brands	Light Beer	Frozen Dinner	Presweetened Cereal
1	1	+	PC/B/BN	B/PC/BN	PC/BN/B
2	2	+	PC/BN/B	PC/B/BN	B/PC/BN
3	3	+	B/PC/BN	PC/BN/B	PC/B/BN
4	1	-	PC/B/BN	B/PC/BN	PC/BN/B
5	2	-	PC/BN/B	PC/B/BN	B/PC/BN
6	3	-	B/PC/BN	PC/BN/B	PC/B/BN

PC - Product Category   + Good Brand
BN - Brand Name   - Bad Brand
B - Body of the Ad

Body/PC/BN, the body of the ad is presented prior to either the product category or the brand name. Therefore, the viewer is not certain what product category or brand the ad is for until the ad is nearly completed.

Brand valence. In order to test the schema activation explanation, we selected two brands from each product category. Fifty subjects, drawn from the same population as the subjects for the main study, completed a pretest. The pretest subjects rated six brands within each category by indicating (on seven-point scales) how good or bad they considered each brand to be relative to the other brands within that product category. The brand consistently rated by the pretest subjects as being better than the average brand in the category was selected as the "good" brand; the brand rated as being worse than average by the most subjects was selected as the "bad" brand. The good brands were rated as being better than average by 89 percent of the pretest subjects for light beer, 80 percent for frozen dinner entrees, and 71 percent for presweetened cereal. The bad brands were rated as being worse than average by 76 percent of the pretest subjects for light beer, 80 percent for frozen dinner entrees, and 75 percent for presweetened cereal.

Product categories. The three product categories used in this experiment were light beer, frozen dinner entrees, and presweetened cereal. Two general principles were used in selecting these categories. First, we wanted to find product categories about which subjects had strongly varying prior attitudes. However, we did not want this variance in prior attitudes to be related to familiarity differences. Second, we selected product categories that contained at least one brand that subjects agreed was a bad brand and one brand that subjects agreed was a good brand.

Fifty subjects, drawn from the same population as the subjects for the main study, completed a product evaluation survey. These pretest subjects rated eight product categories on 7-point scales with respect to how much they liked the product category, how frequently they used the product category, the extent to which they believed brands within that category had important differences, and how knowledgeable they considered themselves to be about the category. For the categories selected, no more than 15 percent of the subjects were neutral about the category. Additionally, no significant differences were found between those subjects who liked the category and those who disliked the category on the questions related to usage, beliefs about the brands within the categories, or knowledge of the categories.

Stimuli

The ads used in this experiment were constructed to manipulate the variables of interest. The ads were built from three video segments: 5 seconds of product category identification; 5 seconds of brand name identification, and 20 seconds of action scenes that represented the body of the ad.

The body and product category identification video segments were taken from movies or existing ads. The brand name introduction segments were filmed specifically for this study. Two brand name segments were produced for each product category—one using the good brand and the other using the bad brand. These two segments were identical, except for the brand (package and product) displayed.

The audio tracks were written and produced especially for this study. They consisted of background music and a spoken message. The product category was mentioned once during the product category video introduction; the brand name was mentioned once during the brand name video introduction; and neither the brand name nor the product category was mentioned during the body of the ad. The audio during the body of the ad related the video scenes to usage of the product. The same segment of background music was used in the ad regardless of the introductory position condition the ad represented. Each product category contained a different piece of music.

Subjects

One hundred thirty-eight subjects, members of a university's subject pool, participated in the main experiment. All members of the subject pool were given a questionnaire that surveyed, among numerous other topics, their attitudes about the selected product categories and brands. Members of the subject pool completing the initial questionnaire were recruited via a letter to participate in a study in which they would evaluate a film used to promote the business school. An incentive of $5 was used to encourage participation.

Procedure

Data indicating the subjects' attitudes toward the product categories and brands used in the study were collected as part of a large data base a month prior to the main study. The main study consisted of groups of subjects viewing in a theater a short program promoting the graduate business school. Three experimental ads and three nontest ads were embedded in the program. Each commercial break contained two ads—a nontest ad followed by an experimental ad. The light beer ad was shown in commercial break one, the presweetened cereal ad in commercial break two, and the frozen dinner entree ad in the last commercial break in all conditions.

Following the program, subjects were asked to recall the names of the products and the services that were advertised. Then they were asked to indicate their attitudes toward the brands advertised; the ads; and the product categories advertised. For each ad, subjects wrote down their reactions to the ad and what they could recall from the ad. Subjects were asked to indicate the extent to which they had experienced each of six feelings in response to each of the ads. Finally, subjects told us what they thought the experiment was testing. Then subjects were debriefed and paid.

Measures

Prior attitude measures were taken from the questionnaires administered a month before the main study. Prior attitude toward the product categories (PA_{pc}) was measured on a 7-point scale anchored by like very much (3), neither like nor dislike (0), and dislike very much (-3). Prior attitude toward the brand (PA_b) was measured relative to other brands in the product category. Subjects were asked to indicate their opinion of the brand on a 7-point scale anchored by very good brand (3), average brand (0), and very bad brand (-3).

Recall of the brand names of the products advertised was unaided. Subjects were asked to recall all of the brands advertised. They were instructed to give the product category if they could not recall the brand name. Attitude toward the brand (A_b) and attitude toward the product category (A_{pc}) were measured on seven-inch lines with the seven inch marks indicated and anchors of dislike very much (left end), neither like nor dislike (middle), and like very much (right end) provided. Attitude toward the ad (A_{ad}) was also measured on a seven-inch line with the seven inch marks indicated and anchors of very unfavorable (left end), neither favorable nor unfavorable (middle), and very favorable (right end) provided. The attitude measures are represented as inches (with two decimal places) from the left end of the scales.

Reactions to the ads were elicited by asking subjects to ''write down any reactions that you had while viewing the commercial. By reactions, we mean any thoughts or feelings you may have experienced during the viewing of the commercial.'' The ad reactions were coded by two judges to indicate whether the reaction was a support argument, a counterargument, a positive ad reaction, or a negative ad reaction. The average correlation across items by the two judges was .91 with discrepancies resolved by a third judge.

Ad recall was elicited with the instructions to ''write down as much as you can remember about the commercial itself—what went on in the commercial, what was said, what was shown, etc.'' The ad recall was coded by two judges to indicate whether the recalled item was from the product category identification segment, the brand identification segment, or the body of the ad. The average correlation across items by two judges was .93. In the cases in which the two judges disagreed on an item, a third judge was used to resolve the discrepancy.

Subjects were also asked to indicate how each of the ads made them feel on six feeling items—alive, disinterested, happy, hopeful, skeptical, and warm. They were instructed to ''tell us how well each of the words listed describes your feelings in response to the ad. If the word describes the way you felt . . . extremely well . . . put a 5; very well . . . put a 4; fairly well . . . put a 3; not very well . . . put a 2; not well at all . . . put a 1.''

RESULTS

Analysis of variance (ANOVA) was used to test for experimental effects. Tests of the main effects of brand valence (good brand, bad brand) and set (the particular introductory position condition, product category combinations) and the test of the brand valence by set interaction used the subjects' within-groups error sum of squares. Tests of the main effects of prior attitude toward the product category (PA_{pc}), product category, and introductory position, and the tests of the brand valence by introductory position interaction, the PA_{pc} by introductory position interaction, the brand valence by product category interaction, the introductory position by product category interaction, and the brand valence by product category by introductory position interaction were tested using the within-subjects error sum of squares. This model is used to analyze each dependent variable, except as noted. Only the introductory position and brand valence by introductory interaction effects are discussed below.

Test of the differences between position are first presented for each dependent variable. These results are then summarized and organized to correspond to the propositions stated above.

Processing

Retrospective, written protocols of reactions to the ad serve as our primary source of data about the processing activities in which viewers engaged. Protocols were divided into four categories: support arguments, counterarguments, positive ad thoughts, and negative ad thoughts. An ANOVA of each of these dependent variables is presented.

Support arguments. The number of support arguments listed varied by introductory position condition ($F = 5.83$, $p < .01$). Subjects gave .01 support arguments when the ad was PC-BN-Body, .10 support arguments for the PC-Body-BN condition, and .03 support arguments for the Body-PC-BN condition. These data are consistent with our expectation that viewers would do more brand evaluation when the structure is PC-Body-BN.

Counterarguments. The number of counterarguments listed did not vary by introductory position condition ($F = .68$, $p > .50$).

Ad thoughts. The number of positive comments about the ad ($F = 1.17$, $p > .30$) and the number of negative comments about the ad ($F = .60, p > .50$) did not vary by introductory position condition.

Overview of processing. The amount of brand processing in all conditions was very low (average number of support arguments plus counterarguments was .25). Subjects in all conditions were evaluating the ads to a much greater extent than the brands (average number of ad thoughts was 1.8). Even with this very small number of brand thoughts, we do see some support for Proposition 2 which indicates more brand evaluation when the introductory position is PC-Body-BN.

Feelings

Proposition 3 suggests that subjects experience stronger feelings in reaction to the ads when the structure is Body-PC-BN than in either of the other two conditions. Two items from each of the three feelings scales identified by J. A. Edell and M. C. Burke (1987) were measured. For each scale, the scores of the two items were summed and the resulting sums are analyzed below.

Upbeat feelings. The extent to which subjects experienced upbeat feelings in response to the ads varied by introductory position condition ($F = 7.93$, $p < .001$). When the ad had the PC-BN-Body structure ($M = 6.19$) or the PC-Body-BN structure ($M = 5.99$), subjects experience significantly more upbeat feelings than when the ad structure was Body-PC-BN ($M = 5.27$).

Warm feelings. The extent of warm feelings experienced in response to the ads also varied by introductory position condition ($F = 4.08$, $p < .05$). The pattern of effects on warm feelings is similar to that displayed with upbeat feelings. The ad with the PC-BN-Body structure elicited significantly more warm feelings ($M = 5.11$) than did the ad with the Body-PC-BN structure ($M = 4.41$), but the ads with the PC-Body-BN structure ($M = 4.72$) were not significantly different from either of the other two conditions.

Negative feelings. Negative feelings show a somewhat different pattern than upbeat and warm feelings. The main effect of introductory position on negative feelings is not significant ($F = 1.34, p > .25$). However, the brand valence by introductory position interaction is significant ($F = 3.29, p < .05$). The interaction occurs within the PC-Body-BN structure. Good brands with this structure elicit significantly fewer negative feelings ($M = 4.64$), but bad brands with the PC-Body-BN structure elicit significantly more negative feelings ($M = 5.77$). When the structure is PC-BN-Body, both good ($M = 4.94$) and bad ($M = 5.05$) brands elicit nearly identical reactions. Similarly, when the structure is Body-PC-BN, both good ($M = 5.34$) and bad ($M = 5.34$) brands generate the same extent of negative feelings.

The findings regarding feelings are contrary to Proposition 3. Our expectation was that more feelings would occur when the subject was unable to evaluate the information about the brand but was still motivated to process the ad. These data indicate that the least warm and upbeat feelings occur when both the product category and the brand name are late in the ad.

Recall

Two indicators of the memory structure for the commercials were collected. Subjects had an unaided brand name recall task and a cued recall task of the contents of the body of the commercial.

Brand name recall. The first task subjects were given after watching the programming was to recall the brand name of the products and services that had been advertised. They were instructed to indicate the product category, if they could remember it but not the brand name. These data were coded into categories: brand name correctly recalled, product category correctly recalled, incorrect brand name or product category recalled, and no recall.

Since the brand recall variable is categorical, the analysis used SAS's CAT-MOD (Categorical Data Modeling) procedure. The main effect of introductory position on brand name recall is not significant (chi-square $= 1.51, p > .40$). However, the brand valence by introductory position does have a significant effect (chi-square $= 21.54, p < .0001$). Table 13.2 shows the recall percentages by brand valence and position. Concentrating on the percentage of subjects that correctly recalled the brand name, we find that for the good brands there is no position effect; however, for the bad brands, the percentage of subjects correctly recalling the brand name fell from 60 percent for the PC-BN-Body condition to 46 percent for the Body-PC-BN condition.

Content recall. Subjects were asked to recall what they could from the ads for each ad under investigation. Here the recall cue was brand name and product category. Thus, if the subject had viewed the ad but had not linked the brand name or the product category cue to the ad trace, then little recall of the ad would be accessible with the brand or category cue. The interest here is what the subjects recalled from the body of the ad.

Table 13.2
Percentage of Subjects Recalling Brand Name Correctly

	PC-BN-Body	PC-Body-BN	Body-PC-BN
Good Brands	63	72	63
Bad Brands	60	54	46

The ANOVA indicates that there is a significant introductory position effect for the recall of the ads' contents ($F = 20.62$, $p < .0001$). For ads with the PC-BN-Body structure, subjects recalled 1.26 items. For ads with the PC-Body-BN structure, the recall was not significantly different at 1.15 items. However, when subjects viewed the Body-PC-BN ad, the recall was .78 items, significantly less than for either of the other two structures. This indicates either less processing of the ad when the introductory position of the product category and brand name were late in the ad or a lack of integration of the ad trace with the product category or the brand name.

Attitudes

Both attitude toward the ad and attitude toward the brand were measured. It is important to recall that the ads were for well-known brands, but new ads.

Attitude toward the ad. A_{ad} was first analyzed using the ANOVA model. A significant effect of introductory position ($F = 5.09$, $p < 01$) and a significant brand valence by position interaction ($F = 3.50$, $p < .05$) were indicated for A_{ad}. The interaction is evident within the PC-Body-BN structure. Good brands with this structure were evaluated most positively ($M = 2.78$); bad brands with the PC-Body-BN structure were evaluated least positively ($M = 2.24$). When the structure is PC-BN-Body, ads for both good brands ($M = 2.67$) and bad brands ($M = 2.80$) are evaluated similarly. Likewise, when the structure is Body-PC-BN, ads for both good ($M = 2.30$) and bad ($M = 2.44$) brands are evaluated similarly. For both good and bad brands, the A_{ad} is more negative when the product category and brand are introduced late in the ad ($M = 2.37$) than when they are both introduced at the start of the ad ($M = 2.74$).

Next we examined to what extent the constructs on which A_{ad} could be formed—PA_b, the positive and negative ad evaluations and the feelings that viewers experienced while they watched the ads—varied in their association with A_{ad} by introductory position. Recall that our expectations were that (1) PA_b would be strongly associated with A_{ad} when the structure was PC-BN-Body, (2)

Table 13.3
Attitude Toward the Ad Regression Coefficients

	PC-BN-Body	PC-Body-BN	Body-PC-BN
Prior A_B	-.04	.13[a]	.14[a]
Positive Ad Evaluations	.31[a]	.31[a]	-.10
Negative Ad Evaluations	-.35[a]	-.42[a]	-.25[a]
Upbeat Feelings	.11[a]	.17[a]	.13[a]
Warm Feelings	.13	-.07	.02
Negative Feelings	-.07[a]	-.09[a]	-.11[a]

[a] - Regression coefficient is significantly (p<.05) different from zero.

positive and negative ad evaluations would be strongly associated with A_{ad} when the structure was PC-Body-BN, and (3) feelings reactions would be strongly associated with A_{ad} when the structure was Body-PC-BN.

To test whether the relative importance of PA_b, positive and negative ad evaluations, and the feelings reactions varied in their influence on A_{ad}, we compared two regression models (Kerlinger & Pedhazur, 1973). Model 1 constrains the coefficient on each of the independent constructs to be the same for the three introductory position conditions. Model 2 includes the variables in model 1 and the interaction of each of these variables with introductory position to test whether the impact of them on A_{ad} is different for different introductory position conditions. Model 2 ($R^2 = .37$) explains significantly more variance in A_{ad} than does model 1 ($R^2 = .22$, $F_{ad} = 7.32$, $p < .001$). Model 2 shows that the strength of the association between A_{ad} and PA_b varies by introductory position ($F = 2.71$, $p < .07$) as does the strength of the association between A_{ad} and number of positive ad evaluative thoughts ($F = 2.68$, $p < .07$). The coefficients by introductory position are shown in Table 13.3. Prior attitude toward the brand was less strongly associated with A_{ad} when the ad structure was PC-BN-Body ($b = -.04$) than when the ad structure was PC-Body-BN ($b = .13$) or Body-PC-BN

($b = .14$). Positive ad thoughts were more strongly associated with A_{ad} when the ad structure was PC-BN-Body ($b = .31$) or when the ad structure was PC-Body-BN ($b = .31$) than when the ad structure was Body-PC-BN ($b = -.10$).

Brand attitude. Both the basic ANOVA model and a regression model were used to examine A_b. The ANOVA model did not indicate any effect of the introductory position of the product category and brand name ($F = .29, = .29, p > .70$) on postexposure A_b. The propositions were based more on the relative impact of the various inputs to A_b varying by introductory position than a main effect. Regression analysis was used to examine this.

The independent variables in the regression model were prior attitude toward the brand, number of support arguments, number of counterarguments, and the interaction of each of these variables with introductory position. While PA_b ($F = 568.43, b = .71$), A_{ad} ($F = 20.79, b = .14$), and the number of counterarguments ($F = 5.50, b = -.46$) each contributed significantly to explaining A_b, none of the interactions of these constructs with introductory position was significant. Thus, the relative influence of the independent variables on A_b did not vary by introductory position as expected.

DISCUSSION

PC-BN-Body Structure

Proposition 1 was based on the belief that introducing the product category and the brand name early in the ad would activate the brand schema associated with that brand. Once the schema was activated, the attitude toward the brand would be activated and processing of the ad could be terminated. If the schema-triggered affect model was followed, then one would see little brand or ad evaluation, a low recall of ad content, few feelings reactions, an A_{ad} that is based on PA_b, and post-exposure A_b that is based on PA_b.

Our results provided little evidence that subjects when encountering the commercial with the PC-BN-Body structure processed it using a schema-triggered affect model. The data for the PC-BN-Body commercials show few brand evaluations, as predicted by Proposition 1. However, the number of ad evaluative thoughts, the extent of feelings reactions, and the brand claims recall are not lower than in the other conditions. Also, contrary to Proposition 1, PA_b is not strongly associated with A_{ad}, and PA_b is no more strongly associated with post-exposure A_b than it is in the other position conditions. Thus, the preponderance of evidence fails to find support for our proposition that the processing of ads with PC-BN-Body structure is schema-triggered affect.

What is the nature of the processing being done when the ad has the PC-BN-Body structure? Our data support an ad central processing strategy. There are few brand evaluative thoughts, so brand central processing is not evident. The thought listings, however, provide more ad evaluative thoughts indicating ad central processing. Consistent with the ad central processing strategy, we find that the A_{ad} is strongly associated with ad thoughts.

PC-Body-BN Structure

Proposition 2 suggests that having the product category introduced early in the ad while the brand name is introduced late in the ad would precipitate central processing of the brand and the ad. If the central processing model was followed, we expect more brand and ad evaluative thoughts, few feelings reactions, good recall of the ad content, an A_{ad} based on the ad evaluations, and a post-exposure A_b that is based on brand evaluative thoughts, as well as PA_b.

Our results provided some evidence that subjects are doing brand and ad central processing of the commercials with the PC-Body-BN structure. The data for the PC-Body-BN commercials show more support arguments than either of the other two conditions, a better recall of the ads' contents, and an A_{ad} based primarily on the ad evaluative thoughts as Proposition 2 predicted. However, the extent of feelings reactions is not lower than in the other conditions. Also, contrary to Proposition 2, the support argument and counterarguments are no more strongly related to A_b in this condition than in any other. Yet, the evidence for ads with the PC-Body-BN structure fits the central processing model more closely than it fits either the ad peripheral processing or schema-triggered affect models.

Body-PC-BN Structure

Proposition 3 suggests that, when both the product category and the brand name are introduced late in the ad, peripheral processing of the ad occurs. If only peripheral processing was occurring, we would expect few brand and ad evaluative thoughts, more feelings reactions, poor recall of the ad content, an A_{ad} based on the feelings reactions, and a post-exposure A_b that is based on A_{ad}, as well as PA_b.

As Proposition 3 suggests, the data for the Body-PC-BN commercials show few support arguments, a poor recall of the ads' contents, and an A_{ad} less strongly related to ad evaluative thoughts than in the other conditions. However, the experiencing of upbeat and warm feelings is lower than in the other conditions. Also, contrary to Proposition 3, A_{ad} is no more strongly related to A_b in this condition than in any other. The evidence for ads with the Body-PC-BN structure shows more lack of fit with the central processing model than it does fits with the peripheral model. Subjects are not processing the ad; they are just waiting to find out what the ad is for.

Limitations

A number of factors limit the generalizability of these findings. The fact that the subjects were exposed to the commercials only one time must certainly limit the scope of our findings. After the initial (two or three) exposure(s), the subject may remember what brand the commercial is for and process all the ads as if the structure were PC-BN-Body.

More sensitive measurements would have given us cleaner data. For example, the use of eye movement equipment would have allowed us to know how long the subject actually processed the ad which would improve our ability to detect schema-triggered affect processing. Similarly, the use of verbal rather than written thought listings may have increased the overall number of items recalled.

CONCLUSIONS

The position in which the product category and brand name are introduced within a commercial changes what consumers do when confronted with that ad. The introductory position changes the nature of the processing that is done, the memory structure that is created, and the attitude toward the ad that is formed. Commercials for well-known brands that introduce both the product category and the brand name early in the commercial are processed more with the ad than the brand as the object being evaluated.

When the product category is introduced early in the commercial but the brand name is not introduced until the end of the commercial, the process changes. Here, the focus of the processing is on the product, although the ad appears to be evaluated as well. It is likely that, by introducing the product category without the brand name, the category information is activated from memory, facilitating the evaluation of the product.

A commercial that does not introduce either the product category or the brand name until the end of the commercial does not appear to be processed. It is not that the commercial is not attended to. Rather, it appears that people view the ad, but that a certain tension has been created by not knowing what the commercial is for, and that interferes with their motivation to process the ad.

Many researchers are asking questions about how various structural properties of an ad impact the nature of consumers' processing. It is our hope that this chapter has shown that another ad structure variable—introductory position of the product category and brand name—is worthy of further study.

REFERENCES

Bettman, J. R. (1979). Memory factors in consumer choice. *Journal of Marketing, 43*, 37–53.

Burke, M. C., & Edell, J. A. (1986). Ad reactions over time: Capturing changes in the real world. *Journal of Consumer Research, 13*, 114–118.

Edell, J. A., & Burke, M. C. (1987). The power of feelings in understanding advertising. *Journal of Consumer Research, 14* (3), 421–423.

Fiske, S. T., & Pavelchak, M. A. (1986). Category-based versus piecemeal-based affective responses: Developments in schema-triggered affect. In R. M. Sorrentino & E. T. Higgins (Eds.), *The handbook of motivation and cognition: Foundations of social behavior* (pp. 167–203). New York: Guilford Press.

Keller, K. L. (1987). Memory factors in advertising: The effect of advertising retrieval cues on brand evaluations. *Journal of Consumer Research, 14*, 316–333.

Kerlinger, F. N., & Pedhazur, E. J. (1973). *Multiple regression in behavioral research.* New York: Holt, Rinehart & Winston.

Mitchell, A. A. (1983). Cognitive responses initiated by exposure to advertising. In R. J. Harris (Ed.), *Information processing research in advertising* (pp. 13–42). Hillsdale, NJ: Lawrence Erlbaum.

Petty, R. E., & Cacioppo, J. T. (1981). *Attitudes and persuasion: Classic and contemporary approaches.* DuBuque, IA: Wm. C. Brown.

Petty, R. E., Cacioppo, J. T., & Goldman, R. (1981). Personal involvement as a determinant of argument-based persuasion. *Journal of Personality and Social Psychology, 41*, 847–855.

Petty, R. E., Cacioppo, J. T., & Schumann, D. (1983). Central and peripheral routes to advertising effectiveness: The moderating role of involvement. *Journal of Consumer Research, 10*, 135–146.

Wright, P. L. (1980). Message-evoked thoughts: Persuasion research using thought verbalizations. *Journal of Consumer Research, 7*, 151–175.

Impact of Emotional Advertising on Consumer Responses

14

Consumer Emotional Reactions to Television Advertising and Their Effects on Message Recall

Basil G. Englis

INTRODUCTION

One aim of advertising is to influence consumer preference; it is presumed that changes in preference will involve changes in attitudes, cognitions, and behaviors. Consumer preference can be inferred from behavior, but more often preference is assessed through verbal measures of consumer attitudes or of cognitive responses. Consumer attitudes and cognitions have long been accorded central roles as mediators of advertising effects; the persuasive content of advertising influences attitudes and cognitions which in turn influence consumption behavior (e.g., Koragaonkar & Bellenger, 1985; Lutz, 1981). Research and theory concerning attitude formation and change has tended to emphasize the cognitive aspects of attitudes and has placed little or no emphasis on the emotional components of attitudes. However, researchers have recently begun to examine the role of consumer emotional experiences in the formation and change of preferences and attitudes (e.g., a recent review by Gardner, 1985). There is a growing acceptance of the need to develop theories of advertising effects that include the influence of emotions on cognitions, attitudes, and behavior.

In addition to the growing theoretical concern for more complete theories of how advertising influences consumers, there are practical reasons for examining consumers' emotional reactions as potential mediators of advertising effects. Although the goal of advertising is usually to motivate behavior (purchase products, use services, vote, or engage in health-related behavior), the effects of advertising on consumption behavior may not show up quickly (e.g., Zufryden, 1981). As a consequence, advertisers often emphasize pretesting techniques which examine the effects of advertising on variables that are presumed to mediate persuasion. Concern over the costs of mounting an ineffective advertising campaign is a powerful incentive for examining all possible mediators of advertising effectiveness. Thus there is a convergence of interests between theoretical concern for identifying the mediators of persuasion and practitioner need for sales-surrogate (or presales) indicators of advertising effectiveness. Consistent with prevailing cognitive theories of preference, research concerning sales-surrogate measures of advertising effectiveness has relied upon cognitive measures of advertising effects. Commonly used measures include recall of product and brand information (e.g., Adams, Mehrotra, & Van Auken, 1983; Coe & MacLachlan, 1980; Singh & Rothschild, 1983; Zielske, 1982) and the formation and change of consumer attitudes (e.g., Belch, 1981; Gresham, Bush, & Davis, 1984; Wright, 1973). In view of recent evidence that emotional reactions are rapid, automatic processes that may precede more elaborated cognitive and semantic processes (e.g., Zajonc, 1980; Zajonc & Markus, 1982), they have the potential to mediate advertisings' initial effects on cognition, as well as later effects on attitude formation and behavior.

Only rarely has emotion been employed as an important mediating variable in examining advertising effects. In many cases where emotion has been studied it has appeared as a contrast with "rational" (or "thinking") advertising approaches (e.g., Vaughn, 1980; Zielske, 1982). The presumption is often made that "emotional" appeals are all similar in a critical way and therefore may be meaningfully contrasted with "rational" approaches. Underlying this reasoning is the assumption that emotions are inherently irrational processes and therefore inappropriate bases for consumer choice. However, behavior that is driven by an emotion is not necessarily irrational as, for example, when an adolescent avoids drugs because of the fear elicited by a television commercial. In addition, treating all emotions as equivalent may obscure important effects; at a more fine-grained level of analysis, it is clear that all emotions are not the same. Emotions "feel" different subjectively (e.g., Izard, 1977; McHugo, Smith, & Lanzetta, 1982); they are manifested in different patterns of expressive behavior (e.g., Ekman, 1972; Ekman, Friesen, & Ancoli, 1980); and they result in different patterns of physiological activation (e.g., Cacioppo, Petty, Losch, & Kim, 1986; Ekman, Levenson, & Friesen, 1983). In view of the growing body of research, which highlights the discrete nature of emotional reactions, it seems plausible to assume that if advertising can elicit such disparate emotions as guilt and joy, then we should expect very different effects on consumer cognitions, attitudes, and behavior.

DISCRETE EMOTIONS IN ADVERTISING

In order to investigate how discrete emotions mediate advertising effects, it was first necessary to identify a form of advertising that was likely to elicit discrete emotions in consumers. Previous research has shown that televised material is particularly powerful in eliciting discrete emotions in viewers (e.g.,

McHugo et al., 1982). The short movie clips used in these studies were structurally similar to the mini-dramas often found in television commercials, and they were similar in duration. Thus television advertising seemed a good arena in which to examine the range of emotions that advertising can elicit and to begin assessing those consumer responses that may be mediated by such emotional experiences. The aims of the first studies of this stream of research were to identify television commercials whose emotional content covered a wide array of discrete emotions, to measure consumer emotional reactions during exposure, and to examine whether the emotions elicited during exposure would influence consumers (the research reported here examined message recall).

Before reviewing the findings of these initial studies, it would be useful to consider the previous research that led to the assumptions and hypotheses that guided the present work. As noted earlier, there has been a general resurgence of interest in emotion and its influence on cognition (e.g., Bower, 1981; Gilligan & Bower, 1984; Isen, Shalker, Clark, & Karp, 1978) and on preference formation (e.g., Aaker, Stayman, & Hagerty, 1986; Zajonc & Markus, 1982). The results of several recent studies suggest that viewer emotions are influenced by exposure to promotional material presented on television and that such emotional reactions may mediate behaviors similar to those of interest to consumer researchers. In a series of studies (reviewed in Englis, 1988), researchers examined emotions as possible mediators of voter attitudes and voting behavior. The findings so far indicate that brief, televised clips of politicians' nonverbal behavior are capable of eliciting discrete emotional reactions in viewers, which may become associated with the candidate (McHugo, Lanzetta, Sullivan, Masters, & Englis, 1985). In addition, repeated exposure to televised coverage that elicited different emotions (like that commonly used in political spot commercials) had different effects on voter attitudes toward the candidate and toward the issues on the national agenda (Englis, 1988; Sullivan, Masters, Lanzetta, Englis, & McHugo, 1984).

In a recent analysis of a large set of television commercials, D. W. Steward and D. H. Furse (1986) included measures of "commercial tone or atmosphere." Among the measures in this category were several items that should relate to the emotional content and emotional impact of the commercials. Adding together the categories that were clearly emotional (warm/caring, happy/fun-loving, uneasy/tense, relaxed/comfortable, humorous) shows that 33.9 percent of their total sample of commercials was described by viewers as having some form of emotional content. This is probably a conservative estimate of the true frequency of emotion in advertising because they did not sample exhaustively from all possible emotions. Moreover, in combining their categories in this estimate, this author did not include several categories which, although not clearly emotion labels, might have reflected some emotional content (e.g., somber/serious, cool/laid-back, etc.). Stewart and Furse (1986) also present data concerning "commercial structure," which show that more than 75 percent of their commercials had surprise or humor at some point during the execution. The evidence suggests that emotion is a prevalent component of existing television advertising.

Other researchers have emphasized measurement of emotions evoked in viewers by television advertising. The work of J. A. Edell and M. C. Burke (1987) measured the emotions elicited by television commercials and related these responses to consumer product attitudes. These researchers factored their emotional response measures into positive and negative emotion factors and showed that both were related to post-exposure measures of consumer product attitudes. M. B. Holbrook and R. Batra (1987) reported a similar research effort which expanded the range of emotions measured (see also Batra, 1986) and which employed a larger set of commercials. These researchers factored discrete emotion scales into the dimensions of "pleasure," "arousal," and "domination" (Holbrook & Batra, 1987). The results indicate that consumer emotional responses were important predictors of brand and product attitudes and that emotional responses were predictive of attitude change.

Previous research thus clearly indicates that television advertising can elicit emotions in viewers and that these emotions are related to important consumer behaviors. However, there remain several important issues that have not yet been addressed. First, the analyses conducted in these studies were correlational in nature and did not therefore address whether television advertising elicits discriminably different emotional states in viewers. What these studies demonstrate is that exposure to television advertising produces variance on emotion scales which covaries with measures of consumer attitudes and attitude change. In order to understand fully the effects of emotion in advertising, it is necessary to determine whether subjectively distinct emotions are elicited and the degree to which these emotions have differential effects on consumer cognitions, attitudes, and behavior. As noted earlier, a commercial that elicits the subjective experience of fear may differ from one that elicits guilt both in the nature and intensity of the responses mediated.

The question of whether emotions ought to be considered as variations on two or three underlying dimensions (e.g., arousal-relaxation and positive-negative) or as discrete states which cannot be reduced to such dimensions has been the subject of much debate (e.g., Izard, 1971, 1977; Plutchik, 1980). As more research is conducted, this issue may be finally resolved. However, there is reason to favor a discrete emotions approach. First, emotions are subjectively distinctive; the fundamental emotions do not appear to be easily reducible to underlying dimensions by the person experiencing the emotion. Second, recent evidence suggests that the fundamental emotions are not only subjectively distinct, but that they are associated with different patterns of autonomic activation (Ekman et al., 1983) as well as different patterns of expressive behavior (e.g., Ekman, 1972; Ekman et al., 1980). The data from studies that reduce consumer emotions to a small set of dimensions may not reflect the underlying phenomenon, but may rather be an artifact of the sampling procedures used.

There are two sampling issues that need to be addressed in order to identify the full range of emotions that television advertising can elicit. First, the measures used must sample a broad range of emotions. As noted by Holbrook and Batra

(1987), it is possible to derive a set of emotions that are common to the most dominant current emotion theories. If we assume that there is a set of fundamental emotions, as suggested by many theorists, then measures of consumer emotion need to sample the full set in order to reflect adequately the true range of consumer emotional experience. For example, if the set of measures does not include guilt and sadness scales, then the research could not conclude that these emotions were important to understanding the effects of emotion in consumer behavior.

A second sampling issue concerns the television advertising itself. In order to describe the effects of emotion in television advertising, a broad array of advertising must be sampled. If we begin with the assumption that any possible fundamental emotion is a "fair target" for advertising, then the sample of commercials used will critically influence conclusions. Since a structural analysis of emotion response measures will be affected by stimulus sampling, this issue has methodological implications as well. For example, if no fear-inducing commercials are sampled, there is no a priori reason to expect variance on fear scales. Thus, a factor analysis will necessarily indicate a smaller number of dimensions in the measurement space than if fear-inducing commercials had been included in the stimulus set.

In the studies reported in the chapter, measures of consumer emotions sampled a full array of fundamental emotions, and attempts were made to sample broadly from all types of television advertising. This program of research was designed to examine and characterize the emotion-eliciting properties of extant television advertising and to determine whether the transient emotions elicited by commercials can have important and enduring effects on consumer behavior.

EMOTIONAL CONTENT OF TELEVISION ADVERTISING

The aim of the first study in this series was to identify a group of television commercials that represented discrete emotion categories and that were "pure" exemplars of each category (i.e., the emotions were as unblended as possible). In order to maintain a high level of ecological validity, the initial set of commercials was chosen from archival videotapes of existing television advertising. The commercials had all been aired but were no longer being shown in the local viewing area in which the research was conducted. Previous research examining viewers' perceptions of television advertising showed that commercials with some form of emotional content were prevalent (Stewart & Furse, 1986). Although Stewart and Furse did not attempt to distinguish among discrete emotions, it seems clear from the measures they used that a range of emotions are represented in television advertising. Thus it seemed plausible that a set of television commercials could be generated that would represent all or most of the discrete emotions.

The first study in this series began with a set of over 200 television commercials which included examples of product, corporate, and public service advertising. Previous studies have tended to use product-focused commercials, which may

overrepresent positive emotions; stimulus selection may have limited the range
of negative emotions. Forty-four of the commercials were judged as potentially
emotion eliciting and as communicating a single, dominant emotion to the viewer.
(No attempt was made to identify the specific sources of emotional arousal in
these studies.) Of course, it was possible that the author's judgments of emotional
content would not coincide with the perceptions of "naive" viewers. Thus the
commercials were shown to viewers who were asked to judge the dominant
emotion communicated by each. Viewers were asked to circle an emotion term
that best described the principal emotion conveyed by each commercial; participants were permitted to circle more than one emotion term in order to capture
perceptions of emotion "blends." Sixty-six viewers made their judgments using
the following list of emotions: anger, surprise, fear, guilt, joy, pain, sadness,
disgust, and neutral (no emotion). For each commercial, the percentage of the
sample that used each emotion label was computed. A derived measure of
emotion blend was computed as the percentage of the sample that had endorsed
more than one emotion category.

The percentage data were subjected to cluster analyses, which clustered the
44 commercials within the measurement space defined by the nine emotion
categories and the derived measure of emotion blend. The aim of the cluster
analysis was to identify discrete emotion clusters and to find commercials that
were the earliest forming pairs in each cluster; these "early joiners" should
represent the purest exemplars of each emotion cluster and should also be most
similar to each other. In order for a commercial to be considered as a pure
exemplar, it had to be a first- or second-joining commercial in each of the three
clustering methods used (centroid, average, and Ward's methods). Commercials
that joined at either the first or second cluster step were selected for further
study. These early joiners met the general criterion for within-cluster similarity
being among the first to join each cluster (defining the cluster centroid); statistical
analyses of these pairs showed no within-cluster differences. A second criterion
used to select commercials was that the clusters represent meaningful distinctions
in consumer perceptions of emotional content (between-cluster dissimilarity).
Analyses conducted on commercial pairs with all emotion categories showed
that the clusters were perceived as emotionally distinct (these analyses are presented in detail in Englis, 1989a).

Figure 14.1 shows the percentage profiles for each commercial cluster; the
clusters were labeled in accord with the most frequently used emotion label(s);
there were three neutral (or neutral blend) clusters and seven emotion clusters—
guilt, surprise, disgust, fear, happy, warmth (blend of joy and sadness), and
regret (blend of joy, guilt, and sadness). The descriptive data indicate that viewers
were readily able to describe the commercials in emotion terms and were sufficiently consistent in their judgments for stable clusters to emerge across the
various cluster analyses employed. The commercial clusters formed on the basis
of viewer descriptions of content seemed good candidates to elicit discrete emotions. However, the perceived emotional content of a stimulus does not neces-

Figure 14.1
Experiment 1: Emotion Description Profiles for Each Commercial Cluster

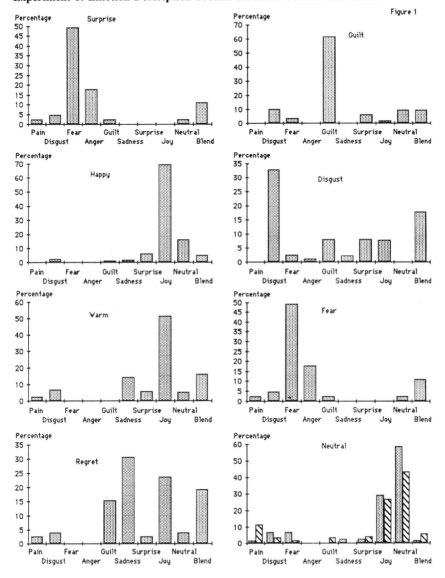

Note: These plots show the percentage of the sample using each emotional descriptor to describe the commercials. In this study, the fear cluster contained one exemplar; a second fear commercial was included in later studies.

sarily match the emotion elicited in the viewer (e.g., McHugo et al., 1985). Thus it was important to determine whether the commercials in each cluster elicited discriminably different emotional reactions in viewers.

EMOTIONAL RESPONSES TO TELEVISION ADVERTISING

A second experiment was designed to examine the nature of consumers' emotional reactions to the commercials. It was possible that the clusters established on the basis of consumer perceptions would not elicit different patterns of emotional response. In order to conclude that the clusters constitute distinct emotion categories, it was necessary to show that they were discriminable from one another on the basis of viewer emotional response measures. In this study consumers were asked to report the emotions they experienced as they viewed each commercial. The principal hypothesis was that viewer emotional reactions to commercials within a cluster would not differ, but that emotional reactions would differ between clusters.

The emotional reactions of viewers were measured using a modified version of C. E. Izard's (1971) Differential Emotion (DE) scales (see McHugo et al., 1982, for a discussion of the derivation of this scale). These emotional response scales present viewers with triads of synonyms describing an emotion and ask them to rate how they felt while they watched each commercial. Each triad was presented with a 7-point scale that ranged from not at all (0), to moderately (3), to very strongly (6). The triads used represented Izard's fundamental emotions: happy-delighted-joyful, angered-hostile-mad, disgusted–turned-off–repulsed, sad-unhappy-blue, scornful-disdainful-contemptuous, fearful-afraid-scared, concentrating-interested-attentive, confused-puzzled-bewildered, and shy-ashamed-embarrassed. Also included were measures of tension (anxious-tense-nervous) and relaxation (relaxed-calm-comfortable), which Izard (1977) considers to be combinations of fundamental emotions. With scales of this form, subjects could indicate the absence of a given emotion as well as the presence of more than one discrete emotion. The latter characteristic is important when measuring emotional responses to stimuli that persist through time (commercials of 30 or 60 seconds in length) and which are of sufficient complexity to elicit multiple emotions.

Twenty commercials were shown to 131 viewers who filled out a complete set of DE scales at the end of each commercial (this study is reported in greater detail in Englis, 1989a). The data indicated that the clusters derived from the descriptive data represent distinct groups of emotionally impactful television commercials. Significant discrimination was obtained between all emotion groups. The criteria of within-cluster similarity (no significant differences between commercials within a cluster) and between-cluster dissimilarity (significant differences between all cluster pairs) were met.

Figure 14.2 shows the differentiation between commercial clusters on each of the emotion scales. All of the emotional response scales contributed to the

Figure 14.2
Experiment 2: Self-Reported Emotional Responses to Commercials in Each
Commercial Cluster

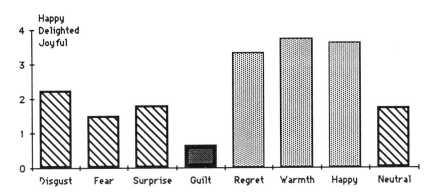

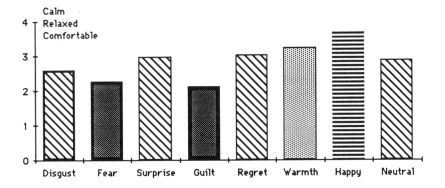

Figure 14.2 (continued)

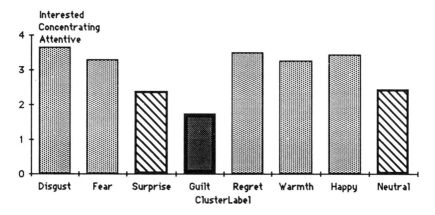

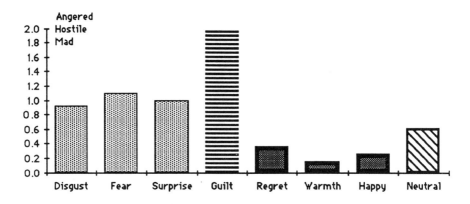

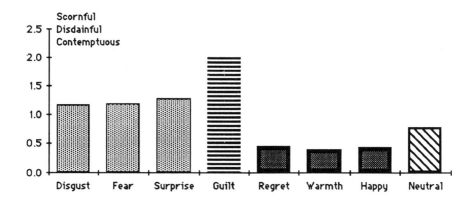

Figure 14.2 (continued)

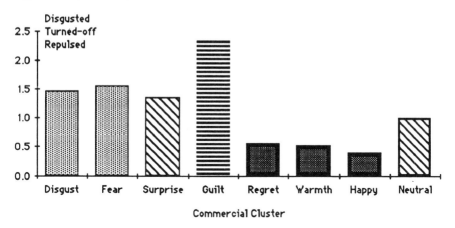

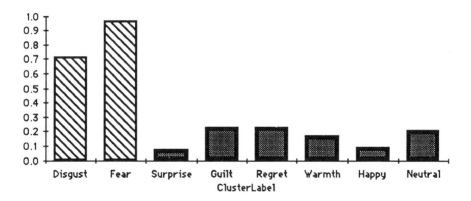

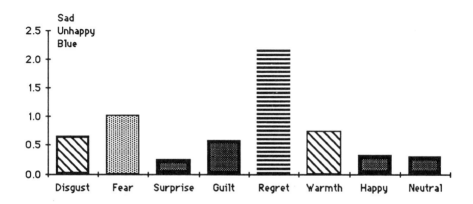

241

Figure 14.2 (continued)

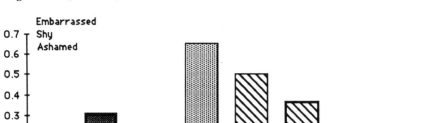

Note: Emotional responses to commercials belonging to seven of Izard's (1971) emotional categories are shown. Since no differences were found among neutral commercials, they were plotted as one category. Cluster labels on the x-axis are based on the descriptive data. Differences in border and pattern indicate significant simple effects comparisons.

overall multivariate discrimination between commercial clusters; main effects for cluster type were also obtained in all univariate analyses of individual DE scales (a structural analysis of the emotional response scales is provided in Englis, 1989a.)

In general, the emotional response data accorded well with consumer descriptions of the commercial clusters. For example, commercials described as containing happiness, warmth (joy and sadness), and regret (joy, guilt, and sadness) evoked higher levels of happiness-delight-joy and very little anger-hostility-madness. However, viewer ratings of sadness (sad-unhappy-blue) differentiated regret commercials from those in the warmth cluster, and warmth commercials evoked more sadness than those in the happy cluster. Commercials in the guilt and regret clusters elicited the highest levels of embarrassment (shy-ashamed-embarrassed), but guilt commercials evoked less sadness than did regret commercials. These examples indicate the need for using fine-grained measures of discrete emotion in order to discriminate among the subtle shadings and blends of emotion present in television advertising. Taken as a whole, the results show that the commercial clusters derived on the basis of viewer descriptions of emotional content elicit distinct patterns of emotional response.

The data collected in this study also permit an examination of one possible source of consumers' emotions. In several previous studies, viewers' responses to commercials were found to correlate with post-exposure attitudes toward the brand and toward the ad (e.g., Edell & Burke, 1987; Holbrook & Batra, 1987).

However, pre-exposure attitudes toward the target of the advertising may influence emotional responses to commercials. This assumption derives from evidence that pre-exposure attitudes toward political candidates influence voter emotional responses to political communications (Masters, Sullivan, Lanzetta, McHugo, & Englis, 1986). In the present study, viewer brand attitudes were measured prior to exposure; for nonproduct commercials, viewer attitudes toward the commercial target (e.g., cigarette smoking) were measured. Preliminary analyses of pre-exposure attitudes suggest that emotional responses are not entirely independent of prior attitudes. However, removal of attitude effects from emotional responses showed that consumer emotional reactions were also not simple read-outs of their pre-exposure attitudes. Rather, the commercials elicited distinct emotions which were independent of the responses predictable by consumer attitudes.

The evidence from these two initial studies supports the assumption that television advertising contains clear-cut emotional content and elicits distinct patterns of emotional response in viewers. The results suggest that such emotions are discrete and not easily reducible to one or two emotion dimensions when the set of stimuli is chosen to represent as broad a range of emotion as possible. The presence of such patterns of discrete types of emotional experience in response to television advertising suggests that mediational properties of emotion may also not be reducible to simple positive/negative or arousal/relaxation dimensions.

CONSUMER EMOTIONS MEDIATE MESSAGE RECALL

The first two studies clearly support the assumption that television advertising evokes a wide range of discrete emotions in viewers. A series of studies is planned which will examine how such emotions mediate other consumer responses (attitudes, cognition, and behavior). The first of these studies examined the influence of the emotions experienced during commercial viewing on the processing of verbal content. This experiment measured consumers' ability to recall the main idea(s) of the commercial and to reconstruct the verbal content of the commercial. However, there are as yet no clear-cut theoretical guidelines for predicting how discrete emotions will influence memory.

Theory and research examining the effects of emotion on memory fall within two general paradigms: (1) "state-dependency," or affect congruency, and (2) attentional mechanisms. In the former, emotion during the encoding of information is assumed to be represented in memory along with other types of information (Bower, 1981; Gilligan & Bower, 1984). Emotion at retrieval acts as an additional cue which facilitates retrieval if congruent, or interferes if incongruent, with the emotion present at encoding. A variant of this approach is exemplified by the work of A. M. Isen and her colleagues who used positive and negative emotional states (moods) and considered the match between the mood and the material retrieved from memory to be important (e.g., Isen et al., 1978). Although this work was an attempt to link emotion per se to information processing, it does not help in predicting the effects of discrete emotions on memory. For example, both anger and disgust might be considered negative emotions, but would they necessarily have the same effects on memory? Moreover, if retrieval is simply mediated by the relationship between the valence (positive/negative) of the emotion and the "valence" of the information in memory, then any negative emotional state should facilitate retrieval of information congruent with any other negative emotional state. This leads to the untenable assumption that when one is angry one would begin remembering information related to guilt, disgust, sadness, and so on.

A second general approach assumes that emotions differ in level of arousal (e.g., Schacter & Singer, 1962); increased arousal should increase attention and thereby facilitate encoding and retrieval (e.g., Cornsweet, 1969; Kanungo & Dutta, 1966; also Kroeber-Riel, 1979). Two problems exist with using this approach to understand the effects of discrete emotions on memory. First, arousal may be high with two subjectively different emotions; e.g., fear and anger may both be associated with increased arousal. Moreover, a single emotion such as joy may be associated with arousal or with relaxation. In addition, recent evidence (Ekman et al., 1983) shows that different emotional states are associated with different patterns of autonomic activation; the type of arousal present in, for example, anger, is different from that in, for example, disgust. Given the complex relationship between emotion and arousal, it seems unlikely that emotion effects would be mediated in a simple manner by different levels of arousal.

The theoretical approach of Izard and others (Izard, 1977; McClelland, 1985; Tomkins, 1962, 1963) suggests a way of linking discrete emotions to differences in consumer cognitive processes. These theorists assume that discrete emotions represent evolved adaptive mechanisms which act to facilitate associations between features of the environment and specific forms of coping behavior. Beginning with such an analysis may shed light on how the memorability of information might be influenced by the quality of the emotional experience during encoding. From this perspective, discrete emotions may be characterized in terms of the nature of the behaviors they instigate. More specifically, the coping behaviors instigated by discrete emotions can be characterized in terms of *environmental versus self orientation* (see Table 14.1). For example, interest-surprise, which instigates feeling curious or exploratory, should result in greater attention to stimuli in the environment. This should lead to greater elaboration and depth of processing and consequently better retrieval. On the other hand, emotions that focus attention more on self and less on the environment, such as sadness (grieving over loss), should result in more superficial encoding and decreased ability to recall information processed during that emotional state. This general model was used to generate hypotheses for this study; as shown in Table 14.1, encoding and retrieval should be facilitated by emotions which focus attention on the environment and inhibited if the emotion focuses attention on self.

In order to test this general proposition, viewers were shown the pretested

Table 14.1
Hypothesized Relationships Between the Fundamental Emotions and Focus of Attention[a]

Fundamental Emotion	Subjective State	Focus of Attention[b]
Interest-Surprise	Feeling curious or exploratory	Environment/external
Anger-Excitement	Feeling strong, excited Self as causal agent	Environment/external
Joy-Happiness-Pleasure	Feeling loved, loving, peaceful, happy	Self/internal
Fear	Feeling fearful or anxious	Environment/ external[c]
Disgust	Feeling repelled Rejecting	Environment/external
Sadness-Distress	Feeling unhappy Grieving over loss	Self/internal

----

a. This material has been adapted from McClelland, 1985.

b. Focus of attention refers to a hypothesized relative allocation of processing resources. An environmental focus of attention indicates that more resources are allocated to processing information from external (environmental) than internal (self) sources. The reverse is the case for a self/internal focus of attention.

c. Intensity of aroused fear may be important in distinguishing between fear and anxiety. Low levels of anxiety may not generally be associated with clear environmental antecedents and may therefore result in a focus of attention on self.

commercials and then responded to a cued recall task either immediately following exposure, after a four-day delay, or after an eight-day delay. Respondents were presented with a product, company, or service label as the cue and were asked to recall the main idea (message) for each commercial (word-for-word recall data were also collected and are presented in detail in Englis, 1989b). Independent judges viewed each ad and provided their judgments of the main idea(s) present in each commercial; these were used as the criteria in scoring the message recall data from the study's participants. A relatively liberal recall criterion was used inasmuch as viewers were scored as correct when the main idea they recalled matched any one of those coded by the judges. Since there were two exemplars of each emotion category, recall of at least one main idea from each ad yielded a score of "2"; recall of a main idea from only one of the commercials, a score of "1"; and errors of recall for both commercials in a group, a score of "0."

As expected, there was a general effect for delay; less material was remembered as the interval between viewing and the recall task lengthened. There was also a main effect for emotion. Commercials that elicited disgust or surprise were the best recalled, but surprising commercials were as well recalled as those evoking embarrassment (guilt). Fear and happy commercials were better recalled than neutral. Finally, regret, warm, and neutral commercials were indistinguishable in their effects on recall. The effects of emotion also interacted with delay (as shown in Figure 14.3). This interaction suggests that pairing messages with some emotions (e.g., disgust) may result in greater resistance to decay of the memory trace over time. In contrast, emotions such as happiness may result in high levels of recall immediately following exposure, but memory may decay more rapidly over time. The effects of emotion were also analyzed within each delay condition; as shown in Figure 14.4, significant effects of emotion on viewer recall were found within each delay condition. In general, the effects of emotion elicited by these commercials on recall became more pronounced at longer delays.

Overall, the results accord well with prediction. Disgust and surprise led to the best recall; both emotions are associated with a strong environmental focus of attention. Guilt commercials elicited the highest levels of anger and scorn, which should also be associated with an environmental focus of attention; these commercials were also among the best recalled. Recall of fear commercials was not very good at eight days after exposure, but was quite good immediately after and at four days after exposure. This finding conforms to prediction if it is assumed that fear in this case is more like a form of anxiety than true fear. As such, it is possible that attention would be more self-directed since feelings of anxiety often have a less clearly identifiable external instigator. Commercial clusters labeled as regret, warm, and happy were the least well recalled, especially at eight days after exposure. This is also consistent with prediction because the emotions of happiness and sadness-distress are associated with a greater focus of attention on self and should therefore interfere with encoding and retrieval.

CONCLUSIONS AND DIRECTIONS FOR FUTURE RESEARCH

Taken as a whole, these initial studies suggest that television commercials contain a wide range of emotional content. In addition, the findings show that the described content of television advertising can evoke distinct patterns of emotional response in viewers and that these emotional reactions are not simple read-outs of viewer attitudes toward the target of the commercial. Of course, in these studies, no effort was made to specify the nature of the advertising stimuli that were responsible for viewer perceptions of emotional content. Clearly, additional research is needed to investigate the possible sources of emotion in television advertising. What elements of commercials lead consumers to label

Figure 14.3
Experiment 3: Effect of Emotion and Delay on Main Idea Recall for Commercial Clusters Plotted Within Emotion Conditions

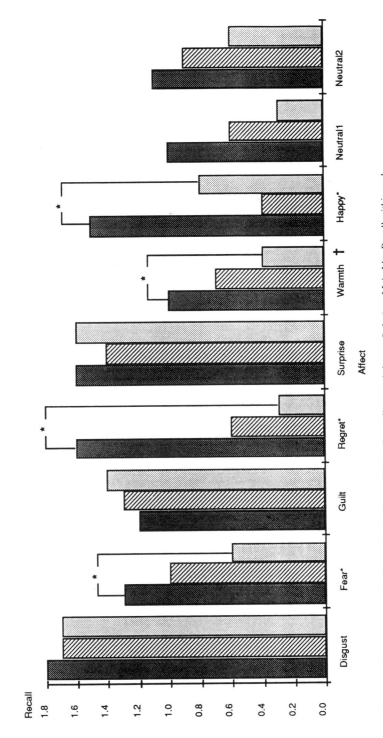

Note: Asterisks indicate the significant simple effects of Delay (immediate vs. 4-day vs. 8-day) on Main Idea Recall within each Emotion Condition.

Figure 14.4
Experiment 3: Effect of Emotion and Delay on Main Idea Recall for Commercial Clusters Plotted Within Delay Conditions

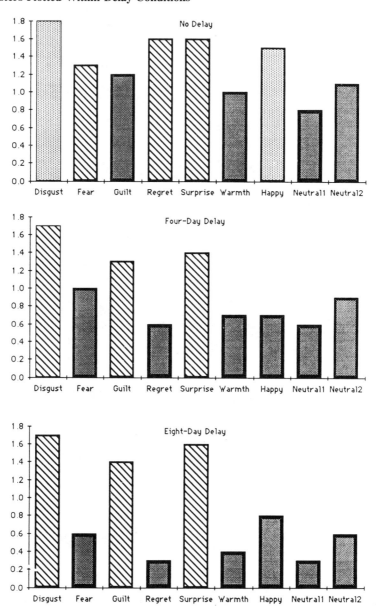

Note: Border and pattern differences indicate the significant simple effects for this interaction between Delay (immediate vs. 4-day vs. 8-day) and Emotion of commercial. The main effects of Emotion on Main Idea Recall were significant within each Delay condition.

the content as emotional, and do these stimulus characteristics reliably elicit emotional reactions in consumers? A large body of research suggests that the facial expressions (e.g., Englis, 1990; Friedman, DiMatteo, & Mertz, 1980) and the gestures and bodily posture (e.g., Haley, Richardson, & Baldwin, 1984) of communicators can elicit emotions in viewers. Other researchers have investigated the role of music (e.g., Macklin, 1988; Stout & Lekenby, 1988) as a possible source of emotion in advertising. Finally, the recent work of B. B. Stern (1988) suggests that allegorical referents in a commercial's "story" may influence viewer emotional reactions. Future research should catalog the range of emotion contained in television advertising and begin to analyze the relationship between emotion and the structure and content of commercials.

These initial studies suggest that distinct emotional experiences can occur in consumers when they view television advertising. The subjective experiences reflected in the verbal reports of these studies may well indicate meaningful changes in the emotional and motivational states of consumers, and these changes may mediate subsequent cognitions, attitudes, and behaviors. Alternatively, the subjective reports of viewers in these studies may be wholly cognitive events that reflect an appraisal of commercial content and perhaps retrieval of subjective "feelings" consistent with commercial content. These latter responses might include some of the cognitive components of emotions but not the physiological changes that normally accompany emotional experience. In addition, although the self-reported emotions of viewers revealed highly differentiated responses, it is unclear to what extent these represent "true" emotions and not a simple cognitive labeling of the ad content and the viewer's perception of how he or she should feel. These considerations lead to the need for research that utilizes psychophysiological measures of emotion in order to determine the degree to which viewer self-reports reflect the physiological activation normally associated with discrete emotions. In generating models of the role of emotion in understanding advertising effects, it may be important to distinguish between emotional reactions that are composed wholly of cognitive responses and reactions that also include physiological responses such as changes in arousal.

The emotional reactions of viewers were found to influence memory for the content of advertising, thus demonstrating a potentially important relationship between the "fleeting" emotions induced with a 15-to-60-second commercial and meaningful consumer responses. Of particular note was the finding that some emotions may result in more enduring memory for commercial content; future research needs to address the specific mechanism whereby viewers can more readily recall material as a function of their emotion during exposure. In this research, a cued recall task was used to test consumer recall of commercial content. However, recognition memory may be another important measure of the effect of emotional responses during advertising exposure on consumer information processing. In particular, recognition memory may be a closer reflection of consumer responses at the point of purchase since product-related stimuli comparable to those often presented in television advertising would also be available as cues for consumer memory. It is also plausible to assume that such product cues can become associated with the emotions that consumers experience during commercial viewing; these emotions, when reexperienced at the point of purchase, may influence choice behavior.

As suggested by previous research, the emotions elicited by television advertising may influence consumer attitudes toward the ad and toward the ad target (e.g., Edell & Burke, 1987; Holbrook & Batra, 1987). However, the mechanism whereby the transient emotions experienced during viewing influence enduring dispositions is not well understood. Several alternatives should be addressed by future research. For example, the emotions elicited during ad exposure may have direct effects on consumer attitudes; this might occur through an associative process whereby the emotion is conditioned to cues presented in the ad (e.g., Gresham & Shimp, 1985). Alternatively, the effects of emotions on attitudes may be more indirect. Since the emotions experienced during commercial viewing influence the information available to consumers when their preferences are evaluated at later points in time, this may influence self-attributions of attitudes. Finally, it is possible that emotional reactions during exposure to advertising may influence consumers' interpretations of ad messages and thus influence attitudes in different directions. Future research should be designed to test among these alternative explanations of the process whereby emotions influence attitude formation and change.

One aim of these initial studies was to identify commercials that would elicit "pure" emotions in viewers. However, much advertising utilizes a blend of different emotions; for example, surprise or anxiety at the beginning which is then resolved into a positive emotion. Future work should consider which emotional transitions and blends are particularly important in influencing consumer behavior. Even if the intention of the advertising is to elicit a particular emotion (or group of emotions) in viewers, it is also possible that programming context will alter viewer responses. There is a need to examine more naturalistic viewing contexts in order to address the issue of how programming context may influence the nature and intensity of the emotions elicited by television advertising. Previous work has examined the impact of differentially arousing programs (e.g., Douglas, 1982) and of "happy" and "sad" programs (Goldberg & Gorn, 1987) on embedded advertising. Future work should expand the range of discrete emotions studied and examine the interactions between the emotions elicited by television programming and those elicited by commercials.

REFERENCES

Aaker, D. A., Stayman, D. M., & Hagerty, M. R. (1986). Warmth in advertising: Measurement, impact, and sequence effects. *Journal of Consumer Research, 12*, 365–381.

Adams, A., Mehrotra, S., & Van Auken, S. (1983). Reliability of forced-exposure television copytesting. *Journal of Advertising Research, 23*, 29–32.

Batra, R. (1986). Affective advertising: Role, processes and measurement. In R. A. Peterson, W. D. Hoyer, & W. R. Wilson (Eds.), *The role of affect in consumer behavior*. Lexington, MA: D. C. Heath.

Belch, G. E. (1981). An examination of comparative and noncomparative television commercials: The effects of claim variation and repetition on cognitive response and message acceptance. *Journal of Marketing Research, 18*, 333–349.

Bower, G. H. (1981). Mood and memory. *American Psychologist, 36*, 129–148.

Cacioppo, J. T., Petty, R. E., Losch, M. E., & Kim, H. S. (1986). Electromyographic activity over facial muscle regions can differentiate the valence and intensity of affective reactions. *Journal of Personality and Social Psychology, 50*, 260–268.

Coe, B. J., & MacLachlan, J. (1980). How major TV advertisers evaluate commercials. *Journal of Advertising Research, 20*, 51–54.

Cornsweet, D. J. (1969). Use of cues in the visual periphery under conditions of arousal. *Journal of Experimental Psychology, 80*, 14–18.

Douglas, R. M. (1982). Arousal from violent television programming and the effects on associated advertising messages (Doctoral dissertation, Hofstra University, 1982). *Dissertation Abstracts International, 43* (6-A), 2077.

Edell, J. A., & Burke, M. C. (1987). The power of feelings in understanding advertising effects. *Journal of Consumer Research, 14*, 421–433.

Ekman, P. (1972). Universal and cultural differences in facial expressions of emotion. In J. K. Cole (Ed.), *Nebraska Symposium on Motivation: 1971*. Lincoln: University of Nebraska Press.

Ekman, P., Friesen, W. V., & Ancoli, S. (1980). Facial signs of emotional experience. *Journal of Personality and Social Psychology, 39*, 1125–1134.

Ekman, P., Levenson, R. W., & Friesen, W. V. (1983). Autonomic nervous system activity distinguishes among emotions. *Science, 221*, 1208–1210.

Englis, B. G. (1990). The role of affect in political advertising: Voter emotional responses to the nonverbal behavior of politicians. In E. M. Clark (Ed.), *Advertising and Consumer Psychology*, Hillsdale, N.J.: Lawrence Erlbaum Associates, Inc.

Englis, B. G. (1989a). *The structure of self-reported emotional reactions to television advertising*. Unpublished manuscript.

Englis, B. G. (1989b). *Consumers' emotional reactions to television advertising influence message recall*. Unpublished manuscript.

Friedman, H. S., DiMatteo, M. R., & Mertz, T. I. (1980). Nonverbal communication on television news: The facial expressions of broadcasters during coverage of a presidential election campaign. *Personality and Social Psychology Bulletin, 6*, 427–435.

Gardner, M. P. (1985). Mood states and consumer behavior: A critical review. *Journal of Consumer Research, 12*, 281–300.

Gilligan, S. G., & Bower, G. H. (1984). Cognitive consequences of emotional arousal. In C. E. Izard, J. Kagan, and R. B. Zajonc (Eds.), *Emotions, cognition, and behavior*. Cambridge, England: Cambridge University Press.

Goldberg, M. E., & Gorn, G. J. (1987). Happy and sad TV programs: How they affect reactions to commercials. *Journal of Consumer Research, 14*, 387–403.

Gresham, L. G., Bush, A. J., & Davis, R. A. (1984). Measures of brand attitudes: Are cognitive structure approaches really needed? *Journal of Business Research, 12*, 353–361.

Gresham, L. G., & Shimp, T. A. (1985). Attitude toward the advertisement and brand attitude: A classical conditioning perspective. *Journal of Advertising, 14,* 10–17.

Haley, R. L., Richardson, J., & Baldwin, B. M. (1984). The effects of nonverbal communications in television advertising. *Journal of Advertising Research, 24,* 11–18.

Holbrook, M. B., & Batra, R. (1987). Assessing the role of emotions as mediators of consumer responses to advertising. *Journal of Consumer Research, 14,* 404–420.

Isen, A. M., Shalker, T. E., Clark, M., & Karp, L. (1978). Affect, accessibility of material in memory, and behavior: A cognitive loop? *Journal of Personality and Social Psychology, 36,* 1–12.

Izard, C. E. (1971). *The face of emotion.* New York: Appleton-Century-Crofts.

Izard, C. E. (1977). *Human emotions.* New York: Plenum.

Kanungo, R. N., & Dutta, S. (1966). Retention of affective material: Frame of reference or intensity? *Journal of Personality and Social Psychology, 4,* 27–35.

Koragaonkar, P. K., & Bellenger, D. N. (1985). Correlates of successful advertising campaigns: The manager's perspective. *Journal of Advertising Research, 25,* 34–39.

Kroeber-Riel, W. (1979). Activation research: Psychobiological approaches in consumer research. *Journal of Consumer Research, 5,* 240–250.

Lutz, R. J. (1981). The role of attitude theory in marketing. In. H. H. Kasarjian and T. S. Roberts (Eds.), *Perspectives in consumer behavior* (pp. 233–250). Glenview IL: Scott Foresman.

Macklin, M. C. (1988). The relationship between music in advertising and children's responses: An experimental investigation. In S. Hecker and D. W. Stewart (Eds.), *Nonverbal communication in advertising.* Lexington, MA: D. C. Heath, Lexington Books.

Madden,T. J., & Weinberger, M. G. (1984). Humor in advertising: A practitioner view. *Journal of Advertising Research, 24,* 23–29.

Masters, R. D., Sullivan, D. G., Lanzetta, J. T., McHugo, G. J., & Englis, B. G. (1986). The facial displays of leaders: Toward an ethology of human politics. *Journal of Social and Biological Structures, 9,* 319–343.

McClelland, D. C. (1985). *Human motivation* (pp. 124–129). Glenview, IL: Scott Foresman.

McHugo, G. J., Lanzetta, J. T., Sullivan, D. G., Masters, R. D., & Englis, B. G. (1985). Emotional reactions to the expressive displays of a political leader. *Journal of Personality and Social Psychology, 49,* 1513–1529.

McHugo, G. J., Smith, C. A., & Lanzetta, J. T. (1982). The structure of self-reports of emotional responses to film segments. *Motivation and Emotion, 6,* 365–385.

Mitchell, A. A., & Olson, J. C. (1981). Are product attribute beliefs the only mediator of advertising effects on brand attitude? *Journal of Marketing Research, 18,* 318–332.

Plutchik, R. (1980). *Emotion: A psychoevolutionary synthesis.* New York: Harper & Row.

Schacter, S., & Singer, J. E. (1962). Cognitive, social, and physiological determinants of emotional state. *Psychological Review, 69,* 379–399.

Singh, S. N., & Rothschild, M. L. (1983). Recognition as a measure of learning from television commercials. *Journal of Marketing Research, 20,* 235–248.

Stern, B. B. (1988). Medieval allegory: Roots of advertising strategy for the mass market. *Journal of Marketing, 52,* 84–94.

Stewart, D. W., & Furse, D. H. (1986). *An analysis of 1001 television commercials.* Lexington, MA: Lexington Books.

Stout, P. A., & Leckenby, J. D. (1988). Let the music play: Music as a nonverbal element in television commercials. In S. Hecker and D. W. Stewart (Eds.), *Nonverbal communication in advertising.* Lexington, MA: D. C. Heath, Lexington Books.

Sullivan, D. G., Masters, R. D., Lanzetta, J. T., Englis, B. G., & McHugo, G. J. (1984). The effects of President Reagan's facial displays on observers' attitudes, impressions, and feelings about him. Paper presented at the 1984 annual meeting of the American Political Science Association, Washington, D.C.

Tomkins, S. S. (1962). *Affect, imagery, consciousness: The positive affects* (vol. 1). New York: Springer.

Tomkins, S. S. (1963). *Affect, imagery, consciousness: The negative affects* (vol. 2). New York: Springer.

Vaughn, R. (1980). How advertising works: A planning model. *Journal of Advertising Research, 20,* 27–33.

Wright, P. L. (1973). The cognitive processes mediating acceptance of advertising. *Journal of Advertising Research, 10,* 53–62.

Zajonc, R. B. (1980). Feeling and thinking: Preferences need no inferences. *American Psychologist, 35,* 151–175.

Zajonc, R. B., & Markus, H. (1982) Affective and cognitive factors in preferences. *Journal of Consumer Research, 9,* 123–131.

Zielske, H. A. (1982). Does day-after recall penalize ''feeling'' ads? *Journal of Advertising Research, 22,* 19–24.

Zufryden, F. S. (1981). A tested model of purchase response to advertising exposure. *Journal of Advertising Research, 21,* 7–16.

15

The Memory Impact of Commercials Varying in Emotional Appeal and Product Involvement

Thomas J. Page, Jr., Esther Thorson, and Maria Papas Heide

INTRODUCTION

With the large number of commercials occurring during television programming, the question of how to make a particular commercial more memorable becomes highly significant, both from a practical and a theoretical standpoint. From a practical standpoint, advertisers want to ensure that their commercials are the ones that viewers store and have readily available for later use. From a theoretical standpoint, examination of the factors that affect advertising recall is important to the development of models of the process by which commercial structure affects memory.

One influence on memory that has received a lot of attention lately is the emotional response experienced by the viewer during the commercial (e.g., Edell & Burke, 1987; Holbrook & Batra, 1987; Holbrook & O'Shaughnessy, 1984). There is conflicting evidence about the usefulness of trying to elicit an emotional response in the viewer when recall of the commercial is the dependent variable. D. Berger (1981), L. L. Golden and K. A. Johnson (1983), and H. Zielske (1982) have argued that emotional commercials are not well remembered. E. Thorson and M. Friestad (1989) and M. E. Goldberg and G. J. Gorn (1987), on the other hand, have shown that emotional commercials are more likely to be recalled than neutral ones. The objective of the research reported here is to investigate specifically how emotional impact affects memory by examining the results of two experiments in which emotional impact was a key variable.

LITERATURE REVIEW AND HYPOTHESES

The research reported in this chapter builds on a model of memory developed by Thorson and Friestad (1989) and partially tested by Thorson and T. Page (1988). This model is based on the assumption that commercials are stored in memory as episodic traces. These traces are recordings of events as they occurred over time. For commercials, episodic traces contain all of the elements of the commercial (e.g., brand name, product category, product claims, and executional elements) as well as the background elements that were experienced by the viewer during the commercial. These background elements can include, among other things, feelings about the programming, comments by fellow viewers, and, most important for the present study, the emotional response experienced by the viewer while watching the commercial. According to the model, any one of the background or commercial elements could serve as a cue to reactivate the entire trace and allow the viewer to "remember."

K. Keller (1987), in testing a very similar model of ad trace memory, has demonstrated the usefulness of retrieval cues (i.e., information originally contained in the ad) in ad recall. However, the question of what happens when no retrieval cues are presented is also important. In this case, the probability of recalling a particular ad trace is totally dependent on the strength of the elements that make up the trace. This is where the creation of an emotional response can be beneficial. Presumably, the emotional response experienced while viewing a commercial is laid down in the memory trace of that commercial. The presence of an emotional response in the ad trace is hypothesized to have two effects. First, previous research (see Thorson & Friestad, 1989, for a detailed review of this research) has shown that the presence of an emotional response element in an episodic memory trace strengthens the trace relative to traces that do not contain an emotional element. Second, this increased strength enhances the likelihood of recall of the entire trace of the commercial, particularly under conditions of free recall. At least two studies (Thorson & Friestad, 1989; and Thorson & Page, 1988) have provided support for these effects.

As a viewer encounters more commercials, the likelihood of recalling a particular commercial decreases. Indeed, interference theory states that something is forgotten primarily as a result of learning new, related information (Keller, 1987). Given the existence of the interference process, it is reasonable to assume that many commercials are forgotten as a result of exposure to other commercials. If the goal of a commercial is to create a trace that can be recalled for later processing (e.g., as part of the purchase decision process), then, according to the model just described, an ad that is capable of creating an emotional response in the viewer should be less likely to be interfered with by other commercials and be more likely to be recalled for later use. This leads to our first two hypotheses.

Hypothesis 1: Commercials that create an emotional response in the viewer are more likely to be recalled than those that do not.

Hypothesis 2: Commercials that create an emotional response are more likely to be recalled sooner, due to their stronger traces, than commercials that do not create an emotional response in the viewer.

Another aspect of the ad memory trace model is that a cue for one trace can serve as a cue for another trace. For example, a product category cue might serve as a cue to activate all traces for ads in a particular product category. In the absence of an external cue, it is reasonable to assume that an element of one trace may serve as a cue for other traces that contain the same element. This is more likely to occur with strong memory trace elements such as emotional responses. Thus, an emotional response element may cue an entire series of traces all of which contain an emotional response. This leads to our third hypothesis.

Hypothesis 3: The recall of a commercial that generates an emotional response in the viewer is likely to be followed by other commercials that also generate an emotional response.

The fourth prediction arising from the ad trace model is that, because an emotional response is likely to increase the probability of a particular ad's being recalled, the other elements ·in that trace are also more likely to be recalled. As already mentioned, these other elements may consist of brand identification and information as well as executional aspects of the ad (Keller, 1987). This leads to our fourth hypothesis.

Hypothesis 4: Commercials that generate an emotional response in the viewer will exhibit greater recall of the brand name than commercials that do not create such a response.

The ability of a commercial to produce a strong memory trace in a viewer may depend on factors in addition to emotional impact. While the research reported here will not attempt to enumerate or test all of the possibilities, one factor that may have an effect is product category involvement. R. Petty and J. Cacioppo (1985), in their elaboration likelihood model (ELM), have shown that, under conditions of high situational involvement, subjects pay more attention to such factors as argument quality, whereas in low-involvement conditions they may be more affected by cues such as source credibility. Thus, it may be reasonable to expect that, under conditions of high involvement, the emotional response may not be as strong an element of the trace as other factors such as product claims. Conversely, under conditions of low involvement, the emotional response may be a very strong element of the trace.

It should be noted that most of the research on the ELM has manipulated situational involvement in a between-subjects design. For example, one group of subjects is told that the product will be available to them while another group is told it will not be available to them. The research reported does not manipulate this kind of situational involvement with the product. Instead, naturally occurring levels of product involvement were used in a within-subjects design. It is not clear whether a high level of involvement with a product category would be strong enough to motivate the viewer to engage in central processing of a commercial which may result in a weaker emotional element in the trace compared to a low level of product involvement. For this reason, the impact of product involvement in relation to emotional appeals must be considered. However, this part of the research is exploratory, and no specific hypotheses are offered.

EXPERIMENT 1

For both experiments, the procedures were very similar. The procedure is discussed in detail for Experiment 1; only the changes for Experiment 2 are noted.

Method

The first task was to identify the level of involvement of student subjects with various product categories. J. Zaichkowsky's (1985) Product Involvement Scale was given to a sample of 79 business students. The 40 product categories chosen to be tested were determined by the pool of available television commercials as well as the researchers' prior expectations about what categories would produce high and low involvement scores.

Based on the distribution of product involvement scores, 27 commercials were chosen for the emotion pretest. All of the commercials appeared to produce a positive emotional response. These commercials were shown to a new sample of 81 business students who rated them on three 7-point bipolar adjective scales (emotional-neutral, warm-cold, and personal-impersonal). The two pretests yielded 12 commercials that fit a 2 (high and low emotion) by 2 (high and low product involvement) design. There were three commercials in each of the four resulting cells.

In the main study of Experiment 1, a new group of 67 students was shown the 12 commercials in a forced viewing laboratory setting. Each commercial was played for 30 seconds with 10 second intervals. Subjects were tested individually, and the order of commercials was counterbalanced with three different orders. No order began or ended with a high-emotion or high-involvement commercial to reduce any possible favoring of these commercials as a function of primacy and recency effects.

After viewing the commercials, subjects were asked to recall as much of each ad as they could. No time limit was placed on this task because doing so might artificially have put a ceiling on the amount recalled and thereby yield misleading

Table 15.1
Experiment 1: Probability of Recalling a Specific Type of Commercial
Through Any of the First Three Commercials Recalled

===

Order of Recall	Expected Probability	Observed High Emotion	Observed High Involvement
First	50.0%	58.5%*	53.8%
Second	77.2%	86.2%**	76.9%
Third	90.9%	92.3%	90.8%

----

*p<.10

**p<.05

results. Subjects were next asked some attitude questions which are not relevant to the information presented in this chapter. In addition, manipulation checks were obtained on the emotional impact and the level of involvement with the product category. These consisted of three semantic differential scales for each construct: for emotion, emotional-neutral, warm-cold, and personal-impersonal; for involvement, of concern to me–of no concern to me, involving-uninvolving, and boring-interesting. The recall protocols were coded by judges who were very familiar with each ad. Thus, the commercials recalled could be identified by brand name, product category, product claim, or execution features.

Results

The manipulation check of emotion showed that the subjects did indeed view the emotional commercials (mean $= 4.8$ on a 7-point scale) as more emotional than the neutral commercials (mean $= 3.4$, $t = 11.58$, $p <.05$). The involvement manipulation was also successful in that the high-involvement products (mean $= 4.5$) were seen as significantly more involving than the low-involvement products (mean $= 3.2$, $t = 9.7$, $p <.05$).

Hypothesis 1 stated that emotional commercials were more likely to be recalled than neutral commercials. The average number of high-emotion commercials recalled was 4.41. For the neutral commercials, the mean was 4.21. This difference, although in the expected direction, was not statistically significant. Thus, the first hypothesis was not supported.

Hypothesis 2 stated that emotional commercials were likely to be recalled sooner in the recall process than neutral ones. Table 15.1 contains the expected

Table 15.2
Experiment 1: Probability of Recalling
Similar Types of Commercials in Sequence

Order of Recall	Expected Probability	Observed High Emotion	Observed High Involvement
First	50.0%	58.5%*	53.8%
Second	22.7%	33.3%**	27.7%
Third	9.1%	15.4%**	7.7%

*p<.10

**p<.05

and observed probabilities of subjects recalling at least one emotional commercial among either the first, second, or third commercials recalled. Of the first messages recalled, 58.5 percent of them were emotional. This percentage was marginally significantly greater than chance ($p < .10$, one-tailed test). For the second position, the difference between expected and observed was significant ($p < .05$). However, at the third position, the observed percentage was not significantly different from chance. These results can be interpreted as moderate support for Hypothesis 2.

Hypothesis 3 suggested that, once an emotional commercial is recalled, it is likely to be followed by a second emotional commercial. Recalling an emotional commercial first was marginally greater than would be expected by chance ($p < .10$), as shown in the test of Hypothesis 2. As can be seen in Table 15.2, significantly ($p < .05$) more subjects recalled two or three emotional commercials in sequence than would be expected by chance. The observed probabilities were significantly greater than the expected until the fourth commercial recalled. Hypothesis 3 was therefore supported for the first three opportunities to recall a commercial.

Furthermore, it should be pointed out that this is a relatively stringent test of Hypothesis 3 since only those subjects who recalled an emotional commercial first were considered in the analysis. Support for Hypothesis 3 does not depend on whether an emotional commercial is the very first one recalled or not, but only on the fact that one emotional commercial be followed by a second one. A further inspection of the data revealed numerous instances of strings of emotional commercials. There were 21 strings of 3 emotional commercials, 5 strings of 4, and 5 strings of 5. However, a chi-square test failed to detect a difference

Table 15.3
Experiment 1: Probability of Recalling a High Emotion–High Involvement
Commercial Through Any of the First Three Commercials Recalled

Order of Recall	Expected Probability	Observed High Emotion and High Involvement
First	25.0%	26.2%
Second	45.4%	46.1%
Third	61.8%	63.1%

in the distribution of emotional strings and neutral strings, both for the total set of commercials recalled and for the first half of each subject's recall list.

To test Hypothesis 4, a repeated measures analysis of variance was performed on the number of brand name mentions for each commercial recalled. This analysis of variance produced a significant main effect of emotion ($F = 3.99$, $p < .05$) with high emotion producing more brand name mentions than the neutral commercials. Thus, Hypothesis 4 was supported.

Equivalent analyses were performed for the involvement manipulation. The average number of commercials recalled for the high-involvement product categories was 4.23. For the low-involvement categories, the average number recalled was 4.41. This difference was not significant. As shown in Table 15.1, the probability of recalling commercials for high-involvement product categories through the first three positions was not significantly different from chance. As can be seen in Table 15.2, there was also no evidence that high-involvement commercials were clustered together in the recall protocols. Furthermore, the difference between the probability of a high-emotion cluster and a high-involvement cluster was not significant. However, there was a significant ($F = 8.66$, $p < .01$) main effect of involvement on brand name mentions with high-involvement commercials producing more brand name mentions than low-involvement commercials.

The interactive effects of emotion and involvement were also examined. Table 15.3 shows that there was no significant difference between the observed and expected probabilities of recalling a high emotion–high involvement commercial through the first three commercials recalled. However, there was some mild evidence of clustering: if the subject recalled a high emotion–high involvement commercial first, the probability of recalling a second commercial of the same type was greater than chance ($p < .05$), but this was not true at the third commercial recalled. For brand name recall, the interaction was not significant.

Discussion

Experiment 1 provided some support for the hypothesis that emotional commercials would be likely to be recalled sooner than neutral ones (Hypothesis 2) and strong support for the clustering of highly emotional commercials (Hypothesis 3). Hypothesis 1 was not supported inasmuch as emotional and neutral commercials were equally likely to be recalled. Two possible factors could account for the failure to support Hypothesis 1. First, subjects were shown only 12 commercials. Given that the recall test followed soon after exposure, 12 commercials may not have been sufficient to produce strong enough interference to allow emotional commercials to demonstrate superior recall.

Second, manipulation checks showed that the commercials were not perfectly balanced across conditions for familiarity of the brand name.[1] Since familiarity of the brand name may create a strong ad memory trace by allowing the incoming information to fit into existing schemas fairly easily, this factor may have masked the effects of the emotion and involvement manipulations. To test these two possible explanations, a second experiment was conducted.

EXPERIMENT 2

Experiment 2 was designed to replicate Experiment 1, but with a change in the design to include more commercials and to include brand name familiarity as a variable crossed with product involvement and emotion.

Method

Based on extensive pretesting, 16 commercials were chosen. The design was a 2 (high and low emotion) by 2 (high and low involvement) by 2 (high and low familiarity with the brand name) with two repeated measures in each cell. Seven of the commercials from Experiment 1 were used together with nine new ones. Again, three different orders of commercials were used, and no order started or ended with a commercial that was high on all three factors.[2] The remainder of the procedure was the same as described in Experiment 1. Forty-two business students took part in the main phase of Experiment 2.[3]

Results

The average number of high-emotion commercials recalled was 5.14, and the average for the low-emotion commercials was 4.66. This difference was marginally significant ($t(41) = 1.86, p = .07$). Thus, Hypothesis 1 received some support. For high- and-low involvement commercials, the average number of commercials recalled was 4.93 and 4.90, respectively, which were not significantly different from each other. The averages for high and low familiarity with

Table 15.4
Experiment 2: Probability of Recalling a Specific Type of Commercial
Through Any of the First Three Commercials Recalled

===

Order of Recall	Expected Probability	Observed High Emotion	Observed Involvement	Observed Familiarity
First	50.0%	59.5%*	47.6%	61.9%*
Second	76.6%	92.8%**	66.7%**	95.2%**
Third	90.0%	100.0%**	78.6%**	97.6%**

----

*p<.10

**p<.05

the brand name were 5.38 and 4.45, which were significantly different (t (41) = 3.04, $p < .01$).

Table 15.4 contains the results of the test of Hypothesis 2 for all three manipulated constructs. The probability of recalling an emotional commercial first was marginally significantly ($p = .10$) greater than chance. However, the probability of having recalled an emotional commercial through the second and third positions was significantly greater than chance ($p < .05$). In fact, by the third commercial recalled, all 42 subjects had recalled an emotional commercial. These percentages provide strong support for Hypothesis 2.

Perhaps the most unexpected results were obtained for involvement with the product category. Table 15.4 shows that the probability of recalling a high-involvement commercial first was not significantly different from chance. The probability of recalling one in the second position, however, was marginally less than chance ($p < .10$), and in the third position, it was significantly ($p < .05$) lower than chance. For familiarity, the probabilities followed the same pattern of significance as high emotion through all three positions. Moreover, the probabilities for the familiar commercials were not significantly different from those for the high-emotion commercials.

Table 15.5 contains the probabilities of recalling commercials that are high on two of the three factors simultaneously. None of the observed values differed significantly ($p < .05$) from the expected values. Also, the two commercials that were high on all three constructs did not show any superiority of recall through the first three positions.

The results for Hypothesis 3 are shown in Table 15.6. For the first position, the results were the same as for Hypothesis 2. For the second position, only familiarity showed evidence of clustering. Through the first three positions, the

Table 15.5
Experiment 2: Probability of Recalling a Commercial that Is High on Two of the Three Factors Simultaneously Through Any of the First Three Commercials Recalled

===

Order of Recall	Expected Probability	Observed Hi-E & Hi-F	Observed Hi-E & Hi-I	Observed Hi-I & Hi-F
First	25.0%	28.6%	26.2%	28.6%
Second	45.0%	47.6%	52.4%	42.9%
Third	60.7%	71.4%*	66.7%	57.1%

----

*p<.10

Table 15.6
Experiment 2: Probability of Recalling Similar Types of Commercials in Sequence

===

Order of Recall	Expected Probability	Observed High Emotion	Observed High Involvement	Observed High Familiarity
First	50.0%	59.5%*	47.6%	61.9%*
Second	23.3%	21.4%	28.6%	33.1%*
Third	10.0%	11.9%	14.3%	14.3%

----

*p<.10

probability of recalling three of the same type of commercial was not significantly different from what would be expected by chance. Furthermore, compared to Experiment 1, there were fewer strings of high-emotion commercials in the recall protocols. There were 11 strings of 3, 3 strings of 4, and 1 string of 5. Again, a chi-square test failed to reject the hypothesis that the distribution of strings of emotional commercials was the same as the distribution of neutral strings. This was true for all commercials recalled and for the first half of each subject's recall list. Therefore, the second experiment did not support Hypothesis 3.

For recall of brand name, only brand familiarity showed a significant ($F = 74.31, p < 0.01$) main effect; highly familiar brand names were mentioned more often. There was a significant interaction between emotion and involvement ($F = 6.94, p < .05$) and between emotion and familiarity ($F = 14.34, p < .01$). These interactions would seem to indicate that emotional impact, product involvement, and brand familiarity may have additive effects on the strengthening of memory traces.

Discussion

Experiment 2 provided evidence that emotional commercials were more likely to be recalled than neutral ones (Hypothesis 1). It also provided strong evidence that emotional commercials were likely to be recalled sooner than neutral ones (Hypothesis 2). However, the second experiment did not provide any evidence of clustering of emotional commercials in the recall sequence, hence failing to support Hypothesis 3.

It is not surprising that commercials for familiar brands were better recalled than those for unfamiliar brands. Commercials for familiar brands were more likely to be recalled and to be recalled sooner; they showed some evidence of clustering; and they had a large impact on brand name mentions. This result could be interpreted as providing evidence that information that activates a schema about an already known brand will have a greater effect on the salience of that brand than would similar information for an unknown brand.

In Experiment 2, the highly involving commercials did not perform well on the recall measures. In fact, they were significantly less likely than chance to be recalled through the first three commercials recalled. There are two likely explanations for this finding. First, involvement with the product category may not be sufficient to trigger in-depth processing of a commercial for a particular brand in that product category. In other words, high involvement with a product category may not result in high involvement with all brands in that product category. Second, it may be that individuals with high levels of involvement with a product category are sufficiently aware of the brands in the category that they may actually "tune out" commercials for that product category. These questions remain for future research to address.

GENERAL DISCUSSION

Overall, the two experiments provided evidence for the superiority of emotional commercials over neutral ones in terms of their recall strength. When the number of commercials was increased from 12 to 16, the emotional commercials began to show evidence of increased probability of being recalled out of the set of commercials to which the subjects had been exposed. Thus, it appears that the presence of an emotional response in the ad memory trace does make the commercial more memorable. The next step is to increase the number of commercials the subject is exposed to even more to determine whether the effect becomes more pronounced.

Both experiments provided support for the hypothesis that emotional commercials tend to be recalled sooner than neutral ones. This result also indicates that generating an emotional response in the viewer is beneficial to memory processes. As the model described earlier predicts, the presence of an emotional response in the trace strengthens the trace and increases its likelihood of being recalled compared to traces without an emotional response element.

Experiment 1 demonstrated clustering of emotional responses, but Experiment 2 did not. One possible explanation for these discrepant results is that in neither experiment did the commercials produce an extreme emotional response. While the emotional commercials were seen as significantly more emotional than the neutral ones, they still scored near the middle of the scale used to assess emotional impact. Thus it may well be that, due to the lack of stronger emotional impact of the commercials, the manipulation produced the expected results in the first experiment but not in the second one by chance. This possibility seems particularly likely given that a 30-second television commercial, seen only once, is limited in the degree to which it can induce an emotional response in the viewer. This issue can be resolved in future research by using messages, such as some public service announcements, that are capable of producing much greater emotional impact. The limitations of this research are very similar to those discussed by Keller (1987). The commercials were shown in the absence of any programming, exposure was forced, and exposure to all commercials took place in a relatively short period of time. These limitations are not necessarily damaging to the results obtained in this research, however. Although the ads were viewed in the absence of a program, the presence of a program, even a relatively neutral one, could have interacted with the commercials in some way and biased the results. Forced exposure is a fairly common technique in this kind of research, and since steps were taken to eliminate potentially confounding effects of fatigue (i.e., rotated orders), the procedure is not likely to have had any major effects on the results.

The question of timing may be more relevant to measurement issues than to exposure. It might have been beneficial to have had a delayed recall test as part of the research design. On the face of it, a delay of a day or a week in measuring recall may appear to provide more opportunity for emotional commercials to demonstrate superior recall because the neutral ones will be more likely to be forgotten with increased time. However, allowing subjects to leave the laboratory would also allow them to view other commercials which would create additional interference. Since different students may be exposed to different levels of interference, and it is not practical to expect a student not to watch television for any extended length of time, the delay measure would be interesting but undoubtedly unreliable. The validity of any study is always open to question. Two issues impinge on the validity of the research reported here.

The first issue concerns the fact that real commercials were used in the experiments. Using real commercials could threaten the internal validity of the experiments in that what was thought to be an emotion generated by the commercial could have been confounded with other variables such as language differences or differences in styles of execution. However, steps were taken to reduce this possibility through the use of expert judges, pretests, and multiple executions. Furthermore, the use of artificial commercials would have been impractical and would have severely reduced the external validity of the results.

The second issue concerns the external validity of any laboratory study. As Goldberg and Gorn (1987) state, the testing procedures "may have induced a higher level of situational involvement than would a normal home viewing situation" (p. 401). If this had been the case, one would not necessarily have expected to find an effect of emotional commercials since subjects presumably would have been more motivated to process the information content of the commercials rather than the emotional content. It may therefore have been the case that the emotional commercials outperformed the neutral ones in spite of the handicap of equalized processing of all the commercials, which is atypical of normal home viewing.

The limitations in the present study serve as areas for future research. The same design could be replicated with the commercials embedded in programming. Or, to substitute for a delay period, subjects could be given a distraction task before gathering the recall measures. Keller (1987) also speculated on the differing effectiveness of retrieval cues for emotional and informational commercials. It may be that the type of cue might interact with the type of commercial to produce enhanced recall, in other words, an emotional cue for an emotional commercial and an informational cue for an informational commercial. Since only positive emotional commercials were used in the research reported here, another important area for future research would be to test the effect of negative emotional commercials in a similar setting. For example, strong fear appeals may depress recall rather than enhance it because the viewer may actively distort or suppress these elements in the ad memory trace. Finally, as mentioned earlier, the number of commercials required to produce interference is an important question to be resolved in future research.

NOTES

1. However, it was not the case that all of the familiar brands were high-emotion commercials. Thus, support obtained for the hypotheses in Experiment 1 is not diminished.

2. In fact, to guard against recency effects in the recall test, no order had a commercial that was high on all three factors in the last two positions. Going beyond this would have resulted in clustering of the commercials on some factor which could have resulted in a biased test of Hypothesis 3.

3. Since the two experiments were conducted a year apart, there was no duplication of students in any phase of the experiments.

REFERENCES

Berger, D. (1981). A retrospective: FCB recall study. *Advertising Age, 26,* 5–36.
Edell, J., & Burke, M. (1987). The power of feelings in understanding advertising effects. *Journal of Consumer Research, 14* (3), 421–433.

Goldberg, M. E., & Gorn, G. J.(1987). Happy and sad TV programs: How they affect reactions to commercials. *Journal of Consumer Research, 14* (3), 387–403.

Golden, L. L., & Johnson, K. A. (1983). The impact of sensory preference and thinking versus feeling appeals on advertising effectiveness. In R. Bagozzi & A. Tybout (Eds.), *Advances in consumer research* (vol. 10, pp. 203–208). Ann Arbor, MI: *Association for Consumer Research.*

Holbrook, M., & Batra, R. (1987). Assessing the role of emotions as mediators of consumer responses to advertising. *Journal of Consumer Research, 14* (3), 404–420.

Holbrook, M., & O'Shaughnessy, J. (1984). The role of emotion in advertising. *Psychology and Marketing, 1* (2), 45–64.

Keller, K. (1987). Memory factors in advertising: The effect of advertising retrieval cues on brand evaluation. *Journal of Consumer Research, 14* (3), 316–333.

Petty, R., & Cacioppo, J. (1985). The elaboration likelihood model of persuasion. In L. Berkowitz (Ed)., *Advances in experimental social psychology.* New York: Academic Press.

Thorson, E., & Friestad, M. (1989). The effects of emotion on episodic memory for television commercials. In A. Tybout & P. Cafferata (Eds.), *Cognitive and affective responses to advertising.* Lexington, MA: Lexington Books.

Thorson, E., & Page, T. (1988). Effects of product involvement and emotional commercials on consumers' recall and attitudes. In S. Hecker & D. Stewart (Eds.), *Nonverbal communication in advertising.* Lexington, MA: Lexington Books.

Zaichkowsky, J. (1985). Measuring the involvement construct. *Journal of Consumer Research, 12,* 341–352.

Zielske, H. (1982). Does day-after-recall penalize 'feeling' ads? *Journal of Advertising Research, 22* (1), 19–23.

16

A Three-Component Model of Attitude Toward the Ad: Effects of the Zipping and Zapping of Television Commercials

T. J. Olney,
Rajeev Batra, and Morris B. Holbrook

INTRODUCTION

Zipping and Zapping

A perennial problem for television advertisers has concerned the problem of people who do not watch television commercials. Traditional nonviewing behavior consisted of talking, reading, and leaving the room (Anderson, 1985, 1987). However, modern technology has given rise to new forms of nonviewing behavior of understandable concern to advertisers. Affectionately known as "zipping" and "zapping," these behaviors are made possible by the advent of private videotaping via the video cassette recorder (VCR) and the deep market penetration of remote control devices of all types. Studies in both the United States (IRI, 1983, 1985; Heeter & Greenberg, 1985; Kaplan, 1985) and Great Britain (Yorke & Kitchen, 1985) have shown that both phenomena and their attendant difficulties for advertisers are extremely pervasive.

"Zapping," or remote channel switching, merely extends the older forms of nonviewing such as leaving the room. Zapping a commercial is the act of using the remote control to change the channel when a commercial appears. This is done in order to see what else is on, to relieve boredom, to check on the news, to watch two programs at once, or for any number of other reasons.

"Zipping," on the other hand, refers only to prerecorded video material which has been recorded with embedded commercials. In zipping, the viewer uses the

The authors gratefully acknowledge the support of the Columbia University Business School's Faculty Research Fund.

remote control device of the VCR to "fast forward" through the commercials. Usually, but not always, the whole commercial pod is zipped through. Depending on the type of VCR and the speed at which the program was recorded, the image in the ad either will be totally unrecognizable or will be seen as happening at rapid speed without sound.

Both zipping and zapping have gained a great deal of attention over the past few years. However, neither has been thoroughly studied, and both are somewhat intractable in the practical problems that they present to the researcher. It is not entirely clear whether zipping and zapping behavior are manifestations of the same phenomenon or how they might be related to one another. Thus, we might ask if they are strongly correlated with one another or if they are at least similar enough in their manifestations so that studies involving one can be generalized to conclusions concerning the other.

This chapter presents a laboratory study in which zipping and zapping environments and behavior are simulated. We report the correlation between these two measures of looking time and examine whether they are one and the same phenomenon.

Attitude Toward the Ad

The other major issue addressed by this research concerns the question of how attitude toward the ad (A_{ad}) will influence the amount of time that one spends looking at a television advertisement. In order to elucidate this issue, we build upon past research on A_{ad} to develop a model which posits that looking time is a function of global affect and three attitudinal subcomponents. We propose a theoretical framework for a three-subcomponent model of A_{ad} and demonstrate that, although all subcomponents contribute strongly to global affect, only two of the three subcomponents show a strong relationship to looking time.

A review of the recent literature on attitude toward the ad indicated that there was probably more to A_{ad} than mere evaluation and that such evaluation might be the synthesis of several attitudinal subcomponents. Specifically, several recent studies have used a four-item index to measure A_{ad} (Gardner, 1985a, 1985b). These four items (good-bad, like-dislike, irritating–not irritating, and uninteresting-interesting) were derived from a study by A. P. Mitchell and J. C. Olson (1981), in which these were the four of seven items that loaded heavily on a first evaluative factor. In that study, this first factor, along with another unidentified second factor, accounted for only 68 percent of the variance in the seven items. This suggests that there is more going on in A_{ad} that might be captured by additional measures.

Work by R. T. Batra and O. T. Ahtola (1987) on attitude toward the brand (A_b) lends support to the notion that attitude has more to it than just the overall evaluative dimension. In that study, Batra and Ahtola found two dimensions of A_b: a "hedonic" aspect (e.g., pleasant-unpleasant) and a "utilitarian" aspect (e.g., useful-useless). Meanwhile, "interesting" has been used as an indicant of A_{ad} by other researchers as well as those already mentioned (Lutz, MacKenzie, & Belch, 1983; MacKenzie, Lutz, & Belch, 1986). This suggests the existence of a third ("collative") aspect of potential importance, one conceptually different from simple evaluative or affective responses (Berlyne, 1960, 1971).

Our work thus builds upon these earlier efforts by proposing a multicomponent structure of A_{ad} and by further suggesting how A_{ad} might mediate advertising effectiveness by determining whether an ad is watched. Based on the above considerations, a set of scales to assess A_{ad} was developed by borrowing from the literature cited above and by expanding each of the theoretical constructs using a thesaurus to generate additional items for the measurement of each construct. Four indices consisting of four items each were developed. These four indices are (1) hedonism component of A_{ad}, (2) utilitarianism component of A_{ad}, (3) interestingness component of A_{ad}, and (4) global affect toward the ad. (For a list of individual items, see Table 16.1.)

Purpose of the Study

Each of these aspects of viewing behavior and attitudes toward ads holds considerable import for the marketing manager. This study and several others before it have demonstrated that it is relatively easy to gather judgments from content analytic judges which reliably measure the attitude toward an ad. If we can demonstrate that there are strong correlations between the attitudes generated toward various ads and the degree to which those ads will be zipped or zapped (rather than watched) relative to other ads, then we shall have established a very powerful copy-testing tool. In other words, it can be argued that all the sophisticated persuasive devices that advertisers may undertake are in vain if the advertisements that result are not watched by the viewing public.

METHOD

Unit of Analysis

The present study evolved from a continuation of the work by D. W. Stewart and D. H. Furse (1985), C. Pechmann and Stewart (1985), M. B. Holbrook and Batra (1987), and others in which the advertisement itself, rather than the subject, is the unit of analysis, and measurements come from independent judges who view the ads and make content analytic assessments on various relevant areas.

Sample

The sample of ads for the present study was created by taping random nights in a week of prime-time television, numbering all of the distinct 30-second commercials that had been taped, and then randomly choosing a sample of 150

Table 16.1
Attitude Questionnaire

```
THE AD IS                                          THE AD IS
UNPLEASANT    ___:___:___:___:___:___:___         PLEASANT

THE AD IS                                          THE AD IS
INFORMATIVE   ___:___:___:___:___:___:___         UNINFORMATIVE

I REACT                                            I REACT
UNFAVORABLY   ___:___:___:___:___:___:___          FAVORABLY
TO THE AD                                          TO THE AD

THE AD                                             THE AD
MAKES ME      ___:___:___:___:___:___:___          DOES NOT MAKE
CURIOUS                                            ME CURIOUS

THE AD                                             THE AD
IS NOT        ___:___:___:___:___:___:___          IS
IMPORTANT                                          IMPORTANT

THE AD                                             THE AD
DOES NOT KEEP___:___:___:___:___:___:___           KEEPS
MY ATTENTION                                       MY ATTENTION

THE AD IS                                          THE AD IS
FUN TO WATCH  ___:___:___:___:___:___:___          NOT FUN TO WATCH


THE AD        ___:___:___:___:___:___:___          THE AD
IS GOOD                                            IS BAD

THE AD                                             THE AD
IS NOT        ___:___:___:___:___:___:___          IS
ENTERTAINING                                       ENTERTAINING

THE AD IS                                          THE AD IS
HELPFUL       ___:___:___:___:___:___:___          NOT HELPFUL

I DISLIKE     ___:___:___:___:___:___:___          I LIKE
THE AD                                             THE AD

THE AD IS                                          THE AD IS
BORING        ___:___:___:___:___:___:___          NOT BORING

THE AD IS                                          THE AD IS
ENJOYABLE     ___:___:___:___:___:___:___          NOT ENJOYABLE

I FEEL                                             I FEEL
POSITIVE                                           NEGATIVE
TOWARD        ___:___:___:___:___:___:___          TOWARD
THE AD                                             THE AD

THE AD                                             THE AD IS
IS USEFUL     ___:___:___:___:___:___:___          NOT USEFUL

THE AD IS                                          THE AD IS
INTERESTING   ___:___:___:___:___:___:___          NOT INTERESTING
```

30-second commercials. These ads were then edited by a professional video production company onto three different tapes. Because of problems in the production, four of the 150 ads were lost, and only 146 were used in the final sample.

This process created a sample of ads that represents what viewers are actually exposed to and thereby departs from other work where ads have been chosen to represent a particular range of emotions or executions of interest.

Judges

For the measures of attitude toward the ad, the 146 commercials were rated by 12 paid judges drawn from a pool of Columbia University graduate students who had not participated in the behavioral task. The behavioral measure of looking time was created by having subjects view the ads under two separate conditions—one designed to simulate zipping behavior ($N = 50$) and the other designed to simulate zapping behavior ($N = 52$).

Measures

Attitude toward the ad. For each ad, paid content judges filled out one sheet of paper, indicating on the top line a word or phrase which identified the ad as a cross-check to be sure that the correct ad was being judged and that the respondent actually watched the ads rather than just filling out the response sheets in a haphazard manner. Attitude toward the ad was assessed using the 16-item questionnaire shown in Table 16.1. Each judge rated each of the 146 ads on the 16 items, four for each of the theoretical indices developed earlier. Beginning at a randomized starting point, each judge watched each ad, stopped the tape, and then responded to the 16 items for that ad before viewing the next ad.

The zipping tape was used for this attitude measurement. The layout of this tape is described more fully in the section on zipping. Judges were started at staggered points on the tape to minimize the order effects inherent in using taped stimuli. Total time to complete the judging task for attitude toward the ad was approximately two and one half hours per judge. Each judge performed the task in a room by him or herself and went straight through with breaks for the bathroom and an occasional stretch.

Looking time. The looking time measure was generated by combining the two measures from two conditions. We designed these conditions to reflect two of the different processes of not watching ads that are of major concern to television advertisers. The first, zipping, occurs when a viewer is watching a television show that has been taped and uses the fast-forward control of the video cassette recorder to hurry past a commercial segment. The second, zapping, occurs when, while watching broadcast television, a viewer uses a remote control device to change the channel at a commercial break. Both of these phenomena deserve study in their own right, but simulated versions of them serve as the measures of looking time, a real behavioral measure of response to advertising.

In this study, viewers were required to watch 1 hour and 15 minutes of advertisements in either a simulated zipping or a simulated zapping condition. Each day that the measures were taken, subjects were either all in the zipping condition or all in the zapping condition. The days for zipping and zapping were randomly assigned, and viewers did not know before the fact which condition would occur. Fifty viewers saw the ads in the zipping condition and 52 in the zapping condition.

Zipping. In the zipping condition, the 146 ads were recorded on a tape in randomized order with the full order repeated after the last ad. The production company inserted a red and white sign saying STOP in between each of the ads. Watchers were equipped with a remote control device which allowed them to speed up or to pause the VCR playing the tape. First, the operation of the machine was demonstrated while they were shown a demo series of ads. They were instructed to watch the tape and to use the fast forward or pause however they chose with the proviso that whenever they saw a stop sign, they should momentarily stop using the fast forward if they were using it when the sign appeared. Furthermore, they were instructed that they would watch the tape for a total of 1 hour and 15 minutes (the normal running time of the tape) and that if they reached the end of the tape, they should rewind to the beginning and continue watching until the experimenter came and told them to stop. As previously mentioned, viewing began at a random position in the taped sequence. Viewer behavior was recorded by another VCR which registered what the viewer actually saw on the monitor. This recording provided one measure of looking time obtained by timing the segments of commercials seen by the viewer.

Zapping. The zapping condition used two tapes, this time without any pauses between the ads, with a different random order on each tape. Each tape was begun at a random starting point for each viewer in the zapping simulation. Both tapes were loaded into separate video cassette recorders and started simultaneously. Viewers controlled which ad (or tape) they watched by means of an A/B cable push-button switch of the kind used for switching between two signal sources for home installations. This switch was mounted on a stand so that a distinctly satisfying zap could be made from one channel to the other and back. The starting position of the switch was randomized for each viewer. Viewers were instructed to watch the ads and to use the switch as they chose. Before the tapes were started, viewers were asked to push the buttons once or twice in order to get a feel for switching between two channels. As in the zipping condition, another VCR recorded what the viewers actually saw. This recording provided the other measure of looking time obtained by timing the segments of commercials seen by the viewer.

RESULTS

Relationship Between the Zipping and Zapping Measures

Consistent with our expectations, the zipping and zapping showed a high degree of correlation with one another ($r = .75$). For this reason, we created an overall, new, looking-time index by summing the standardized values for zipping and zapping. Subsequent discussion will refer to that index as the measure of looking time.

Scale Reliabilities

The mean interjudge reliability for individual items on the attitude questionnaire (as measured by coefficient alpha) was .80. As shown in Table 16.2, these reliabilities ranged from a low of .65 for the item anchored "makes me curious . . . does not" to a high of .87 for the item anchored "fun to watch/not fun to watch."

When the four items for each of the subcomponents of attitude toward the ad are combined into one index in the manner indicated by Table 16.2 and the reliability of those measures is taken across the 12 judges, we obtain the following levels of alpha: hedonism, .89; utilitarianism, .81; interestingness, .85; and global affect, .79. As a final reliability check, we can calculate the coefficient alpha for the four item indices where each item is the sum of the 12 judges on that scale. Perhaps the most telling of the measures of reliability, this calculation is equivalent to the reliability of the means across judges on each scale and represents the degree to which we can say that using judges tells us something about the advertisements (*cf*. Olney, 1988). For this last method of reliability calculation, we obtained the following levels of alpha: hedonism, .95; utilitarianism, .90; interestingness, .94; and global affect, .79. Hence, these indices are quite reliable and support the method of using judges as expert content analysts.

Based on the high degree of interjudge reliability demonstrated above, the data were reduced to mean judgments on each scale for each ad. All subsequent analyses across the 146 ads use these means as the base measure.

Principal Components Analysis

The 12 items which form the three subcomponents of global attitude toward the ad were subjected to a principal components analysis. The first three factors accounted for 91 percent of the variance in the data. These three factors were retained and rotated using varimax rotation. Table 16.3 presents the loadings for each of the scale items on the three rotated factors (multiplied by 100 and rounded to the nearest integer). As can be seen, the principal components analysis

Table 16.2
Reliabilities for Individual Scales Across Twelve Judges Grouped by A Priori Index

Index	Scale	Inter-judge Alpha
HEDONISM	Pleasant/Unpleasant	.8522
	Enjoyable/Not Enjoyable	.8488
	Fun to Watch/Not Fun to Watch	.8734
	Entertaining/Not Entertaining	.8713
UTILITARIANISM	Helpful/Not Helpful	.7465
	Useful/Not Useful	.7167
	Informative/Not Informative	.8673
	Important/Not Important	.7255
INTERESTINGNESS	Interesting/Not Interesting	.7983
	Keeps my Attention/Does not	.8405
	Makes me Curious/Does not	.6543
	Boring/Not Boring	.8723
GLOBAL AFFECT	React favorably/React unfavorably	.7261
	Good/Bad	.7734
	Dislike/Like	.7723
	Feel positive /Feel negative	.7878
	Mean	.7954

faithfully recreated the a priori indices. To keep the independent variables uncorrelated in further regression analyses, scores on each factor were created and used as the measures of hedonism, utilitarianism, and interestingness.

Regression Analysis

The hedonism, utilitarianism, and interestingness components were first used to predict the global measure of affect toward the ad. As shown in Table 16.4,

Table 16.3
Loadings on Varimax Rotated Principal Components

	Hedonism	Utilitarianism	Interestingness
Pleasant/Unpleasant	92	8	7
Enjoyable/Not Enjoyable	88	7	42
Fun to Watch/Not Fun to Watch	85	-5	45
Entertaining/Not Entertaining	78	-7	56
Helpful/Not Helpful	6	96	11
Useful/Not Useful	8	94	21
Informative/Not Informative	-13	90	-24
Important/Not Important	0	67	59
Interesting/Not Interesting	44	9	86
Keeps my Attention/Does not	53	-2	82
Makes me Curious/Does not	23	41	77
Boring/Not Boring	60	-8	76

Note: Factor loadings are multiplied by 100 and rounded to the nearest integer.

Note: Factor loadings are multiplied by 100 and rounded to the nearest integer.

all three subcomponents contribute strongly and significantly to the explanation of global affect (overall $R^2 = .90$). Thus, we have strong support for the three-component model of attitude toward the ad.

Further strong support for the multicomponent model comes from our analysis of looking time as a function of global affect and the three subcomponents (overall $R^2 = .60$). If global affect were a straightforward mediator of the relationship between the three subcomponents and looking time, four conditions would be met (Pedhazur, 1982): (1) the three subcomponents would determine the global affect; (2) the three subcomponents would determine the looking time; (3) the global affect would determine the looking time; and (4) the contribution of the three subcomponents in determining looking time would decline or disappear when global affect was added to the equation, while the effect of global affect

Table 16.4
Standardized Regression Coefficients for the Model of Looking Time

	Dependent Variable			
Independent Variables	Global Affect	Looking Time	Looking Time	Looking Time
Global Affect		0.59		-0.12
Hedonism	0.74 [a]		0.40 [a]	0.48 [a]
Utilitarianism	0.28 [a]		-0.15 [b]	-0.11
Interestingness	0.53 [a]		0.66 [a]	0.72 [a]
Int-sqd	-0.00		-0.04	-0.04
R-sqd	0.90	0.35	0.60	0.60
F	330.57	77.72	53.09	42.43
significance	0.0001	0.0001	0.0001	0.0001

a $p < .001$

b $p < .01$

c $p < .05$

d $p < .1$

itself would maintain its significance. (For further discussion of these conditions, see Holbrook & Batra, 1987.)

By examining the standardized regression coefficients for the four regressions described by the above four conditions as set forth in Table 16.4, we see that, although conditions one, two, and three all hold, the fourth is not satisfied. Instead, when global affect and the three subcomponents of A_{ad} are included in the same regression to explain looking time, the significance of global affect disappears, while hedonism and interestingness maintain significance. This suggests that the construct of global affect contributes nothing further to the independent effects of the three subcomponents in explaining global affect. In other words, the three subcomponents determine looking time directly, with no significant mediating role for the summary measure of global affect toward the ad.

(Because the three subcomponents explain global affect at $R^2 = .90$, a correlation between global affect and looking time does appear at $R^2 = .35$. However, in the regression of looking time on hedonism, utilitarianism, and interestingness, this correlation appears to be spurious since global affect does not play a mediation role.)

Note that the three subcomponents have rather different standardized beta weights: .40 ($p < .001$), $-.15$($p < .01$), .66 ($p < .001$), respectively. In particular, notice that although the effect of the utilitarianism subcomponent of attitude is significant, its importance ($-.15$) is not nearly as great as that of hedonism (.40) or interestingness (.66). Further, the contribution direction of the utilitarianism subcomponent is in the negative direction. This suggests that the appraisal of an advertisement as informative, important, helpful, and useful (see Tables 16.1 and 16.3) actually reduces the likelihood of watching it.

DISCUSSION

We find that the study yields some strong support for a three-component model of attitude toward the ad. The subcomponents of hedonism, utilitarianism, and interestingness all contribute significantly to the overall measure of global affect.

Further, and of major significance to advertisers, they contribute differentially to the determination of whether a viewer will watch a television commercial. As can be seen in Table 16.4, that an ad is judged to be interesting or pleasing is considerably more important in getting people to watch it than that its message has some utility (which, if anything, appears to work against viewership). This result supports an idea that has long been promoted by creative departments. Apparently, in light of the increasing ease of nonviewing associated with zipping and zapping along with the premise that an unwatched message will have no influence, the new evidence dramatizes the importance of listening to the creative people who come up with new ways to make commercials fun and interesting.

Future work in this area should develop methods of checking on zipping and zapping in real-life situations. The chain of effects should be investigated downward to establish the determinants of attitude toward the brand. Further, the amount of time that a commercial is watched needs to be related to brand attitudes and brand purchases. Here, the ultimate study might investigate in-home viewing behavior in a split-cable setting where control can be exercised over the ads cablecast and where data can be gathered about the actual purchase activity of the person whose viewing behavior has been recorded, perhaps by means analogous to those used here to assess zipping and zapping.

REFERENCES

Anderson, D. R. (1985). On-line cognitive processing of television. In L. F. Alwitt &
    A. A. Mitchell (Eds.), *Psychological processes and advertising effects*, (pp. 177–
    199). Hillsdale, N.J.: Lawrence Erlbaum Associates.

Anderson, D. R. (1987, October). *Now you see them—now you don't: Frequency and duration of exiting behavior in a home viewing environment.* Paper presented at the Association for Consumer Research, Cambridge, MA.

Batra, R. T., & Ahtola, O. T. (1987). *The measurement and role of utilitarian and hedonic attitudes.* Unpublished manuscript, Columbia University Graduate School of Business.

Berlyne, D. (1960). *Conflict, arousal, and curiosity.* New York: McGraw-Hill.

Berlyne, D. (1971). *Aesthetics and psychobiology.* New York: Appleton-Century-Crofts.

Burke, M. C., & Edell, J. A. (1986). Ad reactions over time: Capturing changes in the real world. *Journal of Consumer Research, 13,* 114–118.

Gardner, M. P. (1985a). Does attitude toward the ad affect brand attitude under a brand evaluation set? *Journal of Marketing Research, 22,* 192–198.

Gardner, M. P. (1985b). Mood states and consumer behavior: A critical review. *Journal of Consumer Research, 12,* 281–300.

Heeter, C., & Greenberg, B. S. (1985). Profiling the zappers. *Journal of Advertising Research, 25* (2), 15–19.

Holbrook, M. B., & Batra, R. (1987). Assessing the role of emotions as mediators of consumer responses to advertising. *Journal of Consumer Research, 14,* 404–420.

IRI Information Resources, Inc. (1983). *Viewer zapping of TV commercials; pay TV audience accumulation over time; efficiently reaching heavy grocery buyers.* Chicago, IL: Author.

IRI Information Resources, Inc. (1985). *Network audience loss during commercial breaks.* Chicago, IL: Author.

Kaplan, B. M. (1985). Zapping—the real issue is communication. *Journal of Advertising Research, 25* (2), 9–13.

Lutz, R. J., MacKenzie, S. B., & Belch, G. E. (1983). Attitude toward the ad as a mediator of ad effectiveness: Determinants and consequences. In R. P. Bagozzi & A. M. Tybout (Eds.), *Advances in consumer research* (vol. 10, pp. 532–539), Ann Arbor, MI: Association for Consumer Research.

MacKenzie, S. B. (1986). Role of attention in mediating the effect of advertising on attribute importance. *Journal of Consumer Research, 13,* 174–195.

MacKenzie, S. B., Lutz, R. J., & Belch, G. E. (1986). Role of attitude toward the ad as a mediator of advertising effectiveness: A test of competing explanations. *Journal of Marketing Research, 23,* 130–143.

Mitchell, A. A. (1986). Effect of verbal and visual components of advertisements on brand attitudes and attitude toward the advertisement. *Journal of Consumer Research, 13,* 12–24.

Mitchell, A. A., & Olson, J. C. (1981). Are product attribute beliefs the only mediator of advertising effects on brand attitude? *Journal of Marketing Research, 18,* 318–332.

Olney, T. J. (1988). *Viewing time, attitude toward the ad, emotional response and related content as aspects of of advertising effectiveness: Antecedents of zipping and zapping.* Unpublished doctoral dissertation, Columbia University.

Olson, J. C., Toy, D. R., & Dover, P. A. (1982). Do cognitive responses mediate the effects of advertising content on cognitive structure? *Journal of Consumer Research, 9,* 245–262.

Pechmann, C., & Stewart, D. W. (1985). *The multidimensionality of persuasive com-*

munications: Theoretical and empirical foundations. Unpublished manuscript, Vanderbilt University, Owen Graduate School of Management, Nashville, TN.

Pedhazur, E. J. (1982). *Multiple regression in behavioral research* (2nd ed.). New York: CBS College Publishing.

Stewart, D. W., & Furse, D. H. (1985a). Effects of television advertising execution on recall, comprehension, and persuasion. *Psychology and Marketing, 2*, 135–160.

Stewart, D. W., & Furse, D. H. (1985b). *Effective television advertising*. Lexington, MA: D. C. Heath and Company.

Yorke, D. A., & Kitchen, P. J. (1985). Channel flickers and video speeders. *Journal of Advertising Research, 25* (2), 21–25.

Stimulus-Viewer Interactions

17

Message Effectiveness Can Be Increased by Matching Appeals to Recipients' Self-Schemas: Laboratory Demonstrations and a National Field Experiment

Timothy C. Brock, Laura A. Brannon,
and Carol Bridgwater

INTRODUCTION

The failure of dozens of well-designed laboratory studies conducted to identify the individual difference variables that function as strong, consistent predictors of susceptibility to influence has been underscored in authoritative reviews by A. E. Eagly (1981) and W. Wood and B. H. Stagner (in press). Although exceptions exist (e.g., Cacioppo, Petty, & Morris, 1983, and Snyder & DeBono, 1985), Eagly (1981) notes "the weak predictability and the instability of many findings" (p. 195) in the literature on individual differences in persuasion. One objective of these studies was to demonstrate a general condition under which individual differences will affect message acceptance.

The traditional approach toward individual differences in persuasion has suffered from major impediments. First, the mixed outcomes in the literature relating attributes to influence may have stemmed from the use of the same message for all recipients (although exceptions exist, e.g., Snyder & DeBono, 1985). Clearly, in order to influence different persons in face-to-face settings, one uses messages that are tailored to perceptions of the particular values, feelings, needs, capacities, and so on of each target person (Davis, 1982). Hence, it was hypothesized that persuasive messages would be more effective to the extent that they used appeals that were designed to correspond to the self-concepts of the recipients.

A second weakness of the traditional approach is that it attempts to categorize persons along dimensions such as self-esteem. These dimensions, although relevant and valid in and of themselves, may not actually encompass much of a recipient's self-concept. H. Markus defines the self-concept as being a system of self-schemas, or generalizations regarding important, salient aspects about the self (Markus & Sentis, 1982; Markus & Wurf, 1987). Obviously, the self consists of more than where an individual lies on one particular psychological dimension. (The self-concept consists of more than just whether or not a person is an extrovert, or whether or not the person has high self-esteem, although it may contain these schemas.)

Self-schemas are particularly important because they provide a frame of reference from which to interpret various kinds of information, as well as guide behavior (Markus, 1983). Markus and Sentis (1982) summarize the major findings indicating that self-schemas influence information processing about both the self and others:

> With respect to the self, individuals with self-schemata in particular domains: (1) can process information about the self efficiently (make judgments and decisions with relative ease and certainty); (2) are consistent in their responses; (3) have relatively better recognition memory and recall for information relevant to this domain; (4) can predict future behavior in the domain; (5) can resist information that is counter to a prevailing schema; and (6) evaluate new information for its relevance to a given domain. With respect to processing information about others, these individuals: (1) make accurate discriminations in the domain in question; (2) categorize or chunk schema-relevant information differentially; (3) are relatively more sensitive to variations in this domain; (4) select and prefer information that is relevant to this domain; and (5) make confident attributions and inferences about behavior in this domain. (p. 62)

In addition, people are particularly sensitive to self-relevant stimuli and process self-congruent stimuli efficiently (Markus & Wurf, 1987). In short, self-schemas influence information processing, goals, motivations, behaviors, and affect, as well as social perception, comparison, and interaction (Markus & Wurf, 1987). Given the profound and pervasive effects that self-schemas have on information processing and behavior, it is surprising that there has been only one limited attempt (Cacioppo, Petty, & Sidera, 1982) to examine the role of individual differences in persuasion from the perspective of self-schema research.

Markus and Wurf (1987) traced the evolution of self-concept research, from the view of a static, constant self to that of a dynamic, "working" self-concept. The working self-concept is that part of the total self-concept that is accessible at the moment. According to Markus and Wurf (1987), the self-concept, as it is presently formulated, is at once static and dynamic:

> Core aspects of self (one's self-schemas) may be relatively unresponsive to changes in one's social circumstances. Because of their importance in defining the self and their extensive elaboration, they may be chronically accessible. . . . Many other self-conceptions in the individual's system, however, will vary in accessibility depending on the individual's motivational state or on the prevailing social conditions. The working self-concept thus consists of the core self-conceptions embed-

ded in a context of more tentative self-conceptions that are tied to the prevailing circumstances. (p. 306)

Therefore, persuasion researchers must either measure these "tentative self-conceptions," which may change before the individual even receives the persuasive message, or focus on certain core aspects of the self.

Messages Match Recipients' Self-Schemas

To break the logjam of mixed results relating personal attributes to message acceptance, subjects' self-concepts were operationally defined in a way that corresponded directly to persons' sense of themselves (as sets of self-schemas). A schema set is defined as a collection of related verbal, symbolic, and visual schemas. A self-schema set is a set that consists of schemas relevant to the self. Schema sets were used (rather than just one or two, i.e., masculine/feminine schemas, as used in previous research) in an attempt to encompass a larger part of the individuals' self-concepts. Subjects were given sets of schemas and were asked to indicate which set best fit who they were.

Another innovation was the construction of persuasive messages that reflected the recipients' self-concepts (operationally defined as their set of self-schemas). It was hypothesized that persuasive messages would be more effective to the extent that they used appeals that were designed to correspond to the self-concepts of the recipients. In a similar vein, work by B. Schmitt (1988) has shown that an advertisement is more persuasive to the extent that the message makes claims about the product's attitude functions which correspond to the functional state of the recipient. The current studies differ from Schmitt's work, however, in that Schmitt geared persuasive messages to the functional state of the recipient (or the working self-concept), a state which was manipulated in the experiment, whereas the following studies examine the effects of matching persuasive appeals to enduring, core aspects of recipients' self-concepts.

The present research[1] builds on that of J. Cacioppo, R. Petty, and J. Sidera (1982), in which subjects who were legal-schematic rated legal messages as being particularly persuasive, and subjects who were religious-schematic rated religious messages as being particularly persuasive. The current research differs from that of Cacioppo et al. (1982) in two major respects. First, these studies use actual attitude change as the dependent variable; Cacioppo et al. (1982) used a measure of rated persuasiveness of the message as the dependent variable. Since subjects may not always be aware of what will be "persuasive" about a particular message, the present research improved on the principal dependent measure used by Cacioppo et al. (1982). Second, as noted previously, this research examined the efficacy of matching message appeals to sets of recipients' self-schemas, rather than single schemas as used by Cacioppo et al. (1982). Sets of self-schemas were used in an attempt to encompass a considerable portion of the subjects' self-concepts, not just a preference for a legal or religious perspective. Indeed, most persuasive messages, for example, advertising and informal social influence, cannot be composed as either a legal or religious tract. Instead, real-world persuasion capitalizes on a broad array of recipients' values, interests, life-style preferences, and so forth. Significant subsets of recipients' values, interests, and life-style preferences were represented in the present sets of self-schemas.

Role of Topic Familiarity

It was anticipated that familiarity with the attitude object could moderate the effect of matching message appeals to a recipient's self-schemas. Unfamiliar message topics could elicit more attention and more processing effort (Brock, Albert, & Becker, 1970). Furthermore, an unfamiliar message topic would elicit little attitude-relevant data that might provide an informational base of support for counterarguing (Wood & Stagner, in press). Finally, an unfamiliar target implies that the message alone cannot drive information processing, in contrast to a "strong, rich, well-articulated or non-ambiguous stimulus, such that the stimulus activates relevant cognitive structures . . . that drive the consequent processing" (Markus, Smith, & Moreland, 1985, p. 1508).

Assumptions and General Hypothesis

It is assumed that the core aspects of a person's self-concept (one's self-schemas) endure and that the person is aware of these core aspects of his or her self-concept. It is also assumed that sets of persuasive messages can be constructed so that the same arguments use different appeals, appeals that reflect different clusters of self-schemas. Four experiments were conducted in order to examine the effectiveness of matching persuasive messages to recipients' sets of self-schemas. The general hypothesis was that messages would elicit greater acceptance to the extent that they used appeals that corresponded to the self-assigned schema sets of the recipients. It was further anticipated that matching to self-schema sets would be more effective for unfamiliar attitude topics. Experiments 2 and 3 allowed examination of the role of familiarity.

EXPERIMENTS ONE, TWO, AND THREE: METHODOLOGY

Method for Experiment 1

Subjects and site. Subjects were 55 students enrolled in lower level mandatory English classes, grades ten and eleven, at an upper middle-class Ohio high school. These subjects were selected from an initial pool of 105 students because it was determined through pretesting that they were schematic with respect to one of the self-schema sets (see the following section). Note that 52 percent of the subjects were schematic with respect to one of the sets of self-schemas. This is

not a particularly low percentage of schematic subjects relative to related research. For example, Cacioppo et al. (1982) found that approximately 63 percent
of their subjects were either legal or religious schematic.

Materials: Self-concept self-classification. Markus (1977) found that subjects
who had an independent self-schema were consistent across different self-
classification tasks, whereas aschematics were inconsistent across tasks. Therefore, to ensure that the self-schema set matching had succeeded, the analyses
employed only subjects who assigned themselves to the same schema set on two
different occasions, using two different methods. Two methods were used to
enable subjects to type their self-schemas: a card-ranking procedure and an
adjective-ranking procedure. The present aim was to enable subjects to assign
themselves quickly and easily to one of four self-schema sets, which would be
relevant to the subject population (high school and first year college students).

As previously noted, a schema set is defined as a collection of related verbal,
symbolic, and visual schemas. A self-schema set is a set that consists of schemas
relevant to the self. The schema sets stemmed from a four-type scheme proposed
by D. Keirsey and M. Bates (1978), a popular alternative to the 16-fold Myers-
Briggs Type Indicator. Schema sets were used (rather than just one or two, i.e.,
masculine/feminine schemas, as in previous research) in an attempt to encompass
a larger part of the individuals' self-concepts.

The particular sets of schemas used were selected for two reasons. First,
because schemas can be represented in a variety of ways, "representations . . .
are not just verbal propositions or depictions of traits and demographic characteristics. Rather, representations of self may be cognitive and/or affective; they
may be in verbal, image, neural, or sensorimotor form" (Markus & Wurf, 1987,
p. 307). Hence, at least some of the schemas in each set had to be represented
graphically, as well as verbally. Second, the schema sets had to be meaningful
for the subject population (a criterion used by Markus, 1977).

The schema sets chosen were part of a "Discovery" program used in many
California high schools to increase teacher-student understanding and cooperation. The schema sets were found to be relevant and meaningful to high school
students (Lowry, 1987). (Other research has shown that the Keirsey-Bates approach, upon which the present schema sets were based, is meaningful and
relevant to older populations as well, e.g., Hoffman & Betkouski, 1981;
McCarley & Carskadon, 1986). The schema sets, depicted on four cards, did
facilitate quick and easy self-classification by subjects.

As a pretest, subjects received four cards printed in four colors (orange, brown,
blue, and green); each contained four trait adjectives preceded by "I am . . . ,"
a short descriptive paragraph that elaborated the adjectives, and a composite
drawing of persons whose activities and costuming embodied the traits and
descriptive paragraph (see Figure 17.1). A distinct schema set was depicted on
each color card: warm-communicative-compassionate [Blue]; adventuresome-
skillful-competitive [Orange]; versatile-wise-conceptual [Green]; or responsible-
dependable-helpful [Brown]. The printed instructions for subjects were as fol-

Figure 17.1
Four "Color Cards" for Schema Sets

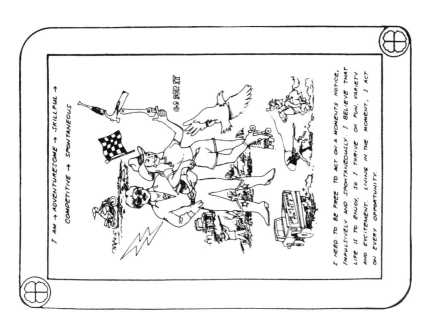

I AM → ADVENTURESOME → SKILLFUL →
COMPETITIVE → SPONTANEOUS

GO FOR IT

I NEED TO BE FREE TO ACT ON A MOMENTS NOTICE,
IMPULSIVELY AND SPONTANEOUSLY. I BELIEVE THAT
LIFE IS TO ENJOY, SO I THRIVE ON FUN, VARIETY
AND EXCITEMENT. LIVING IN THE MOMENT, I ACT
ON EVERY OPPORTUNITY.

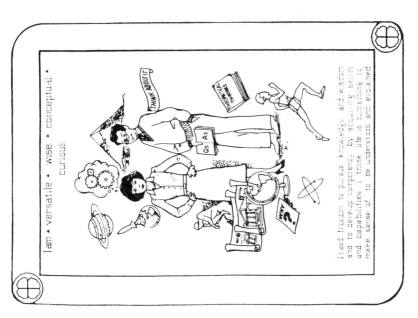

I am ▲ versatile ▲ wise ▲ conceptual ▲
curious

THINK ABOUT IT

THEORETICAL THINKING

Qs As

WHY?

I need freedom to pursue knowledge and wisdom
and to develop competency by acquiring skills
and capabilities. I think life is something to
make sense of, to be understood and explained

291

lows: "Look at the four types of persons represented on the attached cards. Who
are you? I am a (name the color) _____. What color is least you (name the
color) _____." The colors of the cards were used as a nominal category to
allow subjects to choose which set of schemas was most meaningful to them.

An alternative measure of the four schema sets was used in the actual experiment session. A procedure which was similar to, yet not identical with, traditional methods for assessing subjects' self-schemas was employed (Markus,
1977), in which subjects were asked to select the adjectives that described
themselves. Subjects were given five rows of adjective groups and asked to rank
them in terms of how descriptive the adjective clusters were of themselves
(1 = most descriptive and 4 = least descriptive). For example, one row contained the following clusters:

practical	competitive	curious	unique
sensible	impetuous	conceptual	empathetic
dependable	impactful	knowledgeable	communicative

The above columns represent, in order, the schema sets for "Brown," "Orange," "Green," and "Blue," but they were not labeled with color "names."
Column scores were summed to arrive at an alternative determination of the
subject's self-assignment to a relevant schema set. The column with the lowest
score represented the subject's preferred schema set.

It should be noted that, although subjects were forced to choose only one set
of self-schemas, certain schemas appearing in other sets might also have been
self-relevant. By selecting only one set, a subject chose which set of schemas
overlapped most with his or her own self-concept. There is no assumption that
the particular set of schemas encompassed the subject's self-concept.

Consumer messages. One persuasive communication advocated raising the
drinking age to 21 (Age). Subjects read the message shortly before the drinking
age was actually raised in Ohio. The other message promoted the (fictitious)
"No Limits Ski Resort" (Ski). Persuasive messages[2], of about 300 words, were
constructed, one geared to each of the four sets of self-schemas for both Ski and
Age. The text of the messages was not presented like an advertisement, but
rather as blocks of copy. The communications were deliberately written to em-
body appeals that matched the schema sets (Figure 17.1). For example, the Ski
message aimed at "Blues" (warm-communicative-compassionate) stressed the
harmonious, warm atmosphere of the resort:

Come and experience the harmony of No Limits with our warm and cheerful guests
and staff. We like to consider ourselves one big, happy community, one that you
could easily become a part of. Staying at our lodge affords you a wonderful
opportunity to meet other unique and sensitive people.

The Ski message aimed at "Greens" (wise-conceptual-curious) utilized logical appeals and emphasized the learning opportunities offered by the resort:

> We also offer the latest advances in form-analysis. With a sample of your skiing style, we can scientifically profile your technique, highlighting both your strengths and weaknesses. Then our qualified staff can explain how your style should be modified, and why.

The Ski message aimed at "Oranges" (adventuresome-skillful-competitive) stressed the excitement and the competitive environment of the resort:

> The No Limits Lodge offers non-stop fun and adventure to its guests. Imagine yourself racing down one of the most challenging slopes of your life. We provide slopes of all levels of difficulty, for skiers with any degree of experience. So no matter how skillful you may be, there will always be a greater challenge waiting for you around the corner.

Finally, the Ski message aimed at "Browns" (responsible-dependable-sensible) emphasized the quality and reliability of the resort's facilities and staff, as well as the reasonable rates:

> You deserve a weekend off. You've worked hard this week and deserve to be treated with respect, and that's our specialty. Our dependable, well-trained, and responsible staff will be ready to meet your needs at a moment's notice. Also, we offer private lessons with our qualified instructors, at no extra charge, as well as free ski-form analysis. Why not take advantage of such a good opportunity?

Supplementary studies revealed that the messages reflected their intended schema sets and that they were equivalent in persuasiveness. (See note 2.)

Dependent measures. At the pretest, the bulk of the questionnaire items dealt with uses of leisure time, whereas the filler items in the main experimental session were unrelated to leisure time. The critical attitude measures were: "The No Limits ski resort at Mount, Ohio is among the best in the country" and "Ohio law should increase the drinking age from 19 to 21." Agreement was rated on a ten-point scale running from 1, strongly disagree, to 10, strongly agree.

Procedure. At the pretest, teachers told students that the 21st Century Foundation would appreciate their cooperation in a "Leisure time activities study" and that their participation was voluntary. Students identified their "colors" (see Figure 17.1) and then filled out a leisure time questionnaire containing the dependent variable premeasures. Subjects had no difficulty in expressing their opinions about both familiar and unfamiliar attitude objects.

At the main experimental session, five weeks later, teachers told students that researchers at The Ohio State University were conducting a study on "communication and opinions" and would appreciate their voluntary cooperation.

Each subject received one communication which matched their "color type" and one which did not, based upon first session self-ratings. The non-matching message corresponded to the self-schema set "color type" selected as least descriptive. Which communication (Ski/Age) was matching and which was not, as well as the message order (Ski/Age versus Age/Ski), were randomly determined. To ensure that each subject received the correct messages, each booklet had the student's name on it.

After reading the communications, subjects completed a questionnaire which contained the attitudinal dependent measures and the second measure of self-schema set, the adjective-clusters rankings. Subjects completed all materials and questionnaires in less than 30 minutes.

Method (Experiments 2 and 3)

Experiment 2 ($N = 98$, selected because they were schematic with respect to one of the four schema sets, from a pretest subject pool of $N = 189$) and Experiment 3 ($N = 147$, selected because they were schematic with respect to one of the four schema sets, from a pretest subject pool of $N = 263$), using college freshmen, followed the same procedure as Experiment 1. The only changes involved the messages. Experiments 2 and 3 promoted familiar and unfamiliar brands of consumer products. Experiment 2 promoted either a familiar (King's Island) or an unfamiliar (Lake Darien) amusement park, and either a familiar (Clairol's Condition) or an unfamiliar (Abound) hair conditioner. Experiment 3 promoted either the familiar or the unfamiliar amusement park, as in Experiment 2, and either a familiar (Prell) or an unfamiliar (Abound) shampoo. Note that both Abound shampoo/conditioner and Lake Darien amusement park exist; however, they are unknown products in central Ohio. The same communications were used for both the familiar and the unfamiliar brands of the products. For both experiments, the only difference between the messages was the brand name (Lake Darien versus King's Island, Abound versus Clairol's Condition/Prell).

Dependent measures. As in Experiment 1, for both Experiments 2 and 3, the bulk of the questionnaire items at the pretest dealt with uses of leisure time; however, the filler items in the main experimental session consisted of Rotter's Internal-External Locus of Control questionnaire (short version). The critical attitude measures for both Experiments 2 and 3 were: "King's Island [Lake Darien] is among the best amusement parks in the country" and "Abound hair conditioner [Clairol's Condition] is one of the best on the market" for Experiment 2; "Abound [Prell] shampoo is one of the best on the market" for Experiment 3. Agreement was rated on a ten-point scale running from 1, strongly disagree, to 10, strongly agree.

EXPERIMENTS ONE, TWO, AND THREE: RESULTS

Key Findings

Overall message effectiveness. Messages that were ineffective to begin with were not expected to benefit from type matching. Paired t-tests revealed that the Ski messages for Experiment 1 were generally effective and moved recipients in the direction advocated; however, the Age message failed to move recipients in the advocated direction, and, therefore, the Experiment 1 analyses dealt only with the Ski messages. In addition, for Experiments 2 and 3, the King's Island messages also failed inasmuch as postscore acceptance means were actually lower than prescore means. Therefore, King's Island data were not included in the analyses.

Determination of schematic subjects. Markus (1977) found that subjects who had an independent self-schema were consistent across different self-classification tasks, whereas aschematics were inconsistent across tasks. Therefore, to ensure that the self-schema set matching had succeeded, the analyses employed only subjects who assigned themselves to the same schema set at both the pretest and the main experimental session. A subset of these schematic subjects who picked the same self-schema set and rejected the same schema set at both the pretest and the main experimental session was also examined (Me/Not Me Schematic; a term borrowed from Crane & Markus, 1982).

It should be noted, however, that because subjects at the main experimental session first read persuasive messages geared to particular schema sets (which they had not seen again for five weeks) and later described themselves using the adjective-clusters, there could be a problem with experimental demand. However, this appears unlikely, given that, after reading the persuasive messages, subjects filled out a questionnaire (which served as a distractor task) before selecting a self-schema set using the adjectives.

Effects of matching. There were no interactions with Sex and Matching. Therefore, Sex will not be discussed further. As shown in Figure 17.2, messages which reflected recipients' self-schema sets were more persuasive than non-matching messages. The results for Experiment 1 (Ski Resort) are shown in Figure 17.2. An analysis of variance was performed with schema set Matching (versus Nonmatching) as the sole factor.[3] The main effect of Matching to recipients' schema sets was borderline significant [$F(1,48) = 3.71, p < .06$)]; and the main effect of Matching for the Me/Not Me Schematic subset of subjects was also marginally significant [$F(1,24) = 3.10, p < .10$].

The results for the familiar Shampoo/Conditioner are shown in Figure 17.3. The same procedures, communications, and dependent measures were used in both Experiments 2 and 3; therefore, it appeared feasible to conduct an analysis of the combined data in which the two factors were Experiment (2 versus 3) and schema set Matching (versus Nonmatching). For the familiar Conditioner/Sham-

Figure 17.2
Mean Pre–Post Ski Message Acceptance Change (Experiment 1)

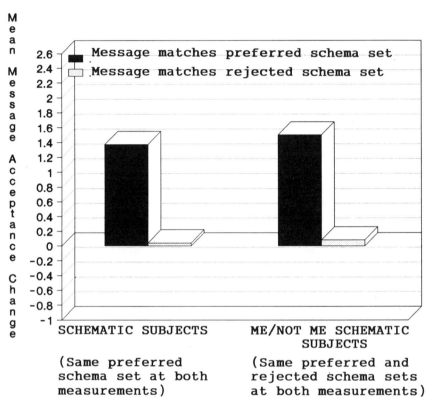

poo message, the schema set Matching main effect approached conventional levels of significance [$F(1, 121) = 2.96$, $p < .09$] and was significant for the Me/Not Me Schematic subset of subjects [$F(1,64) = 5.64$, $p < .02$]. There were no reliable Matching × Experiment interactions. For the unfamiliar conditioner, Abound, there were no effects of matching.

The results for Lake Darien amusement park are shown in Figure 17.4. As for the Shampoo/Conditioner, because the same procedures, communications, and dependent measures were used in both experiments, an analysis of variance was performed on the combined data in which the two factors were Experiment (2 versus 3) and schema set Matching (versus Nonmatching). The means for both the Schematic and the Me/Not Me Schematic subjects were in the predicted direction: messages reflecting subjects' schema sets were more persuasive than nonmatching messages. The schema set Matching main effect approached conventional levels of significance for the Me/Not Me Schematic subjects [$F (1,51) = 2.95$, $p < .09$]. There was also a Matching × Experiment interaction, which revealed that the matching effect was more successful for Exper-

Figure 17.3
Mean Pre–Post Clairol/Prell Message Acceptance Change (Experiments 2 and 3 Combined)

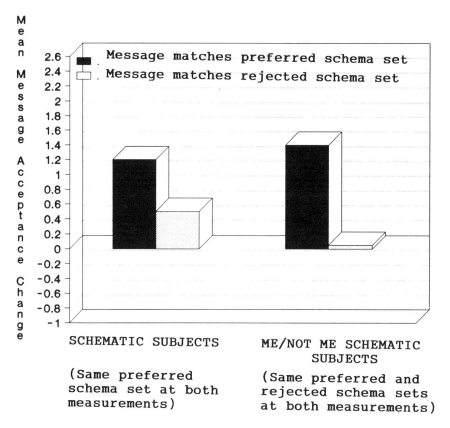

SCHEMATIC SUBJECTS

(Same preferred
schema set at both
measurements)

ME/NOT ME SCHEMATIC
SUBJECTS

(Same preferred and
rejected schema sets
at both measurements)

iment 2 than for Experiment 3 [$F(1,118) = 4.41, p <.04$], but interaction was not present for the Me/Not Me Schematic subjects.

Effects of Matching Within Each of the Four Schema Sets

The effects of matching were examined for each schema set in each of the first three experiments. The data were submitted to analyses of variance as well as sign tests of the patterns of the observed differences between matched and nonmatched cells. In some cases, empty cells reduced the number of possible sign-test comparisons. This approach is illustrated with the results of Experiment 1 for the Ski message and Experiments 2 and 3 combined for the Clairol/Prell messages (see Figures 17.5 and 17.6).

Analyses of variance with Matching and Self-Schema Set as the factors could not be performed for the Ski message in Experiment 1, due to missing cells.

Figure 17.4
**Mean Pre–Post Park Message Acceptance Change (Experiments 2 and 3
Combined)**

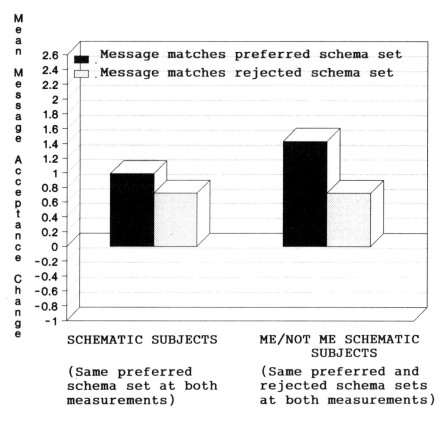

However, a sign test was performed on the possible comparisons of schema set
Matching with Nonmatching mean changes in message acceptance. (See Figure
17.5.) Of the six comparisons, all but one showed that messages which were
geared to recipients' schema sets were more persuasive than nonmatching messages (sign test, p < .11).

As in Figure 17.3, because the same procedures, communications, and dependent measures were used in both Experiments 2 and 3 for both the amusement
park and the shampoo, it appeared feasible to conduct an analysis of the combined
data in which the three factors were Experiment (2 versus 3), Matching, and
Schema Set. However, due to missing cells, sign tests were performed on the
group means for Matching and Schema Set for the two experiments combined.
As shown in Figure 17.6, matching messages were significantly more persuasive
than nonmatching messages across schema sets for Clairol/Prell (seven out of
eight comparisons, sign-test $p < .04$).

Figure 17.5
Mean Pre–Post Ski Message Acceptance Change by Recipients' Self-Schema Sets
(Experiment 1)

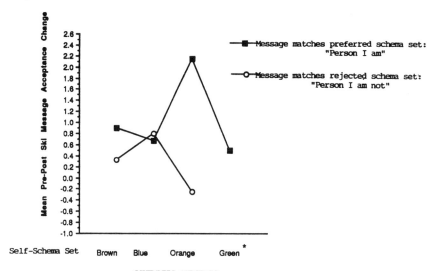

SCHEMATIC SUBJECTS
(Same preferred schema set at both measurements)

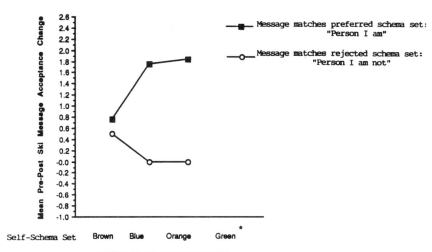

ME/NOT ME SCHEMATIC SUBJECTS
(Same preferred and rejected schema sets at both measurements)

Note: There were no "Green" Schematic subjects in the Non-Matching condition.

Figure 17.6
Mean Pre-Post Clairol/Prell Message Acceptance Change by Recipients' Self-Schema Sets (Experiments 2 and 3 Combined)

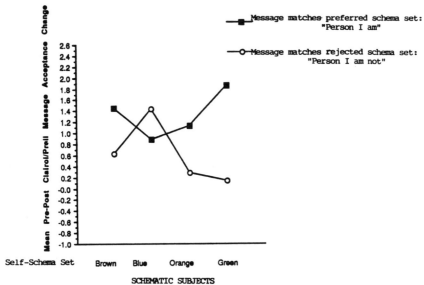

(Same preferred schema set at both measurements)

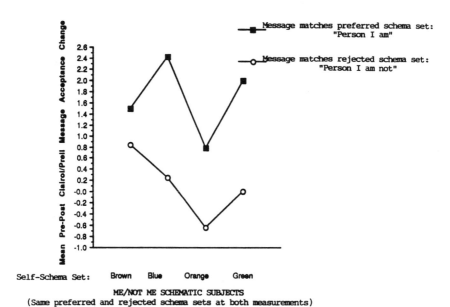

ME/NOT ME SCHEMATIC SUBJECTS
(Same preferred and rejected schema sets at both measurements)

For the Lake Darien message in Experiments 2 and 3, the pattern of differences was similar to that shown for Clairol/Prell in Figure 17.6: acceptance was higher for Matching than for Nonmatching cells across schema sets. The sign-test p value for the Lake Darien message was .19 for Experiments 2 and 3 combined.

Overall, the principal findings of the three experiments demonstrated that the messages that matched the recipients' sets of self-schemas were more persuasive than the nonmatching messages, across the four schema sets.

METHOD FOR EXPERIMENT FOUR: NATIONAL FIELD EXPERIMENT

The schema-matching hypothesis was further tested in a field experiment. Direct-mail persuasive messages were sent to a national sample of real consumers. Although current ideology in direct response marketing invokes measurement of targets' values (e.g., psychographics), actual marketing practice appears to exploit values indirectly by using proxies such as the targets' residence in a particular zip code, their level of education, their previous purchasing behavior, and so forth. Prior direct measurement of targets' values, and subsequent use of that measured information in a mail solicitation, are rarely undertaken.

The present field experiment was conducted in two steps akin to the above laboratory experiments. First, the self-schema sets of former customers of a weight-loss company were measured. Several months later, these lapsed dieters were sent a direct-mail solicitation in which they were invited to reactivate their membership in the weight-loss company. The text of the appeal was matched, or not, to the dieters' previously measured self-schemas. The dependent variable was the return of a business reply card to reactivate membership in the weight-loss program.

Subjects: Dieters

The initial pool of potential subjects included 7,248 past customers of the weight-loss company, the dieters. Names were drawn nationwide from 24 branches to be representative of the metro/suburban/small town mix of the firm's branches across the United States. In the present sample, 2,834 dieters were in metro locations, 2,654 were in suburban locations, and 1,760.were in small towns.

Self-Schema Sets of Dieters

Subjects first received a letter from the (fictitious) Center for Personality Research. They were asked to complete the card-sorting and adjective-ranking measures (used in the previous experiments) at the end of the following letter:

Dear Friend,

Would you take a few minutes to complete this self-description checklist that most people find fun to do?

We are a research organization which is conducting a nationwide study to develop new ways to understand people. We've enclosed some materials which will just take a few minutes to complete. We would appreciate your response so that we can have a representative sample of people from across the country.

Simply follow the instructions shown below and mail back your response using this stamped envelope.

As a token of our thanks we've enclosed a new dollar bill. Can you take a few minutes to complete this now?

Thanks for your help by participating in this research!

Sincerely, (name of President of Center for Personality Research).

Pilot testing revealed that asking subjects to fill out both the adjective checklist and the card sort at the same time did not inflate the correspondence between these two measures.[4]

The order of the schema-set measures, card sort and adjective ranking, was counterbalanced in another version of the letter. The adjective checklist also requested information about sex and age. The label on the business reply envelope included the subject's pre-assigned identification number. In this fashion, some information about the schema-sets of 3,381 lapsed dieters was obtained.

Scoring Schematicity

Since subjects actually wrote the word "Yes" on the card that represented their preferred schema set and the word "No" on the card that represented their rejected schema set, there was no ambiguity about the schema assignment using the card measure. For the adjective-ranking measure, however, it was possible for subjects to show "ties" as to which schema sets were most, and least, self-descriptive. Recall that subjects' adjective scores were determined by summing down the columns representing each "color." Subjects who did not properly follow the adjective ranking were assigned missing values for this task. However, even if a subject correctly followed the self-scoring instructions, it was possible for him or her to report ties. For example, a person could have column totals of eight for both the "Blue" and the "Brown" self-schema sets. In the initial analysis of results, such a subject was assigned to the schema set that corresponded to the one stipulated in his or her card sort; otherwise, a subject who showed a tie received a missing value for the adjective ranking.

Example of scoring with adjective-ranking tie. If a subject tied with respect to his or her most self-descriptive schema set, reporting equal totals for "Blue" and "Brown," for example, and had indicated "Blue" on the card sort, then he or she was considered schematic for "Blue." If, on the other hand, that subject had said he or she was "Orange" on the card sort, there would be no basis for breaking the tie, and the subject received a missing value for the adjective ranking.

Schematic subjects were those whose preferences on both the card and adjective tasks concurred. Thus, the initial analysis of results included some subjects who tied on the adjective measure.

Assignment to Matching, Nonmatching, and Control Conditions

Approximately 90 percent of the subjects were randomly assigned (via a random number generator) to receive a direct-mail solicitation whose appeals either matched, approximately 45 percent, or did not match, approximately 45 percent, their schematic indication. In addition, approximately 10 percent of the subjects received a control solicitation that was neutral to schema-set. The solicitations corresponded to the "colors" of the earlier experiments.

Assignment to Letter "Color" Conditions

In order to know which letter "color" to send to a subject, the preferred and rejected schema sets were taken into account. Card-sort preference was given precedence in the case of discrepancies with adjective-ratings. If a subject did not return cards, or if the cards were incomplete, the subject was assigned to the preferred and rejected schema sets indicated by his or her adjective rankings. Note that such cases were eventually excluded from the principal analyses because these analyses focused upon schematic subjects, that is, subjects for whom both card-sort and adjective-ranking information was available.

Direct-Mail Materials

The direct-mail package included five items: a 500-word letter, a 150-word personal insert, a strip of four "10% off" coupons valid for the weight-loss company's products, a special club membership card, and a business reply card to be returned to the company—the dependent variable. All items, except the coupons, were written to correspond to a particular "color" schema set or were neutral (control condition).

Letter. Each letter described five specific benefits from reactivation of weight-loss membership: a lifetime VIP status at the company's branches, one year's worth of free weekly visits, free two-day counseling sessions, coupons (described above), and 10 percent off fees until March 31, 1989.

Insert. The shorter insert, on a different kind of stationery than the letter, summarized and reinforced the key "color" appeals.

Club membership card and reply card. The membership and reply cards also contained "color" (schema set) rhetoric.

As stated previously, the letter, the insert, and the club membership and reply cards, each were written to correspond to a particular schema set. A "Blue" subject who was assigned to the schema set matching condition, for example, received a "Blue" letter, a "Blue" insert, and "Blue" membership and reply cards.

Control Condition Text

The control condition materials attempted to be schema neutral. The letter and insert focused on benefits, and the membership and reply cards omitted rhetorical embellishment.

Dependent Variable: Reply Card Return

Reactivation of membership in (name of firm) was accomplished by checking "yes" and mailing a first-class business reply card. The cards were collected for 90 days after the completion of the direct-mail drop.

RESULTS FROM EXPERIMENT FOUR: NATIONAL FIELD EXPERIMENT

Distribution of Messages to Schema Sets

A randomization procedure for allocating subjects to matching, nonmatching, and control messages has been described.

Schema set information was obtained from 3,381 subjects; of these, 3,277, or 97 percent, were classifiable as "Brown," "Orange," "Green," or "Blue." The percentages in each set for schematic subjects ($N = 2,804$) are reported in the fourth row of Table 17.1.

Note that the current sample of weight-conscious adults has a higher percentage of "Browns" than the high school and college student samples, the first three rows of Table 17.1. However, the younger adults, under age 34 (row five), showed a schema set distribution pattern that was similar to one of the college samples (row two).

The distribution of messages to schema sets is shown in Table 17.2. Recall the planned assignment of approximately 10 percent of the subjects to a control message, 45 percent to a matching message, and 45 percent to a nonmatching message. In accordance with the randomization procedure, the diagonal cells, for example, "Blue" to "Blue," are all about 45 percent. Each schema set type received approximately 10 percent control messages.

Table 17.2 row totals show that 48 percent of the dieters were "Brown"; 31 percent, "Blue"; 12 percent, "Green"; and about 8 percent, "Orange." These percentages were about the same as those in the general population ($N = 3277$)[5] before sorting for schematics. Note that "Orange" was the most rejected self-

Table 17.1
Self-Assigned Schema Sets Across Experiments: Mean Percentages

Experiment	N	Blue (%)	Brown (%)	Green (%)	Orange (%)
#1: High School	50	22.0	16.0	4.0	58.0
#2: College	98	21.4	31.6	16.3	30.6
#3: College	147	21.1	19.0	9.5	50.3
#4: Dieters					
Total Dieters	2084	31.3	48.5	11.9	8.4
Age ≤ 34	610	39.3	33.3	11.8	15.6
Age > 34	1474	28.0	54.8	11.9	5.4
Returns	119	21.0	61.3	11.8	5.9

Note: Sets of Self-Schemas are particular combinations of verbal, symbolic, and visual schemas (see Figure 17.1) to which schematic subjects readily assigned themselves on two different occasions, using two different techniques. All percentages are based on horizontal row totals. As well as displaying the Total and the Returns for Experiment Four (data rows 4 and 7), the Total for Experiment Four was broken into subjects age 34 and younger (data row 5) and those 35 and older (data row 6). Subjects under age 34 were more comparable to the college samples.

schema and hence the message "color" chosen most often for messages sent to subjects who were randomly assigned to the nonmatching condition.

The percentages of matching, nonmatching, and control messages assigned to each schema set color for schematic subjects are shown in Table 17.3. For example, for 652 "Blues," 46.78 percent received matching messages (i.e., "Blue"), 44.63 percent received nonmatching messages ("Brown," "Orange," or "Green"), and 8.59 percent received the control "schema-free" message.

Principal Findings: Returned Cards

Overall return rate. The mailing of 3,381 invitations resulted in a return of 182 cards, a return rate of 5.4 percent. This rate was somewhat higher than the bulk of the return rates reported in authoritative textbook treatments of direct response behavior. For example, R. Harper (1986) uses 2 percent in many of her worked illustrations; the actual response rates reported in her case studies never exceeded 7.5 percent.

Table 17.2
Experiment 4: Initial Distribution of Messages to Schematic Subjects' Schema Sets

Assigned Message "Color"	Self-Schema "Color"			
	Blue	Brown	Green	Orange
	(%)	(%)	(%)	(%)
Blue	46.8	3.1	10.1	10.3
Brown	6.6	45.5	10.9	16.1
Green	10.3	5.6	47.2	22.4
Orange	27.8	35.4	25.0	43.7
Control	8.6	10.5	6.9	7.5
Total N	652	1010	248	174
Hor. % N	31.3	48.5	11.9	8.4

Note: The first rows contain column (vertical) percentages for Schematic subjects. The seventh row lists the horizontal percentage breakdown for the total Schematic sample. For example, 31.3% of the Schematic subject sample was "Blue," and 48.5% of the Schematic subject sample was "Brown."

Effects of matching to self-schema sets on return rates. Actual card returns for the Schematic subjects in the control, matching, and nonmatching conditions are shown in Table 17.4. In general, the overall results supported the matching hypothesis: of the 182 returned cards, 50 percent were Matching, while only 40 percent were Nonmatching.

Recall from Table 17.3 that approximately equivalent percentages of subjects, 46 percent and 45 percent, were assigned to matching and nonmatching, respectively. The control condition percentage rate of the card return was the same as the population percentage of schematics assigned to the control condition, that is, 9.2. Thus, improvement in acceptance of the re-enlistment promotion appeared to be caused by self-schema matching.

The net improvement from matching is shown in Table 17.5. All schema types, except "Green," exhibited the matching effect, and the overall net gain from matching was 9 percent.

Recall that, in sorting for schematic subjects, adjective-cluster ties were counted favorably. For example, a person who classified himself or herself as

Table 17.3
Experiment 4: Initial Distribution of Matching Versus Nonmatching Messages to Schematic Subjects' Schema Sets

	Self-Schema "Color"			
Experimental Condition	Blue	Brown	Green	Orange
	(%)	(%)	(%)	(%)
Control	8.6	10.5	6.9	7.5
Non-Matching	44.6	44.1	46.0	48.9
Matching	46.8	45.5	47.2	43.7
Total N	652	1010	248	174
Hor. % N	31.3	48.5	11.9	8.4

Note: The first three rows contain column percentages for the Schematic subjects. The fifth row lists the horizontal percentage breakdown for the total Schematic sample. For example, 31.3% of the Schematic subject sample was "Blue," and 48.5% of the Schematic subject sample was "Brown."

"Brown" using the cards shown in Figure 17.1, was classified as "Brown" even if the adjective-cluster scores were tied for "Brown" and some other schema, say, "Blue." A more stringent criterion for schematicity requires that the adjective-cluster score be unequivocal; that is, adjective-cluster ties would not be counted as schematic. One reason for eliminating subjects whose adjective-cluster scores were equivocal is that initially subjects filled out both the adjective rankings and the card sort at the same time. Eliminating ties on the adjective clusters helped ensure that participating in the card sort did not influence subjects' responses on the adjective rankings.

The effects of matching for Stringently-Schematic subjects are shown in Table 17.6. Although the population assignments to matching and nonmatching conditions were approximately 45 percent for the Stringently-Schematic subjects ($N = 1786$), 52 percent of the actual card returns were matching, and 39 percent were nonmatching, while the control condition values were about the same. Again, improvement in acceptance of the reenlistment promotion appeared to be caused by matching the message to the recipients' self-schema set.

The net improvement from matching for Stringently-Schematic subjects is shown in Table 17.7. Note that all schema types, except "Green," exhibited the matching effect and that the overall net gain from matching was 12 percent.

Table 17.4
Experiment 4: Effects of Matching Versus Nonmatching Messages to Schematic Subjects' Schema Sets on Card Returns

	Self-Schema "Color"			
Experimental Condition	Blue	Brown	Green	Orange
	(%)	(%)	(%)	(%)
Control	8.0	12.3	0.0	0.0
Non-Matching	40.0	38.4	64.3	14.3
Matching	52.0	49.3	35.7	85.7
Total N	25	73	14	7
Hor. % N	21.0	61.3	11.8	5.9

Note: The first three rows contain column percentages for the Schematic subjects' card returns. The fifth row lists the horizontal percentage breakdown for the schematic subjects' card returns. For example, 21.0% of the Schematic subjects' card returns were "Blue."

Although it is not clear why "Greens" trended in a direction opposed to matching, it may be speculated that some aspects of the predominant nonmatching message, "Orange," were especially appealing to "Greens." In any case, the occurrence of this opposing trend indicated that there was differential sensitivity to the messages. Because there were only a few "Green" and "Orange" cases among the actual card returns, the differences for "Green," as well as "Orange," probably should not be assigned particular importance.

NATIONAL FIELD EXPERIMENT: DISCUSSION

The return rate in the present direct-mail experiment was near the high end of the range reported in authoritative direct-mail texts (Harper, 1986). Matching messages to dieters' self-schema sets improved the rate of card return in comparison to dieters who received a nonmatching or a control message. For dieters whose schematicity was stringently determined—by both color-card choice and highest ranked adjective cluster—net improvement over the nonmatching comparison condition was more than 12 percent; average improvement over the population percentages was 8.7 percent; and, at the same time, the control message elicited virtually no change. Therefore, the efficacy of matching messages to recipients' sets of self-schemas was demonstrated in the field, as well as in the laboratory.

Table 17.5
Experiment 4: Net Improvement from Matching to Schematic Subjects' Self-Schema Sets: Percentage Card Returns for Schematic Subjects (Table 17.4) Compared to Population Percentages of Schematic Subjects (Table 17.3)

	Blue	Brown	Green	Orange	Overall
			Self-Schema "Color"		
Non-Matching	-4.63	-5.70	18.32	-34.56	-4.53
Matching	5.22	3.87	11.47	42.03	4.50
% Net Improvement	9.85	9.57	-6.85	76.59	9.03
Total N	23	64	14	7	108

Note: Schematic subject population percentages (Table 17.3) were subtracted from the obtained card return percentages (Table 17.4) to calculate the values in the first two rows. Then the decrease due to Nonmatching was subtracted from the increase due to Matching to obtain the net improvement attributable to matching messages to Schematic subjects' sets of self-schemas. For "Greens" the matching effect was not obtained.

GENERAL DISCUSSION

The studies reported here examined the efficacy of matching persuasive messages to recipients' self-schema sets, in both laboratory and field settings. Messages using appeals which reflected recipients' sets of self-schemas were more persuasive than nonmatching messages across the four self-schema sets. This conclusion was further supported by tests of the combined probabilities across seven comparisons (Ski dependent variable in Experiment 1 and Clairol/Prell, Abound, and Park in Experiments 2 and 3). The method of adding Zs (Rosenthal, 1978) yielded $p < .06$ and, for the Me/Not Me Schematic subjects, the corresponding p was less than .004. When the Zs were adjusted for the extent of nonindependence of the comparisons in Experiments 2 and 3, the combined probability became $p < .05$ and, for the Me/Not Me Schematic subjects, the p was again less than .004.

It was demonstrated that gearing persuasive messages to recipients' sets of self-schemas can be done easily and successfully. Although the present studies examined the efficacy of self-schema set matching messages for consumer products, there is no reason to suspect that the matching effect is limited to consumer issues.

Table 17.6
Experiment 4: Effects of Matching Versus Nonmatching Messages to Stringently-Schematic Subjects' Schema Sets on Card Returns

Experimental Condition	Self-Schema "Color"				
	Blue	Brown	Green	Orange	Overall
	(%)	(%)	(%)	(%)	(%)
Control	4.2	13.9	0.0	0.0	9.4
Non-Matching	41.7	35.4	66.7	0.0	38.7
Matching	54.2	50.8	33.3	100.0	51.9
Total N	24	65	12	5	106
Hor. % N	22.6	61.3	11.3	4.7	100.0

Note: The first three rows contain column percentages for the Stringently-Schematic subjects' card returns. The fourth row lists the total frequency for each column and the fifth row lists the horizontal percentage breakdown of card returns for the Stringently-Schematic subjects. For example, 22.6% of the Stringently-Schematic card returns were "Blue."

In this study, self-concept was operationalized as sets of self-schemas, particular combinations of verbal, symbolic, and visual schemas (see Figure 17.1) to which schematic subjects readily assigned themselves on two different occasions, using two different techniques. The persuasive messages were constructed to reflect or not reflect these schema combinations. The present demonstration of the impact of schema set matching no doubt depended upon the global self-assessment of schema set as well as the systematic rewriting of four versions of the core messages to reflect different self-schema combinations. Direct measurement of schema set and tailoring messages to fit those sets of self-schemas appeared to be feasible steps for investigators interested in further examination of the role of the self in attitude change. Refinement of the omnibus tactics used here could lead to answers to questions such as which particular self-schemas (or which aspects of the schema sets) are crucial and to what extent must a persuasive message resonate with a schema set to bring about increased effectiveness.

The present research expands that of Cacioppo et al. (1982), in which messages were found to be particularly persuasive when legal-schematics rated legal messages, and correspondingly when religious-schematics rated religious messages. The current research used actual attitude change as the dependent variable, rather

Table 17.7
Experiment 4: Net Improvement from Matching to Stringently-Schematic
Subjects' Self-Schema Sets: Percentage Card Returns from Stringently-Schematic
Subjects (Table 17.6) Compared to Stringently-Schematic Population Percentages

	Self-Schema "Color"				
	Blue	Brown	Green	Orange	Overall
Non-Matching	-4.56	-7.32	18.74	-46.81	-6.22
Matching	8.51	4.67	-12.75	53.90	5.92
% Net Improvement	13.07	11.99	-31.49	100.71	12.14
Total N	23	56	12	5	96

Note: Population percentages for Stringently-Schematic subjects were subtracted from the obtained card return percentages (Table 17.6) to calculate the values in the first two rows. Then the decrease due to Nonmatching was subtracted from the increase due to Matching to obtain the net improvement attributable to matching messages to Stringently-Schematic recipients' sets of self-schemas. For "Greens" the matching effect was not obtained.

than the rated persuasiveness of the message used in Cacioppo et al. (1982). Actual attitude change is preferable as a dependent measure to rated persuasiveness of a communication because subjects may not always be aware of what they will or will not find persuasive. In addition, the present research also differed from that of Cacioppo et al. (1982) in that the current studies examined the efficacy of matching message appeals to sets of recipients' self-schemas, rather than single schemas. Schema sets were used in an attempt to encompass a larger part of the individuals' self-concepts.

POTENTIAL CRITICISMS

A potential criticism of this research stems from the fact that the combinations of self-schemas used by subjects to classify themselves, namely, the four colored cards, were not derived in a psychometrically rigorous fashion, notwithstanding some research which supports the popular Keirsey-Bates approach (Hoffman & Betkouski, 1981; McCarley & Carskadon, 1986). Even though the meaningfulness criterion for schemas has been used in past research (Markus, 1977), a more refined measure of schema sets would probably suggest rhetoric which more accurately reflected recipients' self-concepts and, consequently, would be more persuasive than the less focused and more global schema sets utilized in the current studies (Figure 17.1). However, the fact that message persuasiveness was significantly improved by matching messages to one of four general schema clusters attests to the robustness of the schema matching effect. Further research using a more refined schema set self-classification, one that better differentiated between subjects' unique self-concepts, would likely reveal an even stronger impact of set matching messages.

Another potential criticism of using the colored cards to allow subjects to type their sets of self-schemas could be a possible confounding of schema set and color preference; for example, who would want to be a "Brown"? However, the schema sets tended to be distributed in a similar fashion to the Keirsey-Bates (1978) type distributions.

IMPLICATIONS FOR FUTURE RESEARCH

Further research could examine the efficacy of gearing persuasive messages not only to recipients' actual self-concepts, but also to their "possible selves" (Markus & Nurius, 1986). In particular, there is reason to suspect that persuasive messages that reflect subjects' ideal selves might be particularly effective, given that "Possible selves represent motivation within the self-concept. They give specific cognitive form and meaning to an individual's hopes, fears, goals, and motives. It is important to assess these aspects of the self-schema because they function as incentives for future behavior" (Sentis & Markus, 1986, p. 173).

Also, another interesting way to examine the efficacy of matching messages to recipients' sets of self-schemas would be to prime recipients in such a way as to make certain types of messages more persuasive (Schmitt, 1988), or, in other words, to activate different aspects of the working self-concept. For example, when subjects are placed in a state of pleasant arousal, they may be more persuaded by messages that use appeals to adventure and excitement than they usually would be.

More research is also needed to explore the possible mechanisms that underlie the self-schema set matching effect. Past research indicates that subjects might more closely attend to, and recall more, message arguments when the appeals reflect their own set of self-schemas (Markus & Sentis, 1982; Markus & Wurf, 1987). Probably even more important, however, is the fact that subjects judge message appeals as being stronger and more relevant when these arguments reflect their own self-schemas (Cacioppo, et al., 1982). Further research will have to examine whether the processes that lead subjects to rate schema-matching messages as being more persuasive (Cacioppo et al., 1982) are the same as those that actually lead subjects to change their attitude toward the message topic.

APPLICATIONS TO DIRECT MARKETING: EXPERIMENT 4

Current ideology in direct marketing invokes measurement of values as well as other psychological elements (e.g., psychographics). Actual practice, however, appears to probe values indirectly by using proxies such as the target's residence in a particular zip code, level of education, previous purchasing behavior, and so forth. The advent of high-speed computers and sophisticated software now makes it possible to design direct mailings that are tailored to recipients' sets of self-schemas. As demonstrated in Experiment 4, competent copywriters and art directors can easily produce alternative versions of selling messages that correspond to the suspected self-concepts of the intended recipients. The self-schemas of recipients were determined beforehand by offering consumers an incentive for assigning themselves to one of several schema sets. When presented engagingly (e.g., the attached cards) together with a real incentive, satisfactory cooperation was achieved. The present demonstration suggested that mass communication to consumers can be individualized in ways that would be more gratifying to both consumer and manufacturer.

INDIVIDUAL DIFFERENCES IN PERSUASION

The failure of psychologists to locate a personality attribute that consistently predicted influence may be due in part to their approaches to the problem. The present studies suggest a solution. The key to the solution may be two procedural steps. First, allow the intended recipients to assign themselves to a particular self-schema set. Second, even more important, coordinate the content of the persuasive messages to the sets of self-schemas of the intended recipients. In the future, alternative self-rating systems of schema sets could be developed, and campaigns could be constructed to facilitate repeated exposure of recipients to their own relevant self-schemas.

NOTES

1. Based in part on an unpublished 1988 honors thesis at Ohio State University by Laura A. Brannon under supervision of Timothy C. Brock. For material assistance we are indebted to the Ohio State University Honors Program and the Ogilvy Center for Research and Development. This material is based upon work supported under a National Science Foundation Graduate Fellowship to Brannon. Any opinions, findings, conclusions or recommendations expressed in this paper are those of the authors and do not necessarily reflect the views of the National Science Foundation. In addition, we express our appreciation to Wendy Wood, Sharon Shavitt, and Diane Mackie for their helpful comments on an earlier draft of the manuscript.

2. A 2 (Experiment 2/3) by 4 (Message type was the message written in a "Brown," "Blue," "Green," or "Orange" way) analysis of variance was performed for each product (ignoring subject schematicity) in order to determine whether the messages were equally persuasive, regardless of matching. The only significant Message Type main effect was for the unfamiliar amusement park, Lake Darien [$F(3, 195) = 2.72, p < .05$]. The "Orange" and "Brown" messages were the most, and equally, persuasive for the amusement park; otherwise, the messages were comparable in their persuasiveness.

In addition, a supplementary study established that the messages used in Experiments

2 and 3 did, in fact, utilize appeals geared to their intended recipients. Twenty-five upper-level undergraduate and lower level graduate students at Ohio State University were each given the four sets of schemas and a booklet which contained eight of the messages from Experiment 3: four of the park messages, one for each schema set, and four of the shampoo messages, one for each schema set. At the top of each message was the statement, "This message most fits the following color (name the color)." Subjects rated each of the eight messages according to which schema set it reflected.

Out of a possible 200 guesses (25 subjects, 8 messages per subject), there were only eight errors. Subjects correctly typed the messages 96 percent of the time. This percentage was obviously significant; therefore, it can be assumed that the persuasive communications used in Experiment 3 (and in Experiment 2 because these messages were almost identical, except that one message dealt with a shampoo, the other with a conditioner) successfully utilized appeals which reflected their intended recipients' sets of self-schemas, as defined by the "color card" and the adjective-cluster self-ratings.

3. An alternative, 4 (Recipients' Set of Self-Schemas) by 4 (Message type) analysis of variance, which would have examined both the main effects of message type and recipient's self-schema sets, as well as the critical Message × Self-Schema Set interaction, might have proven to be more elegant. Unfortunately, there were not enough subjects to conduct such an elaborate analysis. However, there was no evidence for an interaction between the Recipients' Self-Schema Set and the efficacy of schema set matching; self-schema set matching messages were more persuasive than nonmatching messages, across schema sets (see text). That the messages were relatively comparable in their level of persuasiveness has already been noted (note 2).

4. Note that the card-sorting and adjective-ranking assessments were administered at the same time. Pilot studies indicated that when the assessments were administered separately in mailings more than a month apart, the correspondence between schema set from card sort and schema set from adjective ranking was about the same as when both tasks were presented to subjects in the same mailing. Hence, concurrent assessment did not appear to increase the likelihood of indicating the same self-schema set from both the cards and the adjectives.

5. One hundred four subjects did not return information, either properly marked cards or adjective clusters, that would allow for assignment to schema set.

REFERENCES

Brock, T. C., Albert, S. M., & Becker, L. A. (1970). Familiarity, utility, and supportiveness as determinants of information receptivity. *Journal of Personality and Social Psychology, 14,* 292–301.

Cacioppo, J., Petty, R. E., & Morris, K. (1983). Effects of need for cognition on message evaluation, recall, and persuasion. *Journal of Personality and Social Psychology, 45,* 805–818.

Cacioppo, J., Petty, R. E., & Sidera, J. (1982). The effects of a salient self-schema on the evaluation of pro-attitudinal editorials: Top-down versus bottom-up message processing. *Journal of Experimental Social Psychology, 18,* 324–338.

Crane, M., & Markus, H. (1982). Gender identity: The benefits of a self-schema approach. *Journal of Personality and Social Psychology, 43* (6), 1195–1197.

Davis, D. (1982). Determinants of responsiveness in dyadic interaction. In W. Ickes &

E. Knowles (Eds.), *Personality, roles and social behavior*. New York: Springer-Verlag.

Eagly, A. E. (1981). Recipient characteristics as determinants of responses to persuasion. In R. E. Petty, T. M. Ostrom, & T. C. Brock, (Eds.), *Cognitive responses in persuasion*. Hillsdale, N.J.: Lawrence Erlbaum Associates.

Harper, R. (1986). *Mailing list strategies: A guide to direct mail success*. New York: McGraw-Hill.

Hoffman, J. L., & Betkouski, M. (1981). A summary of Myers-Briggs Type Indicator research applications in education. *Research in Psychological Type, 3*, 3–41.

Keirsey, D., & Bates, M. (1978). *Please understand me: Character and temperament types*. Del Mar, CA: Prometheus Nemesis Book Company.

Lowry, D. (1987). Nonverbal communication: A new perspective. In S. Hecker and D. W. Stewart (Eds.), *Nonverbal communication in advertising*. Lexington, MA: Lexington Books.

Markus, H. (1977). Self-schemata and processing information about the self. *Journal of Personality and Social Psychology, 35* (2), 63–78.

Markus, H. (1983). Self-knowledge: An expanded view. *Journal of Personality, 51* (3), 543–565.

Markus, H., & Nurius, P. (1986). Possible selves. *American Psychologist, 41* (9), 954–969.

Markus, H., & Sentis, K. (1982). The self in social information processing. In J. Suls (Ed.), *Psychological perspectives on the self*. Hillsdale, N.J.: Lawrence Erlbaum Associates.

Markus, H., Smith, J., & Moreland, R. (1985). Role of the self-concept in the perception of others. *Journal of Personality and Social Psychology, 49* (6), 1494–1512.

Markus, H., & Wurf, E. (1987). The dynamic self-concept: A social psychological perspective. *Annual Review of Psychology, 38*, 299–337.

McCarley, N. G., & Carskadon, T. G. (1986). The perceived accuracy of elements of the 16-type descriptions of Myers and Keirsey among men and women: Which elements are most accurate, should the type descriptions be different for men and women, and do the type descriptions stereotype sensing types? *Journal of Psychological Type, 11*, 2–29.

Rosenthal, R. (1978). Combining results of independent studies. *Psychological Bulletin, 85* (1), 185–193.

Schmitt, B. (1988, October). *Situational determinants of attitude functions: Effects on the perception and evaluation of advertisements*. Paper presented at the meeting of the Association for Consumer Research, Honolulu, Hawaii.

Sentis, K., & Markus, H. (1986). Brand personality and the self. In J. Olson & K. Sentis (Eds.), *Advertising and consumer psychology* (Vol. 3, pp. 132–148.) New York: Praeger.

Snyder, M., & DeBono, K. (1985). Appeals to image and claims about quality: Understanding the psychology of advertising. *Journal of Personality and Social Psychology, 49*, 586–597.

Wood, W., & Stagner, B. H. (in press). The role of recipient attributes in persuasion. In T. C. Brock & S. Shavitt (Eds.), *Psychology of persuasion*. San Francisco: W. H. Freeman.

18

The Relationship Between Advertising and Consumers' Moods: A Synergistic Approach

Ronald Paul Hill and Debra L. Stephens

Few consumer researchers doubt the pervasive and important influence that mood has on consumers' information processing and decision making. Strong evidence suggests that individual choice behavior can be based on affective as well as rational factors (Zajonc, 1980). Furthermore, the impact of mood states on the consumer decision process appears to be a function of the valence of the current mood (Gardner & Hill, 1986).

Most of the studies that have investigated the role of mood or emotion in advertising have looked at the ability of ads to elicit different affective states (Holbrook & O'Shaughnessy, 1984). This work has popularized the "attitude toward the ad" stream of research, which typically views this construct as an intervening variable that mediates the effects of the advertising message on brand attitudes and preferences (Edell & Burke, 1984, 1987). According to this perspective, the purpose of many ads is to create a favorable ad attitude by leaving the viewer/listener/reader in a positive emotional state after processing the ad (Hill & Mazis, 1986). The assumption underlying this approach is that consumers are hedonistically motivated by the desire to feel good (Hirschman & Holbrook, 1982).

Other investigators have looked at the effects of consumers' current affective states on subsequent evaluations of advertisements (Milberg & Mitchell, 1984). The ads used in these studies are primarily informational, and subjects' moods are manipulated outside the context of the advertisement. Evidence suggests that mood may impact the encoding and retrieval of information contained in an ad (Srull, 1984). For example, consumers who are in positive moods upon exposure to an advertisement should encode more favorable information about the advertised brand. This process may result in more positive brand attitudes than would occur under different mood-related conditions. The gap in our current knowledge involves an understanding of both effects simultaneously. In particular, how does a consumers' mood state interact with the different characteristics of an advertisement to produce ad and brand attitudes? The purpose of this chapter is to provide possible answers to this question.

RATIONALE

Consumer behavior that is motivated by affective desires has been termed "hedonic consumption" (Hirschman & Holbrook, 1982; Holbrook & Hirschman, 1982). The basis of this approach is that the search for emotional arousal is an important motivation for individuals when selecting products to consume. Implicit to this perspective is the assumption that consumers consciously or unconsciously utilize the buying process to manage their moods (Hill & Gardner, 1987).

Recent evidence suggests that consumer behavior activities may result in the extension of an individual's positive mood or the transformation of his or her negative mood. In a study by M. P. Gardner and R. P. Hill (1986), subjects in positive moods, who used an experiential strategy while making a purchase decision, had more positive postprocessing moods than those who used an informational strategy; and subjects in negative moods, who used an informational strategy, had more positive postprocessing moods than those who used an experiential strategy. Interestingly, subjects in positive moods were more likely to use an experiential strategy than those in negative moods, and subjects in negative moods were more likely to use an informational strategy than those in positive moods. This finding suggests that subjects may have been employing a mood-management strategy during decision making.

With regard to advertising, the elements of an advertisement that have the potential to impact a consumer's mood are the contextual factors, product focus of the ad, and attribute-based information (Hill, 1988). Contextual factors are those aspects of the ad designed to create a particular mood. Included in this category are factors such as scenery, background music, facial expressions, and voice tones as well as nonattribute-based information designed to reinforce this mood.

The product focus of an advertisement is the good or service that is being suggested for purchase to consumers. In terms of their impact upon mood, products can be characterized as mood specific, mood general, and nonmood. Mood-specific products are goods and services that are associated with the cause of a consumer's preexposure mood (Hill, 1988). For example, if a teenager is currently anxious about his or her social acceptability, an ad for Clearasil might be seen as mood specific. Mood general products are more global in their impact and are associated with the physical and emotional manifestations of the consumer's preexposure mood. An example of these products would be the "mood-

Figure 18.1
Interactive Relationship Between Advertisements and Consumers' Moods

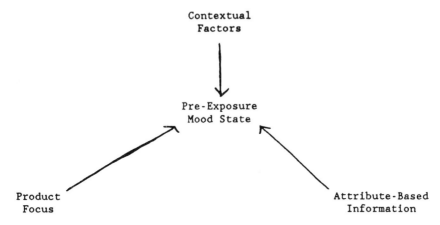

ameliorating'' cookies described by Gardner (1986) which were used to place subjects in good moods despite their negative mood conditions. Finally, nonmood products would be all the remaining goods and services which are not associated with either positive or negative moods by consumers.

   The last element of an advertisement that has the potential to impact consumers' mood states is the attribute-based information contained within the ad (Mizerski, White, & Hunt, 1984). This information might describe how use of the focal product will lead to the transformation of a consumer's negative mood or the extension of his or her positive mood (i.e., emotion as a benefit). Conversely, this information might describe how use of the focal product leads to the transformation of a positive mood (e.g., teen ''partying'' leading to a fatal car accident) or the extension of a negative mood (e.g., continued addiction to cocaine). This approach can be referred to as emotion as a cost. These elements interact with the consumer's preexposure mood to influence his or her resulting affective state. This relationship may take the form shown in Figure 18.1.

   These ad components may work similarly to the hedonic and utilitarian affective attitude elements suggested by R. Batra (1986). Through the process of empathy, the contextual factors in the ad may act to reduce, maintain, or improve the mood of the receiver (Hill, 1988). This could be characterized as the hedonic affective response of the consumer. Furthermore, the attribute-based information contained in the ad may be used by the receiver to evaluate the advertised brand's potential to impact current and future mood states. This could be characterized as the utilitarian affective response of the consumer. Gardner (1985) provides additional support for part of this approach by suggesting that ads designed to impact mood states contain two elements: cognitive mood inducers, such as positive or negative statements (information), and noncognitive mood inducers, such as scary or happy music (contextual factors).

Figure 18.2

Effects of the Interaction Between Advertisements and Consumers' Moods on A_{ad} and A_b

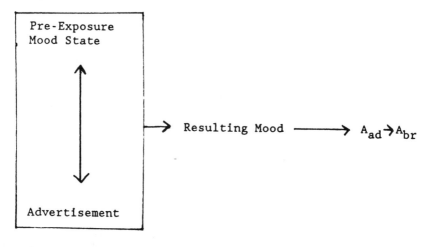

MOOD-MANAGEMENT STRATEGIES FOR ADVERTISEMENTS

According to the mood-management perspective, consumers should prefer advertisements that have the desired impact on their preexposure moods (Mitchell, 1985). Specifically, consumers in positive preexposure moods, whose moods are extended by exposure to an advertisement, will have more positive ad and brand attitudes than individuals whose moods are not extended. On the other hand, consumers in negative preexposure moods, whose moods are transformed by exposure to an advertisement, will have more positive ad and brand attitudes than individuals whose moods are not transformed. A diagrammatic representation of this relationship might take the form portrayed in Figure 18.2.

The mood-management approach provides some insight into the relationship between resulting mood and ad and brand attitudes. What is not clear is how the different components of an advertisement may interact with a consumer's preexposure mood to produce his or her resulting mood state. The following subsections provide a general discussion of this relationship for both positive and negative preprocessing mood conditions.

Positive Preprocessing Mood Conditions

As mentioned previously, consumers should prefer advertisements that extend their positive mood states. Recent evidence suggests that congruency between preexposure positive mood and an ad is likely to result in more favorable evaluations by receivers (Gardner & Wilhelm, 1987). Therefore, ads for both mood-specific and mood-general products that contain contextual factors and attribute-based information that are positive in nature should be preferred by consumers. Specifically, advertisements with upbeat music, attractive scenery, and positive nonattribute information as well as attribute-based information stressing emotion as a benefit should be most effective in extending consumers' positive preexposure moods.

Negative Preprocessing Mood Conditions

In contrast to positive preprocessing mood conditions, consumers in negative preprocessing mood conditions should prefer advertisements that transform their negative mood states. In a study investigating the Acquired Immune Deficiency Syndrome (AIDS) anxiety and consumer behavior, Hill (1988) found that ads which eventually led to the reduction of subjects' anxiety were evaluated more favorably. Furthermore, the preferred ads contained negative contextual factors in terms of nonattribute information (e.g., "Let's face it, sex is risky business . . . ''). However, they also discussed a mood-specific product and provided attribute-based information suggesting emotion as a benefit (''So why take your fears to bed? Use (Brand B) condoms, designed to provide extra protection in today's world.''). In that investigation, it was hypothesized that subjects preferred ads that confirm the cause of their negative moods and, simultaneously, describe a product that deals specifically with the problem.

However, differences may exist between mood-specific and mood-general products. According to Gardner (1986), goods with mood-ameliorating qualities (i.e., mood-general products) such as alcohol and cookies are often used by consumers to ''make life lighter'' without dealing directly with the causes of their current negative affective states. Therefore, with mood-general products, consumers should prefer ads that contain positive contextual factors (''The night belongs to Michelob'') and attribute-based information suggesting emotion as a benefit (''Maxwell House coffee—good to the last drop'').

IMPLICATIONS FOR ADVERTISERS

Consistent with the mood-management perspective, the combination of ad characteristics that potentially is most effective for advertisers is a function of consumers' preexposure moods, the goal of the advertiser, and the focal product. If consumers are in positive preexposure moods and the advertiser's goal is to market a mood-specific or mood-general product, we predict the following:

Proposition 1: Advertisements designed to market mood-specific or mood-general products that contain positive contextual factors and attribute-based information suggesting emotion as a benefit will lead to more positive attitudes toward the ad and focal product for subjects in positive preexposure moods than any other possible combination.

However, differences exist between product categories for consumers in negative affective states. If the consumer is in a negative preexposure mood and the advertiser's goal is to market a mood-specific product, we predict the following:

> *Proposition 2a*: Advertisements designed to market a mood-specific product that contain negative contextual factors and attribute-based information suggesting emotion as a benefit will lead to more positive attitudes toward the ad and focal product for subjects in negative preexposure moods than any other possible combination.

These ads are most effective for mood-specific products since they explicitly recognize the causes of consumers' negative moods and suggest a way to transform these mood states. On the other hand, if the consumer is in a negative preexposure mood and the advertiser's goal is to market a mood-general product, we predict the following:

> *Proposition 2b*: Advertisements designed to market a mood-general product that contain positive contextual factors and attribute-based information suggesting emotion as a benefit will lead to more positive attitudes toward the ad and focal product for subjects in negative preexposure moods than any other possible combination.

These ads are most effective for mood-general products since they avoid the reasons behind the consumers' negative moods and, instead, focus their attention on associations with future positive affective states.

Occasionally, the goal of advertisers is to demarket the focal product (e.g., the reduction of alcohol consumption among teenagers by Mothers Against Drunk Driving). Under these circumstances, advertisers will select the combination of ad characteristics that are expected to negatively impact product attitudes. Specifically, ads will be designed to transform positive or negative moods associated with particular product categories. Therefore, if the consumer is in a positive preexposure mood and the advertiser's goal is to demarket mood-general or mood-specific products, we predict the following:

> *Proposition 3*: Advertisements designed to demarket mood-specific or mood-general products that contain negative contextual factors and attribute-based information suggesting emotion as a cost will lead to less positive attitudes toward the ad and focal product for subjects in positive preexposure moods than any other possible combination.

Since these ads should worsen consumers' preexposure moods, they are expected to dislike both the ad and the focal product. Finally, if the consumer is in a negative preexposure mood and the advertiser's goal is to demarket mood-specific or mood-general products, we predict the following:

> *Proposition 4*: Advertisements designed to demarket mood-specific or mood-general products that contain negative contextual factors and attribute-based in-

formation suggesting emotion as a benefit will lead to more positive attitudes toward the ad and less positive attitudes toward the focal product for subjects in negative preexposure moods than any other possible combination.

These ads result in a different outcome. Since no longer using the focal product is expected to improve consumers' moods, these advertisements should result in more positive ad attitudes with subsequently less positive product attitudes.

DISCUSSION

This chapter suggests that consumers prefer advertisements that help them manage their current moods by aiding in the extension of positive affective states and the transformation of negative affective states. Furthermore, successful use of mood manipulation by advertisers may depend on their ability to understand this process. The above propositions are based on this perspective.

Advertisers should consider carefully the following issues when conducting research in this area. First, they should exercise caution in the selection of the methods used to manipulate and measure consumers' preexposure moods. Recent research by Hill and J. C. Ward (1989) demonstrates that common mood manipulations in psychology may impact mood states as well as a host of other psychological variables. Therefore, the methods selected should be pretested to determine whether potential confounds exist. Multimethod, multimeasure investigations may resolve some of these issues.

Second, researchers should select advertisements for testing that can be broken down into the component parts of focal product, attribute-based information, and contextual factors. Advertisements that provide a mix of one or more of these factors may be inappropriate during the early stages of testing since their influence on resulting mood will be difficult to determine. The use of ads prepared specifically for the purposes of this study may provide a good starting point. Eventually, more complex ads should be utilized across the full range of available media.

Third, researchers should investigate the nature and effects of resulting moods. For example, how long does the mood state exist? Do multiple ads in a program segment each have a separate or a combined effect on mood? Is the mood state "retrievable" at a later point in time such as the point of purchase? What effects do the match or mismatch of the resulting mood with the desired mood have on attitude toward the ad, attitude toward the product, and purchase intentions? Each of these questions suggests streams of research that will involve considerable resources and commitment by advertisers.

REFERENCES

Batra, R. (1986). Affective advertising: Role, processes, and measurement. In R. A. Peterson, W. D. Hoyer, and W. R. Wilson (Eds.), *The role of affect in consumer behavior: Emerging theories and applications* (pp. 53–85). Lexington, MA: Lexington Books.

Edell, J. A., & Burke, M. C. (1984). The moderating effect of attitude toward an ad on ad effectiveness under different ad conditions. In T. Kinnear (Ed.), *Advances in consumer research* (vol. 11, pp. 644–649). Provo, UT: Association for Consumer Research.

Edell, J. A., & Burke, M. C. (1987). The power of feelings in understanding advertising effects. *Journal of Consumer Research, 14* (3), 421–433.

Gardner, M. P. (1985). Mood states and consumer behavior: A critical review. *Journal of Consumer Research, 12* (3), 281–300.

Gardner, M. P. (1986). *Responses to emotional and informational appeals: The moderating role of context-induced mood states.* Unpublished manuscript, New York University.

Gardner, M. P., & Hill, R. P. (1986). Consumers' mood states: Antecedents and consequences of experiential vs. informational strategies for brand choice. *Psychology & Marketing, 5* (2), 169–182.

Gardner, M. P., & Wilhelm, F. O., Jr. (1987). Consumer responses to ads with positive versus negative appeals: Some mediating effects of context-induced mood and congruency between context and ad. In J. H. Leigh & C. R. Martin, Jr. (Eds.), *Current issues and research in advertising*, (pp. 81–98). Ann Arbor, MI: University of Michigan.

Hill, R. P. (1988). An exploration of the relationship between AIDS-related anxiety and the evaluation of condom advertisements. *Journal of Advertising, 17* (4), 35–42.

Hill, R. P., & Gardner, M. P. (1987). The buying process: Effects of and on consumer mood states. In M. Wallendorf & P. Anderson (Eds.), *Advances in consumer research* (vol. 14, pp. 408–410). Provo, UT: Association for Consumer Research.

Hill, R. P., & Mazis, M. B. (1986). Measuring emotional responses to advertising. In R. J. Lutz (Ed.), *Advances in consumer research* (vol. 13, pp. 164–169). Provo, UT: Association for Consumer Research.

Hill, R. P., & Ward, J. C. (1989). Mood manipulation in marketing research: An examination of potential confounding effects. *Journal of Marketing Research, 26* (1), 97–104.

Hirschman, E. C., & Holbrook, M. B. (1982). Hedonic consumption: Emerging concepts, methods and propositions. *Journal of Marketing, 46* (3), 92–101.

Holbrook, M. B., & Hirschman, E. C. (1982). The experiential aspects of consumption: Consumer fantasies, feelings, and fun. *Journal of Consumer Research, 9* (2), 132–140.

Holbrook, M. B., & O'Shaughnessy, J. (1984). The role of emotion in advertising. *Psychology & Marketing, 1* (2), 45–64.

Milberg, S., & Mitchell, A. A. (1984). *An examination of alternative hypotheses of how mood may affect brand attitudes and intentions.* Paper presented at the American Psychological Association Conference, Toronto, Ontario, Canada.

Mitchell, A. A. (1985). Some issues surrounding research on the effects of 'feeling advertisements'. In R. J. Lutz (Ed.), *Advances in consumer research* (vol. 13, pp. 623–628). Provo, UT: Association for Consumer Research.

Mizerski, R. W., White, J. D., & Hunt, J. B. (1984). The use of emotion in advertising. In R. W. Belk (Ed.), *1984 AMA Educators' Proceedings* (pp. 244–248). Chicago: American Marketing Association.

Ray, M. L., & Wilkie, W. L. (1970). Fear: The potential of an appeal neglected by marketing. *Journal of Marketing, 34* (1), 54–62.

Srull, T. K. (1984). The effects of subjective affective states on memory and judgment. In T. Kinnear (Ed.), *Advances in consumer research* (vol. 11, pp. 530–533). Provo, UT: Association for Consumer Research.

Zajonc, R. B. (1980). Feeling and thinking: Preferences need no inferences. *American Psychologist, 35* (2), 151–175.

Epilogue

19

Consumer Psychology's Potential Contribution to Social Science

John C. Maloney

INTRODUCTION

In a best-seller which criticizes American universities for abandoning the goals of liberal education, philosophy professor Allan Bloom (1987) complains that social sciences are no longer taught by liberally educated wise men. They are left in the hands of business school professors, artificial intelligence experts, and others who merely skim the classic philosophies for ideas that can be used for mercenary ends. Too much attention is given to the study of public opinion; too little attention to rationality and principles which apply universally at all times and in all places. We are not paying enough attention, Bloom insists, to the classic old philosophies, and, as a result, there is no unity, nor even a chance for unity, in the social sciences.

Bloom is right in some ways. We applied social scientists do pick the bones of philosophy for ideas that may help us to cope with problems in the world of practical affairs. He might be especially chagrined if he were to review the proceedings of a recent meeting of the Consumer Psychology Division of the American Psychological Association. There is a paper on phenomenology, replete with references to Edmund Husserl, Martin Heidegger, and Jean-Paul Sartre (Jennings, 1988), followed by a paper on consumer psychologists' possible uses of hermeneutics (Packer, 1988a), based on the ideas of Heidegger, a philosopher severely criticized by Bloom.

I cannot deny it. As we scavenge for ideas, we seldom think about the grand scheme that is needed, as Bloom says, to "place man in the universe." But we cannot unify today's social sciences by rehashing ancient philosophies. The best chance for unity comes from a potential merger of applied social science with the modernist philosophies that Bloom abhors.

New Theories Needed

Today's complex governmental and business institutions are not merely enlarged versions of the forum and marketplace of Socrates' Athens. A global economy is emerging with increased exchanges of goods and services between nations. Using worldwide telecommunications networks, major brokerage houses "pass the book" from New York to Tokyo to London, and back to New York each business day.

Live satellite television broadcasts permit millions to watch the president of the United States addressing students and faculty at the University of Moscow, or strolling through Red Square with the head of a government so recently regarded to be "an evil empire." Marshall McLuhan was right. Communicating more than the linear logic of the printed word, such "global village" broadcasts immerse us in picture-in-the-mind/sound-in-the-mind mosaic impressions which profoundly affect our views of "man's place in the world." And, although Heidegger wrote during the era of silent movies and the earliest days of radio broadcasting, none of the ancient philosophers ever saw a television set or a computer. None of them could have imagined the social, economic, or political implications of worldwide satellite networks.

Increased attention to tacit knowledge and everyday behavior. Heidegger's philosophy appeals to consumer psychologists because it acknowledges everyday thinking and action and the importance of tacit knowledge—"the things that we know without knowing that we know them." For philosophers such as Bloom, emphasis on such trivial aspects of thought is an unwelcome distraction from the rationality which presumably sets man apart from lower animals. But applied social scientists have discovered that few of the things that we do in our everyday lives are based on rationally pondered deliberations. In many of the things we do, we rely on prior learning.

For example, when we learn to drive a car, we consciously study the rules of the road and the meaning of various traffic signals. We learn the functions of the clutch and brake pedals and the accelerator; we learn how to shift gears and to steer properly under various conditions. But, as we become experienced drivers, "decisions" about how and when to perform appropriately become habitual. The light turns red and we stop; it turns green and we go; we need not recompute each braking, gear shifting, steering, and accelerating action.

Most of our everyday behaviors are like that—less deliberate and more dependent on preconscious recognitions of relevant cues than many would suppose. (As a case in point, the average brand choice in supermarkets is made in from 3 to 5 seconds.) It is not that we are irrational; it is just that ponderous recomputations of the consequences of each action would be prohibitively inefficient.

At the same time, virtually all of the disciplines concerned with communication and information processing have begun to pay attention to what actors, musicians, and other artists have always known about the importance of nonverbal communication. Linguists, for example, have become increasingly interested in meaning communicated through facial expressions, gestures, and tone of voice (Grice, 1981). And neuroscientists are starting to pin down the neurological basis of our interpretations of nonverbal information (Miller, 1988).

Advances in "neurophilosophy." Bloom laments the lack of attention to the mind-body problem. But, in recent years, neuroscientists have made stunning advances in understanding how our thoughts, moods, and creative capabilities are chemically mediated. With "split brain" studies, Positive Emission Tomography (PET) scanners, and in vitro laboratory studies of animal nervous systems, they have observed the patterns of neural energy flow that underlie a broad variety of sensory, learning, and memory processes. These new brain research technologies are surely comparable, for the behavioral sciences, to the invention of the microscope for the physical sciences. One can hardly say, in any case, that the mind-body problem is being ignored.

Consumer psychologists should be interested in what Patricia Churchland (1986) has to say about such matters. A philosophy professor of a different stripe than Allan Bloom, her intent is to explain neuroscience to philosophers, and philosophy to neuroscientists. Meanwhile, although she is embarrassingly clear about the limitations of "folk psychology" concepts which most of us take for granted, her scholarly and eminently readable book provides valuable insights about many of the problems with which consumer psychologists are now tussling. She explains, for example, why the latest advances in neuroscience suggest that it is not the brain's style to either number crunch or sentence crunch its way to understanding.

The point that I wish to make here is simply this: today's disunity among the social sciences does not stem from an ignorance of, or a vulgarization of, old philosophies. We are witnessing an explosion of behavioral and social science knowledge from many sources: knowledge spun off from the development of information technologies; knowledge about chemical and neural energy mediations of mind-body relationships; and applied social science knowledge of everyday thought and action. There is simply more information, and more kinds of information, than can be tucked into old philosophies or theoretical frameworks. The "centrifugal force" of these developments spreads well beyond the boundaries of old curricula (Altman, 1987; Spence, 1987). New theory is needed. And, to the extent that social scientists can get useful guidance from philosophy, it is unlikely to come from the ancient, classic philosophies.

CONSUMER PSYCHOLOGISTS' USES OF PHENOMENOLOGY

Phenomenology is the study of what goes on inside of our minds relative to what is going on outside in the world. The method of phenomenology is introspection—reflection upon the moment-to-moment stream of consciousness or the felt experience of thought and emotion.

From the philosopher's point of view, phenomenology began with Husserl's protest against psychophysics and experimental psychology.[1] Husserl's opposition to experimental psychology deserves consumer psychologists' serious consideration. He insisted that the experimentalists' procedures are so intrusive, and therefore so likely to distort naturally occurring thoughts and feelings, that they almost inevitably lead to erroneous conclusions.

Heidegger, Husserl's student and successor at Freiburg University, brought phenomenology much closer to the views of today's consumer psychologists. Although it has often been said that "philosophy bakes no bread," Heidegger wanted phenomenology to be a guide for practical action. He wanted the introspective method to be more than a tool for the philosopher's examination of his own thoughts; he was interested in interpreting, and influencing, the thoughts and actions of others.

In his landmark work (*Sein und Zeit*, published in 1927), Heidegger noted that we have several modes of engagement with the world and that most of our actions in everyday living involve much less logical deliberation than is suggested by most philosophies of human thought and action (Packer, 1988a). Thus, his modes of engagement foreshadowed consumer psychology levels of cognitive involvement. He was otherwise interested in the thoughts of others, not just his own introspections, and he had a temporally oriented view (consistent with the view that the trial of a product, or exposure to an ad today, may affect the purchase or repeated use of the product tomorrow or at some later time). And, like many of today's consumer psychologists, he was interested in the study of moods as well as literal perceptions.

But even Heidegger's method is ill-suited for use by consumer psychologists. (Philosopher phenomenologists might be interested in people's thoughts about products or advertising if and when such thoughts should come to mind. But it would be verboten to call attention to, or to ask questions about, specific products or advertisements.[2] So it is not really phenomenology that interests us so much as phenomenology's impact on "phenomenal" psychology—and that comes to us primarily through gestalt psychology which grew up beside phenomenology in Germany in the late 1920s and early 1930s.

The Psycholization of Phenomenology

The early Gestalt psychologists, completely unlike the philosopher phenomenologists, were preoccupied with neural interpretations of perception. But as phenomenology, under Heidegger's influence, became more pragmatic, it needed the psychologists' insights. And, as the gestaltists became interested in more abstract mental processes than they could hope to explain on a neurological basis, they needed the phenomenologists' mode of discourse. (It was as though a group of physicists had become interested in city planning. They did not renounce their old theory, but, in order to get on with it, they had to supplement their fine-grained physiological concepts with "psychological field" concepts.)

During World War II, the famous gestaltist Kurt Lewin, who was, by then working in America, applied his psychological field theory, in eminently prag-matic ways, to studies of mass persuasion. He noted, for example, that persuasion does not always occur in terms of sudden conversion; it often requires the "unfreezing" of old attitudes prior to "refreezing" the relevant percept or attitude referent within a new meaning context. Meanwhile, mass persuaders should try to shore up tentative new beliefs with a flow of belief suppor-tive information. (In this sense, Lewin anticipated the product adoption pro-cess of sociologists' "diffusion of innovations" theories: Aware-ness→Interest→Mental Evaluation→Trial→Adoption.)

Such practical applications of Gestalt theory encouraged the development of directive state theory by social psychologists Leo Postman, Jerome Bruner, David Krech, and others in the 1950s. Experimental psychologists had long since discovered that people see things in the light of past experience, but directive state theorists saw people's interests and learned perceptual tendencies to be something more than pesky little "intervening variables." They not only wanted to control for them; they wanted to study them.

Emergence of "Cybernetic Phenomenology"

The concepts of selective attention and selective perception were more learning oriented that Husserl could have tolerated. (Husserl was primarily interested in universal principles of perception which are unaffected by personal experience.) Nonetheless, Husserl had acknowledged that some perceptions are "prejudiced" by biases implicit in a particular individual's fulfilling intuitions. The directive state theorists adapted the fulfilling intuitions concept to develop their own hypothesis theory. According to such theory, people compare new information with their already existing hypotheses, and information that conforms to those hypotheses is easily believed or accepted.

But there is more involved here than simple acceptance or rejection of message content. As suggested by Lewin's unfreezing-refreezing analogy, information that conflicts with preexisting hypotheses may destabilize those hypotheses— and it is often such instability (uncertainty, doubt, or curiosity) that gives rise to selective attention. Meanwhile, subsequent efforts to restabilize the hypothesis may lead to distortions of relevant information to make it more congruent with the preexisting hypotheses. It was a short step from hypothesis theory to the cognitive balance and cognitive dissonance theories of Fritz Heider, Leon Fes-tinger, and others, in the 1950s, a variety of such theories became known as "new look" perception theories.

Philosopher critics pounced on these theories with a vengeance, criticizing them for their "teleological fallacies of functionalism."[3] But their emphases on cognitive balances and selectivity of attention and perception were remarkably compatible with new cybernetic and biological systems theories—theories which emphasize input-regulating feedbacks which maintain semistable states within servomechanisms, computers, and living organisms. So, during the 1950s, concepts from computer science and biology started to impact theories of learning and perception (e.g., Allport, 1955), theories of personality development and mental illness (e.g., Menninger, Mayman, & Pruyser, 1963), and virtually all theories of information processing. It was the start of what we now call cognitive science.

But, before we stray too far from phenomenology, let us discuss some phenomenological and phenomenal principles which have important practical implications for applied psychology. (I use the word phenomenal to denote concepts implicit in psychological theories inspired by, or closely related to, philosophical phenomenology.)

Principle of Dynamic Structure

Philosopher critics of cognitive psychology (e.g., Fodor, 1981) insist that meanings (beliefs, cognitive connections, attitudes, opinions, images, and so on) are mere figments of psychologists' imaginations—or that they would be if psychologists had imaginations. Needless to say, phenomenologists agree that meanings are valid mental phenomena. But, for them, meaning associations are not fixed patterns of things known; they are loosely structured happenings—currents and eddies, so to speak, in a stream of consciousness.

Latent meaning structures are, of course, assumed. Ideas absent from the stream of consciousness at any given moment may be more or less enduring in terms of their potential for recurrence in consciousness. But different facets of meaning are likely to recur under different circumstances. Thus, impressions of a food product may be impressions of the product as it appears in the store as one of several products which might be bought, impressions of the product in the kitchen as a meal ingredient, impressions of the product on the dinner table as something to be eaten, or fairly abstract thoughts about the product as a source of nutrition or a threat to health.

Moreover, different facets of meaning are more salient (more "top of mind") at different times. Thoughts about a product as a potential purchase choice may be highly salient for someone going to the store expressly to buy that product. On the other hand, such thoughts could be subordinate and fleeting parts of a broader felt experience (e.g., a general shopping experience). And, while felt experiences, or streams of consciousness, sometimes come to mind fairly spontaneously, meaning is affected by the situation or circumstance (e.g., the store display, or the interviewer's question) that brings them to mind. It is doubtful, then, that, the meaning of any event, person, place, or thing is precisely the same on any two occasions.

Principle of Indeterminant Meaning

None of us have direct access to the consciousness of others. We can only infer what others think or feel by observing their actions or listening to what they say about their thoughts and feelings. The problem here is that leading questions produce biased reports of thoughts and feelings, and any question is a leading question since any question intrudes upon the stream of consciousness. It must be noted, moreover, that the "leading question problem" remains when we interrupt the normal stream of consciousness with nonverbal questions (e.g., happy versus sad faces card sorts) or when our questions are posed via experimental manipulations.

This problem is akin to the Heisenberg principle of indeterminacy in physics; what one must do to observe the phenomenon is sure to change that which is being observed. This was Husserl's basic argument with psychologists, and he surely had a point.

"Meaning" often imposed by our procedures. The procedures which produce the most persuasive meaning patterns (i.e., charts, "perceptual maps," and so on for our presentations and journal articles) are most problematic in this regard.

For example, we often use factor analyses and cluster analyses of multiple choice or rating scale responses (e.g., for brand positioning studies) to show how concepts or meanings go together in people's minds. We are, quite rightly, encouraged when our factors or clusters are internally consistent in terms of both statistical homogeneity and common sense. It is gratifying when cross-validation data from different groups of respondents produce nearly identical results. If repeated applications of the method produce consistent meaning clusters (except, for example, for changes which should occur because of product redesigns or new product introductions), we can feel reasonably confident that the procedure is working as it should. But we must remain alert to the possibility that, in any given instance, such results may represent meaning attributions or nonattitudes (Rosenberg, 1968). They may, in other words, have little to do with what consumers actually think, or would think, in natural situations.

Such problems can be particularly troublesome when we probe for the meanings of related objects or events (e.g., when we ask the same people, on the same interview occasion, to rate attitudes toward an ad and attitudes toward the advertised product). In such instances, we may not only draw nonattitudes out of our consumer subjects, we may also elicit a spurious relationship between the nonattitudes. (I call this the "Silly Putty" problem because the simultaneous "massage" of ad-related and brand-related meanings reminds me of the intermingling which occurs when children simultaneously knead two different colors of putty.)

Our measures as snapshots of the stream of consciousness. Our measures of what people think, or how they think, are static representations of dynamic stream-of-consciousness processes. So, as we analyze, we must synthesize. We should, in other words, try to follow French philosopher Henri Bergson's advice

(1944) to ''intuitively reconstitute movement'' or mentally fill in the dynamism of the underlying process.

By way of analogy, our measures are like photos of a parade, photos taken with an imperfect camera from a single vantage point, or just a few vantage points, along the parade route. Such photos do not show where the parade started; they do not show where it ends. No one of them shows the speed at which the parade is moving. If such photos show the tuba players on the near side of the street, they probably miss the tuba players on the other side of the street. And, unless we take a lot of photos, we may miss the baton twirlers and the fire trucks altogether. Even if we used several movie cameras and used thousands of frames of film, we could never capture the total, dynamic reality of the parade or know how it felt to be in the parade. However, if we know how to interpret those photos—if we know enough about parades and the distortions that can be caused by our camera—parade photos can tell us a great deal.[4]

Some of our measures are so intrusive that it is as though we had stopped the parade and insisted on posing the marchers in contrived ways before letting the parade move on. For example, group discussions may call to mind much more detailed ideas about a product than would ever come to mind, even in a tacit knowledge sense, in that mental parade that occurs as people normally march up and down supermarket aisles. And the process is, of course, very intrusive when we force the discussion into areas unrelated to the natural flow of the conversation. Or, when we force people to choose between predetermined response alternatives to questions that never would have occurred to them (or when we purposely alter their thoughts or moods with contrived ''manipulation'' procedures!), we are using extremely intrusive measures.

I do not suggest that we must refrain from using intrusive measures. Such measures often work well for the purposes for which we use them, even though they fail to produce perfect representations of people's felt experiences. But, the more intrusive the measure, the more concerned we should be about validating our results. (More about this later.)

Principle of Multiple Causes

While formal model building is not part of the phenomenological method, phenomenologists advise researchers to explicate (make explicit) contextual issues, ''activating change conditions'' which may be implicitly embedded in our ''all other things being equal'' assumptions (Jennings, 1988).

Lessons from early communications research movement. One of consumer psychology's early encounters with the importance of what is involved here came from summary overviews of the communications research experiments conducted during the 1940s and 1950s.

Hundreds of persuasive message experiments had been undertaken to study such things as the effects of communicator credibility (e.g., the value of authority figures or celebrity endorsers); the effects of message repetition, timing, and orders of presentation; and the use of countless rhetorical devices, such as emotional appeals, fear appeals, one-sided versus two-sided arguments, and conclusion-drawing messages versus messages with implicit rhetoric. But, once the evidence was all laid out and comparisons were made between findings from related studies, the answers to most such questions were "It all depends . . . ." And, even when there seemed to be consistent answers, few of the experimental results were confirmed by studies conducted out in the "real world."

Most of these disappointments resulted from experimenters' failure to appreciate the importance of specific contexts. (To whom should this message be addressed if it were to really have the desired effect "in the real world"? What does that audience already know about the subject matter of the message? What will they otherwise be hearing about it from other sources? How important is this message to the intended audience? Do they typically appraise the subject matter in terms of studied rationality, or in terms of generalized impressions? How easily can the audience comply with the persuasion? Are the necessary channels of action readily available? And so on and so forth.)

In looking for broadly applicable generalizations, those early communications research experimenters commonly controlled for, or held constant, the relevant-to-the-issue selective attention and selective perception biases and the situational factors that have the most to do with how or whether persuasion works in the real world. So experimental controls used to "tidy up" the experiments often rendered them sterile. (After years of experience with such experiments, Yale's Carl Hovland, 1959, discussed many of these problems in his presidential address to the American Psychological Association.)

This explains the difficulties, I think, that some advertising researchers are having today in studying moods and emotions. Instead of doing the necessary "phenomenological homework" (Jennings, 1988) regarding the relevance of mood/emotion for specific product/service purchase-use contexts, they look for "one size fits all" definitions for emotion and universal ways to evoke those emotions.

Importance of competitive context. The principle of multiple causes was discovered in another way by communications researchers who used surveys and quasi-experimental procedures.[5] This was the approach used by Paul Lazarsfeld's group at Columbia University. After reviewing hundreds of their own and others' studies, the Columbia group formulated a "minimal effects" model of mass media impact. Joseph Klapper called it the "phenomenistic" view of media effects, explaining that single-cause interpretations of media effects do not suffice because the media normally work "among and through a nexus of mediating factors" (Klapper, 1960).[6]

Advertisers of that era wanted to believe that the minimal effects model and multiple-cause interpretations of mass media effects did not apply to advertising. But quasi-experimental advertising–sales analyses for dozens of product classes convinced me that Klapper's conclusions apply at least as much to advertising as to the other forms of mass media persuasion studied by the Columbia group.

This has since been confirmed by single-source measures which compare purchases, on a household-by-household basis, with measures of exposure to advertising and observations of a host of in-store influences and promotional activities.

The multiple-cause principle is especially obvious to those who have built laboratory test market models to forecast new brand sales. They soon discovered that their forecasts had to take account of sampling, couponing, or other inducements of new brand trial; advertising weight budgeted to introduce the new brand and a factor for translating weight to brand awareness among prospective buyers; competitors' pricing and counterpromotional efforts; and, most important of all, retail distribution levels (the availability of the new brand to those who wish to try it). In fact, the success of such sales forecasting often has more to do with those ''other things'' than it has to do with experimental measures (e.g., measures of interest in trying the new brand following advertising exposure and measures of repeat purchase intent following brand trial).

And it is not just the relationship between persuasion and behavior that is mediated by other things. Competitive context has much to do with how much persuasion can occur in the first place. For example, when persuasion is defined in terms of changes in simulated brand choice following exposure to advertising, two-thirds of the variance in persuasion can be traced to the number of brands competing in the product category; consumers' propensities for brand switching within the category; and the proportion of the audience which already favors the advertised brand (Research Systems Corporation, 1987).

As W. E. Baker and R. J. Lutz (1988) put the matter from an advertising research perspective, studies of response on the advertising exposure occasions should take account of the circumstances that will prevail on the brand response occasion. Indeed, when we are working in the dark, with little knowledge of choice alternatives and competitive context, we seldom have good records of behavior prediction.

All of this is consistent, incidentally, with Heidegger's ontological emphasis on in-the-world experience (as contrasted with an epistemological emphasis on people's ways of knowing). Consumer psychologists attuned to this view recognize that all determinants of the ways in which people experience products and services (e.g., in terms of the competitive relativities of product design and quality, pricing, distribution, and promotion) lie within the province of consumer psychology.

Principle of Integrative Learning

Phenomenal-cognitive theories assume that perception involves the integration of information into preexisting frames of reference or meaning structures. As is implied by phenomenology's fulfilling intuitions and the directive state theorists' mental hypotheses, preexisting meaning structures provide both the ''storage compartments'' for meaning and the ''meaning templates'' against which new information is ''judged.''

Reminder learning versus reintegrative learning. This is not to say that all information is literally or consciously judged for truth value. Most information simply ''fits in''—just as food, during the process of digestion, fits into, or becomes a part of, existing cells and tissues. Or somewhat novel information may lead to ''tack-on'' learning which moderately adds to old meanings—a reminder with a twist, as we say.

On the other hand, when new information sharply contradicts complex old meanings (e.g., elaborate theories or religious beliefs), adaptation may require gradual, time-consuming change in a whole network of meanings before balance is restored. Learning theorists call that reintegrative learning. (Reintegration sometimes occurs as sudden insight resulting from the bisociation of two previously unrelated matrices of thought—the so-called Eureka experience, à la Newton under the apple tree or Archimedes in the bath tub.[7] But this usually follows lots of cognitive ''percolation.'')

Origins of new meaning. One of the main persuasive functions of the mass media is to put new issues on the agenda. (Even the minimal effects models of mass media effectiveness suggest that the media have much influence in spotlighting candidates or issues or putting them on the agenda for the public's consideration.) But, if information can be interpreted only in the light of existing frames of reference, how do new meanings come into existence? The answer to that question relates to the dynamism and interrelatedness of meaning structures—and the fact that we cannot get entirely new issues on the agenda.

Since meanings never exist as isolated entities, new meanings are likely to be formed from ''subfiles'' of existing meanings. (Although meaning structures are more fluid than computer records, the phenomenal view implies a process crudely analogous to the opening of memory subfiles within existing files.) For example, the mental image of a new luxury model Ford may arise from information tacked onto connections between preexisting images of Fords, images of luxury cars, and other preexisting images which Ford wishes to use to position the new model. (Before people had images of motor cars, cars themselves were introduced as ''horseless carriages.'') In any case, entirely new meaning, totally unrelated to preexisting frames of reference, is a non sequitur within the context of phenomenal-cognitive theory.

Descriptive Rhetoric of Phenomenal Response

When we apply this phenomenal orientation to observations of the mental processes of others, we commonly apply our frames of reference to describe how they (e.g., advertising audiences) make sense of things vis-à-vis their internal frames of reference. Thus, if learning or attitude change occurs which is consistent with the advertiser's intention (e.g., when consumers accept an advertisers' new selling idea), that learning or attitude change is called belief or persuasion. On the other hand, when perceived meanings are interpreted differently than intended, the result is called confusion, disbelief, or message distortion. (From this point of view, an unbelievable message may become believable if the advertiser changes his intention. And, believe it or not, that sometimes happens in advertising.)

The 1940s–1950s "new look" theorists and communications researchers developed a jargon to describe information response phenomena in greater detail. (Churchland would call it "folk psychology" jargon.) For example, a commercial may have failed to penetrate to brand or product meaning because it stirred up the wrong train of thought. In terms of our jargon, it was, as compared with the advertiser's intention, misindexed.

For example, the commercial may be seen as a commercial for a competing brand. Or it may be seen simply as a commercial so that it is interpreted solely in terms of the meanings of scenes, settings, or characters which were meant to communicate brand meaning.

If it is properly indexed, the message may still have been leveled (if the audience overlooked advertiser-intended but, to them, unexpected meaning), or it may have been sharpened (if the audience reads unintended meaning into the message.)

Message elaboration (a term which came somewhat later) may involve message sharpening of the sort that leads to message distortion. Or it may represent a message sharpening train of thought which is essential for the success of an implicit message. And so on.

Such "entry level" phenomenal concepts are the basis for a variety of "judgmental" theories (For example, adaptation level theory, social judgment theory, schema theory, and perspective theory)[8] which are often good enough first approximations to explaining people's ways of making sense of things. Ray Bauer and I introduced such concepts to the literature of marketing and advertising research twenty-five years ago (Bauer, 1963; Maloney, 1963). I was looking for a way to explain that advertising believability is not a property of advertising so much as it is a phenomenon which occurs inside of the audience's headbones. (See later discussion of "curious nonbelief.") But such concepts imply more literal response to the sights and sounds of advertising than may be warranted in the light of more "scientifisch" theories.[9]

WHAT WE CAN LEARN FROM NEUROSCIENCE

As mentioned earlier, phenomenal-cognitive theories have borrowed strength from cognitive science (e.g., as input-regulating feedback concepts from cybernetics and biological systems theory helped to legitimize the selective attention concepts of cognitive psychology). However, neuroscience has largely spurned phenomenal-cognitive theories and it is now moving even farther away from the computational/linguistic baggage which comes with most phenomenal-cognitive theories. Meanwhile, it is moving toward nonnumerical, nonverbal associative memory theories. We might think of these as the neuroscientists' version of the tacit knowledge principle.

Neuroscientists' Version of Tacit Knowledge

Neuroscientists are increasingly convinced that living nervous systems have little in common with the number-crunching computers of the past forty years in terms of the ways in which they process information. This is to say that nervous systems are not step-by-step serial processing computers which seek perfect solutions. Instead, they are analog devices which use parallel distributed processing strategies. They adapt to environmental change through activation of nerve cells which excite associated nerve cells. This mutual excitation and "co-operative search" for a fitting balance of energy continues until balance is restored and the system relaxes into a semistable state. Such patterns are loosely structured and error tolerant.

Given the difference between traditional computers' and living organisms' information processing strategies, it is easy to see why human brains cannot compute as quickly or as accurately as today's cheap calculators. But, because nervous systems are so ready to deal with approximate information, even a fly's or a garden slug's nervous system can recognize complex, ambiguous patterns which would stump a high-powered digital computer.[10] (This discovery is the basis for an emerging nondigital, "neural network" computer technology for pattern recognition tasks.)

Churchland (1986) suggests that, as neuroscientists deal with more abstract responses to information, the higher order processes will be found to involve similar sequences of mutual excitation, "cooperative search," and "relaxation into a minimal energy state." But, as the brain looks for a fitting combination of hypotheses (Churchland's "folk neuroscience" term for abstract responses), the mutual excitations and relaxations will not simply involve nerve cell inter-actions; they will presumably involve global connections between many local nerve cell clusters.

In other words, there seem to be hierarchies of simple to complex patterns of neural excitation, cooperative search, and relaxation. And, while higher order patterns are obviously able to deal with number computations, word symbols, and linguistic structures, the logic of the system is not formal logic or the logic of verbal semantics. As Churchland notes, it clearly does not seem to be the brain's style to either number crunch or sentence crunch its way to a relaxed state. What is stored nonverbally can sometimes be expressed verbally on de-mand. But experienced consumer psychologists must surely agree that "some-times the background assumptions that affect behavior and problem solving can be verbalized only with immense effort or perhaps not at all" (Churchland, 1986, p. 392).

This is another statement of the "indeterminant meaning" principle—another way of saying that, when we draw meaning out of people with questionnaires and rating scales, we are almost surely getting an artificial expression of the "felt experience" of genuine thought or feeling. But how about thought and feeling? Can we, in the interests of developing a unified theory of thought and action, reconcile phenomenologists' and neuroscientists' views of such phenomena?

What about Mind, Emotion, Curiosity, and Interest?

Let us suppose that the neuroscientists are right in assuming that information processing in living organisms has more to do with energy balance than logic. But what happens when we move up the line from the fly's or garden slug's (or human being's) basic pattern perceptions to levels at which many, many local excitations and relaxations interact on a global basis? Is it just more of the same times 10, or 1,000, or 1,000 to the nth power?

Or does something happen along the way, in the hierarchy of lower to higher order processes, to explain the possible validity of the notion of "mind over matter" (or, more precisely, "mind over energy")? Indeed, is there such a thing as mind? Are there points at which the excitations and relaxations are so intense, or so richly diffuse, that energy patterns become consciousness? Do those complex patterns of excitation and relaxation interact with the autonomic nervous system and/or the endocrine system, as many psychologists have supposed for nearly 100 years, to account for the differences in the feeling qualities that we call moods and emotions?

Such questions have profound implications for theologians and humanists.[11] And, from a psychologist's point of view, they bear upon questions of how, or whether, higher order associations (e.g., the curiosities, interests, and ego defenses, of our folk psychology) can exert control over the lower order processes.

Churchland goes to great lengths to argue that consciousness is a disreputable, nonscientific concept (1986). She realizes that living organisms may selectively attend to, or react to, the environment in terms of preexisting internal states[12], and she acknowledges that it makes sense to talk about mental states causing brain states. But her generosity on the latter point stems from her conviction that all mental states, once they are understood, will be recognized to be brain states.

The gestaltists concluded that consciousness is an emergent property of neurological processes—the "greater than" in the expression that "the whole is greater than the sum of its parts." I am ready to bet not only that the gestaltists are right, but also that the principle of emergentism will be vindicated by neuroscience itself.[13]

Consumer Psychology's Interface with Neuroscience

If we psychologists are to contribute to a unified theory of human thought and action, we must reach out to both neuroscience and phenomenal psychologies and, like the gestaltists of an earlier time, strive to fill the space between them.

If meanings which we had supposed to be verbal meanings are really "background assumptions which can only be verbalized with great difficulty," that is fine. That is part of the business that we consumer psychologists are in—the business of getting good enough surrogate measures of meaning. And, if the consciousness and emotions of the phenomenologists' felt experience are inaccessible through neural network theories, that is another part of the challenge which we must be willing to accept.

The neuroscientists' recent discoveries are awesome. (In both a philosophical and scientific sense, it is profoundly interesting to discover that all information, as it is transmitted by communication media or as it is processed in the nervous system, is patterned energy.) But, more than half a century ago, the gestaltists were also interested in neural energy interpretations of mental experience. They too discovered principles of self-organizing, error tolerant pattern recognition, for example, the principles of Pragnanz and perceptual closure.[14] Their hypotheses about the ways in which information from the outside world is represented inside the nervous system were similar to those of today's neuroscientists.[15] But they found, as we do today, that as one studies behaviors of more practical consequence, more broad stroked theory is needed.

As Pylyshyn (1980) has observed, too much attention to "actual pumps and pulleys of the embodiment of mental life" can be a hindrance in doing cognitive research. It would be as foolish for psychologists to ignore neuroscience as it would be for architects to remain ignorant of the laws of physics. But, it would be as silly for us to try to study or explain human thought and action in terms of neural network theories as it would be for architects to do all of their plans and measurements in terms of molecular structures or the principles of quantum mechanics.

We may expect, moreover, that our theories will give neuroscientists some of their most fruitful hypotheses when they are ready to deal with the ways in which "cooperative search for energy balance" reaches out into the environment. They will discover, in other words, that "selective attention" is a natural extension of what we have called "selective perception." And as they discover more about the circularity of arousal-relaxation processes, they will discover what many psychologists have known about (excuse my naive teleology!) "motivational tendencies toward" both aroused and relaxed states.[16]

CONSUMER PSYCHOLOGISTS' VERSION OF TACIT KNOWLEDGE

The most important innovations in consumer psychologists' theories in recent years are like the most important innovations in philosophy and neuroscience; they have to do with nonliteral/nonverbal information processing and tacit knowledge.

The tacit knowledge implicit in Freudian concepts of preconscious motivation inspired consumer psychologists, in the 1950s, to do motivation research for marketing planning[17] and analyses of nonverbal meaning in advertising.[18]

In the mid–1960s, H. E. Krugman's insights about low-involvement responses to advertising (1965, 1966–1967) made an important contribution to advertising theory. His measure of involvement, like my own measure of "positive product response" (discussed below), was based on content analyses of thoughts stirred by television commercials. Involvement was defined in terms of the number of "cognitive connections" between message content and self. (My own measure was based on the occurrence or nonoccurrence of connections between advertised brand and self.)

Krugman's work generated the first widespread acknowledgement that advertising might enhance the probability of action (i.e., purchase) through a form of learning which requires no change in what is known or believed about the advertised brand—learning in the form of enhanced salience, or potential salience, of the brand. Although this seemed to run counter to the traditional cognition→affect→conation paradigm which had been thought to be the basis for attitude formation and change, it was demonstrated that learning, feeling, and action need not take the form, or follow in the sequence, suggested by that paradigm (Ray, Sawyer, Rothschild, Heeler, Strong, & Reed, 1973).

During the 1970s, many other psychologists (e.g., those interested in linguistics or verbal learning) discovered, or finally acknowledged, that literal/verbal sentence crunching is only one of the modes of response to information. In the early 1980s, R. E. Petty and J. T. Cacioppo (1981) conducted a detailed review of the contemporary academic literature of attitude and persuasion research. They tried to put these newer insights into perspective by distinguishing between (1) the central route to persuasion, when people focus on literal persuasive arguments and learning becomes the basis for attitude change, and (2) the peripheral route to persuasion, when attitude change seems to follow attention to nonliteral issue-relevant cues. Echoing consumer psychologists' 1970s views of cognitive involvement (e.g., Robertson, 1976), they suggested that the "central route" messages may serve the persuaders' interests best when the audience is motivated and able to think about substantive claims arguments; but "peripheral route," nonliteral messages may be best when the audience is less interested or unable to weigh relevant arguments.

Convergence of "Scientifisch" Theories and Creative Judgments

Refining these concepts, consumer psychologists have spelled out depth of processing continua, in terms of the cognitive effort devoted to advertising decoding (Greenwald & Leavitt, 1984). Others have described varying degrees of cognitive effort devoted to brand choices or persuasion-relevant decision making.

There has, meanwhile, been a growing awareness, to put things in the folksiest of "folk psychology" terms, that:

- Unless people are especially interested in a product/service category (unless they need detailed information to make brand choices), they are unlikely to work very hard at digging substantive, choice-relevant information out of advertisements.
- When people have already learned what there is to learn about familiar brands, or when the perceived risks associated with brand choice are trivial, advertisers' use of contrived basic selling ideas or brand attribute claims may be counterproductive.[19]
- In such cases the perceived attractiveness or interest value of the ad itself may affect attitude toward the advertised brand. (When people are not very interested in what is said, advertising effectiveness may depend more upon how it is said.)
- And, even when people are attending to information of interest, nonverbal cues can importantly affect nonliteral comprehension and familiarity.

(See, for example, Batra & Ray, 1985, and Baker & Lutz, 1988.)

Such points of view have focused consumer psychologists' attention on the effects of nonverbal, as well as literal/verbal, forms of communication.[20] And they have helped to liberate advertisers and advertising researchers alike from the constraints of unduly literal dogmas, thereby narrowing the gap between researchers' concepts and the intuitions of creative directors, producers, and others who create advertising.

New Kinds of Confusion

But, as always, new answers bring new questions, and there is more than a little "creative confusion" about whether involvement should be defined in terms of message elaboration and internalization (as in Krugman's original message content–self-cognitive connections measure), or whether involvement, or depth of processing, is a matter of the presence or absence of brand comparison thinking, the focus or nonfocus on claims or beliefs about brand attributes, the use of verbal versus nonverbal information processing, and so on.

I suspect, moreover, that the pendulum is swinging too far away from literal learning theory. It has been noted that peripheral route or learning without involvement persuasion may affect attitudes toward the advertised brand even though the audience may pay no attention to brand-relevant information of either a literal or nonliteral/nonverbal sort. Indeed, in some of today's studies, ratings of commercials, and opinions of commercials as commercials (the A_{ad} in the journal articles), seem to be treated as ends in themselves.[21]

But, if it is sometimes unwise to evaluate ads in terms of literal learning, it may be even less wise to focus on response to ads simply as ads. As I have suggested in earlier comments about the "Silly Putty" problem, ad liking→brand liking "rub off," without any stirring of thoughts about the brand, is a phenomenon that may be more apparent than real; it may, in other words, be the product of interviewing procedures, rather than the result of advertising exposure. And, if it occurs as a genuine phenomenon, it may be very transitory (Lutz, 1985). Meanwhile, we know little about how or why it occurs, if it occurs.

Like Baker and Lutz (1988), I find it hard to believe that advertising can be persuasive without being relevant to consumers' perceptions of the brand. And, although such relevance could conceivably occur simply through brand registration, brand registration has received little attention in most of the studies that focus on reactions to ads as ads.

Let me be clear about what I am saying here. I do not argue that effective response to advertising must be a cognitive response in the usual literal/verbal sense of that term. I do not deny that "liking ruboff" may occur as affect referral in a classical conditioning sense (Shimp, 1981). It may even occur as a mere awareness phenomenon (cf., Zajonc, 1980). In either case, recognition of the brand in the liked advertising could produce an affective upgrading of current brand meaning.[22] But, if "liking ruboff" were to occur simply in terms of response to advertising attributes, without a brand relevance link, the "liking" would "rub off" on any or all brands. However, the brand registration issue seems to have been ignored or taken for granted (or treated in a way in which the research itself would establish the ad-brand link) in most studies which focus on ad liking.[23]

My point is that, until these phenomena are further explored and validated in terms of sales effectiveness, preoccupation with audience response to advertising as advertising could be bad business for those who hope to get a reasonable return on advertising investments. It could also be counterproductive for our search for a unified theory of thought and action.

My views on such matters can be better understood in the light of my own theory of persuasive communication, which I think illustrates how real-world pressures on consumer psychologists can become "mothers of invention" for social science theory.

A GENERAL THEORY OF PERSUASIVE COMMUNICATION

I mentioned earlier one of my old articles on believability. In that article (Maloney, 1963) and in an earlier article (Maloney, 1962a), both published while I was a young psychologist with the Leo Burnett Company, I described a principle which I referred to as curious nonbelief.

Curious Nonbelief: The First Step Toward New Understanding

Curious nonbelief is uncertainty or doubt about advertising claims, either explicit or inferred, which have not yet been reality tested by direct experience with the advertised product.[24] It contrasts with the disbelief resulting from contradictions between claims and firsthand experience or disbelief of advertising elements other than brand-related claims.

I was initially interested in the fact that advertising researchers had been dealing with message belief as though it were an either-or event even though there was evidence (à la Lewin's unfreezing-refreezing analogy) that there are many shades of uncertainty between belief and disbelief. It otherwise seemed obvious, once it was pointed out to me by a colleague, that uncertainty often gives rise to information search.

As my friend put it, a lot of what people complain about when we ask them about the believability of advertising has to do with their feelings that "that sounds too good to be true." That often implies, "I won't believe it until I see it." Some follow-up research suggested that this is often the case, although, needless to say, curious nonbelief is not always expressed overtly in terms of "I'll have to see it to believe it."[25]

I did not suppose that curious nonbelief would send thousands of people off in urgent search of information to settle the issue. (Most of the nonbelief that we observed in our research was pretty trivial and probably would not have concerned people if we had not asked them about it.) But, even if such curiosity takes a passive form (nothing more than a heightened reaction sensitivity to the brand if it should be encountered in the store), our evidence suggested that it would be more motivating than "ho-hum" belief.

The curious nonbelief concept seemed iconoclastic at the time. The prevailing advertising theory favored measures of comprehension of, and conviction about, literal advertising claims or selling ideas.[26] Krugman's initial publications on low-involvement response to advertising (1965, 1966–1967) had not yet appeared, and advertising researchers had not yet become aware of the role of less consciously considered responses to advertising. It would be several years before research by M. L. Ray and his associates at Stanford (Ray et al., 1973) would overturn conventional textbook assumptions about the learn→feel→do (cognition→affect→conation) paradigm.[27]

I was convinced that curious nonbelief was simply a manifestation of a need for a wholly new theoretical orientation. But, since my ideas were out of phase with the conventional wisdom of advertising research (and not well received by my employer[28]), I thought it best to keep my most iconoclastic intuitions to myself. But, given the current "creative confusion" among consumer psychologists, you may be interested in an explanation of why I was so convinced of a need for a new theoretical orientation.

Important Further Steps Toward Understanding

I had, by 1960, discovered that the most popular measure of advertising effectiveness, the sales point playback measure, was usually inappropriate for evaluating advertising messages or campaigns.[29] I had, therefore, developed a relatively phenomenal measure for commercial tests—a brand–self-cognitive connections measure much like the message content–self-measure used later by Krugman as an index of involvement.[30]

Demonstrably superior to measures of comprehension and belief,[31] this "positive product response" measure worked as well for new messages as for old messages. (Sales point playbacks are biased in favor of established, easier to remember themes.) It worked for "picture-in-the-mind"/"sounds-in-the-mind" message meanings as well as for literal/verbal messages. (Tabulations of precoded playbacks are biased in favor of literal/verbal claims.) In fact, I found that nonverbal message content often elicits more positive and personally relevant brand-related thoughts than does verbal content, while literal/verbal claims often inhibit positive product response (PPR) by evoking counterarguments.

Importance of symbol relevance. What kinds of nonverbal message content elicited the most PPR? It may come as no surprise that the nonverbal cues which work best in this regard are "product experience cues"—those looks good/sounds good/smells good/feels good nonverbal cues which easily remind people of what it would be like, or has been like, to actually buy, use, or otherwise experience the product or service being advertised.[32]

Mood setting, emotion evoking symbols can enhance PPR when they are relevant to moods and emotions which people often associate with the use of the advertised product or service. But I found that generalized symbolism works poorly. (The sight of a spongy, soft cake, yielding to the pressure of a fork can effectively communicate cake moistness. On the other hand, the sight of early morning dew on a rose with voice-over comments about cake moistness can be very confusing.) It is a matter of the advertiser's sensitivity to what Leo Burnett called "the fitness of things" from the consumer's point of view.

At about the same time, I had started to develop a unified theory of advertising effectiveness to explain my research findings and guide a coordinated program of commercial testing and campaign evaluation tracking surveys.[33] This theory was based on an extensive review of learning and perception theory as well as many new information processing concepts which were then emerging in many behavioral and social science disciplines.[34]

As I have already suggested, the central focus of my infant theory was not on reasoned comprehensions or convictions. I was interested in people's acceptance of, preference for, or interest in the advertised brand for whatever reasons— whether those were literal or nonliteral reasons.

Reaction sensitivity and circuital response to persuasion. To be more specific, I had concluded that curious nonbelief is simply a high-involvement manifestation of the principle of circuital response to persuasion. There is more than ample evidence, it seemed to me, that we never become irrevocably sold on anything on a once and for all basis—certainly not when it comes to advertised brands or products. Linear models of persuasion (and questions about which comes first, attitude change or behavior) miss the point altogether. My idea was (and is) that tentative brand attitudes are both cause and effect of both advertising noting and brand purchase or use. Thus, static beliefs are not the key to action; keep-the-cycle-going interest or reaction sensitivity is the key to action.

The principle of reaction sensitivity had long been implicit in the "attention-holding'' sustaining set[35] and ''attention-stopping'' preparatory set[36] concepts of perceptual set theory. But my interest in reaction sensitivity was really triggered by the input-regulating feedback concepts which cybernetics and biological systems theory were contributing to the nascent cognitive science of the early 1960s. Such concepts were the basis for D. E. Berlyne's theory of epistemic curiosity (1965), and they led Floyd Allport (1955) to the rediscovery that perception is based on ''circuital structures of ongoings and events'' (pp. 525–530).[37]

All of this is remarkably consistent, incidentally, with neuroscientists' recent discoveries that perception involves sequences of arousals and restorations of balance[38], and it all made eminently good sense in terms of what I was finding in my PPR and curious nonbelief studies.

The point is that preparatory set is critical for the cognitive engagement associated with both ad noting and purchase behavior. To be sure, there are noteworthy differences between decisions to read an ad or watch a commercial versus decisions to note a display, listen to a friend's comments about a product, or actually buy the advertised product. (At the very least, the situational factors which compete for attention are different in each case.) But in all such cases, the probability of cognitive engagement depends upon an openness to product-relevant experience—an interest in, a need for, or a curiosity about the product.[39]

It occurred to me, then, that the proper role of advertising is not to convince on a once and for all basis; the purpose of advertising should be to build and maintain interest and openness to experience (i.e., preparatory set).

Depending upon the brand and product or service category, reaction sensitivity can be stimulated in a variety of ways. Some of these (for example, ''sounds too good to be true'' claims which are true) involve fairly literal, though not necessarily verbal, cognitive mediations.[40] Under other circumstances (when all brand-differentiating claims would be old hat or irrelevant to brand-choice decisions, or when the consumer benefit is a nonrational benefit), the advertiser may simply remind prospects of what they know about the brand in nonliterally relevant ways. As Baker and Lutz (1988) suggest, the reminder may involve a product-relevant mood, for example, sexual arousal associated with a perfume. For already well-known and well-liked brands, a brand registration reminder may suffice to enhance top of mindness.[41]

Since all of this depends upon empathy with consumers' views of specific product or service categories, even the best theory is unlikely to obviate the need for phenomenological homework. For example, there are many product or service categories in which a warm and friendly approach can enhance the fitness of things. (I would even suggest, on the basis of my personal commercial testing experiences, if not my theory, that product-experience sharing scenes have remarkably broad applicability.) But the words, music, scenes, settings, gestures, facial expressions, and so on, which are fittingly warm and friendly in one instance are quite different than those which communicate warmth and friendliness, in a brand-relevant way, in another. As Stewart and Hecker have observed with regard to nonverbal communication, meaning only exists within context, and "simplicity is not a virtue in building a theory, since the phenomenon itself may disappear as simplification occurs" (1988, p. 264).

Summary of Theory's Most General Principles

Figure 19.1 crudely summarizes the most general principles discussed so far.

- Advertising affects behavior by altering impressions of the brand.
- Predispositions toward the brand may involve literal impressions of the sort commonly attributed to cognitive processes or nonliteral impressions of the sort commonly attributed to conditioning. This depends, in part, on the nature and degree of cognitive involvement associated with ad noting, from mere focal attention to message elaboration, and the nature and degree of cognitive involvement with brand choice, from mindless to optimizing choice behavior. (The terms in Figure 19.1 are those currently popular, à la Baker & Lutz, 1988.)
- The operant mental impressions are not static beliefs or finished impressions. Salience (awareness) and cognitive uncertainty (e.g., interest or curiosity) are often as important as, or more important than, the meaning associations themselves in determining either brand purchase or use or attention to subsequent advertising.
- Situational factors (brand availability, competitive pricing, sampling and other inducements to trial, and so on) strongly mediate the relationship between the predisposition to choose the brand and the actual purchase or use.
- Finally, as implied by the doubleheaded arrow between brand choice and purchase or use in Figure 19.1, purchase or use experiences are themselves informational inputs which affect impressions of (and interests in or curiosities about) the brand.

Figure 19.1 is what many systems theorists call a logical homology inasmuch as it crudely represents cause-effect principles (i.e., principles of input screening, internal information integration, input-regulating feedback, and so on), which occur at many levels of response to information. (The details vary according to the level of response. More about this very shortly.)

Importance (and complexity) of behavioral validation. As Churchland (1986) points out, studies of information processing unrelated to measures of observable behavior run the risk of being irrelevant, but she was talking about relating pattern recognitions (e.g., a crab's recognition of a food object) to motor behavior (e.g., the crab's here-and-now claw extension and grasping behavior). Needless to say, validations of measures of response to marketing communication vis-à-vis observable mass behavior is very much more complicated.

Whether we are dealing with crab claw extensions or the purchase behaviors of groups of people in the marketplace, the process begins in the same way—with neural response to physical stimuli. But, in the latter case, the time interval between exposure to information and the ultimate criterion action may be days or weeks, rather than seconds or fractions of a second. That means that we are dealing with long-term memory storage, which involves qualitatively different

Figure 19.1
General Overview of Response to Advertising

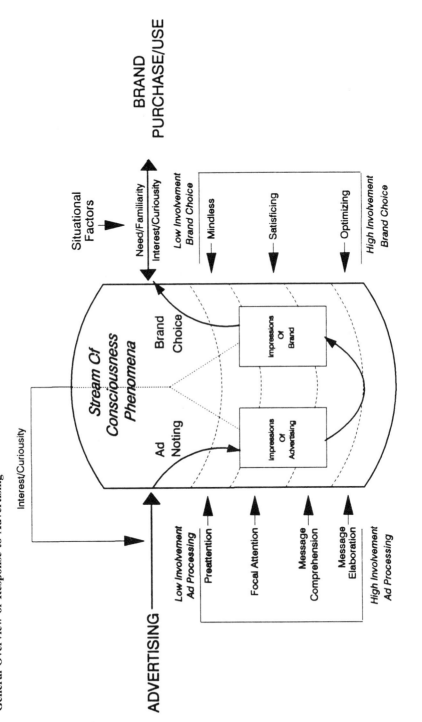

forms of neural energy processing. More to the point, this also means that a great deal of behavior-facilitating or behavior-inhibiting information may be received (for example, repeated exposures to the advertising, exposures to competing advertising, and the opinions of significant others) between information exposure and occurrence of the relevant behavioral response. That means that the information may be processed, reprocessed, and mixed with other information (i.e., as it functions as part of the neural-cognitive template for decoding subsequent information) any number of times before it affects relevant behavior. This is to say that, if advertising has its intended effect, that effect shows up at the end of a long chain of causes and effects.

Hierarchy of Response to Information

From an advertising research point of view, the hierarchy of response to information might be described as follows: the sales effects of the overall marketing mix are partly determined by the effects of the advertising campaign. The aggregate effects of the advertising campaign are partly dependent on the reach and frequency of ad or commercial messages and the persuasiveness (psychological effects) of each of those messages. The persuasiveness of each message is partly dependent upon the effects of separate message elements, and so on, down to those most basic sensory-cognitive responses to media-borne physical signals.

I have often introduced this hierarchy to students with the bit of doggerel verse given in Table 19.1.

I know; the doggerel verse is pretty bad. And the suggested part-whole relationships between the memory forms, (the sensations, perceptions, cognitions, attitudes, and so on) owe as much to poetic license as to sound theory. As Churchland says, our "folk psychology" concepts are "a set of vague notions flying in loose formation" (1986, p. 382–383).

We consumer psychologists are otherwise criticized for inconsistency or relativism as we borrow concepts, theories, and methods from many different disciplines (Anderson, 1986; Siegel, 1988; Anderson, 1988). But, if we handle our validation chores responsibly, our relativism (I prefer to think of it as eclecticism) will be our greatest strength and the basis for an important contribution to social science theory.[42]

Hierarchic Analysis: Key to Measurement Validation and Unified Theory

We now have single-source marketing research technologies which permit us to evaluate advertising on a single-level basis. At least for those products sold through retail outlets with checkout counter scanners, and for advertisers who take advantage of electronically monitored, household-by-household measures of advertising exposure, we can relate sales to advertising exposure with proper

Table 19.1

The Advertising Effectiveness Hierarchy: An Introduction in Doggerel Verse

===

We start with physical signals;
   Then on to symbols of communication.
From symbols we get messages.
   Starting to see the whole relation?

From messages we move on up
   To effects of the whole campaign.
We have to track the whole thing through
   Or the task is all in vain.[a]

So, from sensation to perception;
   From perception to cognition;[b]
From cognition up to attitude
   And right on up to "public mood."

All inputs are with "memories" mixed;
   Things move along this vein.
It's input, "memory" and response. . .
   All three on every plane.

From reverberating neural trace
   Within the nervous system. . .
To "social norms"; they're all forms of "memories."
   How could we have missed 'em?[c]

And, among these many memory forms,
   Things aren't just black or white.
There's curiosity, doubt, "imbalance" -
   Not just agreement that "that's right."

Nor is this just cognition
   Of a literal-verbal kind;
For people also tend to act
   On pictures in the mind.

Do such memories shape behaviors
   Of the audience reacters?
That all depends, we must admit,
   On the situational factors.

But, if we can predict reactions,
   Step by step along the way,
Let 'em ask for a unified theory.
   We'll have of so much to say.

Now don't suppose its simple.
   It's really not, God knows.
Each answer brings new questions.
   That's how understanding grows.

---

[a] That is, one must "track the whole thing through" to examine the level-to-level linkages implied here.

[b] These include perceptions and cognitions of both literal/verbal and nonverbal impression-istic forms.

[c] "Public mood" and "social norms" suggest the aggregate of "consumer demand" for product classes and brands as a result of advertising and other brand/product related experiences.

controls for a host of behavior-leveraging situational factors, such as special deals and in-store promotions.

Such measures are of great value for the program which I propose here. But they cannot, by themselves, help us to understand how sensation shapes perception, what perception has to do with cognition or attitude formation, or how attitude formation affects higher order responses of interest to social psychologists, sociologists, or practitioners of other disciplines concerned with mass behavior. To establish a unified theory embracing all part-whole patterns of response, we need hierarchic analyses.

At the same time, we need hierarchic analyses if we are to handle those measurement validation chores to which I have been referring throughout this chapter. For example, it is unlikely that immediate criterion measures used at the bottom of the hierarchy (e.g., brain wave measures and electrodermal response measures) will ever, by themselves, predict the sales impact of advertising. But they will have proven value when we can interpret them in ways which will predict intermediate criterion measures which have themselves been validated against top level ultimate criterion (sales) measures. And such measures are much more likely to succeed when they are fine tuned within an overall theory-measurement framework which has cataloged the exogenous and extraneous variables, or critical situational factors, at each level of response.

The actual implementation of an adequate hierarchic analysis program requires more knowledge of systems theory principles than can be discussed here. For example, each level specified in a hierarchic analysis system has its own time frame, its own system of feedbacks; its own situational factors or system noises, and its own information chunk sizes—in other words, the momentary physical signals at the bottom of the hierarchy versus the whole marketing mix at the top. In most level-to-level linkages, there are important considerations of both intensiveness and extensiveness,[43] and so on. However, many of these issues allow for practical compromises. This is particularly true when it comes to the number of levels that must be analyzed.

Specifying levels for analysis. Philosophers (and many artificial intelligence experts) have traditionally talked about three levels of response to information: the syntactic, semantic, and pragmatic levels. On the other hand, neuroscientists have identified dozens, or perhaps hundreds, of input-output energy transductions between the most basic perceptual processes and action.[44] As is the case with so many of the issues discussed here, the answer to any question about the number of levels is, ''It all depends.''

The main thing that it all depends upon is the breadth of the response spectrum to be covered by the overall theory. For narrow-spectrum applications of interest to neuroscientists, the top of the hierarchy may be a momentary visual pattern recognition. In that case, one looks at very fine-grained distinctions in defining levels of response. But, for marketing planners, it may be the weeks- or months-long purchase response of a large population of consumers that matters. In that case, it would be impractical and unnecessary to analyze more than a fraction of the response levels that might be identified from a physical science point of view. And, fortunately, we can get on with it by aggregating part-whole levels of response, depending upon the variety and number of measurement schemes one needs to make practical decisions.

There is a further consideration. Some input-output exchanges within information processing systems are chain linked in the sense that they proceed from A to B to C on a now or never basis. Other input-output exchanges are concatenated in the sense that outputs from one level are stored for a time within the system, until needed as inputs for higher order processes (or until the memory of those outputs decays to the point that they are unavailable for use at the higher level). Thus, if exposure to a television commercial has any effect on later purchase or use of the advertised product, it is because a memory residue of that commercial is somehow stored in the system until the time comes for product purchase or use.[45] It is obviously the concatenated linkages, involving stored-for-later-use memories, that matter most in the kind of program that I am talking about.

Figure 19.2 represents the hierarchy I had in mind when I developed my infant theory. Top-level criterion measures are sales or sales share measures. Campaign tracking survey measures provide the second-level criterion. The third-level criterion is based on tests of finished ads or commercials. Bottom-level measures might involve any of a number of immediate response measures (eye scanning patterns, or measures of arousal such as pupil dilation or electrodermal response).

I have no universal set of formulae which will convert bottom-level measures into accurate predictions of top-level sales share effects for all brands or product or service classes. Because of the importance of situational factors (suggested by the dashed arrow inputs at each level), operational details must often be custom built for specific applications.[46] But I have had more encouraging experience with programmatic research of the sort suggested in Figure 19.2 than can be described here. It may suffice to say that considerable progress has been made in understanding the principles and procedural requirements for bridging the gaps—especially those gaps among the top three levels of the hierarchy.

Other marketing and advertising researchers have almost accidentally launched hierarchic analysis programs via fortuitous discoveries of level-to-level relationships. Some of these discoveries involve "postdictions" (e.g., after-the-fact discoveries of correlations between commercial test scores and measured sales responses). That's all right. Such postdictive evidence needs to be confirmed by predictive analyses, but any genuine evidence of level-to-level relationships is too precious to be ignored—and ever so much more worthy of serious consideration than are rhetorical arguments about measures that have never been checked against completely independent higher order criteria.

My theory, or any comparable theory, must ultimately be tested and refined by a rigorous research program. Once empirically established relationships begin to show up in the form of statistically significant level-to-level predictions, the process is under way. One can then tinker with the measurements and refine the theory to establish tighter links between levels.

"Top-down" versus "bottom-up" theory building. Those involved with hierarchic theory building often argue about whether it is better to build the theory from the top down or from the bottom up. Physical scientists tend to argue for bottom-up strategies—with, according to Churchland, psychologists adapting their theories to the latest discoveries of neuroscience. However, consumer psychologists cannot, and need not, wait for more perfect theories of neural network functioning. We have to keep on keeping on with all of the practical tasks that confront us. And, as we do so, we are even more obliged to adapt to higher level realities of mass behavior than to lower level realities of neural functioning.

Notwithstanding the preoccupations of neuroscientists or the platonic speculations of ancient philosophers, behavioral science cannot be content with any studies of mental processes that ignore actions that flow from those processes. Moreover, top-down strategy, such as that implicit in Figure 19.2, provides

Figure 19.2
Hierarchy of Responses to Advertising

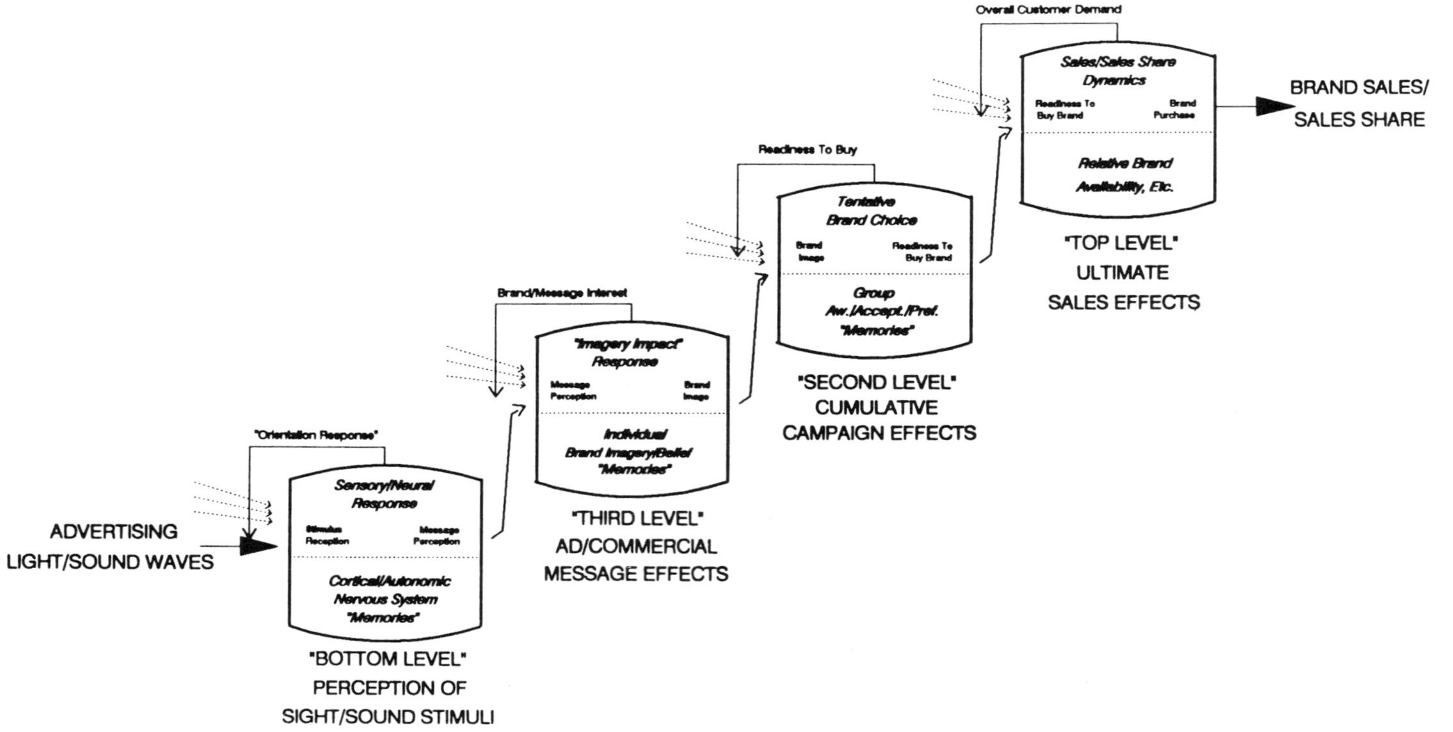

BRAND SALES/
SALES SHARE

Overall Customer Demand

Sales/Sales Share
Dynamics

Readiness To   Brand
Buy Brand   Purchase

Relative Brand
Availability, Etc.

"TOP LEVEL"
ULTIMATE
SALES EFFECTS

Readiness To Buy

Tentative
Brand Choice

Brand   Readiness To
Image   Buy Brand

Group
Aw./Accept./Pref.
"Memories"

"SECOND LEVEL"
CUMULATIVE
CAMPAIGN EFFECTS

Brand/Message Interest

"Imagery Impact"
Response

Message   Brand
Perception   Image

Individual
Brand Imagery/Belief
"Memories"

"THIRD LEVEL"
AD/COMMERCIAL
MESSAGE EFFECTS

"Orientation Response"

Sensory/Neural
Response

Stimulus   Message
Reception   Perception

Cortical/Autonomic
Nervous System
"Memories"

"BOTTOM LEVEL"
PERCEPTION OF
SIGHT/SOUND STIMULI

ADVERTISING
LIGHT/SOUND WAVES

focus for research at lower levels of the response hierarchy. We are less likely to be sidetracked by interesting but irrelevant procedures when we have a clear view of how the game is going to be scored in the final analysis.

It is otherwise easier to keep things in perspective if one has an awareness of the leverage of higher level situational factors. (Because they have had to validate commercial tests, campaign tracking surveys, and new product forecasting procedures against sales criteria, many consumer psychologists have discovered circumstances that must prevail before brand attitudes become relevant considerations.)

I am not just talking about principles of marketing or advertising research. I submit that it is the top of the hierarchy that counts in virtually all social science, just as it is the bottom line that counts in business.

Am I suggesting that consumer psychology can contribute to a unified social science theory only so long as it conforms to sales and profit goals? Of course not. As I have indicated elsewhere (Maloney & Schonfeld, 1973), the principles are the same whether top-of-the-hierarchy behavioral criteria are sales (i.e., buying behavior), voting behavior, or behavioral measures of social change. The point is that real-world behavioral criteria provide the needed dimension of relevance.[47]

SUMMARY

Over the past 30 to 40 years, there has been an explosion of knowledge about human thought and action and response to information. From philosophy to neuroscience, old logically and linguistically oriented theories are giving way to dynamic, new, piecemeal theories which apply to many different levels of response to information. For both practical and philosophical reasons, social science needs a unified theory of human thought and action.

Few consumer psychologists see themselves to be "big picture" theorists. But, because of consumer psychology's eclecticism and engagement with the real world, we should be able to play an important role in formulating a unified theory.

We study a broad range of phenomena. Aware that all marketing communications have their first effects as patterns of physical stimuli impinging on nervous systems, we study autonomic response to products, packages, and advertising. Aware that the ultimate effects of such communications occur in large populations in the marketplace, we study public opinion formation and change. Forced to confront the "errors" which arise from applications of such disparate methods, we have had to improvise. And our experimental and quasi-experimental improvisations are starting to point toward potentially unifying concepts.

Like others who have studied the practical effects of communication, we have discovered that literal beliefs often impact behavior less than people's awarenesses, interests, and openness to new beliefs. We have started to develop procedures for dealing with nonliterally relevant information. Meanwhile, we have probably learned more than any other social science discipline about the ways in which situational factors mediate relationships among thoughts, feelings, and action.

We are sometimes tempted to believe that our procedures work well enough if the client buys them on a given Thursday afternoon. But we cannot simply assert that our newest best-guess concepts and the measures summarized in our multicolored charts are valid, "all other things being equal." As our business patrons look for bottom-line results, they have their eyes on top-of-the-hierarchy mass behavioral sales criteria. Like political pollsters and weather forecasters, we cannot "fool Mother Nature" over the long term. We must eventually prove that the measures that we use at the lower levels of analysis are relevant to, and can predict, events at the higher (more general or more inclusive) levels of analysis. There can be no better impetus for unified theory building.

The challenge is formidable. As we continue to cut and try, refining both procedures and concepts, our unified theory building will have to modify and blend concepts previously thought to be incompatible (e.g., abstract cognitive theories and concrete conditioning theories). But, with access to extraordinary criteria of what actually affects human action, and freed of the strictures of traditional philosophical-theological debates, we have an excellent chance of contributing importantly to an honest to God unified theory of human thought and action.

NOTES

1. William James' *Principles of Psychology*, in 1890, emphasized the stream of consciousness; and turn-of-the-century psychophysicists, especially Edward Titchener, were interested in idea associations and emotions, as well as sensory discriminations. But, for Husserl, phenomenology was a protest against all psychology (Jennings, 1986).

2. There is otherwise a great deal of controversy about the applicability of phenomenological hermeneutic methods, as developed by Heidegger and his successors, for applied research (Barratt & Sloan, 1988; Day, 1988; Packer, 1988b; Russell, 1988).

3. It simply will not do, the critics said, to explain any process in terms of "balance restoring" purposes. What is that mystical structure, they would ask, (i.e., that "hypothesis" or "cognitive structure" or whatever) that does all of that information selecting, sifting, sorting in order to "restore balance"? And how can you contend that the same conditions (curiosities, interests, or whatever) can be both the cause and the effect of learning or response to information out there in the world?

4. Although Bergson's advice about synthesis following analysis refers to a subjective process, such "intuition" may, of course, be aided by hard data. For example, in interpreting results of a commercial test, it may be possible to consider the details of the planned commercial exposure schedule. And, these days, it may even be possible to combine test results with exposure schedules in a mathematical estimate of sales effects.

5. Quasi-experiments, or ex post facto experiments, involve the analysis of data which become available in the normal course of events, without prior imposition of experimental controls. Experimental design standards are then imposed, after the fact, via data analysis

procedures which may, for example, compare sales before and after an advertising campaign interval for reasonably matched groups of exposed versus unexposed consumers.

6. For a recent update of Columbia's minimal effects mass media model, see Katz (1987).

7. The bisociation terminology comes from the theoretical syntheses of novelist Arthur Koestler. I highly recommend Koestler's *The Act of Creation* (1964) to psychologists interested in cognitive process concepts unburdened by overreliance on number crunching–sentence crunching assumptions.

8. See Petty and Cacioppo's (1981) descriptions of judgmental theories.

9. On more than a few occasions, I have "dumbed things up" a bit more by using "mail room" or "switchboard in the mind" analogies. ("We thought we had addressed this message to people's thoughts and feelings about the brand, but the message 'went to the wrong mental department.' So, instead of reminding people of the brand, it was interpreted in the light of people's ideas and feelings about . . . '')

10. Cal Tech biophysicist John Hopfield has directed fascinating research in this area within the Molecular Biophysics Research Department at Bell Laboratories (Draper, 1986).

11. For philosophers, these are questions of antireductionism, reductionism, and emergentism. Antireductionists, often in the interests of protecting the mind or soul from the clutches of vulgar science, argue that the mind functions independently from the brain. Reductionists, in order to establish the unequivocal relevance of neuroscience for understanding mental processes, are just as dogmatic in insisting that the mind is just an aggregation of "brain states." Meanwhile, emergentists see consciousness and emotions to be phenomenal-mental states which emerge from neural/bodily functions. After she strives so effectively to cleanse philosophy of reactionary antireductionism, Churchland, the ultimate reductionist, throws emergentism out with the bath water. But many of today's psychologists (e.g., Sperry, 1988) are increasingly inclined toward a humanistic emergentism.

12. Churchland describes F. H. C. Crick's (1984) hypotheses of attention regulating "searchlight" functions of the reticular complex of the thalamus, and she is aware that there may be higher order feedback mechanisms which are not yet recognizable in physical form. (As she points out, servomechanism engineers refer to input-regulating feedbacks which cannot be attributed to the action of recognizable devices as virtual governors.) But it is doubtful that neuroscientists have yet recognized the extent to which human behavior is affected by selectivity of attention.

13. In my view, consciousness is a part of the "Trinity of Nature." Consciousness may, in other words, be viewed as a natural state which is different than, but related to, resonant neural energy in much the same way that energy is different than, but related to, matter. The unifying formula is still missing (i.e., the counterpart of Einstein's $E = MC^2$). But there are obviously systematic relationships between neural energy and consciousness; that is what anesthesiology is all about.

All of this means, of course, that the defense of spirituality need not be tied to a defense of a disembodied Cartesian soul. Just as psychology rests on neuroscience, neuroscience rests on quantum mechanical physics, and there is more than enough mystery about "God's handiwork" there to satisfy any theologian. But that, as they say, is another story.

14. Examples of closure: our tendency to see a circle as a closed circle, even though

it may have a small gap in it; or our tendency to recognize geometric forms in an almost random scattering of dots.

15. Stimulus patterns (e.g., light or sound wave patterns out there in the world) are assumed to be isomorphic to (corresponding but not identical to) neural energy patterns in the nervous system. Isomorphism for basic pattern recognitions (recognitions of colors, pitches, and edges of forms) is attributable to basic nerve cell structures. But isomorphisms for more abstract recognitions (e.g., recognitions of a friend's voice or a brand's advertising jingle) are obviously "soft wired" as the result of learned associations.

16. As they deal with higher order phenomena, neuroscientists will discover how "aroused associations" take the form of chronic interests, curiosities, and selective attention to the environment as well as cooperative search within the system.

Neuroscientists are likely to discover, moreover, that "information hunger," like food hunger or sexual arousal, is not always a noxious drive state. Thus, psychological theories posit "functional autonomies" (learned expectations of pleasurable "relaxation"??) which may tend behavior toward excitation as well as relaxation. This is presumably the basis for much creative activity and play behavior.

17. Jennings (1988) accuses the motivation researchers of the 1950s of having neglected their phenomenological homework. However, published interviews with both the motivation researchers of that era and their clients indicate that they did a lot of phenomenological homework before talking with consumers (Maloney, in press).

18. "Semiotic" analyses of recent years are very much like the analyses undertaken by E. Dichter, B. Gardner, P. Martineau and other motivation researchers in the 1950s.

19. In the jargon of communications research, forced attention to contrived or irrelevant arguments tends to evoke counterarguments. On the other hand, if the brand has an unknown advantage which may relate to consumers' psychological "modes of evaluation" of such brands, the presentation of that advantage in an entertaining way can help to differentiate the brand, even in a low involvement product category.

20. The proceedings of an earlier conference in this series provide an excellent overview of consumer psychologists' work to date on nonverbal communication. See especially Edell (1988), Hecker and Stewart (1988b), and Stewart and Hecker (1988).

21. One young ad researcher has complained that the early intrusion of the brand in the commercial can have the untoward effect of inhibiting the favorability of attitude toward the commercial. What a far cry from Leo Burnett's dictum that the brand should be "the star of the show!"

22. Even preconscious recognition must be a recognition of something—and "thingness" implies what Donald T. Campbell, my former colleague at Northwestern University, has referred to as entitativity—at least a tacit knowledge of associated properties (Campbell, 1973).

23. In experimental settings, when people are asked about brand liking shortly after ad exposure and just before or after they are asked about ad liking, this may not seem critical, but, in the real world, there are tremendous differences in the brand registration strengths of commercials.

24. The operational definition of curious nonbelief involved content analyses of responses to the question: "What was it that was hard to believe?" This question was asked of any respondent to a series of packaged goods ad tests who had answered affirmatively when asked if there was anything in the advertising that was hard to believe. Examples of curious nonbelief responses: "I doubt that any cake that is that easy to make would taste that good." Or, "They make it look delicious but I doubt that anything that

comes in a can could taste that good." (If respondents criticized the advertising on the grounds that it contradicted their own or trusted friends' firsthand experience, responses were not coded as curious nonbelief.)

25. The criterion measure for this research was pre-exposure to post-exposure shift on a 10-point scale of intention to use the advertised product. Curious nonbelief responses were associated with significantly more upward shifts on the intention-to-use scale than were "nothing hard to believe" responses. Meanwhile, other "hard to believe" responses were significantly less likely to be associated with upward shifts on the scale. These other responses included (1) claims which, in respondents' minds, had already been disconfirmed by firsthand experience with the advertised product and (2) criticisms of message content (e.g., executional elements or "borrowed attention" devices) unrelated to the advertised product.

26. The Association of National Advertisers' DAGMAR report (Colley, 1961) was issued just a few months before my first article was published on this topic. That report's marketing communications spectrum paradigm (unawareness-awareness-comprehension-conviction-action) emphasized comprehension of, and convictions about, literal advertising claims. This encouraged ad message tests and ad campaign tracking surveys based on "sales point playbacks" and/or ratings of advertised brands in terms of advertised benefits or attributes.

27. By the time that Mike Ray and I taught social psychology classes together, during Ray's graduate student days at Northwestern (circa 1966–1968), my nonbelief hypotheses defied literal interpretations of the old paradigm. But it was Ray who later, with his colleagues at Stanford, proved that the cognition→affect→conation emperor was naked.

28. Those articles were the partial result of a long and arduous effort triggered by Leo Burnett's personal request for "some research on believability." However, when the second article was called to the attention of Fairfax Cone at Foote, Cone & Belding, the title alone ("Is Advertising Believability Really Important?") was enough to make Fax call Leo to register a complaint. Unbeknownst to me, Leo and Fax had agreed that "the Chicago school of advertising" distinguished itself by producing inordinately down-to-earth, believable advertising. Any hint that believability was not important was the worst kind of heresy.

29. Reasons for my disaffection with sales point playbacks included the following: (1) such measures are usually biased in favor of old, familiar themes; (2) such measures usually correlated poorly, or not at all, with promising indices of sales effectiveness; and (3) many commercials, which otherwise seemed to have great promise, lacked the kinds of literal/verbal selling ideas which play back easily.

30. This positive product response (PPR) measure was based on a purposely vague, open-ended question: "What went through your mind when you saw that commercial; what did it make you think of?" "Anything else?" The question was asked prior to any other questions about the commercial in order to avoid associations triggered by the interview, rather than by the commercial itself. Although PPR response coding procedures were very detailed, the qualifications for a PPR response were essentially as follows: (1) the viewer had mentally rehearsed a personal experience with the advertised brand (not just the product class) and (2) the rehearsed experience was a positive experience or an experience which would satisfy response coding rules for curious nonbelief.

31. It discriminated in better than chance fashion between different commercials for the same brand and product. It correlated well with a completely independent pre-exposure versus post-exposure brand choice measure used by several of the agency's clients. Follow-

up interviews with commercial test respondents revealed that those who had shown PPR were significantly more likely to have later bought the advertised brand. (In 1970, years after I left the Leo Burnett Co., Leavitt, Waddell, and Wells published an article on my PPR measure and were kind enough to mention that I had developed it.)

32. When brand registration is weak, or when the brand is showcased in a way that fails to suggest brand-person experience, PPR is least likely to occur. But when the advertising "tells it like it is," illustrating the brand as consumers experience it, PPR is most likely to occur. (Examples of product experience cues: a fairly close shot of a coffee lover enjoying the aroma of a steaming hot cup of coffee; the sound of the top popping off of a frosty cold can of beer; or the sight and sound of a crispy, crunchy breakfast cereal pouring into the bowl. Such cues are particularly effective when they are reinforced by evidences—for example, facial expression evidences—of product user enjoyment.)

33. The tracking survey measures were also phenomenal in the sense that they avoided direct questions about the advertising as advertising. If the advertised brand is not part of the consumer's "evoked set" of product-class-related brands we may ask questions about it before the interview is terminated. But, for the basic analysis, we do not suggest, by asking about it by name, that the brand should have been recalled. And, while acceptance/preference measures are derived from comparisons of ratings of brands which come to mind for consumers, direct questions about preference are not asked since most purchases for competitively priced brands are not based on preference.

34. After reviewing a lengthy summary of concepts, which I later used in teaching communication theory at Northwestern University (Maloney, 1962b), my employer gently explained that "You're telling us more about penguins than we want to know about penguins." But my theory-unifying efforts were favorably received by a number of interdisciplinary systems theorists, and one of them (biological systems theorist Ludwig von Bertalanffy) encouraged me to set forth my ideas in a short paper. The resulting essay was eventually published, with essays from 62 representatives of many disciplines and more than 12 nations, in a festschrift honoring Bertalanffy (Maloney, 1973a).

35. Sustaining set (attention-holding power) may be compared with the set that is established with that first handful of peanuts or that first potato chip. For advertisers, this is the keep-going-back-for-more interest which holds people's attention to an ad or commercial, once they start to pay attention to it.

36. Preparatory set stopping power is a more pervasive, longer term attention-controlling feedback which encourages people to pay attention to a particular sort of information whenever it "comes into the psychological field." Thus, people who are in the market for, or generally interested in, a product or service are more likely to note an ad, commercial, display, or other information about that product or service. (The stopping power of an ad is also related, of course, to the relative size of ad, use of color, sound tempo of commercial openings, and so on. And attention-stopping and attention-holding power may both be related to people's interests in the message content other than the product-related content.)

37. This was a rediscovery, Allport (1955) pointed out, since G. W. F. Hegel and any number of nineteenth-century philosophers and psychologists (e.g., Charles Bell, Hermann Lotze, and John Dewey) had recognized the circularity of perceptual cause and effect.

38. Echoing the insights of even earlier gestaltists, Floyd Allport's comments of more than 30 years ago sound like passages out of today's neuroscience literature. After describing the limitations of linear stimulus-response theory, Allport wrote:

We have seen considerable evidence, however, in our study of perception that there is a definite circularity in the arrangement of the perceptual aggregate when set and proprioceptive motor elements are taken into account, or even when perceptual behavior is described in terms of field-theory cycles of disequilibrium and equilibrium, or in the trial-and-check repetitions of the theory of hypothesis-confirmation. (Allport, 1955, p. 525)

39. Advertisers can cheat, of course, by using borrowed attention devices and, as suggested by the foregoing discussion of liking ruboff, one of the most interesting questions in advertising research today concerns the effective use of interesting irrelevancies. (Space limitations preclude a detailed treatment of this topic but, in my view, the crux of the matter relates to the ways in which borrowed attention devices can be made brand relevant.)

40. Appetite appeal food photography is an example of a fairly literal but nonverbal claim. Thus, advertising research increasingly obliges cognitive theorists to pay more attention to nonliteral images. At the same time, as behaviorists pay more attention to the memory associations which link unconditioned stimuli to conditioned stimuli, we are starting to see an erosion of distinctions between cognitive theory and conditioning theory. As J. Edell (1988) has pointed out in reviewing studies of nonverbal advertising communication, such distinctions are already very strained.

41. R. B. Zajonc (1980) suggests that mere familiarity may influence choice behavior by reducing the tension associated with uncertainty. I am otherwise reminded of adman Leo Burnett's concept of "friendly familiarity."

42. As Stuart Tolley (1988) indicated in his presidential address to the Consumer Psychology Division of the American Psychological Association, consumer psychology should be able to make an important contribution to the social sciences because consumer psychologists "stand at the confluence" from which so many behavioral science advances are coming.

43. No matter how much cognitive response (intensiveness) is elicited by a single commercial exposure, it will contribute little to the cumulative effects of a campaign or, at a higher level, to sales, unless there is adequate extensiveness of exposure in terms of reach and frequency. On the other hand, no extensiveness of exposure can compensate for message effects of insufficient intensity.

44. For example, sound waves set up ear drum vibrations; ear drum vibrations become hair cell resonances within the cochlea of the inner ear; these set up piezoelectric impulses which become neural impulses headed through the thalamus to diverse areas of the auditory cortex, and so on. A long series of input-output energy transductions is involved in the simplest act of hearing.

45. Allport (1955) spoke of chained and concatenated linkages in terms of "ongoings" and "events" within the system. He noted that both occur at both concrete (physiological) and abstract (phenomenal or psychological) levels of response.

46. As suggested in the earlier discussion of the principle of multiple causes, a large share of behavior-predicting variance is attributable to situational factors. (For example, predictions of purchase in sales forecasting models for new products usually depend more on measures of product availability, display and pricing, and so on than to measures of literal learning or beliefs about brand or product attributes.) Consumer psychologists have often been reluctant to admit it, but our practical experience suggests that Heidegger was right. Battles for "the minds and hearts of men" are important. But, when it comes to everyday human action, situational factors associated with the ontology of experience often matter more than selling ideas designed to shape the epistemology of knowing.

47. Even for those consumer psychologists who are primarily interested in consumer protection, or those who see marketing and advertising interventions simply as interesting subject matter for academic research or classroom teaching, consumer action (or voter action, etc.) must eventually be the test of concept validity. (There are times, of course, when the higher order criteria may be phenomenal as well as behavioral, e.g., when hierarchic principles are applied to psychotherapeutic objectives.)

REFERENCES

Allport, F. (1955). *Theories of perception and the concept of structure.* New York: John Wiley & Sons, Inc.

Altman, I. (1987). Centripetal and centrifugal trends in psychology. *American Psychologist, 42,* 1058–1069.

Anderson, P. F. (1986). On method in consumer research: A critical relativist perspective. *Journal of Consumer Research, 13,* 155–173.

Anderson, P. F. (1988). Relative to what—That is the question: A reply to Siegel. *Journal of Consumer Research, 15,* 133–137.

Baker, W. E., & Lutz, R. J. (1988). The relevance-accessibility model of advertising effectiveness. In S. Hecker & D. W. Stewart (Eds.), *Nonverbal communication in advertising* (pp. 59–84). Lexington, MA: Lexington Books, D. C. Heath and Company.

Barratt, B. B., & Sloan, T. S. (1988). Critical notes on Packer's 'hermeneutic inquiry'. *American Psychologist, 43,* 131–133.

Batra, R., & Ray, M. L. (1985). How advertising works at contact. In L. F Alwitt & A. A. Mitchell (Eds.), *Psychological processes and advertising effects: Theory, research and application.* Hillsdale, N.J.: Erlbaum.

Bauer, R. A. (1963). The initiative of the audience. *Journal of Advertising Research, 3,* 2–7.

Bergson, H. (1944). *Creative evolution.* New York: The Modern Library, Random House.

Berlyne, D. E. (1965). *Structure and direction in thinking.* New York: John Wiley & Sons, Inc.

Bloom, A. (1987). *The closing of the American mind.* New York: Simon and Schuster.

Campbell, D. T. (1973). Entitativity in language learning. In W. Gray & N. D. Rizzo (Eds.), *Unity through diversity.* New York: Gordon and Breach, Science Publishers, Inc.

Churchland, P. (1986). *Neurophilosophy: Toward a unified science of the mind-brain.* Cambridge, MA: MIT Press.

Colley, R. (1961). *Defining advertising goals for measured advertising results.* New York: Association of National Advertisers.

Crick, F. H. C. (1984). Function of the thalamic reticular complex: The searchlight hypothesis. *Biological Sciences, 81,* 4586–4590.

Day, W. (1988). Hermeneutics and behaviorism. *American Psychologist, 43,* 129.

Draper, J. (1986). Nervy computers. *Proto: AT&T Bell Laboratories report to executives on new technologies, 3,* 6 ff. Murray Hill, N.J.: AT&T.

Edell, J. (1988). Nonverbal effects in ads: A review and synthesis. In S. Hecker & D. W. Stewart (Eds.), *Nonverbal communication in advertising* (pp. 11–17). Lexington, MA: Lexington Books, D. C. Heath and Company.

Fodor, J. A. (1981). *Representations: Philosophical essays on the foundations of cognitive science*. Cambridge, MA: MIT Press.

Greenwald, A. G., & Leavitt, C. (1984). Audience involvement in advertising: Four levels. *Journal of Consumer Research, 11*, 581–592.

Grice, H. P. (1981). Presupposition and conversational implicature. In P. Cole (Ed.), *Radical pragmatics*, (pp. 183–198). New York: Academic Press.

Hecker, S., & Stewart, D. W. (Eds.). (1988a). *Nonverbal communication in advertising*. Lexington, MA: Lexington Books, D. C. Heath and Company.

Hecker, S., & Stewart, D. W. (1988b). Nonverbal communication: Advertising's forgotten elements. In S. Hecker & D. W. Stewart (Eds.), *Nonverbal communication in advertising* (pps. 3–7). Lexington, MA: Lexington Books, D. C. Heath and Company.

Heidegger, M. (1962). *Being and time*. New York: Harper and Row.

Hovland, C. I. (1959). Reconciling conflicting results derived from experimental and survey studies of attitude change. *American Psychologist, 14*, 8–17.

Jennings, J. L. (1986). Husserl revisited: The forgotten distinction between psychology and phenomenology. *American Psychologist, 41*, 1231–1240.

Jennings, J. L. (1988). Marketer heal thyself: What phenomenology can and cannot contribute to consumer psychology's search for models of everyday human action. In L. Alwitt (Ed.), *Proceedings of the division of consumer psychology, 1987 Annual Convention of the American Psychological Association* (pp. 135–139). Washington, DC: Division of Consumer Psychology, American Psychological Association.

Katz, E. (1987). Communications research since Lazarsfeld. *Public Opinion Quarterly, 52*, S25–S45.

Klapper, J. T. (1960). *The effects of mass communication*. Glencoe, Ill.: The Free Press.

Koestler, A. (1964). *The act of creation*. New York: The Macmillan Company.

Krugman, H. E. (1965). The impact of television advertising: Learning without involvement. *Public Opinion Quarterly, 29*, 349–356.

Krugman, H. E. (1966–1967). The measurement of advertising involvement. *Public Opinion Quarterly, 30*, 583–596.

Leavitt, C., Waddell, C., & Wells, W. D. (1970). Improving day-after recall techniques. *Journal of Advertising Research, 10*, 13–17.

Lutz, R. J. (1985). Affective and cognitive antecedents of attitude toward the ad: A conceptual framework. In L. F. Alwitt & A. A. Mitchell (Eds.), *Psychological processes and advertising effects: Theory, research and applications* (pp. 45–63). Hillsdale, N.J.: Lawrence Erlbaum Associates.

Maloney, J. C. (1962a). Curiosity vs. disbelief in advertising. *Journal of Advertising Research, 2*, 2–8.

Maloney, J. C. (1962b). *Psychology of selling communications*. Unpublished manuscript, Northwestern University.

Maloney, J. C. (1963). Is advertising believability really important? *Journal of Marketing, 27*, 1–8.

Maloney, J. C. (1973). Man as an economic subsystem. In W. Gray & N. D. Rizzo (Eds.), *Unity through diversity* (pp. 1059–1104). New York: Gordon and Breach, Science Publishers, Inc.

Maloney, J. C., & Schonfeld, E. P. (1973). Social change and attitude change. In G.

Zaltman (Ed.), *Processes and phenomena of social change.* New York: Wiley Interscience, John Wiley & Sons.

Maloney, J. C. (in press). The first 90 years of advertising research. In E. Clark, D. Stewart, & T. Brock (Eds.), *Advertising and consumer psychology.* Hillsdale, N.J.: Lawrence Erlbaum Associates, Inc.

Menninger, K., Mayman, M., & Pruyser, P. (1963). *The vital balance: The life process in mental health and illness.* New York: The Viking Press.

Miller, L. (1988, February). The emotional brain. *Psychology Today*, pp. 34–42.

Packer, M. J. (1985). Hermeneutic inquiry in the study of human conduct. *American Psychologist, 40*, 1081–1093.

Packer, M. J. (1988a). The hermeneutic approach to action. In L. Alwitt (Ed.), *Proceedings of the Division of Consumer Psychology, 1987 Annual Convention of the American Psychological Association.* Washington, DC: Division of Consumer Psychology, American Psychological Association.

Packer, M. J. (1988b). Hermeneutic inquiry: A response to criticisms. *American Psychologist, 43*, 133–136.

Padgett, V. R., & Brock, T. C. (1988). Do advertising measures require intelligible content? A cognitive response analysis of unintelligible persuasive messages. In S. Hecker & D. W. Stewart (Eds.), *Nonverbal communication in advertising* (pps. 185–203). Lexington, MA: Lexington Books, D. C. Heath and Company.

Petty, R. E., & Cacioppo, J. T. (1981). *Attitudes and persuasion: Classic and contemporary approaches.* Dubuque, IA: Wm. C. Brown Company.

Pylyshyn, Z. (1980). Computation and cognition: Issues in the foundations of cognitive science. *The Behavioral and Brain Sciences, 3*, 111–132.

Ray, M. L., Sawyer, A. G., Rothschild, M., Heeler, R., Strong, E., & Reed, J. (1973). Marketing communication and the hierarchy of effects. In P. Clarke (Ed.), *New models for mass communication research, Sage Annual Review of Communication Research, II* (pp. 147–176). Beverly Hills, CA: Sage.

Research Systems Corporation. (1987). *The advertising research system.* Evansville, IN: Author.

Robertson, T. S. (1976). Low commitment consumer behavior. *Journal of Advertising Research, 16*, 19–24.

Rosenberg, M. J. (1968). Hedonism, inauthenticity and other goads toward expansion of a consistency theory. In R. P. Abelson, E. Aronson, W. J. McGuire, T. M. Newcomb, M. J. Rosenberg, & P. H. Tannenbaum (Eds.), *Theories of cognitive consistency: A sourcebook*, (pp. 73–111). Chicago: Rand McNally.

Russell, R. L. (1988). A critical interpretation of Packer's 'hermeneutic inquiry in the study of human conduct.' *American Psychologist, 43*, 130–131.

Shimp, T. A. (1981). Attitude toward the ad as a mediator of consumer brand choice. *Journal of Advertising, 10*, 9–15.

Siegel, H. (1988). Relativism for consumer research? (Comments on Anderson). *Journal of Consumer Research, 15*, 129–132.

Spence, J. T. (1987). Centrifugal versus centripetal tendencies in psychology. *American Psychologist, 42*, 1052–1054.

Sperry, R. W. (1988). Psychology's mentalist paradigm and the religion/science tension. *American Psychologist, 43*, 607–613.

Stewart, D. W., & Hecker, S. (1988). The future of research on nonverbal communication in advertising. In S. Hecker & D. W. Stewart (Eds.), *Nonverbal communication in advertising* (pp. 255–264). Lexington, MA: Lexington Books, D. C. Heath and Company.

Tolley, S. (1988). On significance, hope, and the role of consumer psychology or: Does this bus go to the center of the galaxy? In L. Alwitt (Ed.), *Proceedings of the Division of Consumer Psychology, 1987 Annual Convention of the American Psychological Association*. Washington, DC: Division of Consumer Psychology, American Psychological Association.

Zajonc, R. B. (1980). Feeling and thinking: Preferences need no inferences. *American Psychologist, 35*, 151–175.

Zukav, G. (1979). *The dancing Wu Li masters—An overview of the new physics*. New York: William Morrow and Company, Inc.

Index

ASI Market Research, 14

Abstract vs. concrete stimuli, 72–73

Achievement motivation studies, 87–88. *See also* Weiner's cognitive-emotion theory

Ad trace model, 256–58, 262, 265–67. *See also* Episodic memory

Advertisements: cognitive vs. affective effectiveness measures, 4–8, 35, 346–49; quality and emotional response, 116–19; structure and elements of, 24, 31–32. *See also* Contextual factors in the ad; Copytesting; Executional formats/styles of commercials; Facial expressions; Message; Preproduction versions of commercials; Pretesting ads

Advertising: role in the marketing mix, 4–5; strategic development, 16. *See also* Four-box model

Affect: congruency paradigm, 243–44; definition, 54; transfer of, 197, 213; vs. cognition, xiii-xiv, 36. *See also* Attitude; Emotion(s); Emotional; Feelings; Schema; Specific feelings; State-dependency paradigm

Affective responses, 113–22. *See also* Episodic memory

AIME (Amount of involved mental effort), 109–10. *See also* Processing; Schema

Amusement, 54–55, 63–64, 203–7. *See also* Smiles; Upbeat feelings; Warmth

Animatics, 176–92. *See also* Storyboards

Appeals: effects on brand loyalty, 13–14; effects on recall and persuasion, 14–16; emotional vs. factual, 199–200, 206–7; rational, emotional, and mixed, 11–14. *See also* Recall

Arguments: counter, 220, 224–25; support, 220, 224–25

Arousal, 199, 203–5, 207, 245–49; and emotion attribution theory, 82–88; measurement of, 55–56; peripheral manipulation of, 84–87; physiological manipulation of, 83–87. *See also* Memory; Physiological changes

Associational commercials. *See* Executional formats/styles of commercials

Attention, 197, 203–7. *See also* Environmental focus of attention

Attentional mechanisms paradigm, 243–244. *See also* Memory

Attitude: central route model of attitude change, 212–13; change, 211–13, 232, 234, 249; and cognitions, 231–32; hedonic and utilitarian affective elements,

About the Editors and Contributors

ABOUT THE EDITORS

STUART J. AGRES is the executive vice president and director of strategic planning at Lowe & Partners. He has worked in both client and advertising agency businesses. Prior to joining Lowe & Partners, he was vice president of market development at the Adolph Coors Company. He has also worked for the Leo Burnett Company, during which time he was vice president, group research director. In May 1985, Agres was co-chair of the American Marketing Association Attitude Research Conference. He received his doctorate in psychology from Michigan State University, and he is a member of various professional organizations in marketing and psychology.

JULIE A. EDELL is associate professor of the Duke University Fuqua School of Business. Her previous work on the role of affect and cognition in advertising has appeared in such journals as the *Journal of Marketing Research*, the *Journal of Consumer Research*, and *Advances in Consumer Research*. In addition, she has been invited to speak about her research at numerous industry and academic conferences. She has also received research grants from both Duke University and the Marketing Science Institute. Currently, Edell serves on the editorial board of *Psychology and Marketing*. She received her doctorate in marketing from Carnegie-Mellon.

TONY DUBITSKY is a group head in the Marketing Research Department at Lowe & Partners. He received a doctorate in psychology from Kansas State University with a concentration in consumer information processing. His research on the comprehension of misleading advertising claims has appeared in *Current Issues and Research in Advertising* and *Information Processing Research in Advertising*.

ABOUT THE CONTRIBUTORS

DAVID A. AAKER is J. Gary Shansby Professor of Marketing Strategy in the School of Business Administration at the University of California, Berkeley. He is the author of several books including *Advertising Management* and *Consumerism*. He has published over 60 articles on advertising, buyer behavior, market research, and business strategy. Dr. Aaker currently serves on the editorial board of several marketing and advertising research journals.

CHRIS T. ALLEN is currently an associate professor in the Marketing Department at the University of Cincinnati. His research projects have focused on the impact of emotional advertising and, in general, emotion as a motivator of behavior. Dr. Allen earned a doctorate in Consumer Psychology with a concentration in marketing from Ohio State University.

HELEN H. ANDERSON is an assistant professor of marketing in the Karl Eller Graduate School of Management at the University of Arizona. She received her doctorate from the Fuqua School of Business at Duke University. Dr. Anderson's research interests center on the role of programming context and advertisement structure on the cognitive and affective reactions to ads.

RAJEEV BATRA is currently an associate professor of marketing in the School of Business Administration at the University of Michigan. His research interests center on the role of emotion in advertising, optimal advertising budgeting and repetition levels. Dr. Batra is also a member of the Association for Consumer Research and the Society for Consumer Psychology.

LAURA A. BRANNON is a National Science Foundation Predoctoral Fellow in social psychology at Ohio State University. Her interests include modeling the effects of the congruence of persuasive appeals to the self-schemas of recipients and to product schemas. She has also investigated the relative efficacy of social influence tactics such as appeals to authority, to scarcity, and to social consensus. Her work has been reported at the annual meetings of the Psychonomic Society and the Midwestern and American Psychological Associations.

CAROL BRIDGWATER is currently principal at Carol Bridgwater & Associates, a marketing research and consulting firm. Prior to that, she was Senior Vice President of Parallax, an applied market research firm. Before joining Parallax, Dr. Bridgwater was at the Oglivy Center for Research and Development and served as Director of Market Research at Wells Fargo Bank. She has published extensively in the areas of clinical psychology and child development.

TIMOTHY C. BROCK is currently a professor of psychology at Ohio State University and president-elect of the Society for Consumer Psychology. During 1988 Dr. Brock was Visiting Scholar at the Oglivy Center for Research and Development. Long interested in attitude formation and change, his co-authored books include *Order of Presentation in Persuasion, Psychological Foundations of Attitudes, Cognitive Responses in Persuasion*, and *Psychology of Persuasion*.

FAIRFID M. CAUDLE is an associate professor of psychology at the College of Staten Island, the City University of New York, where she teaches the psychology of advertising and the history of psychology. Her advertising research interests center upon determining how various components of visual stimuli influence consumer response. Dr. Caudle is a member of the Association for Consumer Research, the International Council of Psychologists, the History of Science Society, and the New York Academy of Sciences.

BASIL G. ENGLIS is currently an assistant professor of marketing in the School of Business at Rutgers University. His research interests have focused on emotional reactions to advertising and psychophysiological responses to marketing communication.

KRISTINA A. FRANKENBERGER is a candidate for a doctoral degree at the University of Oregon where she is studying consumer behavior. Her current research interests include attitudes and emotions as well as information processing issues related to advertising. She earned her BS and MS in advertising at the University of Illinois at Urbana-Champaign.

RONALD C. GOODSTEIN is an assistant professor of marketing at the Anderson Graduate School of Management at the University of California at Los Angeles. He received his doctorate from the Fuqua School of Business at Duke University. Dr. Goodstein's research focuses on the influence of schemas, goals, and affect on advertising processing and effectiveness.

MARIA PAPAS HEIDE is an assistant professor in the Department of Marketing at the University of Akron. Her research has focused on two key areas: the determinants and consequences of commercial avoidance behavior, such as zipping and zapping; and promotional strategies, with an emphasis on the use of coupons and ancillary tools. She is currently completing the requirements for her doctorate in marketing with a concentration in consumer behavior at the University of Wisconsin-Madison.

RONALD PAUL HILL is an associate professor of marketing in the College of Commerce and Finance at Villanova University. His ongoing research program examining consumer mood states has focused on such diverse areas as AIDS-related anxiety and condom advertising, the effects of promotional games, and the possible psychological effects of "beauty" advertising on teenage females.

He has published in numerous marketing and advertising research journals and is currently on the editorial review boards of the *Journal of Health Care Marketing* and the *Journal of Advertising*.

MORRIS B. HOLBROOK is a professor on the faculty of the Graduate School of Business at Columbia University. His current research interests include consumer responses to advertising, aesthetics and the consumption experience, and product design. His research articles have been widely published and he recently served as president of the Association for Consumer Research.

PAMELA M. HOMER is assistant professor in the Department of Advertising at the University of Texas at Austin. Her major areas of research interest include information processing, various aspects of consumer behavior, affect/emotion in advertising, research methodology, and structural equation modeling. Dr. Homer has published articles in such journals as the *Journal of Marketing Research*, the *Journal of Consumer Behavior*, the *Journal of Personality and Social Psychology*, the *Journal of Advertising* and in several conference proceedings.

ROBERT W. HOYER is president of Decision Dynamics, Inc., a company which employs the methodology of the decision sciences. He received his doctorate in statistics from the Virginia Polytechnic Institute. In numerous publications, Dr. Hoyer has presented formal models of decision making under uncertainty. His current research is devoted to critical analyses of such models and the development of indicators of production process capability.

LYNN R. KAHLE is an associate professor of marketing at the University of Oregon. His primary research interests are in the areas of attitudes, values, consumer behavior, public policy, and communication. He has published research in such journals as the *Journal of Personality and Social Psychology*, the *Journal of Consumer Research*, the *Journal of Applied Social Psychology*, the *Public Opinion Quarterly*, the *Journal of Business Research*, and the *Journal of Marketing*. Currently, Dr. Kahle serves as secretary-treasurer-elect of the Society for Consumer Psychology.

SCOTT S. LIU is an assistant professor of advertising in the Manship School of Journalism at Louisiana State University. He is currently completing the requirements for a doctorate in communications from the University of Texas at Austin. His research interests are in the areas of consumer behavior, market research methodology, and international communication. He has published his research findings in such journals as the *Journalism Quarterly*, the *International Communication Bulletin*, *Psychology and Marketing*, and *Current Issues and Research in Advertising*.

JOHN C. MALONEY has been an applied psychologist for over thirty years. He has managed marketing and research programs in business organizations, a major university, and two advertising agencies. Since 1979, he has headed John C. Maloney & Associates, Inc., a Chicago marketing consulting organization involved in automotive, packaged goods, business-to-business, and direct response marketing.

MARIAN CHAPMAN MOORE is an associate professor of marketing at the Fuqua School of Business at Duke University. She received her doctorate from the University of California at Los Angeles. Her research on the role of affective reactions to ads has appeared in the *Journal of Marketing Research*, the *Journal of Consumer Research*, and *Advances in Consumer Research*. In addition to her research on advertising, Dr. Moore has published in the areas of strategic management and competitive analysis.

T. J. OLNEY is a consumer behavior theorist working in the area of consumer responses to advertising and consumer decision making. He earned his doctorate at Columbia University (1989) and now continues his research as Assistant Professor of Marketing in the Department of Finance, Marketing, and Decision Sciences at Western Washington University.

THOMAS J. PAGE, JR. is an associate professor of marketing in the Department of Marketing at Michigan State University. His current research interests include consumer information processing, attitude structure, and attitude-behavior relationships, as well as the use of structural equations in marketing. Dr. Page has published numerous papers in advertising and marketing research journals and has served as an ad hoc reviewer for the *Journal of Marketing Research*, the *Journal of Consumer Research*, and AMA and ACR Proceedings.

CHEONG-SOUNG PARK recently completed a Master's Degree in Mass Communication at the University of Wisconsin-Madison. He currently lives in Seoul, Korea, where he is serving in the armed forces. He hopes to return to the U.S. to complete his doctorate.

RICHARD W. POLLAY is a professor of marketing and Curator of the History of Advertising Archives at the University of British Columbia. His research on the social effects of advertising has appeared in numerous marketing and advertising research journals. Dr. Pollay has also served as a consultant with the American Advertising Museum, the Smithsonian Institution, the Library of Congress, and the National Endowment for the Humanities. Most recently, he was Program Committee co-chair for the Association for Consumer Research.

TRENT H. PUNNETT is currently the Canadian Sales Manager for Mission Cyrus Corporation, a Vancouver-based personal computer manufacturer. He earned a Master of Science degree in Business Administration with a concentration in Marketing at the University of British Columbia, the thesis for which was the basis for his chapter in this volume.

CHRISTOPHER P. PUTO is an associate professor of marketing in the Karl Eller Graduate School of Management at the University of Arizona. He received his doctorate from the Fuqua School of Business at Duke University. His research interests are in the areas of transformational advertising, industrial buying, and decision framing. Dr. Puto's research has appeared in the *Journal of Marketing*, the *Journal of Marketing Research*, and the *Journal of Consumer Research*.

J. EDWARD RUSSO is currently an associate professor of marketing and behavioral science at Cornell University. His research interests center on decision making, especially the cognitive aspects of decision processes, and aids to decisionmaking. Dr. Russo has published numerous articles in research journals, and is also the author of several chapters and reviews. Most recently, he has co-authored a book on decision making for business executives.

TERENCE A. SHIMP is currently a professor of marketing at the University of South Carolina. His research interests include group and consumer behavior, advertising effects, and, most recently, associative learning. Dr. Shimp is an Officer in the Association for Consumer Research and is also on the editorial review board of the *Journal of Consumer Research*.

MALCOLM C. SMITH is a candidate for a doctoral degree at the University of Oregon where he is studying marketing and consumer behavior. His current research has explored such areas as memory for radio advertising among the elderly; the effects of social values, religiosity, and patriotism on consumption; and strategic planning in universities.

THOMAS SRULL is currently an associate professor of psychology and Charles H. Sandage Professor of Advertising at the University of Illinois at Urbana-Champaign. He has published extensively in the areas of social cognition and information-processing. Recently, he co-edited *Advances in Social Cognition* and co-authored *Memory and Cognition in its Social Context*.

DOUGLAS M. STAYMAN is currently an assistant professor in the Department of Marketing Administration at the University of Texas at Austin. His research interests center on emotional responses to advertising as well as emotional responses to ads and the role of affect in decision making. His work has also involved methodological and measurement issues in the study of emotion as well as theoretical accounts for the effect of emotion. Dr. Stayman has published his research in the *Journal of Consumer Research* and the *Journal of Advertising Research*, and currently serves on the editorial review board of the *Journal of Business Research*.

DEBRA L. STEPHENS is an assistant professor of marketing in the College of Business and Management at the University of Maryland at College Park. Her current research focuses on consumer information processing with an emphasis on the role of affective factors. Dr. Stephens is an ad hoc reviewer for the *Journal of Consumer Research*.

PATRICIA A. STOUT is an assistant professor in the Department of Advertising at the University of Texas at Austin. She received her doctorate in communication from the University of Illinois at Urbana-Champaign and her research has appeared in the *Journal of Advertising*, *Psychology & Marketing*, and the *Journalism Quarterly*. Dr. Stout's research interests include copy research, emotional responses to television advertising, and nonverbal features of advertising. She currently serves as treasurer to the American Academy of Advertising.

ESTHER THORSON is an associate professor and Head of the Graduate Program, School of Journalism and Mass Communication at the University of Wisconsin-Madison. Her research program focuses on how people process television programming and commercials. She is particularly interested in how emotion affects the impact of ads, determinants of attention to commercials, and how various media variables affect memory for ads and the selling success of campaigns. Her work has appeared in such journals as *Journal of Marketing Research*, *Journal of Consumer Research*, and *Journal of Advertising Research*.